DATE DUE

DEMCO 38-296

From Autarchy to Market

From Autarchy to Market

Polish Economics and Politics, 1945–1995

Richard J. Hunter, Jr.,
and Leo V. Ryan, C.S.V.

PRAEGER

Westport, Connecticut
London

ion Data

Hunter, Richard J.
       From autarchy to market : Polish economics and politics, 1945–1995
   / Richard J. Hunter, Jr. and Leo V. Ryan.
       p.   cm.
       Includes bibliographical references and index.
       ISBN 0–275–96219–9 (alk. paper)
       1. Poland—Economic policy—1990– 2. Poland—Economic
   policy—1981–1990.   3. Poland—Economic policy—1945–1981.
   4. Poland—Politics and government—1945– I. Ryan, Leo V.
   II. Title.
   HC340.3.H86   1998
   338.9438—DC21   98–11123

British Library Cataloguing in Publication Data is available.

Library of Congress Catalog Card Number: 98–11123
ISBN: 0–275–96219–9

First published in 1998

Praeger Publishers, 88 Post Road West, Westport, CT 06881
An imprint of Greenwood Publishing Group, Inc.

Printed in the United States of America

The paper used in this book complies with the
Permanent Paper Standard issued by the National
Information Standards Organization (Z39.48–1984).

10 9 8 7 6 5 4 3 2

Copyright Acknowledgments

The authors and publisher gratefully acknowledge permission to use the following material:

Excerpts from *Breaking the Barrier: The Rise of Solidarity in Poland* by Lawrence Goodwyn. Copyright © 1991 by Oxford University Press, Inc. Reprinted by permission of Oxford University Press.

Excerpts from the following articles in *The Polish Review* reprinted by permission of *The Polish Review*:

Richard J. Hunter, "The Management Perspective on Poland's Economic Crisis and Recent Attempts at Reform," Vol. 31, No. 4, 1986.

Richard J. Hunter and John Northrop, "Management, Legal and Accounting Perspectives: Privatization in Poland," Vol. 38, No. 4, 1993.

Richard J. Hunter, Artur Nowak, and Leo V. Ryan, "Legal Aspects of the Transformation Process in Poland: Business Association Forms," Vol. 40, No. 4, 1995.

Richard J. Hunter and Leo V. Ryan, "Uwaga! (Watch Out!) Opportunities and Pitfalls for an American Doing Business in Poland: The Political and Economic Scene," Vol. 36, No. 3, 1991.

Richard J. Hunter, Leo V. Ryan, and Andrew Hrechak, "Out of Communism to What?: The Polish Economy and Solidarity in Perspective," Vol. 39, No. 3, 1994.

▨ Contents

⊕ Acknowledgments

We wish to acknowledge and thank the following individuals for their assistance in this project: Professor John Jordan of the Stillman School of Business, Seton Hall University, for his comments on economic aspects of the work; the late Professor William Mathes, historian and director, Program of Russian and East European Studies, Seton Hall University, for his comments on historical aspects of the work; Henry Kedron, scientist and educator, who was the primary "reader" for chapters 1–4; Professor Jacek Klich of the Institute of Management and Institute of Public Health of the Jagiellonian University, Krakow, Poland, for his comments on chapters 5–8; Jane Gromada Kedron, executive assistant at the Polish Institute of Arts and Sciences of America, and Mariusz Bargielski, administrative assistant, for their assistance in translation and bibliographic references; Ewa Nowakowska, program director, Summer School of Language and Culture, Jagiellonian University, and her son, Piotr Nowakowski, a second-year university student in Krakow, for their assistance in securing Polish bibliographic reference materials; Mary Williams of Seton Hall University and Dianne Cichanski, of DePaul University, who generously, patiently, and repeatedly prepared portions of the manuscript from drafts to final copy; and Carolyn Harden of Seton Hall University who prepared the manuscript for publication.

Co-author Leo V. Ryan, C.S.V., expresses his appreciation to the DePaul University Research Council for a winter 1997 leave to develop this manuscript and to the Kellogg Institute for International Studies, University of Notre Dame, for an appointment as Visiting Scholar for spring 1997, during the writing phase. The Vilter Foundation provided grants for research, travel, and related support. Ben C. Spencer, now with the Smithsonian Institution, served as his graduate assistant at DePaul. Co-author

Leo V. Ryan, C.S.V., also expresses his appreciation to the Polish-American Fulbright Commission for a three year serial appointment as (1993–1995) Senior Lecturer, Program in Marketing and Management, School of Law and Administration, Adam Mickiewicz University, Poznan, Poland. That appointment served to deepen and quicken his interest in Polish economic and political transformation. Co-author Richard J. Hunter acknowledges the support of Seton Hall University for fall 1996 sabbatical leave.

List of Abbreviations and Acronyms

AWS	Solidarity Election Action (led by Marian Krzaklewski)
BBWR	Non Party Bloc to Support the Reforms (created by Lech Walesa before the 1993 elections to the Sejm)
CEFTA	Central European Free Trade Association
CIS	Commonwealth of Independent States
CK	Central Committee (of the Polish Communist party)
COMECON	Committee on Economic Cooperation (Eastern European equivalent of the Common Market), also termed CMEA
CRM	Command-rationing mechanism (the system of central planning)
CRZZ	Central Council of Trade Unions
CUP	Central Planning Office (1945–1949)
EBRD	European Bank for Reconstruction and Development
EC	European Community
EFTA	European Free Trade Association
EIB	European Investment Bank
ESOP	Employee Stock Ownership Plan
EU	European Union
FDI	Foreign Direct Investment
FRG	Federal Republic of Germany (the former West Germany)
GATT	General Agreement on Tariffs and Trade
GDR	German Democratic Republic (the former East Germany)
GUKPPiW	Main Office of Censorship
GUS	Central Statistical Office
IBRD	International Bank for Reconstruction and Development
IFC	International Finance Corporation
IMF	International Monetary Fund

KERM	Economic Committee of the Council of Ministers
KIK	Catholic Intelligentsia Club
KKP	The National Coordinating Commission of Solidarity
KL-D	Liberal Democratic Congress
KO	Civic Committee of Solidarity, formed in December 1988
KOR	Committee for the Defense of Workers (established in 1976)
KP	Planning Commission (1949–)
KPEiR	National Party of Old-Age and Disability Pensioners
KPN	Confederation for an Independent Poland
KPP	Polish Communist Party
KRN	National Homeland Council (created by Gomulka in January 1944)
KSP	Committees of Self Management (Party controlled)
KSS	Committee for Social Self-Defense
KUL	Catholic University of Lublin (1918–)
MKS	Interfactory Strike Committee
MPP	Polish Mass Privatization Program
NATO	North Atlantic Treaty Organization
NIFs	National Investment Funds
NSZZ	Independent Self Governing Trade Union (Solidarity)
OBOP	Center for Public Opinion Research
OECD	Organization for Economic Cooperation and Development
OPZZ	All Poland Alliance of Trade Unions (associated with Alfred Miodowicz and General Jaruzelski)
ORMO	Volunteer Reserve of the Citizens' Militia
PAIZ	National Agency for Foreign Investments
PC	Center Alliance
PETs	Planned Economies in Transition
PGR	State Agricultural Enterprise (collective farm)
PHARE	Poland/Hungary Aid for Restructuring Economies
PKO	Universal Savings Bank
PKWN	Polish Committee of National Liberation (the Lublin government, established in 1944)
PPP	Polish Privatization Program
PPPP	Polish Party of the Friends of Beer
PPR	Polish Workers' Party (1942–1948)
PPS	Polish Socialist Party (1892–1948)
PR	Polish Republic
PRL	Polish People's Republic
PSL	Polish Peasant Party (originally, 1895–1947); formerly headed by Waldemar Pawlak, former prime minister
PW	Freedom Party

PZPR	Polish United Workers' Party (also known as PUWP, in English)
RFE	Radio Free Europe
RMP	Young Poland Movement
ROAD	Democratic Action Civic Movement
ROP	Movement for the Reconstruction of Poland (Jan Olszewski)
ROPCiO	Committee for the Defense of Human and Civic Rights
RTRP	Provisional Government of the Republic of Poland (January–June 1945)
S	Solidarity (Marian Krzaklewski)
SB	Secret Police (formerly UB)
SD	Democratic Party
SdRP	Social Democracy of the Polish Republic
SIEC	Network of Solidarity Workplace Organizations
SLD	Democratic Left Alliance (Composed of the PPS and the SdRP)
SLD/PSL	Governing coalition in the Sejm (1993–1997)
SOE	State-owned enterprise
SP	Labor Solidarity
TKK	Solidarity's Provisional Coordinating Committee
TKN	The "Flying University"
TRJN	Provisional Government of National Unity (June 1945)
TUUC	Trade Union Central Council (official trade unions)
UAM	Adam Mickiewicz University (Poznan)
UB	Security Office
UD	Democratic Union (now the Freedom Union)
UJ	Jagiellonian University (Krakow)
UOP	State Protection Agency
UP	Union of Labor
UPR	Realpolitik Union
USAID	United States Agency for International Development
USD	United States Dollars
UW	Freedom Union (formerly Democratic Union)
VAT	Value Added Tax
VISEGRAD Group	Comprising Poland, Hungary, the Czech Republic, Slovakia, and Slovenia
WERI	World Economy Research Institute
WIDER	World Institute for Development Economic Research
WIG	Warsaw Stock Exchange Index
WOGs	"Great Industrial Organizations" (Industrial Lobbies)
WRON	Military Council on National Salvation
WSE	Warsaw Stock Exchange
WTO	World Trade Organization

ZCh-N	Christian National Union (Jan Olszewski)
ZOMO	Mobile Units of Citizens' Militia (specially trained riot police)
ZPP	Union of Polish Patriots (Moscow based, during WWII)
ZREMB	Association of Building Machinery Repair Works
ZSL	United Peasant Party
ZSP	(Socialist) Association of Polish Students

Chapter One

Introduction

The Challenge of Political and Economic Change

"Za wolnosc, prawo i chleb"
The face of the Monument to workers in Poznan, Poland

During the second week of August 1989, the "chief jailer" of martial law in "People's Poland," General Wojciech Jaruzelski, announced that his "ex-prisoner," Tadeusz Mazowiecki, would become prime minister. Mazowiecki was a 62-year-old journalist, editor of Solidarity's weekly newspaper, *Tygodnik Solidarnosc,* a devout Roman Catholic, and a close advisor and partner to Solidarity leader, Lech Walesa.

Surprisingly, Communist party partners in the Peasant and Democratic parties had refused to support the candidacy of Interior Minister General Czeslaw Kiszczak, Jaruzelski's "chief policeman." Kiszczak had been designated as the choice of the ruling elite of the Communist party and *nomenklatura* for the position of prime minister. No doubt, Jaruzelski, elected to the newly reconstituted position of president, but only after key abstentions by Solidarity members, felt confident that his choice would be summarily ratified by the ever-pliant Sejm. The Sejm would be called upon once again to assure Communist party control of Poland, ignoring the results of the 3 June 1989 elections that had taken place under the terms of the Round Table agreement of 5 April 1989.

The Round Table, which began on 6 February 1989, was comprised of 57 delegates from the government (led by General Kiszczak), the opposition Solidarity movement (led by Lech Walesa), and the Roman Catholic

Church (represented by several laymen affiliated with Catholic publications and organizations).[1] Kiszczak, however, remained steadfast in his view that whatever the outcome, "no national problem will be solved by denying the historical achievements and undermining the socialist shape of Poland."[2] Kiszczak was prepared to offer an increase in opposition representation in Parliament, and a new law on associations that would result in trade union "pluralism" and the relegalization of Solidarity. In return, Solidarity would pledge its support for a program of economic recovery, designed to stifle inflation, restructure industry, and resolve Poland's pressing foreign debt problem. The historic accord of 5 April mirrored Kiszczak's original proposals but included several significant additions, fundamentally altering the political equation:

1. Solidarity would be restored as a "free and independent trade union." Rural Solidarity and the Independent Student Association would likewise be restored to full legal status.
2. A June 1989 election would be held for a two-house Parliament, in which 35 percent of the 460 seats in the lower house (Sejm) would be allocated to candidates of the Solidarity-based opposition and would be contested for in an open election process. The communists were guaranteed 38 percent; and parties formally aligned with the communists, the remaining 27 percent (or a total of 65%).
3. Poland's upper house (a 100-person Senate), abolished in 1946 in a patently rigged referendum, would be restored and chosen in completely free and open elections.
4. The post of president of the Republic would be established. The president would be elected by the two houses of the Parliament for a six-year term. It was agreed that General Jaruzelski would assume this newly created position.
5. Broad changes in the economy were agreed upon, including the indexing of wages, by which workers and retired persons would receive compensation to 80 percent of any increase in the cost of living.

In addition, the government agreed to make the state-controlled press "available" to Solidarity, and to provide the union a half-hour of air time weekly on television and one hour weekly on radio. Solidarity was also permitted to publish its own daily national newspaper. Adam Michnik would assume the position of editor in chief, and Helena Luczywo, who had begun her career at *Robotnik* [The Worker] in 1977, would assume day-to-day operational responsibility. The government promised that censorship would be relaxed, although not entirely abolished. Lech Walesa commented that "either we'll be able to build Poland as a nation in a peaceful way, independent, sovereign and safe, with equal alliances, or we'll sink in the chaos of demagogy, which could result in civil war in which there will be no victors." Kiszczak simply added that "there's only one victor, the nation, our fatherland."[3]

General Kiszczak expected that the move to limited pluralism would be more cosmetic than real and would nevertheless result in continued Communist party domination. The election to the "Contract Parliament" had been predetermined to guarantee the ruling Communist party coalition at least two-thirds of the seats and domination of the political process. However, despite a very limited pre-election period and an extensive pre-election spending spree by the government, Solidarity swept to victory in 262 out of 263 contested seats. Communist leaders had completely misread the mood of the Polish people.

The election in June 1989 had turned out to be a total disaster and a "mortifying rebuke" for the communists and their allies, who lost all but one of the contested seats. Only two of the communist-backed candidates on the National List of 35 "unopposed" nominees attained the required majority of the vote necessary for election. Urged on by Solidarity, voters had pointedly crossed out the names of some of the major Communist party leaders.

Among those who failed to win seats included such notables of the Communist party elite as Prime Minister Mieczyslaw Rakowski, Interior Minister Czeslaw Kiszczak, Defense Minister Florian Siwicki, and the official trade union representative, Alfred Miodowicz. In all, six Politburo members suffered humiliation at the polls.

The winners included Jacek Kuron, twice ejected from the Communist party (in 1953, and again in 1964), a KOR veteran who had organized an important "information service" during the strikes in 1980.[4] Kuron had spent nearly nine years in Polish jails, including a sentence served in 1965 when he was imprisoned for charging that Poland was being run by a "dictatorship of the political bureaucracy." During the election campaign, Kuron had been denounced by security police and some student radicals as that "Jew Kuron," but had nevertheless managed to defeat Wladyslaw Sila-Nowicki, a distinguished lawyer and defender of human rights. Also elected was the author and essayist Adam Michnik, who called Kuron his "spiritual mentor"; the actor Andrzej Lapicki; Jan Litynski, thrown out of the Mathematics Department of Warsaw University in March 1968; longtime union activist and organizer Bogdan Lis; academic historian and coauthor of the 1964 *Open Letter to the Party* Karol Modzelewski; historian, author, and cofounder of KOR Jan Jozef Lipski; the noted film and stage director Andrzej Wajda; Warsaw University mathematician, and later Solidarity press spokesman Janusz Onyszkiewicz; and Bronislaw Geremek, an academic advisor to Walesa in Gdansk during the "Polish August" of 1980, who assumed the position of Solidarity parliamentary leader. Voters in the 108 election districts gave communist-backed candidates "dismal returns," ranging from 25 percent, down to 5 percent or less.[5]

The election results and unexpected collapse of the Kiszczak candidacy in August sounded a death knell to communism in Poland and opened Polish prospects for democracy, pluralism, and real economic reform.

For nearly 45 years, the Communist party had been unable to capture the loyalty or the imagination of the masses, and had squandered whatever support it may have once enjoyed. A new era had begun for Poland, and in retrospect, for the entire region of Central and Eastern Europe.

THE CHALLENGE OF ECONOMIC AND POLITICAL CHANGE

At the outset, we recall the words of Zbigniew Brzezinski, who set the parameters of the nature and scope of change in Poland: "There are no precedents in moving from communism to capitalism!"[6]

Leszek Balcerowicz served as deputy prime minister and finance minister in the government of Tadeusz Mazowiecki. He was the chief architect of the changes in the economy that were initiated after 1989. Balcerowicz provided an important context to the cascade of changes emanating from the region. He noted that there were three special and unique features that together distinguish the changes that have taken place in Poland since 1989 from any other cases of "institutional or systemic transformations" attempted in history.[7]

First, was the broad *range of areas* that underwent simultaneous transformation and transition—changes that would be crucial to the long-range success of the process: both the political and economic systems were the focus of "radical transformation." The political system was in transition from the communist-dominated party-state-*nomenklatura* system, administered by an increasingly isolated Communist party. At the same time, the economic system would be transformed from the monocentric model of state central planning, run by a class of bureaucrats called the *nomenklatura,* to a Western market economy. In this way, Poland would join nations in the region in what former Russian president Gorbachev described as a "common European home."[8] In short, Poland found itself in a period of unique transition, literally "going out" of communism, a system that fit its history and traditions much like "a saddle would fit a cow," to the new day of a liberal, democratic, market-oriented society. There were few patterns or models for the economic-political transformation that would follow. There was no guarantee that society would remain patient during what would turn out to be a very painful process.

In most nations, radical reforms of the type attempted in Poland only had to focus on one of these core systems at a time. For example, in both post-Franco Spain in the mid-1970s and in South Korea at the end of the decade of the 1980s, the aim of reform was essentially political—to *democratize* and open-up the political system while retaining "virtually the same economic system." A market economy was already in place and functioned at a high level. Thus, there was no fundamental need to radically reconstruct the economy. It was only necessary to modify or to modernize it to adapt to changing conditions.

On the other hand, in the past decade under a succession of presidents in Mexico, and in Taiwan, especially after the death of Chiang Kai-shek, reform efforts focused almost exclusively on the *economic system*. The closed political system essentially remained intact. The opening of the economic system in these nations is only now being followed by a political transformation, moves toward pluralism, and the development of democratic institutions, including mature opposition political parties. In Poland and in most of the nations of Central and Eastern Europe (the preferred name for the region), the transformation process has involved both the political and economic systems at approximately the same time.

Is there any wonder that the process has been met with uncertainty, skepticism, and reticence on the part of many in society? Is there any wonder that it has been much more difficult to develop and sustain the societal consensus needed to support reform efforts? The Pentor Poll, commissioned in October 1996, reported that Poles' evaluation of the economy had "significantly worsened," and that "economic optimism has again dropped. A depressed economic mood results in decreasing support for political, social and economic changes."[9]

Balcerowicz argued that the second unique feature of the transition in Poland is the *method of change*. In retrospect, it would be accurate to speak of the changes that occurred in Poland as a true revolution in the institutional and social systems. Poland was a nation that essentially "fell into" communism through the presence of the Russian army at the conclusion of World War II. The Yalta System of delicate balances of power between East and West secured the fate of Poland and Central and Eastern Europe for nearly half a century.[10]

Fortunately, the revolution since 1989 has been largely peaceful, or evolutionary. The major exceptions have thus far been Romania, where the Ceausescus were executed to the international audience of CNN; and Russia, where in 1991 an attempt to overthrow President Gorbachev by disgruntled "old liners" in the military and in the state bureaucracies was thwarted by Boris Yeltsin. Later, in August 1993, Yeltsin, who had become Russian president, mounted an offensive against the Parliament and two of its more reactionary leaders, Alexander Rutskoi and Ruslan Khasbulatov, an action in which the Duma was almost completely destroyed in an effort to "save" the nascent democracy.

The region has also witnessed bloody battles in the former Yugoslavia, in Albania, and in many parts of the former Soviet Union (Armenia, Azerbaijan, and Chechnya). However, these conflicts originated from *national-ism, religion, or ethnicity* (or in the cases of Bosnia and Chechnya, a dangerous mixture of all three), and not generally from social changes or societal dysfunctions related to the radical transformation of political and economic institutions. Save for a small number of "diehards" in Russia, carrying portraits of the last czar or of the "patron saints" of Soviet communism—Marx, Lenin, Stalin—few have clamored for the return of Soviet-style communism to any of the nations of the region.

The result of this essentially bloodless transformation in Poland was that Polish society remained basically intact, with the institutions and the elites of the old system largely preserved. Many of these former elites, "reconstructed communists" and members of the *nomenklatura,* immediately began searching for a role in the emerging system. In 1990, this situation led to a dramatic split between two giants of the Polish Revolution in what has been termed the "War at the Top."

Tadeusz Mazowiecki, the first noncommunist prime minister in Central and Eastern Europe, was a distinguished advisor to Solidarity in Gdansk during the 1980 "Polish August." Mazowiecki advocated a policy of "let bygones be bygones" vis-à-vis former communists and prominent members of the *nomenklatura,* as long as they had not broken any specific laws and would now pledge allegiance to the newly created democratic system.[11] Lech Walesa, the hero of the Solidarity movement, urged a program of rapid decommunization and removal of these individuals from both the political and economic life of the nation. These two former allies became bitter enemies during the presidential election of 1990. In the first round, Mazowiecki finished a disappointing third behind Walesa and the mysterious emigré Stanislaw Tyminski. The role of the *nomenklatura* was a major point of contention.

As Balcerowicz insightfully noted, however, it was inevitable that the *nomenklatura,* given their managerial experience and connections[12] (notably to Western capital), would become active in private businesses and banks, especially as the prospect of advancing their political careers in the new system appeared at first to be more limited. Given the backdrop of nearly half a century of pent-up disdain with the ruling communist elite, it is also not surprising that these persons and their very visible successes would be resented by the society at large. Many had witnessed their performance in communist society and were skeptical about their sudden conversion to democracy and democratic capitalism. What is ironic is that in the 1990s the *nomenklatura,* not only in Poland, but also in Hungary, the former East Germany, Lithuania, Slovakia, Romania, and Belarus have enjoyed a resurgence of power. They have benefited politically from the discontent that is practically unavoidable during economic reforms started under very difficult conditions and circumstances.[13]

In Poland society slowly turned against the "reformers and former revolutionaries" and backed former communists, now masquerading under the banner of "social democrats." This process first became evident in the parliamentary elections of 1993, when the postcommunist Democratic Left Alliance (SLD) and its partner, the Polish Peasant party (PSL), polled only 36 percent of the popular vote but gained 65 percent of the seats in the Sejm. More dramatic evidence occurred in the presidential election of 1995 when President Walesa was defeated for reelection by Aleksander Kwasniewski.

Reacting to this defeat, Walesa himself wryly noted: "In 50 years, there will be monuments for me all over this country and people will lay wreaths every chance they get. Then I'll kick my coffin and shout, 'Where were you when I needed you?'"[14]

The third special feature of the transition is the *sequence of change*. Because significant institutional changes were required in both the political and economic systems, patterns were different throughout the region. The transformation of political life and the movement toward the end of one-party rule were necessary because the former system was characterized by the domination of politics over policy. The change was underscored by holding free elections and by creating such democratic institutions as political parties. In the 1989 parliamentary elections in Poland, a relatively monolithic Solidarity captured nearly 70 percent of the popular vote. In the presidential election of 1990, Solidarity captured just over 60 percent on the first ballot. In the parliamentary elections of 1991, despite difficult economic times, parties "sporting a Solidarity pedigree" still won 55 percent of the vote.[15] Political transformation required less time than the more cumbersome privatization process and the creation of other fundamental institutions of capitalism (central banks, stock exchanges, customs and credit machinery, and clearing houses).

This mode of transformation, which has been described as "mass democracy first, capitalism later," is both the reverse of the history of the 19th century (capitalism first, mass democracy later) and of the cases in Spain, South Korea, and Taiwan in this century.

Because of this sequence of change, important policy questions arise: Did the citizens of the region (and especially Poland) confuse democracy with capitalism? Did their frustration with the slow progress of economic transformation (or the fact that their situation actually worsened) lead to their frustration with democracy, and at least indirectly to the successful reemergence of Communist parties masquerading under the banner of "social democracy"?

This unique sequence of change, which whetted the democratic impulse of the people, gives rise to a series of questions regarding the *relationship* between the emerging democratic political system and the economic system in its seminal transition phase to capitalism. What are the *tensions* between democracy and capitalism? What *kind of democracy* is needed to complete the economic transition successfully? Or more specifically, does political reality dictate that certain groups, or at least the unreconstructed leaders of these groups, be somehow "undemocratically" excluded from the process, as was the case in the Czech Republic? Is it truly possible to build an efficient and strong democracy and to create institutions and a culture able to lead the process of economic transformation? Can the democratic process be truly pluralistic? Can the results of a systematic reordering of society inure to the benefit of society at large? Can the new system yield equal benefits to the legions of workers who created Solidarity and who literally risked their lives in 1956, 1970, and 1976, as well as so dramatically during the "Polish August" of 1980?

GENERAL LESSONS FROM THE POLISH EXPERIENCE

Balcerowicz asserted that some general lessons can be drawn from the economic transition in Poland. We agree wholeheartedly and will attempt to expand on his considered conclusions.

1. *"Initial economic conditions do matter, as far as the pace and effects, of the transition are concerned."* The most important of the initial conditions in Poland involved the existence of the command-and-control economic structure—the monocentric system. It was characterized by poor economic performance and crisis in the decades of the 1970s and 1980s, the burden of heavy industry, and the domination of the military-industrial sector over the production of consumer goods. As the nation began the process of economic reform, the real question was: What effects did nearly 50 years of communism have on the memory of capitalism in Poland? How would it be possible to build capitalism with neither capital nor capitalists?

2. *"The process and outcome of economic transition can be seen as the interplay of both internal and external factors."* No amount of external aid (IMF, World Bank, U.S., Western Europe, the Paris or London Clubs) can offset the need for fundamental economic reform and a clear rejection of inflationary budget-busting policies utilized by the regime throughout the 1970s and again during martial law. These policies were particularly pursued by the Rakowski government during the April–June 1989 preelection period and were specifically designed to curry favor with seemingly unsophisticated voters.

After 1989, communism was no longer seen as a military threat to either Western Europe or to the United States. No longer was Central and Eastern Europe seen as a wedge against Russian expansionism or the uncertainties of German reunification. Balcerowicz noted that blocking access to Western markets through adopting protectionist policies or, in a more political context, delaying Polish entry into the OECD, the European

Union, or NATO would likely reduce substantially the prospects for long-range success, even of the most "sensible economic programs." Such policies might also undermine the political position of those persons and groups who pursued such reforms, as well as chances for success for the capital-starved states in the region.[16]

3. *"The choice of strategy for economic transition depends in part on the initial conditions and especially on the degree of inherited macroeconomic instability."* The experience in Poland is quite instructive. A "radical and comprehensive" economic program, containing the elements of *stabilization, liberalization,* and *privatization,* introduced into a socialist economy under extremely difficult conditions, can be successful! By 1991, GDP had already begun to rise. Real wages, which had declined by 24.4 percent in 1990, rebounded to show a decline of only .03 percent in 1991. The rise in consumer prices had slowed to +35.3 percent during 1993. Poland's convertible currency debt, which had reached nearly $48.5 billion in 1990, had been reduced slightly to $47.25 billion in 1993,[17] and was in the process of being managed and "rescheduled."

Being both radical ("shock therapy") and comprehensive (the "big bang"), the program of transformation was designed to break down the inertia and resistance of the bureaucracy and structures of the monocentric system. Economic and social revolutionaries, of whom Balcerowicz was certainly one, would initially benefit from the political capital and increased goodwill generated among the population in order to weather the painful economic dysfunctions and hardships that necessarily emerge after great political changes or breakthroughs. However, a question persists: How long does this "era of good feeling" last? Professor Mieczyslaw Nasilowski of the elite Central School of Planning and Statistics in Warsaw, and former member of the Council of Economic Advisors under Edward Gierek, posed the question in another way: How long would it take society to reach the "barrier of social endurance"? The answer for Poland was perhaps two or three years. It appears that this barrier had been reached at the time of the parliamentary elections of 1993. The situation had certainly come full circle with the defeat of President Walesa in November 1995.

4. Balcerowicz insisted that *"alternative strategies for dealing with hyperinflation (or even increasing it as former Prime Minister Rakowski did for purely political purposes during the campaign of 1989) and of very limited liberalization of the economy have practically no chance for assuring economic success."* Although such strategies may appear less risky from the "social and political points of view," they are in fact very dangerous in these same respects. Economic problems will not simply solve themselves. Radical transformation will certainly be necessary at some point, and because it has been postponed, or watered down (largely because of political considerations), "such measures will appear in a much worse eco-

nomic and social situation." Postponing radical reform can bring the country "into a spiral of mutually reinforcing and destructive economic, social and political tensions."[18] Thus, society will proceed through a wrenching political crisis involving the destruction of the communist political system and still may not be able to overcome the root economic crisis.

5. Mirroring the prophetic words of Zbigniew Brzezinski that no precise economic models exist for such a massive transformation process, *creating a new economic policy is indeed an "art" that requires making decisions in a timely fashion with both incomplete and imperfect (sometimes erroneous) information*, especially if the radical approach is undertaken during an economic crisis. In such a volatile context, societal support must be assiduously and continually cultivated precisely because there is no clear blueprint for success. A major failing of postcommunist Solidarity governments was that they fell into the trap of becoming elitist, appearing to discount the deep-rooted discontent in society ingrained over nearly 45 years of Communist party–*nomenklatura* rule.

The process of transformation, unfortunately, is one of fits and starts. In an atmosphere of cynicism, demagoguery, and the physical exhaustion of the population (reaching "the barrier of social endurance"), it can lead to pervasive mistrust of those who are "leading the charge" toward the creation of a market economy. The intellectuals who dominated the Mazowiecki government (especially those in the Ministry of Finance) and who created the shock therapy remained true to their academic roots, but over time they became estranged from the daily lives of workers. In this process, they inadvertently broke their bond with the workers who launched the revolution and who were at the heart of the revolution itself.

Several important lessons can be drawn from studying the path of economic change and the process of radical and comprehensive economic reform in Poland since Tadeusz Mazowiecki became prime minister in August of 1989.[19]

1. Poland adopted a wide range of traditional tools perfected by Western capitalist-democracies in order to promote macroeconomic stabilization. These include measures such as reducing the budget deficit through the elimination of state subsidies, controlling the money supply, and creating a stabilized rate of exchange.

The Polish experience proved conclusively that these measures can be successful even in a state–controlled, state sector–dominated economy. They must, however, be supplemented by an additional instrument— strong wage controls especially in the public sector, which in Poland comprised 85 percent of all industrial wage earners in 1989. In this atmosphere, it is ironic that the same workers who helped to "make the Solidarity revolution" were especially harmed by the policies of the economic transformation. Thus, they turned against the government and toward the former communists.

The Democratic Left Alliance (SLD) promised a more traditional "leftist" social agenda of expanded wages for workers, protection of income of pensioners, and maintenance of the social safety net for the unemployed and those who had lost their jobs due to enterprise bankruptcy or dislocations. Ironically, these were the very elements of the program proposed by Solidarity itself in 1981 when it was essentially a trade union, expressing traditional trade union concerns. It is doubly ironic, however, that even when Aleksander Kwasniewski and Wlodzimierz Cimoszewicz of the SLD gained power, they too recognized the necessity of creating a strong private sector. Thus, at least in Poland, the SLD has not fundamentally tampered with the privatization program. Instead, critics accused them of engaging in dilatory tactics or "tinkering around the edges," trying to appeal to popular, often populist, sentiment.

2. Only a radical stabilization-liberalization program is capable of abolishing massive shortages and queues, the main features of the failed socialist system, in a very short period of time and of increasing substantially the range of goods available to consumers in only one or two years. By way of contrast, the Russian program of "piecemeal" reform (also carried out in Poland in the 1970s and 1980s) has been wholly unsuccessful in solving the problem of the lack of consumer goods in any significant way, even into 1997. One problem, however, yet remains: How to generate sufficient income to pay for the abundance of goods in an economy characterized as one of "Western prices and Eastern wages."

3. The Polish experiment shows that it is also possible to solve the currency convertibility problem in a relatively short period of time by moving first to internal convertibility and then to full external convertibility. The zloty is well on its way to achieving this second goal. It is now a "denomination currency," moving rapidly toward becoming a full "settlement currency," where transactions are admitted, cleared, and settled in the national currency and not in dollars, as is presently the case. Thus, through a carefully constructed process, Poland met the criteria for entry into the Organization for Economic Cooperation and Development (OECD) in July 1996.[20] It is anticipated that Poland will be in a position to join the European Union (EU), perhaps by the year 2000.

4. Because of the introduction of the possibility of enterprise bankruptcy and the drastic reduction of state subsidies, the program of radical stabilization and liberalization forced many state enterprises to initiate activities relating to the privatization process. Enterprises were required to sell or lease part of their assets to private parties or firms or to seek private (perhaps foreign) parties as joint venture partners. In short, this process induced enterprises to begin to act as normal participants in a capitalist system.[21]

A radical program also fulfills an important psychological function by changing the mentality of economic activity from "state centered" to "private centered." This change in mentality may be most critical to achieving success in the long run.[22] In light of the new reality of enterprise bankruptcy, however, the question remains: What will society do about those enterprises that cannot be privatized, or perhaps more importantly, with their displaced workers? The example of the former Lenin Shipyard in Gdansk comes to mind.[23]

5. Radical stabilization and liberalization induces or sometimes forces state enterprises to adjust to the "new market" and to the demanding and potentially rewarding conditions of the market economy. It also provides individuals with opportunities not present in the former closed system. These opportunities provide the potential for enormous rewards but also enormous risks.[24]

Few in society were prepared by the former system to confront this challenge. Workers had no practical experience in management or with using entrepreneurial tools. They had no experience whatsoever with such concepts as obsolescence, underemployment, or downsizing. KOR activists were essentially academic and nonmanagerial in their outlook and approach. Walesa and his union-organizing cadre had no experience in a capitalist system that rewards both initiative and risk. They were not prepared to adjust to the implications of creating a "free and independent" trade union within the closed communist system.

Ironically, only the members of the *nomenklatura* initially possessed the "tools" and "connections" necessary to move the economy successfully from socialism to capitalism. The seeds of the current political controversy were born during this formative period when the *nomenklatura* began to adapt to the new economic calculus, even as workers in state enterprises began to feel the reality of the "hard edges" of capitalism. A prime example of this new reality was unemployment, which grew to 15.7 percent of the work force in 1993.

The Poland of 1993 experienced its own "shock"—a reality that some industries would never be fully privatized in the sense that a buyer would be found that would be willing to expend its own and not state capital. Valuation problems plagued the negotiations between Barbara Piasecka-Johnson and the managers of the Lenin Shipyard.[25] Firms that produced no useful products or services but were deemed "politically essential" in the state-controlled socialist economy continued to operate. Such endemic problems led to the creation of the so-called ESOP option, in which workers become the "owners" of state-owned enterprises, and in 1996 to the creation of the National Investment Funds (NIFs) to administer a pool of economically viable enterprises. The NIFs were designed to assure the participation of Polish citizens through the issuance of privatization vouchers. The NIFs were also expected to attract foreign capital to modernization efforts. Under the NIF program, 28 million adult Poles were eligible to buy a single "participation unit" representing a share in 15 National Investment

Funds. The program has been termed an "enormous success." The NIFs currently operate a portfolio of over 500 individual firms.[26]

Professor Nasilowski recognized most accurately that no economic change, especially a fundamental and radical change, can be made in a social vacuum. Attempting such fundamental change was indeed a risky and an uncharted course that gave rise to two strongly opposing tendencies. One tendency was a certain societal contentment that arises from a positive change in the economy—that is, the elimination of shortages, the introduction of consumer goods into the market, reduced levels of inflation, a significant increase in general economic opportunities, and the introduction of a wide range of political and societal freedoms.

There will be individuals in society who can make direct use of these new economic and political opportunities—for example, entrepreneurs, bankers, accountants, management consultants, lawyers, tax specialists, and many managerial and professional private sector employees. These individuals are both excited by and satisfied with their prospects in the "new Poland," where a high premium will be placed on entrepreneurship and risk taking.

However, reform has also given rise to discontent and uncertainty, felt intensely by those who essentially led the revolt against the former system. These individuals include the unemployed and those who fear unemployment; pensioners on fixed and dwindling incomes; citizens who were unable to take advantage of the new economic freedom; and those whose relative or actual pay or prestige has declined in the "new" system. It has often been said that socialism in Poland was meant to be egalitarian, but instead was characterized by the "equal distribution of poverty"—with a curious emphasis on the words "equal" and "poverty." One can point to Silesian coal miners, dock workers in Gdansk, tractor fabricators in Ursus, or textile workers in Lodz as examples of individuals who have experienced decidedly negative effects of the transformation process. More generally, those employed in almost all of the "heavy industries" of the WOGs[27] look with envy on the new economic winners. These winners often include the former members of the *nomenklatura*, placed quite profitably in a variety of private businesses. Many managed to gain control over newly privatized enterprises (some through a unique process called "spontaneous privatization"), playing upon their enormous contacts made during the days of state socialism.

In this situation, political "parties of discontent," usually former communists posing as reformed social democrats, have made political "hay" out of the dissatisfaction that arises in a society in the process of economic reform. Once in power, however, even these chameleons are faced by the sobering fact that the *reforms were necessary and inevitable* and were to a large extent successful.

6. The role played by Russian president Gorbachev and the Holy Fa-

ther, Pope John Paul II, needs to be critically reexamined.[28] It seems clear now that without a clear signal from Gorbachev in 1989 that the Soviet Union would no longer intervene in the internal affairs of nations in Central and Eastern Europe (as it had in Hungary in 1956, or Czechoslovakia in 1968), the process of transformation may have been impossible or may have taken other forms, perhaps turning to violence. *New York Times* correspondent Bill Keller termed this rejection of the Brezhnev Doctrine as the adoption of the "Sinatra doctrine" in Eastern Europe ("Hungary and Poland are doing it their way").[29] On 25 October 1989, Gorbachev announced that the Soviet Union had neither a moral obligation nor a "political right" to interfere in the internal affairs of its Eastern European allies in order to prevent changes in their communist governments.[30] Gorbachev literally "opened the bottle" and the genie of freedom and democracy escaped.[31]

Likewise, the constant spiritual prodding and pressure of John Paul II reminded society that it was not isolated and that freedom was as much a valued "commodity" as was democratic capitalism. Lech Walesa seemed to embody this ideal. He still wears the badge of Poland's national icon, Our Lady of Czestochowa, on his collar lapel as a visual reminder of the deep spiritual aspects of the revolution that has taken place in Poland.

The pope made a historic visit to Poland on 2 June 1979, the first Roman Catholic pontiff ever to visit a communist country. He was met by a virtual "tidal wave" of affection and love. "The Pope stirred an outpouring of faith and affection that no political leader in the contemporary world could hope to inspire. . . . His Holiness seemed to convey an almost tangible sense of strength and joy; joy in adversities overcome, joy in being a Christian and joy in being human."

The words of John Paul II, spoken as he celebrated mass in Victory Square in Warsaw, set a unique backdrop to the impending struggles in his native land. He continued: "It is impossible without Christ to understand the history of the Polish nation. . . . It is impossible without Christ to understand this nation with its past so full of splendor and also of terrible difficulties."[32] In his trip to Poland in June 1983, made during the "dark days" of martial law, the pope verbalized similar sentiments, often including references to principles of "equality and Solidarity." In societal terms, the pope energized Poles who dreamed of the creation of a civil society, dedicated to the principle of the rule of law and based upon the principles of a humane democratic capitalism.

This book is an attempt to explain the core aspects of this process of transformation and change, seen through a blending of historical and economic perspectives. We attempt to view the enormous cataclysms and crises through the eyes of many of its central players: Gomulka, Gierek, Walesa, the founders of KOR, the "simple parish priest," Fr. Jerzy Popieluszko, Balcerowicz, Kuron and Michnik, Mazowiecki, Rulewski,

Pawlak, Kwasniewski, and many others who took center stage in these last 50 years of the emergence of a "new Poland."[33] We seek to identify and detail the unique nature of the Polish experience in a series of chapters that we hope will clarify and highlight significant events and people.

We have purposefully divided the work into nine chapters, in addition to the introduction. Chapter 2 is titled "Economics and Politics: 1945–1980" and deals with the pre-Solidarity period in Poland. We have termed this period first as one of "lost opportunities," and later as one of "misused chances." It is subtitled "Out of Victory—The Rise of Central Planning and the Seeds of Its Demise." Chapter 3 considers the period from 1980 to 1981 and is titled "The Rise of Solidarity." This chapter is subtitled "Sixteen Months that Inspired a Revolution." It outlines the major characteristics of the command-rationing mechanism. It deals with the rise of the Solidarity movement and its origins in KOR, provides biographical vignettes of Jacek Kuron and Adam Michnik, details the events of the summer of 1980, explains economic reform proposals offered by Solidarity in the wake of the "Polish August" of 1980, and describes the general state of Polish economics and politics during this critical period of history.

Chapter 4 looks at the period of martial law in Poland after the "lightning coup" of 13 December 1981. It is subtitled "Economic and Political Consequences of the Polish Coup d'Etat: Failed Attempts at Reform." This chapter considers the contributions of Solidarity to the development of a democratic and capitalist state in Poland, delineates the critical events during the initial period of Solidarity, leading up to the coup, describes the state of Poland's economy during this period, and outlines the reform efforts designed by General Jaruzelski during the difficult period of martial law and immediately after martial law was lifted. We attempt to place the life—and tragic death—of Fr. Jerzy Popieluszko in its proper perspective. The chapter also attempts to answer a simple yet critically important question: Why did nearly 50 years of socialism so fail Poland?

Chapter 5 is titled "The March to the Market Economy: 1989–1993." It considers the period of fundamental change in Poland that occurred with the ascendancy of Tadeusz Mazowiecki to the office of prime minister in 1989. This chapter describes the five pillars of economic transformation and the program of economic stabilization. It focuses on the introduction of the Balcerowicz Plan of shock therapy for the renewal of the Polish economy. By describing the successes and failures of the period 1989 to 1993, we attempt to provide a context to events that would lead to the resurgence of postcommunists in both the Parliament and the presidency by the end of 1995. Chapter 6 is titled "Privatization and Polish Private Sector Development: 1989–1993." It deals with both practical and theoretical questions concerning organizing the postcommunist economy and considers the legal aspects of the transformation process and patterns of private sector development in Poland in the period 1989 to 1993. The chapter outlines the "multitrack" approach undertaken in Poland and the important subtopics of spontaneous privatization, reprivatization, small privatization, *gmina* privatization, cooperative privatization, privatization by liquidation (including the important issue of privatization by leasing), and the "sectoral" approach to privatization. It provides a discussion of the political and economic factors influencing the privatization process, common institutional characteristics, and the stages of privatization and outlines the challenges confronting the entire privatization process.

Chapter 7 is titled "Polish Mass Privatization: Proposals, Plans, and Progress." It outlines strategies and programs implemented to affect the privatization of state-owned enterprises and discusses the creation and implementation of the National Investment Funds. It points out such allied issues as Pawlak's "Procrastination Policy," how privatization efforts were thwarted by political contingencies, and how the path to sustained growth and development through privatization has faced an uncertain, "zigzag" road.

Chapter 8 looks at contemporary Poland and focuses on key political and economic developments. It is titled "Economics and Politics after Shock Therapy." It takes a detailed look at the objectives of the reform effort and the literal "revolving door" of post-1989 governments and it focuses on political configurations and the tragic splintering of Solidarity. Chapter 8 also examines presidential politics leading to the 1995 elections. Chapter 9 represents our efforts to echo the question, *quo vadis?* and is subtitled "Looking Forward to the Third Millennium in Poland and in Central and Eastern Europe." Here, we seek to provide insight into future prospects for Poland as it enters the next century by reflecting on the question: Out of Communism to what? We also look at the "winners and losers" in the transformation process, the reemergence of the *nomenklatura,* and the prospects for a continuing role for Solidarity in the current political and social equation. Chapter 9 offers a series of general conclusions and observations, as well as suggesting several imperatives for the future.

Chapter 10 serves as the epilogue to the book. It describes important political, social, and economic issues in the period after 1995 to the midpoint of 1997. This chapter also raises what we believe are the persistent questions confronting Poland in its continued efforts to join the "family of Europe" and take its place among the family of democratic and capitalist nations.

This work also contains a table of frequently used abbreviations, important economic and political information, and an extensive chronology of important dates and events. We have also provided a selected bibliography to highlight sources used in our research.

The book is based upon a variety of sources and experiences, including visits and interviews. It references many primary sources as well as critical secondary materials—translations, lectures, teaching assignments, and consultations. It also draws from practical business opportunities, conversations, and travels throughout Poland over the last quarter century. We have attempted to provide detailed footnotes in order to assist the reader in appreciating the great amount of sources and materials available to the observer of this period. While we have provided a historical perspective, we have concentrated on politics and economics as the prime focus of this work because these are the subject areas of our background, teaching, and academic and practical experiences. We certainly hope that this book will foster further research and study, as well as vigorous debate, commentary, and analysis.

Chapter Two

Economics and Politics: 1945–1980

Out of Victory–The Rise of Central Planning and the Seeds of Its Demise

"Socialism fits Poland like a saddle fits a cow."
Attributed to J. Stalin

INTRODUCTION

By the spring of 1979, it was evident that the period of growth for the Polish economy of the early to mid-1970s had come to a grinding halt. Indeed, just a few years later, during the summer of 1981, the economy hit absolute "rock bottom" and was practically bankrupt.[1] It was reported that Poland would go into history as the "first country which has borrowed over $25 billion to introduce a system of rationing and worsened living standards."[2] Adam Gwiazda, professor of economics at Gdansk University, aimed a pointed criticism at the bureaucratic system as the root cause for the collapse. Gwiazda noted that even by 1975, every member of the Polish central government and of the Central Planning Commission itself was aware that economic conditions were rapidly deteriorating. Yet, tragically, none were willing to follow the advice of those "more critical and above all more competent experts or advisors" who urged "a fundamental reform of the economic system."[3] The demise of *both* the political and economic systems was clearly at hand.

The rapid deterioration of the economy led to an economic debacle of an unparalleled nature during the period from 1979 to 1982, the "deep years of crisis," a period during which national income declined in real terms for the first time since World War II. In 1979, national income had declined by 3 percent. In 1980, there was a further fall of 6 percent. In 1981, the economy experienced another staggering slide of fully 13 percent, thus reducing economic activity to its 1974 level. In real terms, national income was in 1983 at least 20 percent below the level of 1978.[4]

Pawel Bozyk, chief economic advisor to the Gierek regime, confirmed the private views of Professor Gwiazda in a 1983 book, *Dreams and Reality or an Anatomy of the Polish Crisis*.[5] This book, written from the viewpoint of a policy insider, offers a perspective lacking in critiques of East European political economies.[6] It candidly underscores the attitude of a government that was unable to overcome the structural obstacles of an excessively bureaucratized command structure of central planning and management—a situation that led to a near revolutionary atmosphere. Daniel Singer wrote: "The tensions are such that nobody . . . asks *whether* everything will blow up once again, but *when* it will happen."[7] It was this period of unprecedented economic turmoil that spawned the birth of an independent union movement, Solidarity, the first of its kind in all of Central and Eastern Europe. Solidarity would capture the imagination of workers, intellectuals, and ordinary citizens in Poland and throughout the world. It would galvanize itself into an important economic and political force in Poland during its initial, brief period of legitimacy in 1980–1981 and well beyond into the period of the collapse of the Soviet Empire in Central and Eastern Europe.[8]

In order to better understand this situation, several central questions will be explored: What were the origins of the economic crisis of 1979 to 1982 that led to the birth of Solidarity? What were the contributions of Solidarity to the economic and political equation during the period immediately preceding the imposition of martial law in December of 1981? And finally, what concrete and lasting results may be attributed to the early successes of Solidarity in fashioning a new economic and political system in Poland?

THE GENESIS OF THE CRISIS

Why had the economy of Poland virtually collapsed? What had led Poland, a nation rich in the traditions of hard work, thrift, and economic vibrancy, to such a low level of economic activity and to the precipice of anarchy, violence, economic disaster, and political chaos?

The answers to these questions relate to both economic and political rationales. Successive postwar regimes in Poland,[9] beginning with Wladyslaw Gomulka—first in the immediate postwar period of 1945 to 1948, and again when he returned to power in 1956—had embarked on irrational investment schemes that produced goods (if they produced them at all) inefficiently and wastefully. Poland's traditional major industries—steel, shipbuilding, and coal—failed either to economize or to modernize. Later, under Edward Gierek (1970–1980), what little real economic progress existed was built on a massive amount of borrowing from Western banks, financed by foreign credits and loans. Prices, which were artificially low for a vast array of raw materials and consumer goods, were maintained through a fantastic maze of direct and indirect governmental subsidies. Yet, salaries of workers barely left enough for all but a subsistence level of existence. Bureaucracy, corruption, cronyism, fraud, and waste characterized both the Gomulka and Gierek regimes.

Along with severe economic deficiencies that led inextricably toward the collapse of 1981, there existed a more fundamental and important systemic reason: the "directive and rationing system" of central planning, forced upon Poland by the Soviet Union as an aftermath of the political "realities" of World War II.[10]

Professor John Montias, in his seminal work, *Central Planning in Poland*,[11] delineated three stages characteristic of the directive and rationing system.

1. *Stage I, 1945–1948.* During this period of "national reconstruction," the state expanded its direct control over the economy by nationalizing large scale industrial and commercial enterprises.[12] In 1946 the Sejm passed two important laws: an *Act on the Nationalization of Industry* and an *Act on Taking over the Main Branches of the National Economy*. These laws effected the nationalization of all factories with 50 or more workers and the complete takeover of basic industries such as transportation, mass communications, iron, steel, coal, shipbuilding, and telecommunications.[13] The *Act of Land Reform* nationalized all farms over 100 hectares (about 247 acres) in the former German territory of western Poland that had been receded to Poland as a result of the Yalta Agreements in order to compensate Poland for eastern territories annexed by the Soviet Union. All forest lands over 25 hectares were also nationalized.

All of these acts of nationalization were accomplished through a process of *expropriation,* without compensation to their former owners. These acts, and the system created to administer the "national property," became the basis of centrally planned activity. As a result, industrial and agricultural capacities were rapidly reconstructed.[14] This monumental task was necessitated by the almost total decimation of the prewar economy, and through a recognition of the fact that the prewar "Polish economy bore only a passing resemblance to the classical model of competitive capitalism."[15] Professor Brzezinski noted that the idea of central management may have been suitable for the initial phase of reindustrialization after the conclusion of World War II because of the "imperatives of recovery"[16] that had left Poland and its economy in a state of almost total devastation. During the war, Poland lost 6,028,000 of its citizens—fully 22 percent of all Poles (including over 90 percent out of a prewar population of 3.4 million of Polish Jews who perished in Hitler's extermination or work camps.) Fifty billion dollars, or 38 percent, of the nation's prewar assets were destroyed, as were 60 percent of all work establishments. Eighty percent of the nation's transportation and 60 percent of its schools and scientific institutions were razed; and 20 percent of all farms, 38 percent of all railway lines, 43 percent of all cultural facilities, and 55 percent of all medical facilities were decimated.

2. *Stage II, 1948–1956*. This period was characterized by fundamental "reforms" of the economic system in the Soviet mold. A "one-party state"[17] was created with the merger of the Polish Workers' party (PPR) with the formerly independent Socialist party (PPS) in 1948 under the communist-dominated banner of the Polish United Workers' Party [PZPR].[18] The party soon fell under the control of its "Moscow-trained faction."[19] In 1949, a Russian of supposed Polish origin, Konstantin Rokossovskiy (Konstanty Rokossowski), was appointed commander in chief of the Polish army and minister of defense. All high military positions were awarded to Russian officers. Integration within the Soviet sphere was nearly complete.

The Stalinist system was formalized by the Constitution of July 1952, which officially proclaimed the Polish People's Republic (PRL). These events freed central planners, under the leadership of Hilary Minc, to initiate a number of important economic changes: the comprehensive physical allocation of essential material resources; the imposition of long-term plans for all industrial units; central budget grants to individual enterprises for major investment outlays; an all-out industrialization drive "spearheaded by the growth of heavy industry," especially iron and steel; and a centralized system of price fixing, often at a highly subsidized level, which reflected a pronounced antimarket behavior.[20] For example, in the city of Krakow, a massive project was undertaken with the construction of Nowa Huta, a new suburb created to support the Lenin Steelworks, the largest of its kind in Poland. Lawrence Goodwyn asserted that Nowa Huta "achieved a monotony of such august proportions that it almost seemed to represent a conscious effort by state planners to diminish the self-esteem of the work force."[21]

In agriculture, priority was given to forced collectivization. The government engaged in a campaign to deprive peasants of their private ownership rights and to force them into State Agricultural Enterprises and into cooperatives. Between 1950 and 1955, the number of collective farms rose from 12,513 to 28,955. Professor Sanders noted that the "private peasant faced the prospect of elimination," raising in Poland the specter of the destruction of the kulaks by Stalinist terror in the 1930s.[22]

In the social sphere, the Catholic Church was subjected to a blistering attack, as Stalinism penetrated all aspects of public life. The government, officially atheistic, promoted the schismatic Polish National church, and launched a series of anti-Catholic, political-religious organizations such as

PAX, Caritas, and Veritas. In 1950, all Church property (with the exception of church buildings themselves, churchyards, and cemeteries) was nationalized. Priests were detained and arrested in large numbers. In 1953, Stefan Cardinal Wyszynski, the primate, was arrested and placed under detention in the remote monastery of Komancza in the Bieszczady Mountains of southern Poland.

During this secondary phase of central planning, even the State Price Commission was hemmed in by various limitations on its activities. It was obliged to honor a pledge made by the Bierut government to bar further price increases for any commodity whatsoever. The regulations adopted by the State Price Commission were so complex and fraught with administrative exceptions that there was often "considerable doubt" as to which prices ought to be paid. An article in *Zycie Gospodarcze* [Economic Life] noted that "in many instances, there was no apparent reason at all for wide differences in profitability," and thus in prices.[23]

3. *Stage III, 1956–1970.* During the third stage of central planning, bureaucrats were confronted by a series of inescapable economic conclusions and had to face squarely resource scarcities constraining the modernization and development of the economy. Instead of moving ahead boldly with further collectivism, state planners had to concentrate on how to make the best use of the available resources to achieve goals laid down by political authorities. Economic reality confronted Polish state planners. The Marxist notion of "thesis-antithesis" had come full circle. Central planning simply would not work. Professor Bozyk captured the essential dilemma faced by central planners: "It is no joke that in Poland, a country with the highest per capita production of coal in the world, there is a permanent shortage of coal. In Cuba, there is a shortage of sugar and in China, of labor force. The point of the joke is the hypothesis that if the system existed in the Sahara it would inevitably lack sand."[24]

Thus, as early as 1956, Bronislaw Minc had called for essential reforms in the economic system: "First of all, we must substantially restrict the scope of directives laid down by the central authorities and accord a much wider measure of independence to enterprises and local organs."[25] Stage III saw central planners clearly on the defensive. It was widely recognized that many of the disproportions in Poland's economy that had arisen during the course of the various plans were due to "poor balancing prior to the plan and excessively optimistic forecasts of productivity trends . . . and to strategic errors which common sense and economic experience could have avoided."[26]

Professor Edward Lipinski, the dean of Warsaw economists, was even more pointed in his substantive criticisms, calling central planning an "impediment to economic development."[27] Lipinski believed that it was necessary to decentralize the economy and to grant greater autonomy and initiative to socialized enterprises. Oskar Lange, the economist and diplomat, spoke of a "new economic calculus," where decentralization in planning and management of the economy was both vital and necessary.[28] Lange served as chairman of the State Economic Council. He believed that prices must be fixed on the basis of a "market mechanism," linking necessary state planning to market forces. Lange further postulated that the Stalinist scheme of industry was not suited to a "mechanical translation" to Poland, a country with entirely different economic and political considerations from other nations in Central and Eastern Europe. The council itself favored decentralization and limited restructuring of private enterprise in retail trade, handicrafts, services, and small scale production.[29] In addition, and perhaps more importantly, the State Economic Council recommended the transfer of direct authority to fix annual plans, to improve investments, and to make decisions on new production to the factory or enterprise level.

What was the essential critique of the system of central planning? Why was the economic system itself the major target of fresh criticism by viewpoints even within the Polish ruling strata? The central planning system imposed direct targets on virtually every one of Poland's individual industrial units and carried with it direct plans of implementation, based on the twin concepts of *submission* and *subordination*. The system additionally required a huge bureaucracy and a "heavy apparatus" for planning. The system, to which Professor Wladyslaw Balicki ascribed the notion of the "fetish of the central planner,"[30] attributed to the state the role of the only true economic subject or actor. Balicki continued that one rule operated without exception: "the lower the targets of the plan, and the more means for realization are available," the higher is the probability of its execution. The writer Jerzy Putrament had commented some two months before the Poznan riots in 1956, writing in *Przeglad Kulturalny* [Cultural Review]: "Non-fulfillment of the Plan has become something so terrible that people will do anything to avoid it. . . . The Plan is law. . . . The Plan means bonuses. The Plan means for many workers the achievement of a minimum standard of living."[31]

After the tragedy of Poznan on 28 June 1956, in which 53 persons had lost their lives clamoring for "bread and freedom" and chanting "Russians go home," workers at the ZISPO Locomotive Factory rioted in the streets, assaulted Party buildings, attacked the local police station, and wrecked the radio-jamming towers that had successfully blocked broadcasts of both the BBC and Radio Free Europe. The factory was a huge works, formerly known as Hipolit Cegielski, employing 15,000 workers. The Central Committee of the United Workers' party convened in a plenary session. Edward Ochab, successor to Boleslaw Bierut, who had died while on a visit to Moscow in February of 1956, addressed the systemic question forthrightly: "As a consequence of this system, mistakes, once made, were magnified and became impacted. . . . Local initiative—the initiative of the staff and management of factories—was paralyzed."[32]

The resolutions of the Seventh Plenum of the Party called for the prompt liquidation of "excessive centralization and administration" of the economy. The resolutions also demanded an absolute reduction in the number of central directives binding on individual enterprises. Managers of enterprises were promised more autonomy, and incentive schemes were proposed to encourage the elimination of waste and inefficiency, the compression of costs, and the essential improvement in the quality of goods produced. Comments made at this plenum noted: "In the course of the implementation of the Six Year Plan, an excessive centralization of the planning and administration has taken place, as well as an excessive growth in the state . . . apparatus and bureaucratization of the methods of leadership. These phenomena have hampered the initiative of the masses . . . and have caused waste and have retarded technical progress and economic expansion in general."[33]

Later, when Wladyslaw Gomulka was reinstated as first secretary of the PZPR, a real impetus for reform based upon a popular consensus was anticipated. Gomulka had spoken bravely: "The causes of the Poznan tragedy and of the deep dissatisfaction of the entire working class lie within us, in the Party and in the government."[34] The early optimism was short-lived.

THE HEART OF THE CRISIS–THE ROOTS OF SOLIDARITY

The next period of 25 years (1956–1981) can be aptly characterized as first, that of "lost opportunities," and later, that of "misused chances."

Wladyslaw Gomulka

Much of the history of postwar Poland is the personal history of Wladyslaw Gomulka. By the end of 1943, Gomulka had emerged as first secretary of the PPR, which had been established in 1942. A complicated and complex man, Gomulka remained "unwaivering to communist ideals," and at the same time, managed a "lifelong revulsion to Soviet practices."[35] In the 1930s, Gomulka had received training at a Communist party school in the Soviet Union and had witnessed firsthand the brutal collectivization campaign in the Ukraine. In retrospect, it was fortunate for Gomulka that he had been arrested by the police for illegal political activities. He was thus spared Stalin's purge of the indigenous Polish Communist party (KPP). In 1939, as an official of the Union of Chemical Workers, Gomulka found himself in prison in Lwow in the Soviet zone of occupation, but he returned to his native town of Krosno in the *General-gouvernement,* or Nazi-controlled part of Poland. Later, Gomulka made his way to Warsaw at the height of the Nazi occupation and terror. Professor Norman Davies captured the essence of the man, Gomulka, who would dominate nearly three decades of Polish politics:

> In most other matters, Gomulka remained an orthodox, disciplined, and philistine communist. He had little time for intellectual theorists, or for artistic pursuits, and no interest at all in liberal ideas. The stubbornness of his nature, forged in prison and in the underground, was to prove a stumbling-block not only to Soviet designs for manipulating Poland to their own uses but also at a later date to misguided hopes for "liberalization." . . . For the next twenty-seven years, his outlook stamped itself on the basic aspirations of a movement which did not gain control of its own destiny until 1956.[36]

Gomulka's rise to prominence closely paralleled the rise to power of the communists in Poland. On 22 July 1944, the first postwar government, the Polish Committee of National Liberation (PKWN), was formed in Lublin under Soviet auspices. Gomulka was appointed second deputy prime minister and minister for recovered territories in the West. This land had been given to Poland in compensation for the 70,000 square miles—nearly the eastern one-third of the nation—annexed by the Soviet Union. Gomulka administered a territory that contained the 5,057,000 Germans expelled from the former German provinces of East Pomerania, East Brandenburg, Silesia, Danzig, East Prussia, and Central Poland, on the basis of an agreement reached between the Allies on 14 February 1946.[37]

The settling of these territories became a point of national pride for Poland for both historical and political reasons. Gomulka gained a reputation for dedication, patriotism, and resolve, even as the communist movement itself remained weak and ineffectual and could never have "contemplated open competition" with established democratic parties. It was therefore critical to destroy these rivals for power. Words such as "communist" were carefully avoided—even when coining the party's official name as the Polish Workers' party. Professor Lawrence Goodwyn pronounced the Communist party of this period as a "social failure," led by a "band of functionaries despised by the population, maintained in power solely through military force, politically trapped between its dependence on the Soviet Union and its demoralizing illegitimacy at home."[38] The long-delayed elections promised at both Yalta and Potsdam finally took place on 19 January 1947.

In these elections, the communist-led "Democratic Bloc" garnered 80 percent of the votes cast, in an exercise that was neither "free" nor "unfettered." The list of candidates was heavily screened by the government. Nearly two million voters were struck from the register of those eligible to vote by the government-controlled electoral commission. When the British and American governments lodged official protests that the elections violated provisions of both the Yalta and Potsdam Agreements, the Soviets rejected such assertions.[39] As a result of the elections, the PPR assumed its domination of Polish politics for the first time, engaging in the "systematic extermination of the prewar Peasant and Socialist parties."[40] On 5 February 1947, Boleslaw Bierut, the spokesman for the Lublin government, was elected president. On 6 February, a government under Prime Minister Jozef Cyrankiewicz of the Polish Socialist party (PPS) took offic with Communist support. From this date, all prospects for the reemergence of a free, independent, and democratic Poland were dashed. Stanislaw Mikolajczyk, the leader of the Peasant party, was publicly denounced as both a "foreign spy" and a "collaborator." In October of 1947, Mikolajczyk fled for his life and spent his remaining days in exile in London and in the West.

However, by June 1948, Gomulka's fortunes had changed. Gomulka was now seen as a defender of an unacceptable "national independence" and of the "uniqueness" of Polish communism. He was denounced by associates and was forced to make a formal recantation of alleged "flaws" and "errors." He was replaced as general secretary of the Party by President Bierut. Davies described Bierut as a "stool-pigeon of the most obvious ilk, quite incapable of forming a power grouping in Poland except at the end of someone else's string."[41] However, unlike many others who fell from power and who lost all (including their lives), Gomulka remained as vice premier until January 1949, and as a member of the Central Committee of the Communist party until 1951. Gomulka was never subjected to a public trial or shipped to a "gulag" in the Soviet Union.

In the course of the summer of 1956, Gomulka would resurface from years in exile. His impending resurgence was foretold by the resignation of Hilary Minc as minister of industry, the individual directly responsible for the discredited planning function. On 21 October 1956, Gomulka was unanimously elected as first secretary. He was immediately confronted by a direct challenge from the Soviet Union and Nikita Khrushchev, who had landed at Warsaw's Okecie Airport with the entire Russian Politburo in order to orchestrate a "solution" satisfactory to the Soviet Union and to block Gomulka's return to power. Gomulka achieved instant celebrity status when Khrushchev relented, faced by the clear prospect that the Poles were "prepared to fight" and that it was indeed doubtful that the Polish General Staff would obey Marshall Rokossowski's orders to fire on its own people.

The Period of "Lost Opportunities"

The initial period under Gomulka was seen by many as a time of economic growth because of certain quantitative results. New apartments were constructed. Prices for basic consumer goods were rolled back. The standard of living increased, as Gomulka reversed many of the more unpopular economic decrees of his predecessors, especially those dealing with the forced collectivization in the agricultural sector. Gomulka also attempted to reestablish at least cordial relations (perhaps a truce would be more accurate) with the Catholic church. Stefan Cardinal Wyszynski was freed from his long house arrest. Gomulka stated: "It is a poor idea to maintain that only Communists can build socialism, only people holding materialistic social views."[42]

However, the period of his second stewardship (1956–1970) saw no essential change in the management system, even as Poland embarked on its own "road to socialism." In fact, the second Gomulka period saw the strengthening and institutionalization of the system of central management and planning, as the government reinstated commissions for the control of science, culture, and education.[43] The central planners' response to an increasingly sluggish growth rate was to "attempt to secure even greater control over the economy and to restore high growth by committing greater volumes of inputs to production."[44] Despite clear economic indications to the contrary, the theoretical errors perpetuated by the Gomulka regime became further ingrained in a system that would bring Poland to its knees barely 10 years later. These errors may be summarized as follows:

1. The idea of central management and planning, seen as the only acceptable form of economic functioning at the macroeconomic level, was strengthened and institutionalized;[45] and
2. The inability of reaching the dual social goals of modernization and industrialization, except through the adoption and implementation of a central plan in a centrally managed economy, was never again seriously questioned.

By 1961, Gomulka had gradually lost the respect of his nation, which had universally acclaimed him as patriot and savior in 1956. Professor Davies wrote: "In the course of the 1960s, the drive for economic self-sufficiency, especially in agriculture, ran into difficulties. The promised rise in the standard of living was slow to materialize. The Party bureaucracy prospered ostentatiously, to the disgust of the ordinary people. The First Secretary surrounded himself with a closed circle of cronies, and steadily lost contact with opinion in the Party and in the country at large."[46]

Two separate crises would drive Gomulka from power. One, the crisis of 1968, was sparked by a relatively minor incident concerning a performance of Adam Mickiewicz's classic, *Dziady* [Forefathers' Eve], which was ordered closed after a protest was made by the Soviet ambassador that the play was anti-Soviet. When students took to the streets in Warsaw in protest, they were beaten and arrested, as the press called upon workers to defend the nation against "Zionist traitors." In Krakow, Market Square was surrounded by members of the ORMO factory police, and buildings of Jagiellonian University were attacked by a special riot squad that brandished clubs and tear gas. Professor Davies noted that these actions were "classic examples of political provocation so common in the annals of East European dictatorships."[47]

These events also marked an open political challenge to Gomulka, in the person of General Mieczyslaw Moczar, the minister of the interior, who was most willing to take action against Poland's "enemies." After a series of confrontations between workers, students, and intellectuals, Gomulka was able to reassert his authority, as the Communist party closed ranks around his leadership—at least for the time being. However, Gomulka engineered the dismissal or resignation of many prominent individuals from public life (including Leszek Kolakowski, the Marxist philosopher, and Pawel Jasienica, the historian) in what is now regarded as a most "bizarre episode" with severe antisemitic overtones.

The crisis of 1970 was precipitated by sheer stupidity on the part of the government, which decided to introduce price increases in the range of 12 to 36 percent, curiously during the two-week period preceding Christmas. Professor Goodwyn wrote: "A party leadership without credentials had picked the Christmas holidays to demonstrate yet one more time its disdain for the population."[48] Strikes and demonstrations broke out in various parts of Poland, and Gomulka was forced to order the militia and the army to restore order. However, the most devastating challenge was mounted by workers in the Baltic region in the shipyards of Szczecin, Gdynia, and Gdansk (including an appearance by a 27-year-old electrician and activist at the Lenin Shipyard, Lech Walesa, named by the workers to a strike committee). Professor Davies captured the core of this worker challenge, led by the most highly paid and historically progovernment sectors in the work force:

> Clearly, the root of the trouble lay much deeper than in the immediate problem of food prices; and feelings ran high. In Gdansk, the train bringing workers to the shipyards, where a lockout had been proclaimed, was ambushed, and fired on by armed militiamen. The workers responded with fury. Shops were looted. Party headquarters were besieged. Militiamen were lynched on the street. The Militia Training Centre at Slupsk was burned to the ground. Demonstrators were crushed by armored vehicles. . . . In all, some three hundred people were killed.[49]

On this occasion, however, Gomulka was unable to defend himself from criticisms coming from all fronts—the Party, intellectuals, students, and workers. On 20 December 1970, the Seventh Plenum of the Central Committee accepted Gomulka's "resignation" and confirmed the elevation of Edward Gierek to the post of first secretary. The early promise of the Gomulka era had crashed in economic and political disaster.

In the next decade, Edward Gierek, a mining technocrat and Party bureaucrat with little formal economic training, would eschew Gomulka's view of a unique "Polish road to socialism." Gierek would instead base his vision of technical progress and modernization on a system financed by a direct infusion of foreign credits, Western technology, and external resources.

The Period of "Misused Chances"

Edward Gierek came into office on a tide of goodwill and expectation. Gierek had been the longtime party boss in Silesia. He had spent his early years with the Communist parties of both France and Belgium and was the first Party leader in the Soviet Bloc who had never been trained in the Soviet Union. Gierek appeared to be quite different from Gomulka in both style and substance. His first official act was to order a freeze in food prices for a period of 12 months. He visited Gdansk and spoke with shipyard workers. Gierek "exonerated the workers" and placed blame for the country's social turmoil upon the departed party leadership. He attempted to assuage the fears of peasants by abolishing compulsory deliveries of foodstuffs to the state, by increasing the base prices paid for food, and by extending free health services to nonstate-sector employees. Intellectuals were "wooed" by easing censorship of newspapers and independent magazines (especially the weekly Polityka [Politics], which frequently detailed stories of corruption and scandal on the part of the government) and by lowering restrictions on foreign travel and foreign contacts. Polish patriotism was reinforced by the rebuilding of the Royal Castle in Warsaw, and contacts with Polish emigrés (Polonia) were both encouraged and strengthened. Initially, the period from 1971 to 1975 saw a dramatic increase in real wages, by an average of 7.2 percent.[50] Prime Minister Jaroszewicz said: "The main aim of this plan [1971–1975] is an acceleration in the growth of living standards in comparison with the past ten years."[51]

A series of other early successes, especially in the period from 1971 to 1973, was also evident with a better supply of consumer goods, the stabilization of prices for necessities, and the modernization and industrialization of the economy. However, contrary to what had become a "propaganda of success," it is now widely recognized that Gierek's policies were an objective failure, leading the nation to the brink of economic disintegration and political collapse. Professor George Sanford of the University of Bristol pointedly asserted: "The 1980 crisis had been caused primarily by the Gierek leadership's faulty and authoritarian decision-making processes and by the over-ostentatious personal corruption of its cadres."[52]

Indeed, while Polish exports increased by an average rate of 10.7 percent for the years 1971 to 1975, Polish imports increased by an average of 15.4 percent during this same period. The growth of imports reached a high of 53 percent in 1976. More alarmingly, foreign debt had risen to around $26 billion; by 1983 it would further rise to a staggering $29.6 billion.[53] Policies adopted by Gierek failed to produce the growth required to finance the massive amounts of borrowing and imports. Many Western bankers and financial experts had described Poland's economy as "practically bankrupt."[54] Professor Jan Drewnowski was even more explicit in his criticism: "For some reasons, the centrally planned economies proved neither able to perform or to reform."[55] The "for some reasons" led analysts inevitably to a critique once again of the mechanism of the command structure which denigrated individual responsibility, managerial skill, and economic efficiency.

By 1975, the last year in which the economy would grow in real terms, it was apparent that the "New Economic and Financial System,"[56] launched on 1 January 1973, would not work. This strategy could not be a substitute for deep economic reform. In addition, the burden of the ever-increasing foreign debt became so severe that Poland was unable to produce enough exports to pay the interest on the various loans for the capital intensive improvements that had been begun, some with an investment time lag of up to 10 years.

Under Gierek, funds were improperly allocated and investment priorities were improperly set. Expensive licenses were obtained for Fiat automobiles, Jones cranes, Leland engines, Berliet buses, Grundig electronics, and Massey-Ferguson tractors, which would be adapted for use by Polish peasants who still used methods and technologies developed for farmers of the 18th and 19th centuries.

In all, more than 85 percent of all investments during this period were for projects with an investment cycle of more than five years, most notably in the energy and coal sectors. Many of these projects were high cost, inefficient, and poorly placed, especially those in the chemical, petrochemical, and pesticide areas, and those in textiles, paper and machine tools—further weakening Poland's fragile environment. Resources were wasted through an inherently bad decision-making process, influenced by the rise to importance of the so-called industrial lobbies. These lobbies saw that their economic security and personal success lay in preserving the centrally planned system, in lowering the targets of the production plan, and often in increasing the volume and means necessary for the execution of Gierek's plan. More importantly, the Gierek period was marked by an inefficient motivation mechanism on both the managerial and operational levels, characterized by cronyism, corruption, and waste. Professor Goodwyn noted: "The command economy lurched towards crisis, and the government tightened up on work norms throughout the society; the workers rebelled, and the party promised reforms; when changes did not materialize, the worker mobilization enlarged, and the party attempted new evasions."[57]

The crisis of 1976 was symptomatic of the inherent failure of Edward Gierek. In June of 1976, Gierek ordered prices for food raised by an average of 60 percent. Strikes, protests, and demonstrations spontaneously broke out in almost every town and factory in the nation. In Warsaw workers at the Ursus tractor plant tore up the railway track and laid siege to the Paris-Moscow express. In Radom a Party headquarters was razed to the ground. In Nowa Huta, where just a decade earlier workers had rallied to the defense of the beleaguered Gomulka regime, the army was called upon to continue production in the deserted steelworks. At the Lenin Shipyard in Gdansk, an occupation (sit-down) strike took place. The same was true at Gdynia, Elblag, Slupsk, and Szczecin. Under siege, the government canceled its price increases. It seemed that Gierek had learned little or nothing from the experiences of Gomulka. J. B. de Weydenthal noted: "It had become increasingly obvious that the man whose name had been associated in the minds of many with the exceedingly ambitious program of rapid industrialization and modernization of Poland's economy in the early 1970s had proved to be incapable of adjusting his views and of proposing new policies when the situation became more difficult."[58]

Edward Gierek would continue in office until July of 1980, when another crisis would hit. On 1 July 1980, the government once again introduced increases in the price of meat and meat products. Workers reacted with shock and with a wave of strikes and work stoppages. A little more than two months later, the Gierek era, begun with optimism and hope, would abruptly end with a communique issued by the Polish United Workers' party: "In connection with the serious illness of Edward Gierek, the Central Committee relieved him of the function of First Secretary of the Central Committee and as a member of the Politburo." Gierek was replaced by Stanislaw Kania, a longtime Politburo member and Central Committee secretary in charge of internal and military security issues, as well as church-state affairs. In his address to the nation of 6 September 1980, Kania repeated almost verbatim the words of his predecessor when he assumed power after the fall of Wladyslaw Gomulka: "Serious mistakes in economic policies and disparities in social life have been the basic sources of the great wave of strikes that have rolled across Poland since July and that lasted until today." Kania continued: "Our most important task is that of restoring public confidence in authority, the confidence of the working class, and of all working people in the party. We must build a strong bond between authority and the people. This has been lacking and this has caused an outburst of widespread discontent so dangerous in its consequences."[59]

Tragically, Gierek's years may best be characterized as the period of "misused chances." It is also important to note that as economic failures under Gierek mounted, the system itself, the mechanism of planning, once again came under siege. Professor Balicki noted: "Wherever a centrally planned economy exists, there exists the inevitable shortages or queues in shops" and the situation of permanent and irreversible shortages in the economy of both investment possibilities and consumer goods.

In any command structure, several consequences will inevitably and universally result:

1. Severe disequilibrium of demand;
2. Rapid growth of economic and political bureaucratic (the *nomenklatura*) involvement in the mechanisms of planning;
3. Permanent underdevelopment of the enterprise level, which produces consumer goods, and the nondevelopment of management techniques, objectives, and prerogatives; and
4. Continuous lines in shops, with the burden of inefficiency and failure falling squarely on the consumption sector.

Perhaps most alarmingly, as Professor Balicki reported, there exists no hope of escaping until the economic mechanism is changed. In short, Poland had been tragically transformed into a land of lines and *nie ma*! with a fundamental disconnect between politics and economics.

It is also interesting to note that under Gierek, the Communist party itself had begun to disintegrate. Professor Andrzej Walicki wrote: "The leadership of the party avoided even lip service to the communist ideals, encouraging instead the *nomenklatura's* tendency towards embourgeoisement. The party itself had become a mass organization supporting the regime as it was and caring very little for ideology. Most of its members openly despised Marxist indoctrination, loathed being called communists, and justified their political options on the ground of expediency oriented patriotism."[60]

It was at this point, after the fall of Gierek ("the price of food has been taken as a barometer of political protest"[61]) that a societal consensus began to develop for a fundamental change in the economic system. The foundations of reform[62] were based on four considerations:

1. The system of central planning is not a suitable basis for the functioning of the Polish economy;
2. The system of allocation tended to be both conservative and wasteful and was geared toward favoring the "big industries," the so-called WOGs,[63] well represented in the political and economic apparatus of government;
3. The system of central planning will lead inevitably to breakdown and crisis, and to the dissatisfaction and alienation of the working classes. The dysfunctions of the system of central planning resulted in the recurring, cyclical political crises, riots, and upheavals that had gripped Poland and that toppled Gierek in 1980 as they had Gomulka earlier in 1970;
4. The monocentric system will lead to an unusual mixture of greater centralized control and a kind of economic volunteerism[64] in which

important decisions were made in a totally unguided manner without any reference to any objective principles or any rational purpose, and to the eventual destruction of both the political and economic systems.

It was also this period that saw the rise of a new and vital player in the economic and political sphere—the first *independent* trade union operating behind the authoritarian walls of a communist-controlled socialist economy.

Chapter Three

The Rise of Solidarity

Sixteen Months that Inspired a Revolution

"If a living system drifts too close (to the edge of chaos), it risks falling over into incoherence and dissolution; but if the system moves too far away from the edge, it becomes rigid, frozen, totalitarian. Both conditions lead to extinction."

Michael Crichton, *The Lost World* (1995)

Andrzej Gwiazda was one of the radical leaders and perhaps the most eloquent spokesman for the strike movement in 1980. Lawrence Goodwyn described Gwiazda as an individual who had a "commanding, almost imperial presence, a quick mind, and an iron determination to free himself and the rest of the Polish nation from as much of the party apparatus as was geopolitically possible."[1] Gwiazda had declared: "For thirty-five years, we invest, we invest, we invest and our society has practically nothing to show for it. For years, people asked how much steel was being produced, how much coal was being dug. But nobody looked at what it all meant for the life of the workers."[2]

CHARACTERISTICS OF THE ECONOMIC SYSTEM—THE CRM

It is important to understand the nature of the economic system that would drive critics to the belief that a fundamental change was necessary in order to break the cycle of crisis (1956, 1968, 1970, 1976) that had gripped Poland for nearly 25 years before the birth of Solidarity in 1980.

Leszek Balcerowicz identified certain basic characteristics of the Soviet-type monocentric system.[3] He asserted that these characteristics are endemic; thus, they exist independently and "regardless of the will of the economic actors." These characteristics may be summarized as follows:

1. The most basic feature of the monocentric system is the *command-rationing mechanism* (CRM), which consists of establishing planning targets, coupled with severe administrative allocation of inputs. This feature is expressed in a comprehensive and detailed central plan that is applied to component industries or levels of production during a period that Balcerowicz described as "interlevel bargaining." The CRM replaced a traditional market mechanism with centralized coordination and allocation functions performed by the State Planning Commission.

2. The CRM requires an organizational system involving the strict hierarchial *subordination* of lower echelon managers to superior state and party bodies, termed the *nomenklatura* system,[4] operated by the governing party apparatus. Balcerowicz noted that in the "monoparty system of the Soviet type the distinction between the party and state administration is a fiction."[5] Professor Andrzej Walicki asserted that by the time of the crisis of 1980, the Party itself "was a mass organization supporting the regime as it was and caring little for any ideology."[6] In short, the system had only one real objective—maintaining its position of power and privilege in the state. The *nomenklatura* system also developed into a highly centralized administrative structure—not only for truly national organizations but also for intermediary organizations, whereby smaller enterprises operated only as a part of huge centrally organized bureaucracies. The operation of this system guaranteed the Communist party the right to name the top 150,000 administrators (including enterprise directors) in Poland. By the 1980s, the system had virtually elapsed into a "lunatic collage of incompetence, privilege, pandering and outright corruption," based on a principle of chronic underqualification and a "perverted practice of negative selection."[7]

3. In order to maintain the system, the state apparatus must centralize the right to create, restructure, and dissolve enterprises and ancillary organizations. Private organizations and enterprise managers are barred from taking decisive actions, especially in creating new enterprises. Balcerowicz identified the following additional features dictated by efforts at *centralization*: the assignment of enterprises to specific branches of government (creation of strong and dependent "vertical links" between the government branch and individual enterprise); the prohibition of independent ties between organizations (the inability to create "horizontal links" between enterprises and between workers in these enterprises); and the elimination or restructuring of enterprises through administrative procedures rather than through bankruptcy. This "centralization of organizational rights," which gives a monopoly to state action, precludes spontaneity in the evolution of

the organization and assures that the monocentric system will be preserved, at all costs.[8]

4. The CRM requires a financial structure in order to carry out a major redistribution of funds, accomplished through *state subsidies*. This structure includes a noncommercial banking system, which Balcerowicz described as a "monobank." It is a poor substitute for the creation of a genuine capital market. The monobank distributes credit and automatically funds the state budget according to the imperatives of the central plan and not according to any objective criteria of financial viability. In such a system, a securities market is both unnecessary and undesirable.

Following an analysis of the basic characteristics of the system, Balcerowicz then identified certain "derivative traits" of the CRM:

1. Administrative price fixing by central authorities;
2. The isolation of domestic producers from foreign markets, deriving from the fact that domestic prices are unrelated to the world prices of similar goods or from the price of inputs into the product, the excessive regulation of imports through licenses and import quotas, and a tendency by central planners to engage in "import substitution" (often accomplished through rationing, queues, lines, and coupons);
3. Enterprises' "soft budget constraint" (often requiring that targets of planning be revised downward or that inputs be significantly increased in order to meet the plan), which results from excessive governmental intervention, defective or unrealistic prices, and the lack of commercial financial institutions[9];
4. Monopolization due to "extreme organizational concentration," the centralization of organizational rights (which regards the government as the only true economic actor or subject), and the lack of foreign competition.

All of these monopolistic tendencies make individual enterprises insensitive to market forces and to any fundamental or subtle changes in consumer demand.

These characteristics and traits created a dominant self-centered motivation, significant information limitations on the part of decision makers through the absence of horizontal links, low cost efficiency, and low innovation. Perhaps most importantly, the system created chronic shortages, which placed the inefficiency of the system squarely on the consumption sector.[10] In addition, the CRM involved numerous *motivational factors* that operated to preserve the existing system. The continuance of the system further assured a lack of interest in reform, no matter how minimal or piecemeal such reform may have appeared to an outside observer.

In this context, Balcerowicz noted that only a radical restructuring of the economy can remedy these inherent contradictions and flaws. He also added that "this is why a radical economic reform is much more difficult to introduce than to maintain. The reverse is true of superficial reform."[11] These important questions arise: Who would be able to introduce or suggest these reforms in the context of a closed political system? What group or groups in society could spur the nation to a radically different economic system? What type of system would, in Andrzej Gwiazda's words, make a "real difference in the lives of the workers" who had invested both in their enterprises and society and who had so little to show for their substantial efforts after nearly four decades of Polish socialism?[12]

THE RISE OF SOLIDARITY

During September 1979, 11 months before the events of July and August 1980, *Robotnik* [The Worker], the official publication of the Committee for Social Self-Defense [KOR], published a charter of workers' rights and a program for achieving them. While recognizing that strikes might be effective over the "short run," KOR noted that in order to preserve whatever gains might be won, something more substantive would be required: the rejection of government and party-dominated labor organizations in favor of the creation of free and independent trade unions. "Only they can represent a power the authorities cannot ignore and will have to negotiate with on an equal footing."[13] Among the 65 signatories to the charter was Lech Walesa, an unemployed electrician and union activist from Gdansk. Walesa had been fired from a succession of jobs (the Lenin Shipyard in 1976, a building company, ZREMB, in 1979, and the engineering firm Elektromontaz in 1980) for political activities and for being dubbed a "political troublemaker." This was the same Walesa who in May 1978 had joined with Andrzej Gwiazda and Anna Walentynowicz, later central players in Solidarity, to form the Committee of Free Trade Unions for the Baltic Coast.

KOR as the Foundation of Solidarity

Lawrence Goodwyn noted: "It was as if KOR's ideas, whatever they might be, were somehow understood to have been projected over an invisible social transom and into the consciousness of an unseen group of people, abstractly identified as the workers. In unspecified ways, this information enabled the workers to make the revolution."[14]

After the 1976 crisis, in reaction to the violence and lawlessness of the government in cracking down on workers in Radom, a small group of intellectuals came to the defense of the workers who had been persecuted for their participation in the June protests. In September 1976, a group, led by Jacek Kuron, created the Committee for the Defense of Workers, known by its Polish acronym, KOR. This committee was composed of 14 and later 30 members drawn primarily from the "literary and technical intelligentsia," including Jan Litynski and Henryk Wujec. KOR immediately began to collect funds for the families of imprisoned workers—the money would be used for medical assistance for the victims of police brutality and for legal assistance for those charged with various "offenses against the state." In short, KOR began to act as a traditional labor union, creating a striker fund. KOR also began to publish an open *Information Bulletin,* which contained detailed economic data and a factual refutation of evidence the state was prepared to use in its various "showcase" trials of activists.

From its inception, KOR also assumed the responsibility of speaking for the creation of a "civil society" based on the rule of law, in order to counterbalance the reviled system controlled by the Communist party and the bureaucracy. KOR hoped to demonstrate that unlike its inaction in previous crises, the intelligentsia would rally to the side of workers. In 1977, KOR had attempted to form a "free trade union" in Radom, but the effort was unsuccessful, as the one worker whom KOR located was unable to recruit anyone else to its cause. This effort was centered around the journal *Robotnik.* Its editor, Leopold Gierek (no relation to the first secretary), pledged to fight for the rights of working men independently of the official government unions.[15]

On 23 February 1978, a Workers' Committee was formed in Katowice. It appealed to Polish workers to create "free national trade unions." This appeal was signed by Kazimierz Switon, the owner of a radio shop, Wladyslaw Sulecki, Tadeusz Kicki, and Roman Ksciuczek. The founders noted the "centralization and omnipotence of the government apparat, the lack of independence of the official unions, and their consequent inability to defend the workers' rights." They added that "by uniting [we] will be able to resist the exploitation of the workers by the state and the party apparats."[16]

While these efforts in Katowice succeeded in producing a free trade union with four members, its creation did not immediately produce any major results. One exception was found in Gdansk, where Krzysztof Wyszkowski, a "well-read carpenter" and a non-Party socialist, joined with Andrzej Gwiazda and Antoni Sokolowski in issuing a "founding statement" on 29 April 1978. The appeal pointed out that the creation of free unions was necessary because the official unions had failed to protect workers' interests and had become "a subordinate instrument for the organized exploitation of all social groups by the ruling communist party."[17]

This group was joined by Bogdan Borusewicz (the lone KOR member on the Baltic coast), Gwiazda's wife Joanna, Wyszkowski's brother Blazej,

Lech Walesa, and Anna Walentynowicz. Andrzej and Joanna Gwiazda were both trained engineers. Along with Bogdan Borusewicz, they had been educated at the Catholic University in Lublin (KUL). Anna Walentynowicz was a 53-year old crane operator and a longtime union organizer. Almost immediately, Wyszkowski was beaten up by the security police. Walesa was only saved from being sacked from his job at ZREMB when co-workers threatened a "sympathy strike." Gwiazda was jailed and fined and Blazej Wyszkowski was ruthlessly persecuted by police. Sokolowski, unfortunately, renounced his association with the group—only later to recant his denunciation.

Lech Walesa would later write: "There's no slot in official Poland for people like the Wyszkowskis, just as there's no room for Andrzej Gwiazda and his wife Joanna, human rights activists who tackle needed social reforms head-on."[18] Walesa's view echoed that offered by Professor Goodwyn, who noted: "The episode merely verified the perilous status of working-class organizing in a police state."[19]

Roman Stefanowski identified the activities of eight workers, who on 11 October 1978 set up an unofficial free labor union committee in the western Pomerania region.[20] Their statement captured the essence of the mission that KOR so passionately advanced:

> As a result of the problems that torment us all . . . such as a reform of the work norm to the detriment of the employee, wage losses caused by work interruptions which cannot be blamed on the workers, the unjust division of premiums and of awards, the extension of working hours, inadequate conditions of hygiene and of safety—there is a need for the *defense of workers'* interests, because the existing unions are unable to undertake such defense.[21]

Professor Andrzej Walicki regarded the emergence of an organization such as KOR as a momentous event. KOR provided society with an alternative, an "organized and overt opposition, . . . determined to organize social forces and mobilize them to exert pressure *from without* on the communist rulers . . . a logical consequence of the long process of detotalitarianism, more advanced in Poland than in other countries of real socialism."[22] Goodwyn noted that in this formative period, KOR set a "new standard" for an opposition movement, with its fundamental and unshaking belief in human freedom. Eschewing both excessive religiosity and patriotism, KOR opted instead for its adherents to "participate continually and systematically in public life, to create political facts through collective action, and to propose alternatives."[23] To this end, KOR became an overt antagonist to the Polish State and to the official unions.

KOR's *Information Bulletin* documented police fabrications and denounced the legal system, which perpetuated illegality against its own citizens. It encouraged citizens to attend court proceedings and urged the filing of various writs and appeals in open court, actions that served to heighten public attention to the "principle of law." KOR directed pleas to such organizations as *Helsinki Watch* and *Amnesty International,* actions that would focus world attention and public opinion on the plight of the "courageous workers" of Poland.

KOR also encouraged the creation of many quasi-public institutions such as the "Flying University" (TKN), which offered bitingly critical lectures on matters pointedly ignored by official press organs and state-controlled universities, and created the independent publishing house NOWa, which offered "unfiltered access" to a wide variety of literature, politics, poetry, and economics, despite government harassment, confiscation, and arrests. KOR nurtured a host of student groups in major university towns such as Gdansk, Torun, Lublin, Warsaw, and Krakow.

KOR also inspired the creation of the Committee for the Defense of Human and Civic Rights (ROPCiO) in the spring of 1977; the Young Poland Movement (RMP) by Gdansk students, under the leadership of Aleksander Hall; and a patriotic group called the Confederation for an Independent Poland (KPN), led by Leszek Moczulski, in 1979.[24]

KURON AND MICHNIK

Two individuals merit special attention in discussing the pre-Solidarity period in Poland—Jacek Kuron and Adam Michnik.

Jacek Kuron was born in 1934. He became an assistant lecturer at the University of Warsaw in 1963, where he developed a reputation among students as a proponent of the "liberal Marxist movement." At the university, he became a confidant of Karol Modzelewski, a fellow lecturer, and Adam Michnik, then a student. Kuron was expelled from the Communist party in 1964 when he and Modzelewski wrote an *Open Letter to the Party,* earning both a three-year stint in prison. This letter proved to be decisive in the course of events for Kuron, who had been educated in classical Marxism. Kuron's break with the Party was brought about by an appraisal of his personal experiences as a Party member, compelling him to the conclusion that the Party had unequivocally failed Poland. Kuron wrote that the Party had become estranged from the working classes and had become intrinsically undemocratic. He was convinced that the Party could not reform itself, that it had to be "overthrown" by the workers themselves.

Kuron was released from prison in 1967, but he was rearrested in March of 1968, following student demonstrations that broke out at the university. He was once again sentenced to three-and-a-half-years imprisonment in January 1969. Thus, Kuron was "removed" from the Baltic mobilization of 1970–1971.

Upon his release from prison in September 1971, Kuron resumed his political activities. Along with four other noted dissidents, he signed a congratulatory message to Nobel prize winner Andrei Sakharov. In December 1975, he signed the controversial *Letter of the 59* addressed to the Sejm, in a protest against proposed changes in the Polish Constitution. Kuron remained convinced that previous protests had failed because the intelligentsia had remained politically passive and had not supported the cause of workers. When Gierek's policies resulted in a wave of strikes across Poland in 1976, especially at Radom and Ursus, Kuron played a critical role in the creation of KOR, as one of its original 14 members. Professor Goodwyn has captured the essence of Kuron's views:

> The intellectuals who had sat on the sidelines while the working class challenged the state in 1970 had to redeem themselves by taking a stand in 1976 when the workers protested once again. Kuron said he and other activist intellectuals organized KOR because "we were ashamed the intelligentsia had been silent in 1970, and '71, and we wanted to restore its good name." To do so, effectively, Kuron felt, intellectuals had to go beyond moral stands and social aid, fundamentally important as both were, to organize an effective worker—intelligentsia coalition.[25]

Kuron was initially skeptical that an effective counterbalance to the Party could be created by establishing free trade unions independent of the party. He had concluded that such an emphasis would be inherently self-destructive because independent unions would surely be crushed by the police as soon as they became public. It is therefore not surprising that both Kuron and Litynski (another original KOR founder) opposed the creation of free trade unions by activists in Katowice and Gdansk in 1978. In an effort to broaden the scope of their efforts, Kuron and Litynski succeeded in changing the name of their organization from the Committee for the Defense of Workers (KOR) to the Committee for Social Self-Defense (KSS). Kuron instead began to focus once again on the prospect of reforming the official government unions. In this view, Kuron was not completely isolated. *Robotnik* likewise urged dissident workers to "infiltrate" official union organizational structures in order to make these organs responsive to legitimate demands of the work force. In this way, Kuron exhibited a "profound innocence" that would not be shared by other activists—most especially Lech Walesa, who had learned the hard lesson that "all the worker efforts since World War II in Poland conclusively pointed to the invulnerability of the official unions to this kind of reform."[26]

Between 1977 and 1980, Kuron would stand largely ignorant of the activities of those who, like Andrzej Gwiazda and Bogdan Borusewicz, favored "self-activity," and thus the creation of independent trade unions. Kuron remained true to his belief that workers could not successfully organize outside of the framework of the traditional Party-controlled unions. Kuron naturally *opposed* the first and most fundamental demand of the strikers during the "Polish August" of 1980. Kuron found himself in prison during this critical period (20 August–1 September 1980). Yet, despite this fundamental disagreement, Lech Walesa provided a personal tribute to Kuron: "Jacek Kuron . . . was a man of fixed ideas, and the originator of radical concepts. It was to him, too, that I owed much, especially the help that KOR gave me and many others when unemployed or in personal difficulties."[27]

Adam Michnik was born in 1946. In the mid-1960s, he became involved with a liberal social group, the so-called Crooked Circle Club—an activity that got him expelled from school for illegal activities. He had enrolled at Warsaw University in 1964 where he studied history and political economics. There, Michnik met Jacek Kuron, who became both his mentor and friend. He also met Professor Leszek Kolakowski, who had developed a "liberal" approach to Marxism as editor of *Po prostu* from 1955 until its suppression in 1957, and for this activity he was finally fired as professor in the Department of Philosophy.[28]

In 1964, Michnik was arrested for distributing Kuron and Modzelewski's *Open Letter to the Party*, for which he received a two-month prison sentence. In 1968, Michnik was expelled from the student union and the university for his involvement in the student strikes. In March 1968, he was arrested as one of the chief instigators of the student strike movement (the "March Events") and was sentenced to three years in prison. He served only 18 months as a result of an amnesty declared by the government.

After his release from prison, Michnik took a job as a "simple worker" in Warsaw, and later as the private secretary for the "dean" of Polish writers, a committed fighter for civil rights and liberties, Antoni Slonimski, a position in which Michnik remained until 1976. William Robinson maintained that while Michnik was not one of KOR's founders, he was certainly its "spiritual leader."[29]

In the decade of the 1970s, Michnik wrote extensively on politics and economics.[30] He was greatly influenced by the Soviet invasion of Czechoslovakia in 1968. Michnik wrote: "Czechoslovakia is an example of the fragility of totalitarian stability, and also of the desperation and ruthlessness of an empire under threat." Michnik and the philosopher Leszek Kolakowski proposed a theory termed the "new evolutionism," which asserted that the existing totalitarian regime did not contain any mechanisms "whose development would ensure a meaningful change; hence, its evolution was possible only as a result of external pressure."[31] The theory demanded that the opposition to the system had to organize social forces and mobilize them to exercise suitable pressure *from without* on the totalitarian rulers of the state. Adherents to this theory were quite successful in undermining the authority of the communist regime and in mobilizing its opponents (especially in the intelligentsia) toward nonviolent political struggle.

Michnik was especially assertive in his praise for the Catholic hierarchy in Poland, whom many in the secular left believed had only belatedly come to the position of "defending the civil liberties of working people and particularly their right to strike and to form independent labor unions."[32] He also seemed to demonstrate an unusual insight into the role of workers in this scheme of gradual evolution. He continued: "The new evolutionism is based on faith in the power of the working class. . . . Pressure from the working class is a necessary condition for the evolution of a public life toward a democracy."[33]

However, Michnik seemed unable to understand the "dynamics of shop-floor organizing to appreciate the strategic importance of the emergence of self-organized occupation strikes and, most important, the formula of interfactory strike committees as pivotal instruments of working-class autonomy." Thus, Professor Goodwyn stated that Michnik had misread the politics of 1968 and 1970 and noted that his "strategic vision" and attempts at coalition building (most especially with the Polish Roman Catholic Church) did not extend to building the base of the movement by enlisting workers in the cause of creating unions independent of the official government unions and "did not further expand from 1977 to 1980.[34]

THE EVENTS OF THE SUMMER OF 1980

Three events during the summer of 1980 assumed a critical importance.

1. As circumstances unfolded during August, reports [35] began to surface that "on the more political side, strict observation of freedom of speech and the press is [being] demanded, including ending censorship and reprisals against independent publications, as well as access to the media by representatives of all religious denominations." Tracking KOR's interpretation of the events of 18 August 1980, largely based on the press summaries provided by Jacek Kuron, shows that a new topic in the labor area was introduced into the political equation: "The committee demanded the right of all workers to strike and official assurance that those involved in any labor disputes would not be victimized."[36] These statements did not, however, mention a key worker demand: the creation of "free trade unions independent of the Polish United Workers' party." Only during the negotiations carried out between workers and the two government negotiating teams (Tadeusz Pyka, followed by Mieczyslaw Jagielski) would the issue be raised and the dynamics of the situation be so dramatically altered.[37]

2. The government decided to sharply increase meat prices on 1 July 1980.

3. The final event was the 7 August 1980 firing of Anna Walentynowicz, a 55-year-old widow and crane operator at the Lenin Shipyard. Walentynowicz had been working at the Shipyard since 1950. She had spent 16

years as a welder and had been operating a crane for an additional 14 years. In the summer of 1980, she was just five months short of retirement. Walentynowicz was a well-known activist whose "organizational skills were a godsend."[38] She had "tweaked the noses" of her communist bosses on many prior occasions. In 1978, in an article in *Robotnik Wybrzeza* [The Coastal Worker], she had openly criticized the ostentatious expenditures that had accompanied the visit of Edward Gierek to the Shipyard during the summer of that year.[39] The firing of Anna Walentynowicz was perhaps the single most important event that spurred the strike of her 16,000 fellow workers at the Lenin Shipyard.

The combination of these three seemingly disjointed events led to the "second Polish spring" in August of 1980, and to the historic *Gdansk Agreement*. The name *Solidarity* would not be officially used until 22 September when delegates of 36 independent unions would meet in Gdansk to unite under that banner.

The Summer of 1980 and the "Polish August"

On 1 July 1980, the Polish government increased the price of meat and meat products. The government, however, announced the news rather belatedly, on July 2, the day after the increase had been implemented. On two prior occasions, February 1971 and June 1976, the government had been forced to rescind similar decisions when it was faced with overwhelming negative public opinion, particularly that voiced by Polish workers. Workers countered government actions almost immediately with a series of seemingly unrelated and spontaneous work stoppages, centering around their demands. These demands were essentially economic in nature: higher wages to compensate for the price increases and that management of individual firms bargain with workers' representatives on issues of wages and benefits.

The first strikes broke out in Mielec (where an aircraft factory was located), several plants in Warsaw (including the Ursus tractor and heavy machinery factory), and in the northern town of Tczew. In less than three weeks after the introduction of the meat price increase, more than 30 separate factories were involved in some form of work stoppage, including strikes by railway workers in the city of Lublin, workers in textile mills in Lodz, workers in the shipbuilding centers in the Baltic, more than 900 garbage collectors in the city of Warsaw, and aircraft workers in Swidnik.

Robotnik reported that the workers at Ursus had formulated a list of demands and had elected representatives to present those demands to management. Management reacted in typical fashion, ignoring the demands, and intensified their efforts to intimidate several of the workers. Finally, management was forced to accede to workers' requests for formal negotiations, coupled with a guarantee of immunity from reprisals for workers' representatives who had engaged in the strike. The settlement that was reached included a 10 percent increase in bonuses and wages, as well as a broadening of other benefits in return for worker promises of increased productivity. At the time of the negotiations at Ursus, J. B. de Weydenthal noted: "All these developments suggest the possibility of a significant change in the operations of the Polish political system. . . . If anything has become obvious after the current workers' unrest, it is that until the system finds new ways of involving the workers in its operations, it will only contribute to a situation in which periodic protests and strikes will erupt from time to time."[40]

As the second week of August came to an end, three common characteristics of the strikes were apparent:

1. The disputes were primarily of an *economic nature*—they were distinctly *nonpolitical* and *nonideological*;
2. Both sides desired to keep and maintain a *low profile* and desired to keep the dispute *nonviolent*. Workers in their "unofficial unions" stressed the necessity of remaining within factory premises and the need to display "self-discipline and calmness"; and
3. The movement was *not prepared to assume a nationwide scope*, nor were the individual strike committees designed to become permanent organizations, to rival existing government-sponsored unions.

However, on 9 August, the situation began to change. KOR proposed that it serve as an information agency for strikers and as a contact center for the numerous strike committees, offering them the assistance needed to establish ties (horizontal links) with experts and advisors in various fields. KOR determined that only by establishing "good order and solidarity" can the strike movement guarantee the "permanent betterment of the living conditions of families with lower incomes."[41] The situation remained tense until 16 August.

The Turning Point

A decisive turning point occurred on 16 and 17 August 1980. An estimated 50,000 to 90,000 workers from 21 major industrial enterprises, including shipyard, docks, and transit depots in Gdansk, Gdynia, and Sopot, decided on 16 August to set up a "joint committee" to consolidate their demands. The committee published a 16-point manifesto, calling on the government to establish a bill of rights for workers. Kuron would term this change an "essentially new situation" and an "important step" in arriving at a solution to the conflict.[42]

The creation of the joint committee was an event of enormous import.

It provided workers with a distinct "mechanism of internal communications" that would force the Party into a direct dialogue with them. It would also make the government negotiate with a strike committee that would speak effectively with a "single, compelling voice." Coupled with the tactic of the occupation strike, a device that was seen as essentially defensive in nature, allowing workers to be protected from the massive violence often exhibited by police, the establishment of the joint committee on 17 August 1980 changed the dynamics of the "Polish August."[43]

Ewa Celt of Radio Free Europe identified three problems that characterized the situation during this period:

1. The government continued to exhibit "bad intentions" in spreading false information about both the strike and strikers, including a false report that a deal had been struck and that workers would return to work on 18 August.
2. The government attempted to drive a wedge between strikers and their leadership, including the creation of a fictitious strike committee, a tactic thoroughly denounced by legitimate strike leaders as "dirty tricks" and one that had been a part of the government's continued philosophy of *divida et impera*.
3. The isolation of the coastal workers from the rest of the country continued. On 15 August, the government had cut all telephone and telex communications from Gdansk.

A new Interfactory Strike Committee (known by its initials MKS) was created. It included two representatives from each of the 21 factories involved. Headquartered at the Lenin Shipyard, the MKS drew up a list of demands that would form the basis for direct negotiations with the government:

Their demands . . . include a number of clear-cut, specific issues concerning basic civic freedoms, similar to those demanded by other representatives of the Polish democratic opposition. . . . Moreover, the immediate release of all political prisoners was called for, including several well-known worker and peasant activists still in jail. To lead the country out of the crisis, participation in the discussions on the draft reform plan by representatives of all social groups was imperative, and complete and unbiased information on the social and economic situation in Poland had to be provided. Finally, all privileges enjoyed so far by the security services, police, and party officials—these involve various fringe benefits and family allowances, as well as special shops with goods not generally available—should be eliminated and all citizens put on equal footing economically and socially.[44]

In addition, specific demands were formulated in the labor area, some of which carried clear and important political implications. The MKS demanded that all workers be given a right to strike and official assurances that those involved in any labor dispute would not suffer reprisals. The MKS also called upon Polish authorities to honor provisions of the 87th *International Labor Convention,* to which Poland was a signatory. The MKS insisted that all interference with trade union activities had to end immediately and that the official media should provide accurate information to society on the nature of the dispute and the creation of the MKS. On the economic side, the strikers concentrated on a number of traditional union issues and called for a freeze on all commercial prices; an end to exports (especially of meat products) until a full market supply could be established; the creation of meat sales by coupons until the supply could be stabilized; a wage increase of 2,000 zlotys a month (about $65); and the addition of automatic cost-of-living raises to make up for inflation that had eroded the buying power of workers.

On the same day as the MKS issued its manifesto, the government announced the formation of a government commission under Deputy Prime Minister Tadeusz Pyka, a minor Party functionary and close ally of Edward Gierek, to "negotiate" with strikers in Gdansk.

The situation grew more volatile as strikes spread throughout the Gdansk region, involving more than 260 enterprises. On 19 August, the MKS created a 13-member presidium headed by Lech Walesa, while on 20 August, the government sent Deputy Prime Minister Kazimierz Barcikowski to meet with strikers in Szczecin. Yet, signals remained mixed. While, on the one hand, the government seemed ready to negotiate with "representatives" of workers, it preferred those picked by the official Trade Unions' Central Council. The first secretary of the Gdansk Voivodship, Tadeusz Fiszbach, attacked various "antisocialist elements" operating among the workers. Miroslaw Wojciechowski, the head of the *Interpress* news agency (providing official information to foreign newsmen), reiterated that any political concessions regarding the independence of trade unions or free access to the media were "out of the question."

Authorities also rounded up 14 members of KSS/KOR. Pyka was adamant that he would have "nothing to do" with the MKS (especially Walesa, Walentynowicz, and Gwiazda), maintaining that the MKS was at best illegal and that it did not represent the workers in whose name it spoke. Anna Sabbat noted that the government had "refused to recognize them [the strike committees] as such and to accept the fact that the workers' demands have now gone beyond the level of individual plant management."[45]

Pyka was unexpectedly replaced on 21 August by the deputy prime minister and Politburo member, Mieczyslaw Jagielski. Unlike Pyka, Jagielski had held a variety of important governmental and Party posts. With the ascendancy of Lech Walesa as the chief negotiator for the striker presidium and a change in leadership of the government's negotiating team, clearly, the tenuous situation had reached a new crisis point.

Lech Walesa: "I am a union man."

Lech Walesa was a 37-year-old electrician and father of six children. Walesa had a record of involvement in various strike activities, dating back to 1970 when, as a member of the strike committee at the Lenin Shipyard, he met with Edward Gierek on 25 January 1970. When the 1970 unrest subsided, Walesa returned to his employment, but was subsequently dismissed from his job on 30 April 1970 for continued organizing activities. Following his dismissal, Walesa found work with the Association of Building Machinery Repair Works (ZREMB), as a railway car electrician. There, he came into contact with the publishers of *Robotnik,* later served as a member of the editorial team of *Robotnik Wybrzeza* (the official publication of the Free Trade Unions of the Baltic Coast), and met representatives of KOR. He also became a member of the Founding Committee of the Free Trade Unions of the Baltic coast.[46]

In December 1978, Walesa was arrested after attending a memorial ceremony conducted for workers killed in the Gdansk riots of 1970. He was tried, convicted, and fined 5,000 zlotys for "disturbing the peace" and was dismissed from ZREMB on 31 January 1979. Subsequently, he found employment at the Elektromontaz plant in Gdansk, but was dismissed once again in January 1980 after taking part in yet another "commemorative ceremony." Since 1976, Walesa had been detained more than 100 times by police or various security agents. Yet, Walesa's presence was not noted in any of the reports of the initial strikes on 14 August. However, one of the strikers' demands had been the reinstatement of three dismissed colleagues, including Walesa. As soon as management had agreed to his reinstatement, Walesa scaled the wall at the Lenin Shipyard and joined his colleagues.[47] Described by various journalists as both "charismatic" and a "born leader,"[48] Walesa eschewed any political role and often repeated a simple but forthright statement: "I am a union man." Walesa adamantly refused to comment on a variety of political matters, such as what effect any settlement might have on Polish relations with the Soviet Union and the internal affairs of the Communist party, stating directly that he had no ambition other than to "serve the common cause" of obtaining recognition and respect for the rights of workers.[49]

On 22 August, Jagielski met with a three-man delegation of the MKS, an event that signaled an end to the government's policy of isolating the strikers. On 25 August, negotiations were engaged directly, and matters reached a critical juncture on 26 August, when the Jagielski team arrived at the Lenin Shipyard. The strikers obtained the cooperation of a group of seven academic experts, who would advise them in their negotiations with the government. The decision to invite the participation of this outside expert group was explained by one of its members, Tadeusz Kowalik, in a retrospective account of the academics' role in the crucial phase of the Gdansk negotiations: "My impression is that the choice of the term 'experts' was made by the strikers themselves, perhaps influenced by some myth of intellectual expertise."[50]

The composition of this advisory panel is in itself quite instructive. It included:

1. Bronislaw Geremek, a medieval historian and lecturer for TKN, who was especially aware that Polish workers resented the patronizing attitudes of many Polish intellectuals. Geremek had been an orphaned Jewish child, saved by Gentile parents who had adopted him and given him his name.

2. Tadeusz Kowalik, an economic historian, former Party member, TKN lecturer, and editor in chief of *Zycie Gospodarcze* [Economic Life].

3. Leszek Kubicki, a lawyer, former editor of *Prawo I Zycie* [Law and Life], and a member of the Institute of Legal Sciences of the Polish Academy of Sciences.

4. Waldemar Kuczinski, an economist, TKN lecturer, and a persistent critic of central planning.

5. Tadeusz Mazowiecki, a respected journalist, a leading figure in the Catholic Intelligentsia Club (KIK), editor in chief of the Catholic monthly *Wiez* [Bond], and TKN lecturer. Mazowiecki was initially skeptical of the workers' first demand but was also adamant that their advisory status did not permit the group to alter the content of the strikers' demands. Mazowiecki and Geremek were primarily responsible for the historic "Appeal of the 64" of 21 August 1980, which stated: "With determination and maturity, Polish workers are fighting for the right to a better and more dignified life. The place of all the progressive intelligentsia in this fight is on the side of the workers. That is the Polish tradition and that is the imperative of the hour."[51]

6. Jadwiga Staniszkis, a sociologist, and an activist in the Warsaw Catholic Intelligentsia Club (KIK). Staniszkis has been described as both "haughty and imperious," wedded to the Marxist idea of the "party's leading role" in society. She exhibited a "lack of political poise within the working-class milieu decisively reinforced at a personal level by her enormous psychological distance from Polish workers whose politics she consistently misread."[52] She remained opposed to the creation of independent unions, dismissing them as nothing more than a "utopian dream," and argued for a revision of the official trade unions operating in Poland, a proposal that became known as *Variant B*. She "abandoned" the negotiations on 27 August but remained a most controversial figure of this period. Her departure seemed to rally the remaining advisors strongly to the cause of the workers.

7. Andrzej Wielowieyski, a writer, and the secretary and leading spokesman of KIK.

In the midst of these negotiations, a major leadership reshuffle was announced in the government, including the naming of a new prime minister, Jozef Pinkowski, and the firing of the head of the official trade unions, Jan Szydlowski. Gierek continued to reject worker demands for free trade unions, but held out the prospect of unspecified democratic reforms in the existing trade union structure.

At the 26 August meeting, Jagielski promised that the right to strike would be incorporated into a new law on the official trade unions. However, an editorial in *Trybuna Ludu* continued to echo the Party line, attacking the idea of an independent union and some unidentified "enemies of socialism" who are "striving to destroy the unity of the Polish people, to foster internal fighting, and to encourage social anarchy."[53] Meanwhile, major strikes erupted in at least 12 Polish cities, even as a second government team, headed by Deputy Prime Minister Kazimierz Barcikowski, continued protracted negotiations with strikers in Szczecin. The situation seemed to be moving toward an unresolved impasse.

Then, on 28 August 1980, Lech Walesa expressed his willingness to issue an appeal to workers to temporarily refrain from calling further "solidarity" strikes. Walesa noted that "if we do not get results in three or four days, then let the strikes spread." On 29 August, the strikes spread to Swidnik, Wloclawek, Legnica, Poznan, and Torun, even as the fourth round of Gdansk talks were held. On 30 August, as strikes continued to expand to the northwestern part of the country and for the first time into the industrial-mining area of Silesia (around Katowice, Wroclaw, and Walbrzych), a major breakthrough took place. Walesa proclaimed that "Point No. 1 [the demand for free trade unions] has been 90 percent settled. . . . We see the finish."[54] The logjam was broken.

On 30 August, Deputy Prime Minister Jagielski returned to Warsaw to report the results of the negotiations to the Fifth Central Committee Plenum, intending to return to Gdansk to continue to negotiate on several outstanding matters. On the same day, the strike in Szczecin was declared over as an agreement was officially signed. A few hours later, a similar agreement was reported in Gdansk. Jagielski was quoted as saying: "I accept the formula for a new trade union."[55] Questions remained whether or not the agreement would be limited to Gdansk and to the Baltic region or whether "independent and self-managed unions" would be legalized throughout Poland. Some strikers questioned whether negotiators had unreasonably acceded to the government's insistence that the Party retain its "leading" role in society (as opposed to a "guiding" role). Uncertainty over the status of the 29 detained dissidents, members of KOR, ROPCiO, and KPN, persisted. Nevertheless, the final agreement was signed by representatives of the striking workers and the government on 31 August 1980. Both Walesa and Jagielski spoke eloquently.

Walesa noted: "We have shown that Poles can always come to an agreement, if they want to. It is a success for both sides. . . . We have achieved everything that was possible under the circumstances." Jagielski added: "We have spoken as Poles to Poles. . . . There are no winners and losers. The important thing is that we have understood each other and the best guarantee for what we have done is hard work."[56]

The Protocol

The Protocol[57] closely mirrored the original *Twenty-One Points* put forth by the MKS on 23 August. It addressed a number of important demands for economic and political change: access to mass media; specific guarantees concerning retirement, maternity leave, pensions, and prices; the elimination of Saturday as a mandatory day of work; and religious freedom for both believers and nonbelievers. Of the 21 points of the agreement, the two most important were the guarantee of the right to strike and the acceptance by the Polish government of "free, independent, and self-governing" trade unions.

While Walesa was willing to generalize and even compromise about many of the *Twenty-One Points* (for example, in the area of press censorship and "free" Saturdays), he remained immovable about the first two points: "We [will] have an independent union and we [will] retain our right to strike." These became the essence of the agreement, the sole guarantee that the government would honor future promises. John Darnton, bureau chief of the *New York Times*, summed up the importance of this provision: "The right to strike and to form independent trade unions could be seen as historic an advance for participatory socialism inside the Soviet bloc as the Magna Carta was for Western parliamentarianism."[58]

In the economic sphere, however, Solidarity avoided taking any direct economic responsibility for the crisis because it saw itself primarily as a trade union and not as an institution of public authority. It further declined to do so until the movement could "fashion mechanisms whereby [it could] exert substantial leverage on formulating and carrying out economic policy."[59] This reluctance was expressed by Solidarity spokesman Stanislaw Bury in rather simple yet direct terms: "[The government] got us into this mess, let them get us out. . . . Besides, we're workers not economists."[60] What was obvious, however, was that Poles did have a most consistent idea of what they found repulsive about their lives: "the distant and arbitrary central authority, the repression, the corruption. They also [had] a consensus on what they wanted to replace the system with: some sort of democratic and worker control in the workplace."[61]

Several of the *Twenty-One Points* dealt with the systemic roots of the economic crisis. The Strike Committee demanded that the Gierek regime (soon to be replaced, on 5 September, by one headed by Stanislaw Kania) take "decisive action to get the country out of the crisis" and suggested that the government:

1. Give full information to society regarding the facts of the social and economic situation (during the Gierek regime, the government neither informed people about the true economic situation nor adequately prepared them for necessary austerity measures);
2. Establish the possibility for all social spheres to take part in a public discussion concerning the best ways to overcome the crisis; and
3. Take immediate steps to hasten an economic reform.

After an initial period of optimism and euphoria, a time when "horizons suddenly opened up and the blinders came off," stark reality set in. The next year (the interval between the August 1980 agreement and the Solidarity Congress in September of 1981) would prove critical, as the economic and political situations rapidly deteriorated.

Economically, Poland was in dire straights. With fully 75 cents of every hard currency dollar generated by exports to the West going toward repaying the foreign debt, the GNP fell by 25 percent. Individual output fell by 17 percent. Industries were operating at 60 to 70 percent of capacity. Unions were staging strikes and work slowdowns. There was an obvious drop in the standard of living, accompanied by an average 120 percent rise in food prices and a 200 to 300 percent rise in the price of other consumer goods. "There was a sense that events were spinning out of control and heading for disaster."[62]

Politically, the nation was experiencing a severe "crisis of political authority," as "the Communist Party became totally divorced from the realities of everyday Polish life."[63] After 35 years of Communist party rule, Polish workers ceased to believe in the Party's legitimacy, authority, or ability to rule. The Communist party virtually ceased to exist as a force capable of running and organizing the country.

Yet, as late as 1981, the government media had continued to trumpet a "propaganda of success and disbelief has become endemic. To participate actively in Polish communism was to live a lie. The signs of crisis were everywhere."[64]

As the economy worsened, Solidarity for the first time identified major weaknesses in the economy and entered into a critique of the burgeoning crisis. It reported that the overcentralized nature of state planning was the primary cause of the economic debacle. It further recommended that society must confront the way in which positions in the upper and middle bureaucracy (including heads of enterprises) were filled.[65] Solidarity insisted that "merit, efficiency, and, above all, accountability" replace "membership in the *nomenklatura* as the operating criteria for filling administrative positions in industrial Poland."[66]

As a result, Solidarity turned its focus sharply to two critical issues: *self-management* of the individual enterprises and the *property status* of the enterprises. These two issues would dominate the economic debate for the next decade and beyond. True self-management would include the specific right to elect self-management bodies and to appoint or select enterprise directors who would administer the enterprises.

Gradually, ideas about self-management [*samorzad pracowniczy*] began to dominate political and economic discussions. In March 1981, the first meeting of the Network,[67] composed of representatives of 17 key factories, with the Warski (Szczecin) and Lenin (Gdansk) Shipyard taking the initiative, addressed the question of self-management. Workers would take a more active role in economic renewal through intense participation in the selection of the enterprise director, and the creation of founding committees for self-management of the enterprises. The appointment and dismissal of enterprise directors would be the "acid test" for the success of any proposals for self-management. Employee self-management would be the core issue around which the future of wider economic reform would be accomplished in employment policies, the general direction of economic activity, organizational structures, divisions of income, enterprise cooperation (the creation of horizontal links), and other matters of social welfare.[68]

Karol Modzelewski, publicity director for Solidarity, noted: "Self-management may not solve everything, but we've got to find some way of institutionalizing the integration of the workers' wishes into the decision making process."[69] Polish workers in 1981 were again willing to try to "save the Polish economy" by replacing the "corruption, aloofness and incompetence" of communist administrators with competent, honest, and responsive ones, even though the prior history of *samorzad* [self-management] with Workers' Councils, committees, and factory councils had ended in failure and disillusionment.[70] On these prior occasions, however, nothing substantive had really changed because effective power remained vested in the Party and the bureaucracy. Workers' Councils were simply too weak to stand up to the Party. The absence of horizontal links between enterprises had left workers isolated from each other's concerns and the real agenda, as well as isolated from intellectuals and students who had a common stake in reform of the system.

Solidarity called for a new system whereby the enterprise would rule over a part of the "national wealth," which had been transferred to it by a founding agency. This represented a rethinking of the concept of "social property" along the lines suggested by Oskar Lange 25 years earlier. Such an idea entailed the creation of an entirely new system where managers of enterprises "run their own affairs, set their own prices, pay wages and buy materials out of their own earnings and make capital investments from retained earnings or taking individual bank loans on strictly commercial terms."[71]

The experiment of Solidarity would be short-lived. Between October and December of 1981, tensions grew as the economy further deteriorated. The Communist party once again reverted to its old form and began to attack the various "antisocialist" elements in Solidarity. The government initiated a new round of price hikes for food and tobacco in October. More than 300,000 workers engaged in a series of bitter wildcat strikes. Industrial production declined by an additional 15 percent and exports were down 25 percent. In addition, the Party had ousted Kania and selected General Wojciech Jaruzelski as its first secretary. Jaruzelski would later claim that the nation faced "imminent famine and a collapse of its health support systems."[72] Echoing the official party line that Poland was on the verge of civil war and anarchy, a government spokesman stated: "Poland could easily break apart because there is no government or Communist Party structure left."[73]

The "lightning military coup" and the imposition of martial law like a "sledgehammer" on 13 December 1981 served as General Jaruzelski's response to events that were seen as rapidly steaming out of control.

Chapter Four

The State of Poland's Economy during and after Martial Law

Economic and Political Consequences of the Polish Coup d'Etat: Failed Attempts at Reform

"The people had tasted freedom—the cornerstone of Polish hopes had been laid—and now we had to bide our time."

Lech Walesa, *A Way of Hope*

THE SOLIDARITY BREAKTHROUGH

The initial period of Solidarity (August 1980 to December 1981) contributed mightily to the conversation about the future of the Polish State and Central and Eastern Europe in several important ways.

1. Polish workers reminded the world that they occupied a unique position of power in a state ruled ostensibly for the benefit of, and in the name of, the working class. From a membership of nearly 750,000 on 1 September 1980, Solidarity's ranks swelled to nearly 10 million by December 1980. By the time of its official registration in November 1980 (accomplished only after a threat of a general strike), Solidarity had captured the allegiance of nearly every adult person in Poland. Unlike the events of 1956 in Poznan, of 1970 on the Baltic coast, and of 1976 in Ursus and Radom, the events in 1980 forever changed the political landscape in Poland. By demanding and winning the right to strike and the right to create unions outside of Party structures, Solidarity broke the monopoly of

power exercised by the *nomenklatura*-government-party cabal for nearly 35 years. In addition, by raising issues such as press censorship, public access to information, the appointment by merit of key management personnel, and by forcing a major reshuffling of Party leadership, including the precipitous dismissal of First Secretary Gierek, Solidarity "provided a decisive impetus for the breakthrough of that spirit of innovation and reform the country so desperately need[ed]."[1] In essence, Solidarity created an authentic worker revolution in social, political, and economic relations.

2. The events of August 1980 through the imposition of martial law in December 1981 proved that individuals could attain and sustain power in the face of both hardship and repression. Despite years of disillusionment, workers had become self-disciplined and maintained an innate dignity in the face of unbelievable provocations. Workers generally avoided physical confrontations of the type that had doomed incipient revolutions in Hungary (1956) and Czechoslovakia (1968). By the late 1970s, recognition that the system was "beyond repair and beyond reform" had become so pervasive that, in retrospect, it is truly amazing that workers were once again willing to take a major risk to change a system that had corrupted all those who participated in it. Professor Andrzej Walicki provided this insight into the core of the totalitarian ethos: "What was distinctly totalitarian was the unprecedented intensity and unlimited scope of state control of human life, amounting to the full abolition of the private sphere of individual existence; not only full suppression of independent political activities but also, and primarily, full control over economy and thought, total suppression of the nonpolitical individual freedom, including the most elementary freedom of conscience."[2]

Professor Walicki described this situation as a partocracy, one in which individuals were in constant "apprehension of physical terror with elements of will-paralyzing moral intimidation."[3] In the period of Stalinization (1945–1956), the totalitarian system was created by individuals from *within* Poland (Bierut, Osobka-Morawski, Minc, Cyrankiewicz, Gomulka, and others) who had at their disposal a newly created state apparatus of coercion and a wide variety of social controls. Ironically, they were supported (in some cases enthusiastically) by elements of the progressive, left-leaning intelligentsia, who regarded prewar Poland as "bourgeoisie" or authoritarian (the Pilsudski era). This group has been variously described as "the last genuine millenarians" or "the last true Communists" who possessed both self-confidence and authority in the eyes of the people.[4] Walicki added that "among the population at large the communists were often feared, sometimes hated, but not held in contempt."[5] This is a view not often shared by those who believe that communism was imposed on Poland as a result of the treachery of the West (Yalta, Potsdam), or because of the treason of a "limited few" in the postwar period. This view has become more problematic as we assess the election results in both 1993 and 1995 in which former communists, or "postcommunists," as they now prefer to be called, assumed power in both the Parliament and the presidency.

With the "Polish October" in 1956, however, the situation changed. The worst aspects of Stalinism (terror and murder) disappeared. The sociologist Hanna Swida-Ziemba asserted that "in the sociological sense the period after 1956 was qualitatively different. It changed the character of everyday life of the people. The horrifying darkness, the paralysing fear and the ideological shackles were finally gone."[6] However, the Communist party retained its iron monopoly on power in both legal and institutional structures, and pluralism was not introduced into the mechanisms of power in the Polish State. Walicki described the Gomulka period as the "replacement of communist totalitarianism by communist authoritarianism."[7] Gomulka argued strongly for the maintenance of the Communist party's "stranglehold" on power as the only way to guarantee Poland's political existence and safety within its new borders. By 1968, the Gomulka regime was itself fully authoritarian, insisting on political and economic autarchy, culminating in the shameful antisemitic campaign of 1968.

While the Party maintained its grip on power under Edward Gierek, "Most of its members openly despised Marxist indoctrination, loathed being called communists, and justified their political options on the ground of expediency-oriented patriotism."[8] Gierek's inner circle lapsed into a decade-long period of cynicism, relying on an argument that the Communist party should remain in power sui generis. The Party asserted that political reality dictated that there was simply no alternative to communist rule in Poland, relying on postwar agreements concerning the geographic and political divisions of Europe. It relied on a "propaganda of success" that identified the Party in national terms, arguing that only the Party could guarantee Polish interests, freedoms, and economic gains. The Party asserted that only it could "win the sympathy of the West, obtain from it massive financial aid and use it for a successful modernization of the country and for building an affluent second Poland."[9] Yet, by rejecting a fundamental ideological basis for its existence, the Party may have doomed itself and created the seeds of its own eventual demise.

3. The emergence of KOR in 1976 and the enlisting of the group of intellectuals to the cause of Baltic coast workers in 1980 resulted in a "fundamentally changed situation." KOR became an organized and overt opposition, determined to rally social forces under a banner of free and independent trade unions and to mobilize them to exert pressure from without on their communist rulers. This view was shared by Leszek Kolakowski and Adam Michnik, who argued that the system as it existed did not contain any "mechanisms whose developments would ensure a meaningful change." Kolakowski and Michnik believed that "evolution" was only possible as a result of external pressure. What surprised both Kolakowski and Michnik was that workers, in pressing for unions *outside* party-state

organizations, would in fact become this organized, "outside" social force who would engage the government in a process of collective bargaining. Also surprising was that workers were once again willing to enter into this task, in light of the violence of 1956, the riots of December 1970, and the Gierek regime's use of security police to brutally suppress the unrest in Radom in 1976. What is also astonishing to many observers is that, unlike Czechoslovakia and Hungary, "Poland managed to muster the strength to live through more than two weeks [15–30 August 1980] of dangerously direct confrontation without violence and without attempts at forcible repression of the strikers."[10] John Darnton placed this fundamental change in perspective when he noted on 31 August 1980, "After today, Poland will never be the same."[11]

CRITICAL EVENTS DURING THE "PERIOD OF SOLIDARITY"— TOWARD THE IMPOSITION OF MARTIAL LAW

Before moving to a discussion of politics and economics *during* the period of martial law, it is important to briefly describe the most salient events that characterized the life of the Solidarity movement during its fifteen months of legal existence.

1. Almost the entire population was engaged through a massive self-recruitment during September–December 1980, a period during which Solidarity's ranks swelled to nearly 10 million persons. In addition, negotiations between Walesa and General Jaruzelski resulted in the registration of Rural Solidarity, a union for peasants, an action strongly supported by the Catholic church, in May 1981.

2. It appears that almost from the outset, the Soviet Union was adamant that Solidarity had to be "summarily repressed." Reports from a Polish army officer, Colonel Ryszard Kuklinski, a CIA "mole" planted in the Polish General Staff, make it clear that on at least two occasions—December 1980 and March 1981—the Soviet Union was poised on the brink of direct military intervention.[12]

3. The Communist party remained steadfast in its opposition to the legalization of Solidarity or to the good faith implementation of the Gdansk Accords. These machinations resulted in the Bydgoszcz crisis and the national warning strike of March 1981. The Bydgoszcz affair began quite innocently on 16 March 1981 with a sit-in by activists at the headquarters of the United Peasants' party. This action was heightened because of the participation of Jan Rulewski, the regional Solidarity chairman for Bydgoszcz. On 19 March 1981, 35 Solidarity and peasant activists engaged in negotiations with local officials. Two hundred security police burst into the room and suddenly began beating and arresting the participants. Twenty-seven activists were beaten, among them Rulewski himself. In response to

these actions, a wave of unrest swept across Poland. Press reports showed photos of bleeding union members. Walesa led a delegation of Solidarity's National Coordinating Commission (KKP) to Bydgoszcz to calm the situation.

4. On 4 March 1981, the Soviets summoned Stanislaw Kania and several of his closest associates to receive a warning concerning continued "surrenders" of the prerogatives of the Party.[13]

5. March 1981 witnessed the "appearance and subsequent evolution" of the Network, which focused on drafting legislation on the issue of self-management of the social enterprise. In April, a formal organizational meeting was held in Gdansk that attracted delegates from many of Poland's major industries. The Network saw its role as independent of Solidarity: Solidarity would continue to represent the interests of its members; the Network (elected by "workers from below") would administer the enterprise, select the enterprise director, and engage in negotiations concerning traditional union issues such as pay, funds for recreational activities, vacations, and pensions. The creation of the Network not only constituted a frontal assault on the state-party-*nomenklatura* monopoly, it also challenged the existing structure of Solidarity itself.

Later, on 8 June 1981, the Sejm announced its own draft law on the subject of self-management. It was widely accepted that the Party was barely paying "lip service" to the idea. This action "had the effect of moving the National Coordinating Commission (KKP) into closer strategic proximity to the Network's position."[14] By July 1981, Walesa would publicly state: "Therefore we recognize the initiatives of union activists aimed at organizing workers' self-management groups as undertakings in accord with the needs of society, a most proper way to restore the health of the economy [and achieve] genuine, not formal, national unity."[15]

6. In the fall of 1981, Solidarity held its National Congress and unveiled its Action Program. The chairman of the Action Program Commission was Bronislaw Geremek, historian and TKN lecturer, who had played a prominent role as one of the advisors to the strikers at the Lenin Shipyard. Professor Goodwyn described an insight that delegates brought to this critical meeting: "What united us is a revolt against injustice, abuses of power and the monopolization of the right to speak and act in the name of the nation."[16]

The Action Program tackled issues first raised by the Network and had as its focal point the socialized enterprise. The program called for decentralization of decision making and an end to the command system. The Action Program demanded full employment and stressed the profitability of individual enterprises. Other issues concerned food distribution, control of the media and other general censorship questions, and self-management of scientific and learned institutes. The October convention also reelected Walesa as chairman, with 55 percent of the vote, over three credible opponents. Marian Jurczyk, Solidarity's regional chairman in Szczecin, ran second; Andrzej Gwiazda came in third; and Jan Rulewski (who had recovered from his brutal beating in Bydgoszcz) was fourth.

By the middle of November, over 250,000 Poles were again on strike. The situation was especially tense in Zielona Gora, where both Walesa and Kuron joined forces as "firemen." The situation further deteriorated. Solidarity faced stiffened opposition in the Communist party. Both Tadeusz Fiszbach and Stefan Olszowski had been "sent packing." Since October, the Party had been led by a professional soldier, General Jaruzelski. Kuron was rearrested on 22 November and Walesa was quoted as stating that "confrontation is inevitable . . . and it will take place." Society was literally breaking apart at the seams. "With winter coming, there was not enough heat, not enough winter clothing, not even enough shoes. The shortages could no longer be ascribed to simple mismanagement, even by an apparatus as mature in the art of error as the Polish [Communist] party."[17]

In the early hours of 13 December 1981, "the general called out his army" and placed the society under effective military occupation. A "state of war" had been declared against both Solidarity and the Polish nation!

The State of Poland's Economy during and after Martial Law: First Attempts at Reform

Immediately after the imposition of martial law, General Jaruzelski announced that the first priority of the government was to rebuild the "orthodoxy" of the Communist party. However, while cracking down decisively on Solidarity and its political and intellectual leadership, Jaruzelski realized that the imposition of martial law had alienated the very workers whose cooperation would be necessary to get production back on the track and to overcome the deep economic crisis. In February 1982, barely one month after the state of war had been declared, Jaruzelski announced a program of economic reform based on the principles of "self-management, self-direction and self-financing"[18] that had been prepared by the Communist Party Congress and Parliament in 1981.[19] The document established two objectives for the reform: "increased economic efficiency and restoration and maintenance of the market balance, i.e., elimination of chronic shortages."[20] The reform would attempt to create a "new economic system" to achieve these objectives, abolishing the "directive nature of central planning."

Created at the height of the deep economic crisis that demanded swift and decisive action, the reforms nonetheless were based essentially on "old assumptions." The state would maintain its core responsibilities in three areas: national defense, situations involving natural disasters, and those cases where enterprises were required to "fulfill international agreements entered into by central authorities" with the Soviet Union and nations in

COMECON.[21] The government also announced that manufacturing capacities would henceforth be administered by the "forces of the market," through a system of self-governance and self-direction (using newly energized enterprise workers' councils).

The reforms, however, remained ambiguous about the role and function of planning itself and stated that the economy was to operate "on the principle of central planning with the utilization of the market mechanism." Were these goals and objectives internally consistent or mutually exclusive? Was it possible to maintain the essence of planning while eliminating its most onerous aspects?

Professor Marian Guzek of the Adam Mickiewicz University suggested that the most effective method of introducing reform would simply lie in abolishing central directives, granting true economic independence to enterprises, and then creating a motivation mechanism and a system of incentives for Polish workers.[22] Seweryn Bialer noted that "wthout such reforms, . . . any hopes for a long-range recovery are a pipe-dream."[23]

In this context, two policy questions developed. Would it be possible to create a market system in a nation where there was little private property, where there was a basic aversion to economic risk, and where the system of central planning had ingrained in society habits, attitudes, and a work ethic that was geared toward subordination and submission of workers and managers? In the short run, would it be possible to re-orient the bureaucracy to reflect this change in economic policy? As Robert Ball put it so aptly: "Can the 'old dogs' of Polish industry be taught these new tricks?"[24]

These "old dogs" have been variously described as the "industrial lobbies" and the "red bourgeoisie" of the *nomenklatura*. They were wedded to the old system and had nowhere to go in a Poland where a management-oriented bureaucracy would be required to serve the interests of workers and the state alike. Given this backdrop, what were the results of the policies adopted by Jaruzelski during the five years of effective martial law (1981–1986) and in the period immediately preceding the Round Table in 1989? The economic signals and results were decidedly mixed.

The low point of 1981 saw Poland become a nation of endless queues, where everything people needed was in short supply. In 1983 and 1984, there was a general rebound with a positive growth rate of 6.39 percent and 5.19 percent respectively. In 1985, the increase slowed to 4.44 percent. In 1986, the economy grew at a rate of 5 percent, a level higher than projected by the official plan. In 1987, the trend was reversed and national income only grew "officially" at the rate of 1.7 percent. In 1988, there was a further increase of 4.6–4.7 percent, but *1989 produced a 0.0 percent increase.*

In the area of foreign trade, exports increased by 10.2 percent in 1982; slowed to 8.9 percent in 1984; and further retrenched to 7.2 percent in 1985. In 1987, exports increased by 4.8 percent; in 1988, 9.4 percent; but *declined by 0.2 percent in 1989*. Imports increased 10.3 percent in 1983; 9 percent in 1984; and 1.5 percent in 1985, reflecting a slowdown of reliance on foreign inputs. In 1987, imports increased by 4.5 percent; in 1988, 8.7 percent; *but they declined by 0.7 percent in 1989*.[25]

In 1986, hard currency exports to the West grew by 5.7 percent and imports rose 6.4 percent. While leaving a modest overall hard currency surplus, it would fall short of plans and agreements negotiated to pay off the interest on Poland's convertible currency debt, which had grown to an estimated $39.2 billion by 1987 and to a staggering $40.0 billion by the end of 1989. In 1987, Poland earned a $1.6 to $1.8 billion surplus in hard currency; however, its scheduled payments amounted to $2.5 billion. In 1985, the debt service, if fully paid, would have claimed 81 percent of Poland's hard currency export earnings. In 1987, the percentage was an unmanageable 94.9 percent.[26] In absolute terms, Poland faced an indebtedness trap. If left unmanaged, indebtedness would lead to extreme economic austerity, placing the burden of debt service squarely on Polish society through a reduction of the standard of living for all citizens.

Prices, which had more than doubled between 1981 and 1982, continued to increase by 21.8 percent in 1983, but slowed to more moderate increases of 14.4 percent in 1984 and 12.3 percent in 1985. In 1987, the cost of living increased by 30.7 percent; in 1988, by 68.5 percent; and in 1989, by a crushing 254 percent. Agricultural production (targeted as the "strong link" in the economy),[27] which had declined by 4.1 percent in 1982, increased by 3.3 percent in 1983, 5.6 percent in 1984, but slowed to 0.7 percent in 1985. In 1986, the agricultural sector performed extremely well, with gross output increasing by 5 percent and grain production rising by 5.4 percent. In 1987, agricultural production again was riding on a rollercoaster and rose by only 1 percent; 1988 saw an increase of only 0.6 percent; and in 1989, a gain of 2 percent was recorded.[28]

Considering the wide fluctuations in the period from 1981 to 1989, the question arises as to whether these swings were due to poor economic performance or to interference (or resistance) by the industrial lobbies? Adam Gwiazda noted that while "numerous laws and decrees have been passed, providing for more self-administration and self-financing for the enterprises, in practice these reforms have encountered *administrative obstacles*.[29]

Growth in the aftermath of the "deep years of crisis" continued to be based on the old criteria. That criteria involved extensive development of capital intensive and wasteful industries (coal, steel, shipbuilding), centralized decision making, and an orientation toward Poland's Eastern Bloc trading partners (especially the Soviet Union). Again, "the cost of failure is being automatically transferred to the consumer."[30] Severe price increases in the spring of 1987 led to protests by underground Solidarity, the

Catholic church, and, surprisingly, even the official, state-sponsored trade unions.[31] In addition, the government undertook some concrete initiatives designed to improve its stature within Polish society, especially after martial law was officially ended in 1983. Full amnesty of political prisoners was carried out in 1986. Press censorship was relaxed. The State Consultative Council was created. However, Polish law continued to provide for the existence of only one government-controlled union in the workplace. New laws imposed stiff fines and imprisonment for "activities aimed at disturbing public order or at provoking disturbances." Other laws forbade distributing leaflets in unauthorized places and banned participation in unauthorized gatherings.[32]

One other situation merits special attention. In retrospect, the kidnap and murder of Father Jerzy Popieluszko may have doomed the reform effort and destroyed any real chance for societal support for Jaruzelski's regime.

Father Jerzy Popieluszko

In Warsaw a young priest from St. Stanislaw Kostka parish had become a symbol of the struggles of Poles during martial law. "Fr. Jerzy," as he was universally known, "toured the country soliciting funds for food and medical supplies for the families of thousands of imprisoned Solidarnosc activists. . . . Food, medical supplies, and money poured into St. Stanislaw Kostka from Western Europe and the United States and were judiciously distributed throughout the country."[33]

Fr. Jerzy was regularly subjected to police harassment. A group of Huta Warszawa steelworkers, sympathetic to Solidarity, acted as his personal bodyguard. At a time when public meetings were banned, 15,000 people attended his Christmas mass in 1983.[34] Fr. Jerzy clashed frequently with state agents and his own hierarchy, whom many in Solidarity felt had abandoned them. In July 1984, Father Popieluszko was indicted for "activities against the state," including a charge that he had secreted a vast cache of arms and ammunition in his apartment.

Father Popieluszko was included in the general amnesty announced in August 1984, but he suddenly disappeared on the night of 19 October 1984 while returning from a special mass offered for workers in Bydgoszcz. On 30 October, parishioners were informed that Father Popieluszko had been found dead. His automobile had been intercepted by agents of the state security service. He had been viciously beaten before his body had been thrown into the water above the Vistula dam at Wloclawek. The funeral was attended by an estimated 350,000 persons. Delegations of Solidarity workers arrived from all parts of the country, bearing Solidarity banners, "which were held high as workers marched to the church." Lech Walesa was called upon to speak at a memorial following the funeral mass.

His eloquence may never again be matched: "The entire life of this good and courageous man, this extraordinary worker priest, pastor and leader of the national cause, bears witness to the unity of peace and social justice for our country. Solidarnosc lives on, Father Jerzy, because you gave your life for us."[35]

In retrospect, the Poland of 1981 to 1989 remained a study of contrast and contradiction. Most Poles had lost confidence in the government to gather accurate economic data or to report truthfully to the public. One observation was inescapable: The Poland of the 1980s was a much different Poland than that of the 1950s, 1960s, or 1970s. The Polish working class was urban in character and no longer peasant in origin. It was activist, energized, better educated and trained, and better informed than workers in any prior generation. It understood all too well the forbidding words of Edward Lipinski: "The socialism that was created here was the socialism of mismanagement and inefficiency that brought about an economic catastrophe unequalled in two hundred years. It is the socialism of prisons, censorship, and police."[36]

Reflecting on events of this period, several observations and conclusions may be drawn.

1. "The Polish Communist Party [was] deeply divided, its ideology [was] rejected by the vast majority of Polish workers."[37] The government and the Party continued to issue mixed signals on their willingness to accommodate societal interests. In 1985, the Party was still trying to divide the opposition, even though it had issued an earlier amnesty to its leadership, "the Solidarity Eleven," shortly before their trial in 1984. Bogdan Lis, a former Party member who had been active in the creation of the Baltic movement, Wladyslaw Frasyniuk, regional Solidarity chairman from Wroclaw, and Adam Michnik were arrested, along with Walesa, after a meeting in Gdansk. All were indicted, except for Walesa, who was forced to "testify" at their trial. Michnik was given a three-year sentence; Frasyniuk, three and a half years; and Lis, two and a half years.

Michnik described the trial as a "classic example of police banditry"—no journalists or observers were permitted. None of the accused were permitted to give testimony beyond a simple yes or no response to the questions posed. This incident solidified the resolve of all involved and effected a quite public rapprochement between Walesa and these prominent activists. Then, in 1986, in anticipation of the soon-to-be announced reforms, the government declared another limited amnesty, and Lis, Michnik, and Frasyniuk were released from prison. This limited amnesty was soon followed by a general amnesty that permitted Solidarity leaders to meet publicly. However, without true economic and political reform, Poland continued to lapse into a period of cynicism, confrontation, and isolation.

2. The government lacked the political will to impose unpopular eco-

nomic solutions on its population at this time of crisis. As a result, attempts to resolve the twin crises of the economy and the foreign debt trap led to a political stalemate, with the regime unwilling to permit the degree of political pluralism necessary to gain the support of society at large. The radical political scientist, Stanislaw Milc, was even more direct in his analysis: "Radical economic reform raises in absolute earnest the question of the development of democracy in Poland."[38]

3. Polish workers faced poor housing conditions, a demoralized system of education, increasing shortages, and a collapsing health care system.[39] The only effective means of attaining the societal consensus necessary to introduce economic reform would be a movement on the part of the Polish political leadership toward pluralism. Genuine pluralism would involve society in decision making and provide freedom of expression, public debate, and an accountability of political leadership to the Polish population.

4. Solidarity was not silent during this period. A statement issued by Solidarity in April 1987 rejected the government's main economic thesis. Solidarity argued that the proposed reforms represented the "survival of a primitive approach to economic reform, based mainly on coercion and price hikes."[40] Solidarity urged a return to trade union pluralism, with a guarantee of the right of workers to organize and bargain collectively. Such a change would provide for meaningful participation of workers in their workplaces and would dispose workers to accept measures such as price hikes and "wages tied to productivity." However, Solidarity did not escape criticism for economic conditions in Poland. Even during 1981, public opinion polls reflected a decline in support for Solidarity, as many came to look upon Solidarity and the regime as sharing responsibility for the economic crisis.

5. Poland experienced another "great migration" (a "brain drain"), as young intellectuals, engineers, scientists, doctors, and other professionals opted to leave Poland because of "limited options and opportunities." Likewise, despite "talk" to the contrary, the decade of the 1980s indicated that little had been done to create a bureaucracy competent in managerial, financial, or even general business skills, further limiting prospects for Poland's younger generation.

6. First Secretary Gorbachev's policies of internal reform in the Soviet Union (*perestroika*) and an openness (*glasnost*) precluded opponents of reform in Poland "from using the clear prospect of Soviet opposition" as an effective bar to systemic reform.[41]

7. Economic policies promoted investment in industries that advanced specific Soviet needs (especially in coal and steel production). Because of this perceived "irrationality," Western governments were reluctant to assist Poland in overcoming its debt crisis.

8. It would be essential for Poland to arrange a realistic debt-manage-

ment framework in cooperation with the International Monetary Fund, the Paris Club (public debt), and the London Club (private debt). In order to accomplish this task, Poland would be required to enlist the active support of the United States. However, the United States made it clear that a solution would only be possible in the context of establishing a broad political consensus within Poland. Such a consensus would be based upon democratization and the achievement of political pluralism and stability. U.S. State Department spokesman, Charles E. Redmen said: "Successful economic reform and recovery require genuine dialogue between the government and society . . . [and] in our view, the dialogue must allow the expression of working people's rights . . . including those of Solidarity."[42]

In May 1987, Jaruzelski (now president of the Council of State) admitted that the economy had not "evolved" according to projections. Jaruzelski also seemed to grasp the importance of gaining societal support for the second stage of the reform. He stated: "We are now at a historic moment of implementing the economic reform. The sense of turning from the present state to the new, higher state of economic reform is a policy of releasing social energy and the system of controls in the state will be simplified and coordinated."[43]

Jaruzelski recognized that this was the time when society could no longer turn back and that the future of Poland depended on the success of economic growth, social renewal, and reconciliation with all elements in Polish society. Jaruzelski declared: "The active participation of the milieux involved, openness of work and the freedom of discussion, and broad consultation will . . . be necessary."[44]

1987: A Second Attempt at "Reform"

Intent upon following a reform strategy, Jaruzelski rejected the call of "hard-liners" for a return to centralized controls. In October 1987, Jaruzelski announced another ambitious program of economic and political reform, combining a mixture of decentralized planning, expanded private enterprise, and changes in ownership structures in the state sector. The reforms also promised to streamline the central bureaucracy and to introduce the elements of a Western-style market.

Zycie Gospodarcze summarized the four general aims of the reform:

1. Attainment of "market equilibrium" through increased supply;
2. Reduction of inflation (which had averaged 28% in the previous three years);
3. Growth in private consumption by the stabilization of real earnings; and
4. Improvement of the housing and utilities sectors.[45]

Professor Zdzislaw Sadowski, deputy premier and chairman of the State Planning Commission, was asked a pointed question in an interview in *Polish Perspectives*: "How can you avoid the malpractice committed by your predecessors?" Sadowski answered candidly: "It has been pointed out that in the past, there was talk of the need for surgery, but it was never followed up by an actual operation."[46] In an effort to legitimize his regime, the general attempted to rally a weary nation behind his policies. Jaruzelski also hoped to encourage foreign creditors and Western bankers to extend new lines of credit and loans.

To this end, Jaruzelski scheduled a referendum for 29 November 1987, an action unprecedented in the Eastern Bloc. The electorate would be asked to vote on the following two questions:

1. "Are you in favor of full implementation of the program presented to the Sejm for the radical revitalization of the economy which aims at a marked improvement of the standard of living of society, knowing that it will require going through a difficult two-three year period of rapid change?"
2. "Are you in favor of a Polish model of profound democratization of political life whose aim is reinforcement of self-government, broadening of civil rights and expansion of citizen participation in government of the country?"

To many, this represented a desperate (and perhaps last) attempt to "turn the economy and the nation around." For others, it was apparent that the regime had already waited too long and had not gone far enough to implement the program of industrial democracy demanded by Solidarity. What surprised observers was the rebuff the electorate dealt Jaruzelski. In an area of the world where referendums are regularly supported by 99 percent of voters, nearly one-third of the electorate refused to participate. More than 30 percent of those who voted said no.[47] Solidarity called for an election boycott. Surprisingly, leaders of the Catholic Church supported a positive vote. After a meeting with Jaruzelski on 16 November 1987, Cardinal Glemp said: "Even a difficult reform is better than chaos."

What was clear from the results of the referendum was that the program of austerity, coupled with vague promises of democracy and pluralism, was regarded with skepticism by the vast majority of Poles.

Leszek Balcerowicz has offered valuable insights into the first and second stages of economic reform carried out under General Jaruzelski. Balcerowicz noted that the economic system that evolved during these critical years did not achieve the objectives stated in the reform: an increase in economic efficiency and the elimination of chronic shortages.[48] Balcerowicz asserted that the basic reason for this failure was due to the fact that the reform was neither comprehensive nor radical. He noted that the basic features of the economy remained essentially unchanged, even in the face of several partial changes, which we have termed "piecemeal reforms."

These features included widespread *central intervention* in industrial production and in the allocation of resource inputs; continued and pervasive *price controls,* with strong internal disincentives to reduce prices;[49] continued organizational concentration and the related monopolization of the WOGs; massive redistribution of assets from and to socialized enterprises by state financial institutions"; the continued existence of the monobank; continued severe constraints on the private sector (both the tax structure and limits on employment did not allow private sector firms to grow[50]); and continued *dependence of enterprise directors* on both Party and state bodies. Goodwyn wrote: "The party's tentative introduction of selected market mechanisms succeeded principally in demonstrating to the population that members in good standing in the *nomenklatura* could enrich themselves through forms of state-chartered monopolies in a manner that had more in common with the early days of post-feudal mercantilism than with the structural invigoration of a modern industrial society."[51]

Balcerowicz added that due to the survival of the basic negative features of the economy, the reforms resulted in a lack of competition among state-controlled suppliers and a "massive bargaining by enterprises with superior bodies about the most convenient terms of activity."[52] Finally, and perhaps most importantly, the reforms made no real effort to create organizational competition, that is, the creation of a management-oriented bureaucracy determined to find "new paths" and "new solutions" to the economic stalemate.

Balcerowicz argued strongly against such piecemeal reforms undertaken by the government in 1982 and 1987. He termed these attempts as essentially self-defeating and futile. He concluded that "what the Polish experience shows is . . . that a move from such a system must be more radical."[53]

TOWARD THE ROUND TABLE

In retrospect, five events during 1988 foretold that deep economic and political change, not cosmetic tinkering on the fringes, would be necessary if society were to advance. Lawrence Goodwyn noted that "the tepid pace of party-generated 'reform' from 1986 to 1988 verified the final collapse of its martial law and post-martial law politics. . . . Events proved—one last time—that the party could not govern without some sort of agreement with society."[54] These events included the following:

1. Two rounds of industrial strikes, centered in the Lenin Shipyard in Gdansk, took place in May and August 1988.

2. General Kiszczak and Lech Walesa met in negotiations on 31 August 1988—by coincidence, it was the anniversary of the signing of the original Gdansk Accords. The divisions in society were so deep that Walesa had great difficulty in persuading strikers to suspend strikes so that the talks could begin. Walesa himself was bitterly attacked by his more radical associates for being "soft" on the regime and having "sold out" the interests of workers.

3. In November 1988, Walesa took part in a nationally televised debate with the head of the official trade union, Politburo member Alfred Miodowicz. Lawrence Goodwyn noted: "Walesa's public humiliation of the cliche-quoting party apparatchik seemed to have given the government a much-needed final push into serious preparations for the Round Table."[55]

4. In December 1988, the government enacted the *Law on Economic Activity*. This law nullified many of the regulations, directives, and restrictions adopted since 1945[56] that had established the preferential treatment of the socialized sector of the economy over most forms of private economic activity. The act made significant changes in employment law, established a broad-based tax structure, and brought to an end attempts by central authorities to stifle and regulate the activities of the private sector. These changes in the legal structure of Poland were accompanied by the elimination of the rationing of consumer goods and the freeing of prices for many consumer goods and products.[57] They resulted in a dramatic growth in the private sector: the total number of private retail trade and catering units increased by 66 percent in 1989.[58] The opening up of the economy proved to be a strong impetus to the "opening up" of the closed political system.

5. In December 1988, Walesa and Henryk Wujec, a longtime KOR activist and physicist "with wide connections at Warsaw University," invited 128 oppositionists to a gathering in Warsaw. The group was later expanded to a final membership of 232. The group announced the formation of the Solidarity Citizens Committee, which was ready to enter into negotiations with the government. The committee was heavily dominated by "intellectuals and Warsaw intellectuals in particular" who were quite willing to "leave the workers to Lech." It is ironic that in the creation of the Citizens Committee, the working-class base of Solidarity disappeared, as did the significant participation of farmers, women, and "Poles of any description from outside the capital city." The committee was heavily influenced by representatives of the Polish Academy of Sciences to the disappointment of many "veteran movement activists who felt slighted and whole cities and even regions of Poland that were transparently under-represented."[59]

The Solidarity of 1988–1989 never regained overwhelming popular support. During the initial period of Solidarity (1980–1981), it truly existed as a quintessential democratic institution, staffed by over 40,000 people who were financed out of local dues and were directly accessible and re-sponsible to the people who paid their wages. This exercise in "self-gener-ated democracy" resulted in the creation of the Network and its insightful and penetrating critique of the system. These efforts resulted in plans for enterprise self-management, the Action Program, Rural Solidarity, and lit-erally hundreds of local labor organizations dedicated to teaching the dy-namics of worker-democracy and political pluralism. In mid-1989, the relegalized independent trade union counted two million members, while its ranks had swelled to nearly 10 million in its formative period. The new focus of organizing activities was clearly on the local citizens committees.

The composition of the Citizens Committees in 1988–1989 was later reflected in the leadership of the Sejm after the June 1989 elections. The elimination of workers from leadership may have been a portent to the failure of post-Solidarity parties in the elections of both 1993 and 1995, when many workers who made up the core of Solidarity voted for the new-ly reconstructed "former" communists.

All factions, however, agreed that the risks were enormous and the stakes extremely high. "Living standards continued to decline even as trumpeted 'rounds' of reform limped along aimlessly."[60] Anthony Lewis of *New York Times* noted insightfully: "The trouble is that the police cannot make the economy function. Neither can just giving in to extravagant wage demands."[61] Events presaged an imminent and fundamental change in tac-tics, as the short-term results from 1987 to 1989 resulted in an acute dise-quilibrium in the economy along with high unemployment, reduced gov-ernment subsidies, and high prices for staples such as meat and bread. The political situation had degenerated into rancor and stalemate. Would the lessons of history be lost on the regime once again? The Round Table would begin on 6 February 1989. It would end in agreement on 5 April 1989 in time for June elections.

◈ *Chapter Five*

The March to the Market Economy: 1989–1993

"Poland's transition to capitalism is a great puzzle, hard for social scientists to decipher and to put into a cohesive analytical framework."

Kazimierz Z. Poznanski

When President Wojciech Jaruzelski invited several hundred representatives of the Polish United Workers' party, the United Peasants party, the Democratic party, and the Citizens Committees of Solidarity to a series of meetings that came to be called the "Round Table," it was an act of desperation.

Both the PZPR and the communist system had failed to meet a series of economic and political challenges that had developed between 1980 and 1989. At the end of the decade, the governments of Prime Ministers Zbigniew Messner (1988) and Mieczyslaw Rakowski (1989) failed because of their politically manipulative and inept management, as well as their irresponsible monetary and fiscal policies. The economy in 1989 was in a state of "near collapse."

In February 1988, Prime Minister Rakowski introduced an economic plan, *Income and Price Operation*. The Rakowski program incorporated two aspects. In the economic sphere, the plan involved a number of institutional adjustments. Included for all practical purposes was the elimination of all restrictions on private sector activity. The program also introduced the idea of privatization of State-owned Enterprises (SOEs), limited internal convertibility of the zloty, and established a two-tier banking system to replace the monobank.

The second aspect of the Rakowski plan was clearly political. Professor Kazimierz Poznanski observed that at the time the Rakowski government was making decisions on food prices and farm subsidies, voices were being raised that these moves were politically motivated and that the outgoing government elite wanted its opponents to be left with "as difficult an economic situation as possible."[1]

Branko Milanovic, a researcher at the World Bank, suggested that it was difficult, if not impossible, to determine how far Rakowski was willing to go. It seemed that Rakowski was unaware where concessions would lead and held a "too optimistic view of his own popularity."[2]

Milanovic further noted that the key reason for the failure of the program was political unwillingness to resist wage increases, combined with the inability of those who designed the program to control the budget-busting policies of the National Bank of Poland.[3]

Political events would overtake the Rakowski regime. Rakowski simply lost control of the state budget and money supply. The Communist party had lost its credibility and legitimacy. So when President Jaruzelski finally asked Tadeusz Mazowiecki to become prime minister and to form a new "coalition" government, he was offering Mazowiecki no prize, only problems. On 24 August 1989, Mazowiecki became the first truly "noncommunist" prime minister in postwar Poland. He formed a coalition government involving Solidarity, elements of the existing communist government, and their political party satellites in the Sejm.

Jeffrey Sachs has pointed out that among the deep and intrinsic flaws of "market socialism" that contributed to the failure of the pre-1989 reforms were "the timidity of the reforms; the power of the *nomenklatura* to avoid a real opening of the economy to international competition, and even the introduction of domestic competition; the political illegitimacy of the regime; and the corruption and arrogance of the Communist party."[4]

Professor Jan Mujzel, former director of the Institute of Planning and deputy chairman of the Economic Council of the Prime Minister, described the situation facing Mazowiecki: The first independent and democratic government of the postwar period inherited a collapsing economy from the communist past, with declining and inefficiently structured output and investments, a destroyed natural environment, a huge monetary overhang, high foreign and internal debt, unbalanced markets, a damaging rate of inflation, highly distorted and over-regulated prices, a weak nonconvertible currency and, last but not least, a predominant public sector, consisting of mainly obsolete and badly managed enterprises. Economically the transition was therefore extremely difficult and politically risky.[5]

With the support of Solidarity and the electorate, Prime Minister Mazowiecki "brought about a radical change in social attitude toward the government, which gave it a chance to tackle difficult economic problems in the conditions of popular support, confidence, and consent to the introduction of radical economic reforms."[6]

The Mazowiecki government faced a desperate situation. Production and imports were stagnated; budget deficits reached 60 percent of total expenditures, which equaled 4 billion USD for January to June 1989. Inflation rose from 60 percent in 1988 to 90 percent in July 1989. By August 1989, inflation was running at the rate of 700 percent per year. Domestic shortages became acute. Foreign debt service was suspended due to lack of any convertible currencies. Political tensions and social unrest threatened to further destabilize an anemic economy. However, Jan W. Bossak of the Warsaw School of Economics noted that "the political breakthrough and social confidence enjoyed by the government enabled the implementation of the economic program that under other conditions would be deprived of social consent. Political, social and economic changes taking place in Poland have also won the support, both political and economic, of countries performing a leading role in the world economy."[7]

Before considering the immediate and specific actions undertaken by Mazowiecki, it is important to recall several *structural characteristics* of the Polish economy in 1989 that were an outgrowth of over 40 long years of communist rule.[8]

Professor Jeffrey Sachs of Harvard University was destined to play a critical role in the economic transformation. Sachs wrote that he had the great honor to meet with Prime Minister Mazowiecki on his first day in office—even before his economic team had been selected.[9] From that day forward, Sachs became a key advisor to the coalition government on transformation possibilities. Sachs cited six structural features in the discussion of "reform strategy and the early results of reform":

1. Poland was highly industrialized;
2. Poland still has a large peasant agriculture sector;
3. The Polish economy was overwhelmingly state owned;
4. Poland lacked small- and medium-sized industrial enterprises, whether public or private;
5. Poland's international trade was excessively directed to the East, especially the Soviet Union; and
6. Poland was *egalitarian* in the distribution of income and wealth, that is, almost everyone in Poland at the beginning of this transition was relatively poor and without wealth.[10]

Aleksander Vacic, director of the Division for Economic Analysis and Projections of the Economic Commission of Europe, examined the situation at the time of the transition. He cited three positive structural components. First, the private sector dominated the agricultural sector, contributing about one-sixth of the nation's net material product. Second, central planning was shorter lived in Poland than in the Soviet Union and had been fundamentally questioned in Poland as early as the mid-1950s and in almost every decade thereafter. Third, Polish authorities restricted postwar economic legislation largely to the state and cooperative sectors, while maintaining general civil legislation. This kept alive basic notions of a market economy or at least "prevented negative social and political connotations" from arising.[11]

From a negative perspective, however, Vacic observed that the overall level of economic development on the eve of the 1989 revolution remained very low. Hence, conditions were not conducive to sudden economic reform, especially as industrial output in 1989 was roughly where it had been in the pre-crisis year of 1978.[12]

ENTER THE BALCEROWICZ TEAM

Mazowiecki was said to have been "looking for his Ludwig Erhard." Indeed, he found him in the person of Dr. Leszek Balcerowicz, professor of economics at the Warsaw Institute of Economics, as well as chairman of two Warsaw institutes, The Center for Social and Economic Research (CASE) and the Foundation for Economic Education. Balcerowicz graduated in 1970 from the Faculty of Foreign Trade of the Warsaw School of Planning and Statistics (now the Warsaw School of Economics). Between September 1972 and January 1974, he studied business administration, specializing in economics, at St. Johns University, New York City. In 1974, he returned to the Central School of Planning and Statistics from which he received his doctorate in 1975. His academic interests and dissertation topics included the economics of technological change and the social costs of speeding up product innovations.

In 1978, Balcerowicz made a far-reaching decision. He organized a "think tank" from which proposals would eventually come that shaped the program of economic reform adopted by the Mazowiecki government and subsequent Solidarity governments. Dr. Balcerowicz got together an informal group of 10 young economists who met regularly (almost weekly for two years) to discuss and debate possible programs for economic reform. The group considered such issues as how to prevent workers in cooperatives from consuming profits, what instruments of indirect control the state might and should have in the economy, how to design a two-tier banking system, and, in general, what powers local governments should have in the economy. As a result of these meetings and later because of considerable publicity about the group, the members became known, after August 1980, as the "Balcerowicz Group." Most important was the fact that their ideas for economic reform had been discussed and debated over the years. They were prepared to act boldly and decisively.

In June 1989, Harvard professors Jeffrey Sachs and David Lipton were invited by the leaders of Solidarity to share their previous experiences in privatization and to present their ideas on strategies for a program of comprehensive economic reform. Both Sachs and Lipton had extensive experience with privatization in Argentina, Bolivia, and Chile. In mid-July, Sachs was invited by Mazowiecki to submit an outline of his proposals for reforms. A proposal was circulated to the Parliamentary Club of Solidarity. The Solidarity leadership decided to pursue a course of *radical reform* and so informed Sachs.

Sachs explained that Solidarity's decision was predicated on "several crucial reasons":

> They recognized that they had a unique opportunity to make an econom-ic breakthrough to a market economy and a political breakthrough to democracy. They understood the economic and political logic of radical reforms. Their own experience had taught them that tinkering within the old system would produce no results. They knew that the economy bordered on hyperinflation. Economic logic also underscored the need to move comprehensively, as each aspect of the reform was intimately connected with the other dimensions. And Solidarity's lack of experienced personnel in the ministries also led the new government to rely on market forces as much as possible.[13]

Balcerowicz was a natural choice to join the Mazowiecki government. He was named deputy prime minister and minister of finance in September 1989. Several economists from the Balcerowicz Group came with him into the government. Others were to follow. The importance of these appointments was that the group not only had discussed and debated issues related to economic reform, but they were also armed with specific proposals for that reform. Their ideas, which were clearly radical and which stressed comprehensive and immediate reforms, had matured as a result of experience and their extended and continuous academic interaction. These ideas generated intense interest among many persons involved with the Solidarity movement. By 1989, Solidarity was increasingly perceived as much more than a trade union. Solidarity had become a cultural, social, and political phenomena that had suddenly inherited the responsibility for a functioning government.

Balcerowicz entered government with a strong "anti-gradualist attitude towards economic reform," not only based on the experiences of previous reforms, but also on Leon Festinger's *theory of cognitive dissonance*. This theory holds that people are more likely to change their attitudes and behavior if they are faced with "radical changes in their environment, which they consider irreversible, than if those changes are only gradual."[14]

With his dual appointment as deputy prime minister (for economic affairs) and minister of finance, Balcerowicz was invited to name his economic team, subject only to approval by the prime minister. Immediately, some of the Balcerowicz Group accepted appointments in the government. This group joined with others of like mind, shared vision, and common convictions, and soon they became identified in and out of government as the "Balcerowicz Team."[15]

External advisors and consultants also provided expert assistance to this new "team." The ideas that Sachs and Lipton had presented earlier that summer to the Solidarity leadership were similar in concept to what Balcerowicz was prepared to propose. As a result, Sachs, Lipton, and others were invited to collaborate with the team.[16]

Reflecting on the situation, Sachs wrote that Balcerowicz and his team confronted a legacy of communism that was negative in almost all dimensions. The economy was both bankrupt and deeply scarred through 40 years of communism. It was also reeling from a deep financial crisis and the emerging hyperinflation that resulted from fundamental structural problems, as well as the "political and administrative collapse" of the former system.[17]

Time was of the essence. The Balcerowicz Team established the year-end as the target date for completing their plans, so that their strategy for reform could become operative on 1 January 1990. The drama of meeting the December deadline was yet to unfold. Meanwhile, simultaneous activities at home and abroad were essential to inaugurate the proposed reform program.

LAUNCHING THE TRANSITION

The Mazowiecki government took immediate action in a series of crucial areas at home. Simultaneously, the government began overtures to Western countries, especially to creditor nations like West Germany, England, and France and the International Monetary Fund (IMF), seeking support for the efforts proposed by the new government to undertake radical plans for economic stabilization.

Balcerowicz believed that a major challenge would be to implement a process of transition that could be undertaken quickly while still ensuring long-term economic development. He concentrated his early planning on three kinds of changes: *stabilization*, microeconomic *liberalization*, and *privatization* of the economy. Professor Ben Slay noted that the transition program was based on the view that harsh measures were required to repress hyperinflation and set Poland on the course to a market economy. Slay acknowledged that the near-hyperinflationary conditions in which the transition began were highly unfavorable and resulted in an emphasis on the stabilization aspect of the program.[18] Balcerowicz maintained that the main reason for the success of the economic reform was the great speed of its early phase ("shock therapy"), when the fundamentals of a "liberal" economic system were firmly established.[19]

The Balcerowicz Plan was constructed around *five pillars of economic transformation*: (1) macroeconomic stabilization; (2) liberalization; (3) privatization; (4) construction of a social safety net; and (5) mobilization of international financial assistance to support the process.[20]

Balcerowicz believed that radical reform was essential and that timing was critical. His motivations were economic, psychological, and political. The goal was to break decisively from the communist system, end half-hearted and piecemeal reforms, and, in the words of the Solidarity leadership, "jump to the market economy." The government wanted to create an economy "in the style of Western Europe," based on private ownership of property, free markets, and global integration. The economic program focused on stabilization and liberalization, and on a realistic understanding that the period of "extraordinary" political cooperation was temporary.

Balcerowicz often used the expression *extraordinary politics* to describe the political situation in the last six months of 1989 and early 1990. He explained his expression in this way: Extraordinary politics is a period of discontinuity in a nation's history; it is a period of deep economic crisis, a breakdown of the institutional system, or a liberation from external domination, or an end of war. Nearly all of these phenomena converged in Poland in 1989.

He further noted that in the period of extraordinary politics new political structures, including genuine political parties and interest groups, are "fluid" because there are usually no "professional" politicians. The former political elite has been discredited, and politicians representing "the new order" have either not yet emerged or have not had sufficient time to become professional. Balcerowicz believed that among the political elites and the population at large, "there is a stronger-than-normal tendency to think and to act in terms of the common good."[21]

Meanwhile domestic legislation was necessary. Two overriding considerations governed the immediate planning process: A *market economy* was preferred over a centrally planned economy and a *private enterprise market economy* was preferred over "market socialism." The government needed to give immediate attention to the international scene and to begin extensive negotiations surrounding Poland's foreign debt.

The first of January 1990 was selected for the launching of the new economic program because it was the first day of the new fiscal year. The date was selected soon after the new government began (24 August in the case of the prime minister; 1 September for Minister Balcerowicz) in order to take advantage of a "honeymoon" period during which the Sejm and the Senate would be disposed to accept the new program. In October, the Council of Ministers gave "approval in principle" to the anticipated economic program of the government.

It was also essential to develop an agreement with the International Monetary Fund before world interest in Polish reform diminished or attention was distracted by other events. The scope and the intensity of those negotiations are described in some detail later in this chapter, following a few preliminary comments on the domestic timetable.

LEGISLATION DEVELOPS

The Sejm established 17 December 1989 as an absolute deadline for any new or revised legislation. New legislation and proposed amendments to existing laws involved a three-phase process. First, new statutes or revisions of existing statutes were initially studied by a specially appointed task force, chaired by a deputy minister of finance or by a department member of some other related department. Second, draft laws were then forwarded to the Economic Committee of the Council of Ministers (KERM). To simplify the process of evaluation, the responsibility of KERM was limited by the new government to dealing with interdepartmental projects and then only after they had previously been carefully prepared.

The third phase in the approval process was that of the Council of Ministers, which received proposed legislation from KERM. The deadlines were tight, the scope of new legislation comprehensive, and the thrust of the economic program, while familiar to the drafters, was essentially foreign to the Council of Ministers and many others at the intermediate levels of government. Drafting, discussion, debate, and some decision making were required.

Balcerowicz reported that his team prepared 11 proposals, essentially changing the legal framework of the economy. These proposals included a new tax law, a banking law and foreign exchange law, a law regulating foreign investment, a law on customs, legal foundations governing credit, and a law on taxing excessive wage increases. From this point on, the efficiency of the Sejm was critical. To debate these laws in the normal way would have taken at least several months. Special legislative procedure was required.[22]

As December approached, Balcerowicz met with the leaders of the Sejm and the Senate and with the leaders of all the political factions. He sought an agreement on their respective modus operandi, in view of the limited time available to satisfy all deadlines. The legislative leadership agreed to the establishment of an "extraordinary special commission" to facilitate the legislative consideration and adoption process. Before the government program was fully developed and unveiled, its direction and thrust were apparent and the elements that comprised the Balcerowicz Plan were a source of intense controversy."[23] On schedule, 17 December, Balcerowicz unveiled the plan in the Sejm with a TV broadcast in which he stressed that the task of transforming the economic system, difficult in itself, had to be undertaken under circumstances that were unfavorable: hyperinflation, lack of foreign exchange reserves, and the strenuous burden of foreign debt. The tasks that Poland faced were truly overwhelming and without precedent, and it was necessary to take quick and decisive action.[24]

The parliamentary approach to collaboration with government economic ministers was unprecedented. Patriotism supplanted partisan politics. Legislative groups and political parties gave the benefit of the doubt to the reformers and adopted extraordinary mechanisms to address the challenge of debating extensive and radical legislation within a highly compressed time frame.

The parliamentary session ended on 17 December and created an "extraordinary commission," comprised of members of Parliament from diverse political parties and from various parliamentary commissions. The work of this commission was critical and marked a "high-water mark" for the Parliament. Its members later recalled that it was "a romantic endeavor" when political divisions virtually disappeared. Members worked a dozen or more hours a day, even during the holidays, to get everything ready before the "zero hour" of 1 January.[25]

Ordinarily, the Senate would debate legislative acts only after they had been approved by the Sejm. To accommodate the compressed time frame, the Senate leadership agreed to receive proposed laws in "draft" form, ones that had been submitted to and tentatively approved by the extraordinary commission of the Sejm. These legislative drafts went to a similar extraordinary commission of the Senate for immediate study.

The Sejm and the Senate were in almost constant session, receiving, examining, debating, and generally approving "the government economic program" and exhibiting extraordinary cooperation in order to accommodate the calendar countdown.

Concurrently, Dr. Balcerowicz in his capacity as minister of finance was involved in implementing a series of internal measures that required remedial action in order to set the stage for the proposed 1 January economic start up. A series of currency devaluations preceded the unification of the exchange rate in 1990; interest rates were increased; the existing system of subsidizing coal mining was restructured; and the indexation of wages was abolished, with a substitute system introduced as a forerunner to wage restraints after 1990. Two successive budgets were prepared for the remaining months of 1989.

The race for the deadline on domestic legislation was won by a margin sufficient to secure the necessary presidential signatures by 31 December. The Sejm passed the new and revised legislative package for the government's economic program on 27 December. Minister Balcerowicz, who had previously met with President Jaruzelski and had advised him of the ongoing legislative processes, secured his concurrence and prearranged his availability on 30 and 31 December to sign the multiple statutes. So, the almost impossible became reality.

THE FOREIGN DEBT CRISIS

Simultaneously, Deputy Prime Minister Balcerowicz and another Ministry of Finance "team" were engaged in a parallel race in the international arena to renegotiate Poland's foreign debt. Balcerowicz observed that foreign debt was a major burden on the economy, inherited from its socialist past. The debt problem could only be solved by a rather unusual "triangle": Poland, the International Monetary Fund, and creditors officially represented by the Paris Club as well as over 500 Western banks represented by the so-called London Club.[26] The debt situation was serious; renegotiations were essential; and the time frame was the same December 31 year-end date.

Between 1970 and 1997, Poland borrowed about $20 billion from Western governments and banks. Poland's debt grew exponentially, especially during the decades of the 1970s and 1980s:

- 1975—$8 billion
- 1978—$25 billion
- 1989—$41 billion
- 1991—$45 billion

In the decade of the 1980s, the situation was exacerbated by domestic difficulties and international reactions. In 1981, a severe balance of payment crisis prevented Poland from making debt service payments. In April 1981, the government signed an agreement with the Paris Club (holders of public debt) that permitted Poland to postpone 90 percent of its principal repayments for 1986 to 1989. The agreement, however, obligated Poland to repay the interest. Then came martial law. Western governments, that is, the Paris Club, severed official ties with the Polish government. Consequently, Poland made no debt payments for several years; however Western banks, represented by the London Club, did not break their commercial relations. They came to a new agreement about restructuring Polish debt by shifting the payment obligation forward to 1988–1989.

Not only did the Mazowiecki government face enormous domestic challenges, but the debt crisis threatened to overshadow and sabotage any domestic economic program. In September 1989, the government estimated that U.S. 500 million USD were necessary just to cover essential imports. Without an agreement with the IMF, there was almost no hope of meeting current government obligations or implementing the government's proposed economic package of reform. Moreover, without IMF endorsement there was little hope of securing concessions from either the Paris Club or the London Club. The cooperation of all parties was essential. Securing that cooperation became yet another challenge for the Balcerowicz Team. To do so by the 31 December deadline for the implementation of the domestic program created another set of pressures and another race against the clock.

These negotiations were considerably less under the control of the Balcerowicz Team than the forging of domestic economic reform had been. In September 1989, in his capacity as minister of finance, Leszek Balcerowicz met with his Western government counterparts and pressed for a 500 million USD emergency credit. The Basle Bank for International Settlement granted Poland a bridging loan of 215 million USD. Negotiations with the IMF continued unabated. The spirit of cooperation evolving between the economic planners representing the new government and the Sejm made it possible to initiate and continue negotiations with the IMF. By December 1989, Poland and the IMF had reached an understanding. The IMF agreed to receive a "letter of intent" from the Polish government.

The letter of intent confirmed the "goodwill intent" to obtain full relief from payments of both capital and interest in 1990, an enormous presumption in itself. The letter of intent further committed the government to reach agreements with creditors on the *permanent reduction* of the debt burden. This commitment was likewise daring since such a proposal for debt reduction was as unprecedented as it was unconventional.

Negotiations about the reduction of debt continued throughout 1990. In January 1990, Prime Minister Mazowiecki wrote to the heads of state of every creditor nation requesting consideration for debt reduction by debt forgiveness. Balcerowicz used his IMF appearances and trips abroad, as well as his Warsaw meetings with ambassadors and visiting government dignitaries, in order to "lobby" for debt relief.

The proposals of the Polish government were unconventional. At the outset Poland was seeking an 80 percent debt reduction. The concept of such a steep debt reduction had no precedent. By March 1991, the Polish government had reconsidered its percentage of reduction rate, based primarily on the advice of deputy U.S. secretary of the treasury, David Mulford. He persuaded the Balcerowicz team that a 50 percent rate was possible, but that 80 percent was unrealistic. To insist on 80 percent risked loss of any agreement. By March 1991, the preliminary agreement signed between Poland and the Paris Club in February 1990 to temporarily forego debt service was about to expire. Again, time was of the essence.

On 20 April 1991, Poland and the Paris Club reached a historic agreement. The governments that constituted the Paris Club held two-thirds of Poland's foreign debt. They agreed to forgive one-half of this debt (about $15 billion), provided that Poland continued to make progress toward the economic reform introduced in 1990. The agreement to forgive 50 percent of the net present value of Poland's debt was to be effected in two phases: 30 percent in the first phase, and 20 percent in the second phase, assuming that Poland met the requirements of its IMF agreement.

The London Club, consisting of over 500 of Poland's commercial bank creditors, also reached agreement. The London Club agreed to forgive 45 percent of the outstanding debt (or slightly over $13 billion). The Ministry of Finance agreed to fully service Poland's remaining debt, which had not been accomplished since 1981.

These concessions, together with the support of the IMF and the World Bank, essentially confirmed the confidence of the international financial community in the Balcerowicz Plan.

THE POLISH CURRENCY PROBLEM

Still another Ministry of Finance negotiation with Western governments was in process. Poland was seeking contributions of 1 billion USD from Western governments to a stabilization fund to support the stabilization-liberalization package; it was especially concerned with the convertibility of the Polish zloty. This campaign also had a 31 December 1989 deadline because the convertibility of the zloty was crucial to the economic program to be launched on 1 January. Globally, the creation of such a fund was designed to convey a message to the public that the about-to-be launched Polish program of economic reform had the endorsement, and therefore the confidence, of Western governments.

Domestically, the stabilization fund increased the confidence of reformers in the possibility of full convertibility of the zloty. Balcerowicz noted that without the creation of the stabilization fund, zloty convertibility would not have been launched.[27]

Sachs had earlier insisted that a program based on a convertible zloty in the first six months of the transition was essential.[28] He further argued: "In my view, the single most important reform that this government will take in its first six months of office, indeed, one of the most important reforms it will ever take is the creation of a convertible currency linked to the international exchange rate system."[29]

The commitments of credits and grants to the stabilization fund continued to be made by Western governments, but it was crucial to receive these funds in time to meet the launch date. On 29 December, the last of these commitments were still "in process." Working over the normal Christmas holiday, Minister Balcerowicz engaged in telephone negotiations with IMF managing director, Michel Camdessus, ensuring the IMF that Poland had met the conditions of the "letter of intent" but that Western governments were delaying their payments. In a state of desperation, Balcerowicz contacted David Mulford, deputy secretary of the treasury, who served as the U.S. chief of mission for world debt issues. Secretary Mulford had earlier represented the United States in confirming to the Polish government the favorable disposition of the United States toward the government's reform package. Mulford responded promptly. Before the end of December, 400 million USD were confirmed, with the balance assured by 7 January 1990.[30]

Another deadline had been met. The economic reform package was now complete. On 1 January 1990, the Balcerowicz Plan became a reality.

THE PLAN AS A REALITY

On 1 January 1990, Poland's stabilization and liberalization program with its stringent macroeconomic measures was introduced as promised. The Balcerowicz Plan contained two broad strategic goals that also reflected the austerity expected by IMF: *stabilization* of the economy (elimination of hyperinflation) and *transformation* of the economic system to a market economy. The government faced a choice between a gradual, step-by-step approach or a shock treatment. The government chose the latter; hence the plan is called "the big bang" or "the shock program," or simply, "shock therapy."

The stabilization plan was radical and ambitious. Economist Marian Paszynski noted that the main goal of the program was to restore normal conditions for economic activity by means of eradicating galloping inflation in the first six months and limiting price increases to one-digit figures per month in the middle of the year. Overcoming hyperinflation was considered to be the only feasible strategy of combating inflation and was treated as a priority in economic policy.[31]

Sachs contended his "five main pillars" of reform were the essence of the Balcerowicz Plan: macroeconomic stabilization; liberalization of the range of actions needed to allow markets to function, including the end of central planning, bureaucratic controls over prices, international trade, and the use of raw materials; the establishment of a legal environment to support private property, including a commercial code, corporation law, and a system of judicial enforcement of contracts; privatization—the transfer of ownership of state assets to the private sector; the creation of an adequate "social safety net" and the introduction of an unemployment compensation system; and mobilization of international financial assistance to support the transformation process.[32]

The stabilization package consisted of five major components:

1. There would be a restrictive monetary policy, a drastic reduction in the money supply, and the establishment of a high interest rate (exceeding inflation in real terms from March 1990), accompanied by a law regulating

credit operations by introducing interest rate adjustments in all previous credit agreements. The law restricted the so-called preferential credit arrangements of the former system.

2. It called for the elimination of the budget deficit, predominantly through further drastic reductions in subsidies for food, raw materials, production input, and energy carriers, as well as the removal of tax exemptions.

3. There would be a further liberalization of prices (since January 1990, 90% of prices were to be determined by the market), as well as a significant increase in prices that were still under administrative control, for example, fuels and energy, transportation, rents, and pharmaceuticals. Some other price deregulation steps were taken during 1990 (e.g., a liberalization of coal prices from 1 July 1990). Rents were partly deregulated only in 1994.

4. The zloty was made convertible for transactions at a single exchange rate. The exchange rate was stabilized at 9,500 zlotys per 1 USD. There was also liberalization of foreign trade (elimination of import quotas and most export quotas and unification and reduction of tariffs).

5. There would be a restrictive income policy, through the elimination of general wage indexation in the state enterprise sector; it was introduced in July 1989. In addition, severe tax penalties on wage increases in the state sector (so-called *popiwek*) were introduced. This policy allowed only a modest growth of wages with respect to prices. The excess wage taxation was gradually relaxed, especially after 1992, and was abolished in 1994.[33]

The transformation package aimed to alter fundamentally the economic system by introducing market economy institutions and mechanisms. While some actions were undertaken immediately, and others staggered, the original intention was to implement all of them within a two-year period.

Additional actions necessitated by the Balcerowicz Plan included:

1. Transformation of ownership of enterprises, privatization of state-owned or cooperative enterprises, and the competitive sale of state assets;
2. Demonopolizing and creating conditions favorable to unrestricted competition between enterprises, both private and public;
3. Liberalization of foreign trade and payments, eliminating trade quotas and reducing tariffs and cumbersome restrictions on the licensing of the foreign exchange market;
4. Liberalization of the rules concerned with the ownership of land[34];
5. Establishment of capital markets, including a Securities Exchange;
6. Modification of labor laws to create conditions favorable to a free labor market;
7. Upgrading administrative and managerial skills of the business community;

8. Developing a comprehensive reform of the tax system, including the introduction of individual income taxes and value-added taxes; and

9. The enactment of a new *Joint Venture Law* designed to attract foreign investors.

Professor Bossak wrote that the long-range success of the program rested squarely on "social acceptance and support by all meaningful political and social forces, including trade unions and the Parliament."[35] Public support would be critical to success!

Professor Sachs commented that certain aspects of liberalization were easier to effect than might initially appear possible. The previous regime had undertaken a number of steps to resurrect the legal structure of the interwar period, such as the *1934 Commercial Code.* There were well-trained lawyers who could negotiate and enforce contracts. There was also a judicial system, "which was rusty to be sure," but which could enforce a wide range of private arrangements. That aspect of liberalization did not represent an impossible task.[36]

We have examined the goals and the theory of the stabilization-liberalization plan. We next move to an analysis of the crucial implementation stage. Now we need to ask: What were the steps that were required by the introduction of the new economic transformation package? The Mazowiecki government immediately undertook 10 actions:

1. Reduction in consumer and producer subsidies;
2. Ending of almost all price controls;
3. Elimination of central planning;
4. Devaluation of the zloty-dollar exchange rate with a pegged rate at the new level;
5. Opening of foreign trade;
6. Full convertibility of the currency for current account transactions;
7. The introduction of *popiwek* (the tax on excessive wages);
8. Legal changes designed to promote new private firm development;
9. Introduction of competition; and
10. Demonopolization.

Beyond the stabilization program, additional measures were planned for 1990 in order to stimulate economic activity and ensure transformation to a market economy. Seven programs were scheduled, including (1) the completion of the legislative enactments essential to the creation of the legal base for private ownership; (2) beginning of the sale of state assets; (3) creating conditions for demonopolization and facilitating competitiveness; (4) initiating agrarian reform by removing all restrictions on sale of farmlands and launching efforts to foster village industry and services; (5) updating bankruptcy legislation; (6) updating the labor code; and (7) organizing investment banks.

A third phase was planned for the second half of 1991 that would focus on a complete reform of the tax system, including the imposition or levying of an income tax for all legal persons; value-added taxes to replace turnover taxes; and a personal income tax to be levied on all income.[37]

Additional legislation was passed in 1990, including laws strengthening the Central Bank, laws governing insurance, an antimonopoly law, and a law disbanding the compulsory Association of Cooperatives. The process continued into 1991. A new securities law and the law reestablishing the Warsaw Stock Exchange were enacted. The Warsaw Stock Exchange reopened 16 April 1991.[38] An important new *Foreign Investment Law* replaced the *Foreign Investment Law of 1988*.[39] An income tax law and a new budgetary law were also enacted.

In May 1991, the zloty was devalued and pegged to a "basket" of currencies rather than to the dollar. In October 1991, a "crawling peg" was introduced. The government also modified the wage control mechanism, against the protests of the labor unions.

Any system of change creates negative personal and public reactions. A radical macroeconomic program such as that introduced in 1990 and 1991 had the potential for considerable economic and social disruption, as well as possible eventual political repercussions. The transformation in Poland proved to be no exception.

Stabilization and price liberalization were painful. Inflation initially turned out to be higher than expected; the decline in production was deeper than previously thought. Measured real wages decreased. Unemployment became a new phenomenon in Poland. However, inflation quickly began to go down, that is, 80 percent in January 1990; 23.8 percent in February; 4.3 percent in March; and 1.89 percent in August. In September 1990, however, inflation had grown to 4.6 percent, reversing the initial downward trend. Inflation was never again as low as in August 1990 until 1996/1997.

The average inflation (as calculated by the EBRD) for the 1990s was as follows:

- 1990 — 585.8 percent
- 1991 — 70.3 percent
- 1992 — 44.2 percent
- 1993 — 37.6 percent
- 1994 — 29.5 percent
- 1995 — 21.6 percent
- 1996 — 18.5 percent
- 1997 — 14.6 percent (first half)

Stabilization and price liberalization also had positive effects. The variety and quality of consumer goods, domestic and especially foreign, increased noticeably. Queues disappeared. The new internally convertible zloty held stronger than expected, and exports to the West expanded dramatically.

AN ANALYSIS

In 1990, the World Economy Group within the World Institute for Development Economic Research (WIDER), a United Nations university research center, studied three aspects of "Eastern Europe Reform": (1) stabilization and liberalization, (2) privatization, and (3) restructuring.

While the economists involved in the study recognized that "the Polish stabilization is still unfolding," they concluded that "from the first few months we have learned at least three main lessons about stabilization in a previously socialist economy." Those three lessons were:

1. "Price liberalization was associated with a large increase in prices over wages.
2. Stabilization has been associated with a sharp demand-induced contraction.
3. The decrease in sales has been substantially larger than the decrease in employment."[40]

Why this disparity? The removal of subsidies from firms, together with firms in monopoly positions that elected to raise prices, contributed to price increases. The disruptions in the distribution systems, previously controlled by the Communist party, also contributed; but there was also a decline in consumption. Firms reduced production or held production in inventory, which contributed to a supply-demand pressure and which increased prices without a corresponding increase in wages. The "squeeze" that many families felt between rising prices and a decrease in measured real wages tended to weaken public enthusiasm for various liberalization and stabilization programs throughout Eastern Europe, and especially in Poland.

The World Economy Group reported that the evidence "points to demand rather than supply as the main factor behind the contraction of output." Before stabilization, demand had exceeded output. Based on the evidence, they concluded that "part of the decrease in consumption behavior comes from the adverse shift in the income distribution; part of it comes also from uncertainty as to what the future may hold."[41]

Managers reacted to the decrease in sales, not by adjusting employment, but essentially by increasing inventories. Ownership was uncertain, but what was recognized by managers was that workers had control in most firms. So, managers acted to keep employees on the payroll. They were able to do so because managers still exercised monopoly power in SOEs (state-owned enterprises). At the same time, SOEs had large amounts of retained earnings, and because of hyperinflation, firms had little debt and low interest payments. Managers had no incentive to invest their retained earnings because of the uncertainties related to the future and the likelihood that eventually they would no longer be in charge. Whatever funds were available were used to retain and pay workers.[42]

The World Economy Group concluded that "price liberalization and stabilization have to be implemented simultaneously. . . . Partial liberalization is incompatible with convertibility, to the extent that convertibility allows for highly destructive speculation against a price structure that differs from that of the rest of the world."[43]

A NOTE OF CAUTION IS RAISED

As early as the first year of the Balcerowicz Plan, some economists were urging caution and concern. Professor Marian Paszynski of the Warsaw School of Economics identified the following seven areas of concern that he foresaw as risks or potential problems associated with the uncertainty surrounding the government's economic program. In retrospect, these concerns were both insightful and revealing.

1. The path of overcoming inflation might not be as short as it was programmed.
2. The impact of the program on the financial position of the enterprises and their chances for survival was not at all clear.
3. Though the foreign exchange market seemed for the time being to be stabilized, it was not certain whether, in the case of persistent high inflation, the maintenance of the exchange rate level would be feasible in the longer run.
4. It was not certain that the inflow of external resources and economic assistance would be forthcoming on a scale commensurable with the growing import requirements.
5. Keeping the budget in balance could be endangered in the case of a higher than expected drop of industrial output that might in turn cause a more pronounced narrowing of the tax base with a concurrent growth of expenditures for unemployment benefits.
6. Any delay in enforcing the proposed changes in the economic system that might give precedence to implementation of the stabilization program would have a negative impact upon the growth of supply.
7. Although the wage restraints built into the stabilization program related to the wage fund of the enterprises and not to individual wages, the reaction to the enforcement of such restraint was not yet clear.[44]

From the beginning, the Mazowiecki government recognized a wide range of risks and uncertainties. Many situations were immediately evident; others had the possibility of becoming more serious and exacerbated in the future. From the outset, the government decided to move boldly. In looking back at this dynamic and challenging period, it is apparent that policy risks and implementation uncertainties could be identified by seven interlocking concerns. This by no means exhausts the possibilities, but it captures the major concerns under discussion at the outset of the program of economic transformation.

1. *Attitudes and Lack of Change Models.* Professor Stefan Kurowski of the Catholic University of Lublin observed: "It's possible to nationalize an economy by one decree and overnight going the opposite direction inescapably becomes a long and difficult process which needs deliberation and careful handling."[45] Peoples' ideas, patterns of thought, and spirit of action or inaction had been shaped for 40 years in the centrally planned, decreed, and enforced mode. The shift to entrepreneurial, open, risk-taking, and free market approaches to economic and social issues came neither easily nor quickly. Moreover, there were no precise models to follow for transitions from socialism to market economies. "A lack of experience in transition and unpredictability of the behavior of economic entities in the process causes all the assumptions [about] the course of this process and of its outcome to lie in the sphere of conjectures," wrote Professor Paszynski.[46] Reorientation of the population, combined with positive reenforcing experiences, requires time and usually long-suffering patience.

University of Warsaw professor Jacek Kochanowicz reminded us that "the experience of late comers shows that their ability to modernize and compete internationally was conditioned on the presence of a supply of skillful managers, engineers, administrators and workers."[47]

By 1991, "better tomorrow was yesterday" graffiti was beginning to appear. To some, the hardships, risks, and uneasiness of the promised "new order" evoked a nostalgia for the security of the "old order."

2. *Continued Social Acceptance.* Calmness, discipline, and sacrifice characterized the early months of the Mazowiecki government after the introduction of the Balcerowicz Plan. Initial positive acceptance was widespread. Early opinion polls showed overwhelming support for the new government's efforts; but social acceptance proved to be tenuous. Dariusz Filar remarked that "in the long run the extent that democracy develops in the country will define the extent that Poland is able to emerge from its economic gloom."[48] Jeffrey Sachs concurred: "The glue holding together the reforms is the basic social consensus that success will be achieved by returning to Europe."[49]

Uneasiness existed about the political future because of the division in the Sejm, the multiplication of political factions, legislative delays, the continuing role of the *nomenklatura,* and the next election. Social tensions were on the rise. Unions routinely threatened strikes. Farmers created roadblocks, occupied the Ministry of Agriculture, and on 11 July 1990, staged a nationwide two-hour blockade of all highways to protest union wage concessions, loss of subsidies, and low prices for their produce. In the face of growing unemployment, loss of purchasing power, and deterioration of the quality of life, the question was beginning to be asked: How long will it be before society reaches its limit of endurance?

3. *Unemployment.* Unemployment was relatively unknown in "real socialism." From the outset, unemployment rose rapidly and far outdistanced the estimates of economic planners. Originally estimated at 400,000, by December 1990, the number of unemployed had reached between 1.3 and 2 million.

The early unemployment rates were unevenly distributed by regions and by local areas. The social cost of unemployment proved to be high. Erosion of confidence and loss of hope opened society to the possibility of demonstrations, strikes, riots, and increasingly demagogical societal behavior. Unemployment benefits, however modest, added a further strain on the budget.

4. *Controlling Inflation.* Controlling hyperinflation was a priority that met with success. Keeping inflation low and preventing a reoccurrence of galloping inflation demanded constant vigilance to resist the many pressures to adjust wages and prices, and for increased government spending.[50] Unemployment benefits greatly exceeded original budget estimates. Productivity declines, increased budget pressures, growing unemployment, consequent benefits, payments and group layoffs, and the possibility of reduced tax revenues would all impact the government.

5. *Achieving Privatization.* Developing the institutions of a free market economy constituted an immediate challenge. Legislation on privatization of state-owned enterprises was finally approved after months of delay. Implementation of privatization suffered from a lack of uniform accounting standards, the absence of valuation systems, and a paucity of capital markets and savings in the economy generally. Bankruptcy and shutdowns affected one out of every three private enterprises. Industrial production declined. The continuing presence of a great number of *nomenklatura* in state firms who lacked enthusiasm for conversion from monopoly to capitalism would further impede privatization. Foreign investment and joint ventures were in the infant stage. Some further barriers to privatization included a poor service sector and technical infrastructures, the lack of qualified managerial and operating personnel, a dearth of managerial and marketing technology, limited telecommunications facilities and transportation networks, and the continuing uncertainty of the socioeconomic environment.[51]

6. *Parliamentary Structures.* The Round Table Protocol preordained the profile of the Parliament by authorizing that 299 seats would be reserved for the government coalition (173 members were from the Communist party), and restricting the initial free electoral process to contests for

161 seats in the Sejm. Thus, the Communist party, its satellites, and the *nomenklatura* held 65 percent of the seats in the Sejm. That majority succeeded in delaying legislation and in obstructing many of the reforms proposed by Prime Minister Mazowiecki. Early commentators foresaw parliamentary complications but did not realistically predict the parliamentary maneuvers that would arise as political parties multiplied, as electoral results continued to change the composition of the legislative assembly, and as intra- and interparty rivalries emerged.

7. *Need for Immediate Economic Aid.* The worldview of Poland's turnaround was immediate and widely approved. However, Polish authorities noted that, in practice, actual agreements, concessions, debt forgiveness, and other forms of aid were not so rapidly forthcoming. Polish foreign trade continued to be heavily dependent on COMECON countries (especially the Soviet Union), all of which were undergoing enormous economic and political upheavals themselves. Unresolved issues such as Polish-Soviet debt and zloty-ruble convertibility rates affected trade revenues.

The preoccupation of Germany in the merger of FRG and GDR, and of the Soviet Union, later Russia, with internal political and economic pressures, left both trading partners politically distracted. The restructuring of the European Union (EU) consumed the attention of Western European countries. Whether Poland looked East or West, its immediate neighbors were preoccupied with their own self-interest and had few resources to devote to Polish economic rehabilitation. FRG economic aid packages for GDR subtracted from the funds available for Poland. Aid from the United States, friendly to Poland but geographically much farther away, was slow in coming. Poland needed a massive injection of foreign aid in order to maintain political equilibrium and economic and fiscal stability, and in order to get on with the transformation program. As late as 1993, Sachs noted that given the attitude of the West, and the documented cases of "rapacious" Western investors intent on profiteering from the gaps in the legal structure, there was a clear risk of a "xenophobic backlash" in the region.[52]

The preoccupation with stabilization and liberalization delayed implementation of the other three pillars of economic transformation: mass privatization, creating a social safety net, and mobilizing continuing international financial assistance and investment.

These were the doubts and uncertainties that preoccupied the attention of academics and the public during the initial year of the political transition and economic transformation. How then did the situation play itself out in the intervening years? Chapter 6 discusses the movement toward privatization with special references to the various patterns of Polish private sector development. Chapter 7 presents in detail the efforts of the Mazowiecki government and all subsequent governments to resolve the challenge of implementing a nonconventional voucher certificate mass privatization program.[53] Chapter 8 examines economics and politics after shock therapy. Chapter 9 evaluates the consequences of the Polish economic and political experiment with an assessment of what this experiment means for the future. Chapter 10 is an epilogue of the period from 1995 to 1997.

THE BARRIER OF SOCIAL ENDURANCE

The comments of several leading economists provide an important context to the delicate transition process. Professor Kazimierz Poznanski of the Henry M. Jackson School of International Studies at the University of Washington suggested: "From the very beginning, economists have wondered whether it was rational for the newly formed political leadership to invest its future in such a radical program. The question has also been raised of the practicality—and economic cost—of such an approach as compared to a more evolutionary type of reform. Moreover, debate has emerged on the more technical aspects of this transition (e.g., choice of instruments, sequencing of reforms, etc.)."[54]

Jeffrey Sachs, who was a leading architect in the development of the Balcerowicz Plan, asserted that a key fact about economic reform is that several years must pass before the fruits of reform are apparent. The intervening period has been called a "valley of tears," and it has occurred in nearly every country that adopted radical economic transformation, from postwar Germany and Japan, to Chile and Mexico in the 1980s. "The time in the valley depends on the consistency and boldness of the reforms. If there is wavering or inconsistency in economic measures, it is easy to get lost in the valley. Argentina has been lost for forty-five years."[55]

Economics professor Jacek Kochanowicz of the University of Warsaw remarked that experience demonstrates that the transition to capitalism and modernization cannot be quick and easy—if it is to succeed.[56] Tsuneaki Sato, professor of economics at Japanese Nihon University, provided a more generalized critique: "There is no short-cut in the transition to a market economy as was imagined amid the euphoria of the Revolution," though there will be no turning back on the chosen path of a shift away from socialism.[57]

Part of the difficulty in the transition was the gross *underestimation of the time required to implement changes* and the *longer period required to assimilate the changes*. During the period of initial euphoria, the Mazowiecki government estimated that the decline in production and the increase in unemployment would be short-lived, perhaps lasting only six months. The optimism was predicated on the expectation that deflationary measures were needed to reduce inflation and to remove imbalances inherited from the Rakowski government, even though there was a possibility that these measures would bring about a recession. The error in judgment was the belief that the recession would be "shallow" and limited. In fact, the recession was seen by most as a depression. It was very deep and extended over a three-year period. By 1992 GNP was 20 percent below 1989; and industrial production had fallen 30 percent below its 1989 level.

This drop turned out to be much greater than had been envisioned by almost every official and independent forecast, observed Jan Mujzel, former deputy chairman of the Economic Council, who concluded that this situation "revealed both the weakness of the theory and a limited capacity for achieving any meaningful progress under such extreme circumstances."[58]

Both John P. Hardt, senior specialist in post-Soviet economics, and Philip J. Kaiser, consultant with the Library of Congress Congressional Research Service, pointed out that "all countries committed to a transition to a market system were faced with an inevitable period of recession, inflation and unemployment."[59] Professor Sato noted that privatization was not free from the impact of the depression, which proved to be deeper and longer than anticipated. Since the economy was still dominated by the state or "quasi-state" sector, "priority given to stimulating production is bound to affect the pace, methods and forms of privatizing large state-owned enterprises. How to reconcile these two requirements will be crucial in the course of further privatization, at least for several years to come."[60]

THE ECONOMIC RECORD

What did the record reveal? According to official figures, the gross domestic product (GDP) fell by 18.3 percent between 1989 and 1991. Industrial production dropped by 33.2 percent; construction by 11.0 percent; and transport services by 24.8 percent. Unemployment—an unknown phenomenon until then—rose by over 2.2 million, and by the end of 1991 involved 11.8 percent of the economically active population. At the end of July 1993, it rose to over 2.8 million, or 15.2 percent. It should be noted that some official indicators, especially those concerning GDP and unemployment, are somewhat suspect because of the strong rise of the unregistered "gray" economy, a phenomenon discussed in greater detail below.

The recessionary trend persisted into the first quarter of 1992. By April 1992, there were signs of recovery in industry, construction, trades, and services. The sale of industrial products in 1992 exceeded the 1991 level by 4.2 percent in real terms. The rate of unemployment slowed down sharply, from about 1.1 million in 1990 and 1991 to 354,000 in 1992. There was an estimated increase of 1.0 percent in GDP. If this trend continued and if economic policy was carefully formulated, the rate of GDP growth in 1993 had the potential of reaching around 4 percent. In fact, the GDP in 1993 reached 3.8–4.0 percent.

Hardt and Kaiser further described the situation "in most countries of the region" when they said that "the expectation for prosperity to come with freedom in this revolutionary period [was] ... disappointed." They offer reasons for the economic downturn (or "great depression" in their terminology) between 1989 and 1994 in all of the former Soviet Bloc countries.

The reduction in demand for heavy industrial and military-related products was combined with recession, political instability, and a general collapse in trade. German reunification led to the cancellation of many contracts between former East German and Polish companies. The freeing of prices, the Soviet oil price shock, continued deficit spending, and the exposure of hidden inflation contributed to a substantial increase in real inflation. The fall of industrial output, the closing of unprofitable enterprises, and a recognition of "hidden unemployment" led to higher rates of reported unemployment. The "foreign debt trap" further exacerbated negative performance measures. Inter-enterprise debts and a withdrawal of subsidies resulted in a fall in real wages. A disparity in income distribution began to appear. The rise in real interest rates put a damper on domestic investment. Continued political and economic uncertainty encouraged the flight of capital and discouraged foreign investment.[61]

Slay challenged these assessments by pointing out that because the transformation process makes extensive use of statistics, *standard* macroeconomic statistics are problematic as measures of real change. He contended that the reported 20 percent decline in GDP during 1990–1991 should not be equated with wholesale "economic devastation"; rather, it reflected the cessation of activities that could not survive a market economy. Slay offered this rationale: "The immediate damage caused to enterprises, workers and communities closely tied to those activities should neither be denied or minimized, this damage generally speaking is an unavoidable cost of the restructuring needed to create economic institutions capable of surviving and competing in the global economy."[62]

Slay further believed that a reference to official unemployment rates (from 0.0 percent at the start of 1990 to 16.0 percent at the end of 1994) is also misleading in three respects: (1) some persons classified as unemployed were not, prior to 1990, gainfully employed; (2) many persons officially classified as unemployed work in the "secondary" or "gray" economy; and (3) some structural unemployment is the by-product of industrial and labor-market restructuring. Slay insisted that the contention that structural unemployment is "both an unmitigated disaster and an unavoidable calamity brought on by policy mistakes—is difficult to accept."[63] However, he asserted that economic reform has been generally viewed as anything but an "unqualified success" within Poland.[64]

Keith Crane, director of research at PLANECON Inc., a research firm specializing in socialist/postsocialist economies, mirrored Slay's views. He commented that the results of the "big bang" have been mixed. On the positive side, he noted that private sector activity has "soared" and has created a substantial number of jobs. However, because of the lack of reliable economic statistics and data collection mechanisms, these jobs have not been captured, thereby causing Poland's performance to appear "bleaker" than it actually was.[65] Other positive aspects of the "big bang" effort that Crane considered include: (1) better foreign trade performance and (2) the first convertible currency current account surplus since the Gomulka regime. He also offered the opinion that movement toward the creation of a convertible zloty was one of the most important achievements of the transformation program.[66]

On the negative side, Crane stated that the major failures of the program have been much steeper reductions in real incomes than expected and a decline in industrial output, as consumer demand literally collapsed. He believed that the government would have achieved a greater measure of success in controlling inflation if its fiscal and monetary policies had been "tighter" and the reliance on wage restraints less severe.[67]

Poznanski believed that the priority of balancing the budget at almost any cost and the choice of a fixed exchange rate policy at the initial stage of shock therapy were shortcomings. He called the stabilization program "destructive." It was imposed on an economy exhausted not only by years of underinvestment, but also suffering from the obsolete institutional setting inherited from the communist past. Poznanski further thought that Poland slipped into recession/depression without achieving deep structural adjustments because the harsh measures applied by the government were unable to work under conditions of a "property vacuum." He saw that "unhealthy state enterprises" were practically bankrupt, had persistent overemployment (especially in the WOGs), engaged in excessive enterprise borrowing without fear of intervention from commercial banks, and for all practical purposes, continued to operate as agencies of state central planning.[68]

Crane, however, contended that the result of shock therapy offers four worthwhile lessons for other countries undertaking similar reforms. First, given an appropriate exchange rate of the national currency (in Poland's case, the zloty), domestic currency convertibility can be established in a very short period of time. Second, despite a monopoly in the production sector and state ownership of the factors of production, markets can be created and operate in these systems simply by making it legal for them to function. Third, inflation takes a substantial and sustained political commitment to conquer. Fourth, shock therapy leads to substantially better economic performance than policies that seek to delay the rapid introduction of a market economy.[69]

Probably more important than Balcerowicz personally remaining in government was the fact that the logic of his reform program survived the "populist" government of Mazowiecki's successor, Jan Olszewski, the succeeding five governments, six prime ministers, and six ministers of finance, and even the postcommunist SLD-PSL coalition of Jozef Oleksy and Waldemar Pawlak.

Slay observed that the three post-1989 national elections (the presidential election of November–December 1990 and the parliamentary elections of October 1991 and September 1993) "were widely described (both within Poland and the West) as dangerous, if not catastrophic, for the economic transition. In fact, however, deviations from the policies begun in 1990 have occurred. They have on the whole been fairly insignificant. . . . By 1992, the Polish economy . . . (was) beginning to function according to its own logic."[70]

Balcerowicz himself, however, did not "survive" the first fully free election in October 1991. Competition and then conflict developed between the two most prominent Solidarity personalities, Mazowiecki and Walesa, when they ran against each other in the first round of the presidential election. Their initial collaboration in the Solidarity movement, which carried over to the early phases of the Mazowiecki government, symbolized the collaboration between the intelligentsia, represented by Mazowiecki, and the workers, represented by Walesa. The election of Walesa resulted in the formation of a new "right" populist government with Jan Olszewski as prime minister (December 1991 to June 1992). The election brought new personalities into government. As Balcerowicz commented: "From my first meeting with Prime Minister Olszewski, it was clear on both sides that I would not be participating in a new government, even though that was never mentioned directly during our conversations."[71]

Balcerowicz believed that the main reason for the success of the reform was the great speed of its early phase when the fundamentals of a liberal economic system and macroeconomic stability were established.[72] He credited his program with "the sustainability of Polish economic returns." He cited the following:

1. Independence of the Central Bank (introduced in December 1989 and further strengthened in 1991);
2. Convertibility of the currency for current account operations;
3. Rapid elimination of shortages with the accompanying free price system; and
4. Growth of the private sector.[73]

Balcerowicz remained positive in his assessment of the situation: "The Polish economic programme has been a success."[74] Balcerowicz offered the following lessons, alluded to in chapter 1, as proof of his assertion:

1. Traditional tools of macroeconomic stabilization will work in a socialist economy, but such measures need to be supplemented by strong wage controls.
2. A radical program is capable of abolishing massive shortages in a short period of time and of increasing the range of goods available in the market in the course of perhaps as little as one or two years.
3. It is possible to introduce "internal" currency convertibility in one step instead of doing it gradually over a period of two to three years.
4. A radical program will force many state enterprises to sell or lease part of their assets to private parties, contributing to the rapid growth of the private sector and thus to the eventual privatization of the entire economy.
5. The program induced many state enterprises to adjust to the more risky but also potentially more rewarding conditions of a market economy.
6. The program induced wholesale restructuring of industrial output and rapid reductions in the ineffectiveness of industry, which had prevailed under socialism.
7. Poland achieved a better economic performance from 1990 to 1993 than other countries of the region.[75]

Professor Barbara Blaszczyk and Marek Dabrowski, former vice-chairperson and chairman, Council of Ownership Transformation in the Office of the Prime Minister, took a more reserved view. They asked: "What is the general balance for the first three years of Polish Privatization?" They responded with a truism: "The results achieved are better than the skeptics feared and worse than the enthusiasts of privatization hoped." Their analysis indicated that in this first three-year period, "the real shift from the state to private sector amounted to 20 percentage points in GDP creation and almost 11 percentage points in employment."

Additionally, the majority of the cooperative sector became genuine cooperatives during this same period. Previously, most of the cooperatives had been actually controlled by the Communist party and the state administration.[76]

We should not underestimate the significance of this conversion of government-controlled and party-dominated cooperatives. Cooperatives up to 1989 were only pseudo-cooperatives. The combination of consumer, municipal, and housing cooperatives put a stranglehold on the economy and on all property rights.[77]

In chapter 6 we discuss at some length the wide ranging significance of the conversion of consumer, government (*gmina*), and housing cooperatives and their impact on "small privatization." Consumer cooperatives provide an immediate example.

Prior to 1989, consumer cooperatives were the largest owners and operators of retail firms and catering businesses in Poland. Cooperatives ran approximately 96,000 stores (65% of the total and 80% of the socialized sector) and 44,000 other outlets. They operated 13,000 restaurants and other catering businesses (42% of the total and 81% of the socialized sector) and 13 percent of all sales of services.

Consumer cooperatives were greatly centralized under two giant retail organizations: Spolem, serving cities, and Samopomoc Chlopska, serving villages and rural areas. In the 1980s, Spolem had over 30,000 retail outlets in cities. Samopomoc Chlopska had over 69,000 retail outlets in rural areas. Both of these organizations were represented on the Central Planning Committee and were accountable to the committee. Ruch was a separate cooperative, subordinated directly to the Central Committee of the Communist party. It was a huge conglomerate that owned most newspapers and magazines, as well as an extensive network of publishing firms, and enjoyed under Party patronage a wide system of distribution. Ruch enabled the Party to control the print media. Ruch not only sold books, newspapers, and magazines, but also cigarettes, cosmetics, and miscellaneous items. Ruch operated kiosks in almost every Polish village as well as throughout Polish cities. Ruch was a Party-owned cooperative and was the chief source of Party revenues.

Spolem, Samopomoc Chlopska, and Ruch were pseudo-cooperatives, fully controlled by the Communist party and the state administration. The decision to "unhinge" these pseudo-cooperatives from the Communist party and permit them to reorganize under the *Law Governing Changes in the Organization and Activities of Cooperatives* (January 1990) had widespread consequences for privatization.

Commenting from their respective experiences on the Council of Ownership Transformation, Blaszczyk and Dabrowski offered two insightful conclusions.

1. "The real privatization process began too late in Poland." Time was lost ("dissipated") in conceptual discussions. The loss of time reduced the potential for government initiative. The political climate changed and social consensus began to erode.

2. In hindsight, "the significant part of the big privatization debate in 1990 seems to have been pointless." They pointed out that the multitrack privatization system was accepted by almost all academics and politicians alike. Everyone agreed that employees must participate in the privatization process.

As late as 1993, Professor van Brabant believed that it was far too early to draw any firm conclusions from the initial experiences with privatization. He noted that "though the *whether* to privatize the PETs (Political Economies in Transition) is no longer a matter of economic, political or social debate in the vast majority of economies, the question of why there should be privatization and how it should be accomplished in the face of multiple obstacles certainly are."[78]

However, he thought that it is possible to compile tentative positive and negative indicators that will provide useful "warning signals" for PETs that are designing core elements of their own privatization agenda. These were his findings:

1. Privatization cannot be pursued solely for economic reasons or in a political vacuum.

2. The process is bound to be protracted and costly, even when a broad societal consensus is maintained.

3. Revenues obtained from the sale of state assets will remain well below estimates made at the outset of the process, regardless of how these estimates were derived.

4. Neither the sale nor free distribution of assets or shares will overcome the need to come to terms with key obstacles to the privatization process. Van Brabant foresaw that for public purposes the government may seek to stimulate private initiatives on a selective basis by tackling not only wages but also the cost and risk of capital formation. In the case of "free distribution" of certificates or vouchers, systems must be designed to identify and reach beneficiaries, select the manner of distribution, and design ways to get these new owners to exercise their rights in corporate governance.

5. The process of privatization is far more complicated than a mere change in ownership. It involves a complex social and economic process aimed at changing "the way every firm is run and every decision is made."[79]

6. PETs that have advanced the most in the privatization process have paid close attention to the creation of a capital market. However, "skimpy market regulation . . . is an open invitation to chicanery." Potential conflicts of interest, insider information, collusion, and shady deals suggest possible widespread risk of malfeasance and should be a concern.[80]

Slay suggested that corruption was perhaps the most serious problem facing privatization efforts. He admitted that while the roots of corruption predate the postcommunist era, the problem was exacerbated by deregulation of the private sector, which was not accompanied by the creation of appropriate regulatory, fiscal, and legal mechanisms. The general weakening of state authority that accompanied the transition further prevented the state from adequately dealing with the issue of corruption.[81]

Charles S. Maier, writing in *Foreign Affairs,* cited "a new impatience with long-tolerated patterns of corruption. Bribery and kickbacks, which have long been shrugged off or ignored as a transaction cost of public business, now become perceived as an intolerable symptom of decay."[82]

A purely economic assessment of shock therapy is insufficient. As discussed earlier in this chapter, the political aspects of the move to the free market have been almost overwhelming. Poznanski observed that shock therapy was as much a "political maneuver" as an "economic cure," with key economic choices having political implications for major social groups. In addition, many economic choices had to take into account political constraints that seemed at times insurmountable. This intimate correlation between economics and politics makes it difficult to determine whether politics has dominated economics, or whether economics has dominated politics.[83]

Professor Slay made a pertinent observation about the apparent contradiction between political instability and the revolving door in the government, which occurred at the same time that the "march to the market" continued forward. Slay wrote that by 1992, the economy was increasingly insulated from political instability and was beginning to function according to its own logic. The economy's increasing insulation from the politics of the transition was perhaps the greatest cause for public optimism.[84]

However, Balcerowicz disagreed and suggested that "with hindsight one can see that the Polish political calendar was not very opportune." He observed that the political timetable negotiated at the Round Table proved to be a "liability." He explained that first there was a radical economic program and only then the dismantling of the "contractual political system." In addition, this dismantling took place in the reverse order, beginning with presidential elections (1990), while parliamentary elections were moved to the end of 1991. In 1990 and 1991, two electoral campaigns took place, and the government changed twice. In addition, Balcerowicz noted that the more the economy is in state hands, the more susceptible it is to politicization.[85]

Despite political interference, any number of systemic outcomes can be measured in the aftermath of the Balcerowicz Plan. These systemic outcomes are measured in the changes in the relative prices and the institutional framework of the economy. In measuring the "march to market," Balcerowicz assessed the following primary changes as achievements:

1. The greatest volume of transactions (about 90%) were conducted at free prices.
2. The role of money as a medium of exchange increased significantly as the zloty became freely convertible, and goods became widely available.
3. The liberalization of property rights and foreign trade made for free entry into the Polish economy. Between 1990 and 1993, it is estimated that more than one million new private firms were organized.
4. Exit mechanisms were redefined, but the process was slower than anticipated. A gradual form of exit (downsizing by sale or lease of assets to the private sector) became the dominant exit model.

5. Poland's economy became increasingly more private. Fast development of the private sector, growth of small firm activity, downsizing of SOEs, and demonopolizing of a number of industries all contributed to a rapid organizational deconcentration of the Polish economy.
6. The banking sector changed from a monobank structure, with no clear separation between the banking systems and the state budget, to an independent system with a network of commercial banks.
7. Nonfinancial institutions, including the organization of the Stock Exchange, were set up.
8. The tax system was reformed from the complicated and fragmented tax system of a socialist economy to a modern Western system.
9. The expenditure side of the fiscal system was reformed and made more integrated and transparent.
10. Unemployment and social assistance programs proved to be problematic then and into the present.

Reviewing these systemic outcomes, Balcerowicz concluded that "Poland has made large strides towards a competitive, private-enterprise market economy."[86]

Balcerowicz conceded that the development in the pension system has been the weakest part in the economic transition, together with the tepid pace of privatization. He also assessed the "remaining agenda," which includes privatization of the remaining state-owned enterprises and banks, the development of the financial sector, and the institution of major reforms in health services, education, and the social security system.[87]

Professor Poznanski, in the introduction to the volume *Stabilization and Privatization in Poland,* observed: "Clearly, Poland's transition to capitalism is a great puzzle, hard for social scientists to decipher and put into a cohesive analytical framework. Importantly, it is equally hard for policymakers to understand the reality of transition, which means they are often forced to make uninformed choices and move ahead with half-ready projects."[88]

Aleksander Vacic, director of the Economic Commission for Europe's Economic Analysis and Projections, provided a fitting insight into this fascinating period of Polish transition:

> Thus, the main failure of the privatization in Poland so far seems to have been its largely textbook, doctrinal and, occasionally even, ideological reasoning, without the necessary linkage of the objectives, scope, pace and means of privatization with the economic realities of Polish society. The transition to a market system and the transformation of that society are altogether inseparable from the resumption of normal economic development and the complete technical and technological restructuring of the Polish economy.[89]

Vacic then concluded with a note of recognition for the stalwart character of Polish citizenry on the road to the market economy that also reflects the sentiments of the authors of this volume: "For an external observer, who is not familiar with all the necessary details and whose knowledge is derivative, perhaps the most important achievement in Poland is the changing climate of society and the patience with which the population has withstood all the shocks and experiments to which it has been subjected. It appears, however, that their patience should not be either overestimated or abused."[90]

Both the successes and the failures of this initial period (1989–1993) would determine policy perspectives and initiatives during the next crucial stages of economic transformation, leading to the ascendency of postcommunists in both the Parliament and the presidency by the end of 1995.

Chapter Six

Privatization and Polish Private Sector Development: 1989–1993

"The concepts and practice of privatization turned out to be much more complex than was thought at the beginning of transition."
Marie Lavigne, *The Economics of Transition:*
From Socialist Economy to Market Economy

The World Economy Group asserted that when "the shocks of price liberalization and stabilization eventually subside, the main items on the agenda will be restructuring and growth."[1] Jeffrey Sachs set the proper context for a full discussion about the nature of private sector development in Poland, delineating two important perspectives. The first is the timing and content of the reforms; the second is the timing and content of the restructuring that will take place as a result of the reforms. While the reforms themselves can and should be introduced quickly (in three to five years), the restructuring will of necessity last for a much longer period (possibly a decade or more), since there must be sufficient time for a substantial investment to occur in new sectors of the economy in response to the newly introduced market.[2]

Restructuring of ownership relations is recognized as the fundamental task. Both experts and the general public are "in agreement that the essence of restructuring is denationalization, and that the key element in denationalization is a significant growth of the share and importance of private ownership, that is, so-called privatization."[3] Unfortunately, privatization is not the simple reversal of the process of nationalization and expropriation carried out in Poland between 1944 and 1952. As Wladyslaw Jermakowicz pointed out: "In the 1940's nationalization measures were undertaken with the aim of creating a just, class-free social system, governed according to scientific principles of labor management and by the collective intelligence of the working class, (whereas) the present privatization program aims at the creation of an effective economy, driven by the 'invisible hand' of the market."[4]

In one context, privatization involves the increase in the private sector in the economy through the development and growth of new private enterprises. Privatization also includes all activities contributing to the *destatization* of economic activity through the legal transfer of former state-owned property rights from the state into private hands.

Professor Marie Lavigne pointed out that "the concepts and practices of privatization turned out to be much more complex than was thought at the beginning of transition."[5] This is so much so that Professor Tsuneski Sato commented that one is often perplexed by the sense in which the term "privatization" is used.[6]

One of the principal scholar-commentators on the privatization process is Jozef M. van Brabant, principal economic affairs officer, Department of Economic and Social Information and Policy Analysis at the United Nations. He considered that "privatization is political economy. *par excellence*."[7] He defined privatization as "a policy process designed to take the 'state'—that is, the political commanding heights, including their subordinated bureaucratic layers and the notorious *nomenklatura*—out of the decision making about at least the allocation of the usufruct of state-owned assets as quickly as possible."[8]

Van Brabant distinguished between what he termed "big" privatization and "petty" (others call this category "small") privatization: "Big privatization refers in particular to divestment through the sale or free distribution of shares of State-Owned Enterprises (SOEs) that tend to be large, organized in conglomerates, and highly monopolistic which may first have to be broken up into meaningful units." He termed less complex situations or smaller privatizations as "petty" privatization and explained that "the layer of economic operations between the 'petty' and 'big' assets—the medium size firm—has traditionally been ignored in most privatization debates for planned economies in transition (PETs), fundamentally because there were not that many to begin with."[9]

Under the terms of the letter of intent signed by the government of Poland with the IMF, privatization was to achieve both short-and long-run benefits. The sale of SOEs was designed to provide liquidity, reduce the budget deficit, and stabilize the economy. Privatization was seen as the means of developing a middle class and contributing to the stable development of democratic processes.

One of the questions raised in chapter 5 is whether or not firms should be reconstructed before or after privatization. In responding to the question, Why not privatize first?, the World Economy Group insisted that "privatization is urgent and has to take place long before firms are reconstructed."[10]

In 1988-1990, the economic situation in Poland was in a state of near collapse. Hyperinflation prevailed. A concept like privatization was sufficiently new and radical to provoke extended public discussion and debate. Developing an agreeable method of privatization and then implementing such a system for thousands of SOEs would take years.

Jeffrey Sachs contended that any significant progress on privatization before resolving the issues of stabilization and price liberalization was simply not possible because the government would have been "swept away" well before the public had concluded its debate over the various approaches to the privatization process.[11] In addition, Leszek Balcerowicz expressed his conviction that the *spontaneous* growth of the private sector should be as fast as possible, but the optimal pace of privatization is still a much disputed question.[12]

Sachs was adamant that there was a "real race against time" in taking the final step in transforming state property into private property. He reasoned that Poland's macroeconomic successes could be reversed because the constant financial pressures from the state sector could force Poland into a situation of sustained macroeconomic instability.[13]

Sachs expanded on his concerns. He foresaw two problem areas: (1) the lack of self-discipline in wage setting, and (2) a fear that state enterprises would not properly manage decisions over long-term investments. He reasoned that "enterprise managers and workers might very well paralyze the future of the privatization process because as insiders they have a natural tendency to object to any type of privatization" that does not substantially benefit themselves. Sachs projected that if privatization was delayed too long, pressures would rise to give the enterprises directly to the workers and managers, a solution that he viewed with "serious ethical and efficiency shortcomings."[14] The situation is not a simple one. Sachs has concluded that although much is known about stabilization and liberalization, there is not a clear precedent for privatization on a massive scale.[15]

Professor Wojciech W. Charenza believed that the speed and efficiency of privatization are, at least in relation to the state sector, "rather pessimistic." Much of the pessimism had to do with the high rate of unemployment that persisted for an extended period of time.[16] Van Brabant pointed out that:

> the most cogent arguments for rapid and comprehensive privatization in PETs derive from failures of past reforms and two anomalies of socialism. Foremost in favoring substantial and rapid privatization are

noneconomic considerations, although they undoubtedly exert repercussions on economic affairs too. There are two critical ones: the overpowering influence of Party politics over economic affairs and the hold of government bureaucracy over a highly monopolized enterprise sphere.[17]

Professor Tadeusz Kowalik of the Polish Academy of Sciences concluded that "the obsession with acceleration is an obstacle to sober discussion not only on privatization itself; it is part of a broader question. There is a side effect to the shock theory the period . . . of fast cumulative changes over a few months in 1990 was followed by a period of fairly low adjustments."[18] In the presidential campaign of 1990, the conflict between Mazowiecki and Walesa was heavily laden with both personal and policy differences. One of the rallying cries of Lech Walesa was "acceleration."

Analyzing Polish domestic politics of that period, Professor Louisa Vinton described the situation in this way:

> The presidential contest also centered on the proper tempo of political and economic change. Walesa's campaign slogan was a call for *przyspieszenie*, or to "speed things up," whereas the Mazowiecki campaign proclaimed its faith in *sila spokoju*, or "the force of calm," that the prime minister embodied. Walesa's followers charged that the Mazowiecki government was moving too slowly to take advantage of the opportunities presented by the collapse of communism.
>
> Mazowiecki stood for evolutionary, gradual, and, above all, legal means of procedure, whereas Walesa argued for pragmatic shortcuts, such as the granting of special powers to the government to enable it to bypass the roundtable Sejm. Walesa demanded a decisive break with the past; Mazowiecki emphasized the need for stability.[19]

Frydman, Rapaczynski, and Earle asserted that the privatization process in Poland has been characterized by an essential tension "between the centralist schemes of post-communist governments and the pressure of enterprise insiders to decentralize control over ownership changes at the enterprise level."[20]

Was the situation in Poland qualitatively different from the experiences of the other nations in Central and Eastern Europe? In 1989, Poland was no longer a completely centrally planned economy. It was already in transition to a market economy because of the program agreed upon at the Round Table and economic developments.[21]

Vacic provided three examples of the Polish situation that confirmed his assessment: (1) agriculture remained primarily in private hands; (2) central planning had a shorter history in Poland and had been seriously questioned as early as the 1950s and in every decade thereafter—even by members of the government itself; and (3) Polish authorities wisely limited postwar economic legislation to the state and to the cooperative sectors while retaining the general *Commercial Code of 1934* for other business and commercial activities. As a result, he concluded that privatization was understood from the beginning not as a comprehensive ownership restructuring but as a simple divestment of state assets.[22]

The Mazowiecki government formulated the initial privatization plan in an atmosphere of considerable optimism. It soon became clear that this early optimism was premature. The interests of "insiders" were more deeply embedded in the system than had been perceived by the reform planners. Spontaneous (and often illegal) appropriation of state property by local *nomenklatura*, "sweetheart" deals with a supposed "outside" partner, and the power of Workers' Councils at the enterprise level to stop or slow down the process were among the significant obstacles to privatization that were encountered. It soon became evident that privatization through the type of sales predicated on the United Kingdom privatization model simply was not appropriate for Poland. In the United Kingdom, only a few firms were designated by the government for privatization and then they were offered to the public, one at a time. At first the Mazowiecki government favored the British approach. However, the number of SOEs to be privatized and the time-consuming process of selecting individual firms and nurturing them to a level of profitability would take too long. Moreover, Poland lacked the capital market necessary for the success of this type of privatization.

As with any new and experimental program, mistakes and even *policy errors* were to be expected.[23] Professor Slay wrote that while mistakes were certainly made during the transition, many of Poland's economic problems resulted either from developments entirely beyond the control of policy makers or from the nature of the postcommunist transition itself, much of which was unexpected and unprecedented.[24] Sachs admitted that mistakes were made in implementation and in the theoretical basis of the privatization process. First, he believed that the adoption of the British method of privatization was a "fateful mistake" for Poland in 1990.[25] He suggested that "of equal significance" was the strategic decision to make privatization essentially a voluntary procedure for each enterprise, leaving each enterprise the option of remaining a state-owned enterprise. The ultimate decision to privatize rested with the Workers' Council of each individual firm, its management, and the central ministries in Warsaw. While the government had the power to force a firm to privatize, the legislation implied that this power would be used sparingly.

As Sachs perceived the situation, the voluntary approach to privatization was a wholly "unsatisfactory response" to a very real problem: Workers' Councils in enterprises were already exercising some of the authority of ownership (without the responsibility). The councils strenuously resisted the privatization of several important enterprises. Rather than considering the views of insiders in the privatization process, authorities instead gave them an effective veto power over the process. As a result, the program was excessively delayed in its implementation.[26]

Professor of Economics Jacek Klich of the Jagiellonian University in Krakow asserted that the British model was not appropriate for Poland:

> In a typical Western country that has recently privatized some state enterprises, only a handful of firms have been sold by the government to the private sector. These sales may have made an important economic difference in some sectors but they have not involved a fundamental transformation of the economy. Even in the UK case the amount of capital transformed through privatization has generally been a rather small proportion of total business capital and national income, and the Western economies typically had large, private industrial and financial sectors before privatization.
>
> In Poland privatization is a very different task, involving the complete redefinition of property rights for over 8.5 thousand of enterprises.[27]

In September 1990, a new Ministry of Ownership Changes (Ministry of Privatization) prepared and published its Privatization Program. The Privatization Program was based on four main requirements that had to be satisfied if a privatization plan had any real chance to succeed. Roman Frydman and Andrzej Rapaczynski have delineated the four main requirements as:

1. Privatization must be accomplished quickly;
2. Privatization must be socially acceptable;
3. Privatization must assure effective control over the management of privatized enterprises; and
4. Privatization must assure access to foreign capitals and expertise.[28]

The Privatization Program was based on the following objectives:

1. To move the economy from a centrally planned system to a competitive market system, which would encourage the development of a competitive and dynamic private sector;
2. To improve the performance of enterprises through more efficient use of labor, capital, and management skills;
3. To control the process so as to avoid the sale of assets at unduly low prices;
4. To reduce the size of the public sector and the burden of the public budget and administration;
5. To generate funds from the sale of enterprises or their shares;
6. To ensure a wide diffusion of ownership of privatized assets;

7. To provide an effective system of corporate governance; and
8. To start a program of debt-to-equity swaps in privatized enterprises.

THE MULTITRACK APPROACH

The privatization strategy adopted by the Mazowiecki government envisaged a multitrack approach, comprising separate privatization paths for the various categories of enterprises. Often the process contained a simultaneous use of different techniques of privatization within a given category.[29]

Professor van Brabant acknowledged that privatization in the "planned economies in transition" (PETs) could have "a virtually endless variety of objectives." However, he believed that six objectives stand out and are paramount:

1. Buttressing democracy and personal freedom;
2. Raising the efficiency of managing state-owned assets through market discipline and competition, and by eliminating government interference;
3. Raising revenue for and reducing outlays from the budget to run and monitor SOEs;
4. Allowing firms to raise capital in commercial markets, but not necessarily a stock market, which as a rule is dominated by secondary trading;
5. Contributing to anchoring adaptable capital markets, possibly to encourage savings (such as through stock-owning incentives); and
6. Undercutting entrenched positions of interest groups (such as trade unions, the Communist party, and the *nomenklatura*). As a rule, in most countries the goal of privatization is to maximize some combination of these objectives.[30]

These multiple goals immediately suggest that no one plan for privatization would meet all expectations. For that reason, from the outset legislation provided for a multitrack approach.

Frydman, Rapaczynski, and Earle observed that the Polish approach to privatization was one that provided for a range of different programs and techniques, and that the relative emphasis of the Polish authorities with respect to privatization has changed over time. They recognized that this multitrack approach embraced all of the following options: *reprivatization*, the *small privatization* process, eventual privatization by *liquidation*, various *mass privatization* plans, and the *sectoral approach* (i.e., a grouping of like firms in an industry for analysis and evaluation for potential privatization). However, they emphasized that the first objective of authorities was to end the uncontrolled appropriation of state property by insiders (so-called spontaneous privatization).[31]

Before discussing the multitrack options, the importance and negative effects of "spontaneous" privatization should be addressed.

"SPONTANEOUS PRIVATIZATION"–THE *NOMENKLATURA* APPROPRIATES STATE PROPERTY

So-called spontaneous privatization began even before the collapse of communism in Poland, before the movement toward the market system gained momentum, and before the adoption of any legal provisions to privatize SOEs. The *1981 Law on State-owned Enterprises* gave directors of SOEs considerable freedom in the management of the assets of their firms. After the *Law on Business Activity* (23 December 1988) came into effect, many enterprise directors exercised their authority and disposed of SOEs by transferring their assets to newly established private commercial companies in which they themselves were partners or directors. "Spontaneous privatization" was the term applied to these "inside" transactions. Many directors of SOEs exercised their legal prerogatives and derived generous capital gains through the sale to themselves of assets at or below the fair market value. Regulations were introduced in 1991 to prevent these "ownership experiments," but much damage had already been done.

The World Economy Group pointed out that "in the legal no-man's land in which state firms are de facto no longer responsible to the state, their opportunities for personal gain by managers and their friends are clearly unbounded."[32] For example, the systematic underevaluation of assets, or "sweetheart" deals between managers and their associates, enterprise councils, or outside investors, in effect, helped transfer state assets into private property. Most often former *aparatchiks—nomenklatura* were, by this process, transformed into operatives and potential "new capitalists" in the emerging private sector. As the World Economy Group reported:

> the legal vacuum and the lack of effective state control since the middle of 1989 has led many managers to stitch their own golden parachutes. Knowing that they may not keep their jobs for very long, they have through outright sales, or pseudo-leases to dummy corporations, or through joint ventures (sometimes with foreigners) found ways to improve their interest to the detriment of their firms. Some of those practices are definitely illegal. But they will be hard to prosecute and even hard to undo.[33]

State enterprises were transformed into joint stock companies using the authority granted under the new *Law on Business Activity*. Directors and managers exercised their new authority to split up state companies, to spin off or divest them (most often, the best and most profitable sections) into limited liability companies or other new joint ventures. This process ensured employment for themselves, as well as permitted them to acquire new proprietary rights with guaranteed profitability. The most skilled workers were often transferred to the new enterprises. Many "communist" directors and managers of SOEs took advantage of this new legal opportunity to become "capitalists." They derived income and capital gains from applying "transfer prices" to items that were sold in asset deals, or they simply contributed assets to already existing commercial companies that they controlled.[34]

Frydman and Rapaczynski pointed out that the pressure for spontaneous privatization comes from a curious alliance between workers and managers "who are intent on resisting significant departures from the status quo: it is precisely the opposition to a restructuring that is likely to result from a genuine privatization that motivates the alliance."[35] One of the primary incentives toward spontaneous privatization was the attempt by workers to avoid the stiff tax on wage increases [popiwek] that applies to the employees of state enterprises, but that may be relaxed or eliminated for companies that privatize. The pressure for spontaneous privatization was primarily political in nature. The result of this process essentially impedes rather than promotes restructuring. The Law on State-owned Enterprise (25 September 1981) was amended in 1990 and de-legalized these arrangements.[36]

Spontaneous privatization should not be confused with a type of privatization authorized and initiated by SOEs themselves. Spontaneous privatization has created different reactions in different countries. In Hungary, the reality was simply accepted; in Czechoslovakia, the process did not exist because there was no legal framework that might have permitted such self-serving activity; in Russia, spontaneous privatization has a semi-legal appearance, and is sanctioned by the law.

Professor Marie Lavigne wrote: "It is very difficult to reach a sober assessment on this issue. Eastern governments and Western experts alike are very much against this form of privatization. It looks too much like Western inside trading and legacies of Communist nomenklatura's privileges combined."[37] In fact, Jeffrey Sachs said that spontaneous privatization is simply "what in the West would be called stealing."[38]

Lavigne raised two different but interesting viewpoints, writing that "this might be in fact the most common way of privatizing, and in any case an unavoidable one."[39] One viewpoint relates to the thousands of managers needed in economies in transition. Lavigne asks:

Is the process bad per se? The question is hardly relevant as there is no real choice on a large scale. The countries in transition each need thousands of managers. While it was relatively easy to find a few dozen experts among former dissidents or quasi-dissidents to take jobs in the new state administration, it is impossible to find enough good managers to replace the previous managerial class. This class may be trained. The former communist managers are able to act with a view to maximising their own economic interests, which they did in the past, and which is after all the quintessence of capitalism. As most of them (if not all) never really believed in communism but just pretended to, there is no risk that they would help to bring the old regime back. And if not them, who else?[40]

The second perspective asks the question: Is there a link between spontaneous privatization and the return to power of the parties originating from the former Communist parties? In fact by mid-1994, many countries "in transition" were once again ruled by coalition governments led by former Communist parties, often masquerading as reformed social democrats.

Lavigne then commented: "These governments all declare themselves committed to market reforms, sometimes just paying lip service to the reforms, in any case lagging behind in implementation. In contrast, the *ex-nomenklaturists* that in fact manage the enterprises, both state and privatized, are certainly more earnestly committed to the market as their aim is to maximize their gains."[41]

In any event, despite severe limitations and inconsistencies, spontaneous privatization was one of the earliest privatization processes and one that gave considerable momentum to the Polish economic transition despite its decidedly negative social, ethical, and practical consequences.

REPRIVATIZATION: HOW TO COMPENSATE FORMER OWNERS

Early legislation recognized the necessity of addressing the question of reprivatization or restitution to former owners. Returning property that had been nationalized in the 1940s and 1950s was believed by many to be almost impossible or at least extremely difficult. Various attempts have been made to enact reprivatization legislation. The Office of President during the tenure of Lech Walesa attempted to pressure the Sejm for such legislation. Legislative proposals were drafted and even debated in the Parliament, but without coming to a final decision. Poland is somewhat unusual among the Central and Eastern European countries because it does not yet have a reprivatization or restitution law. Eventually some form of reprivatization law will certainly be enacted. Meanwhile, over 100,000 individual claims for restitution have been filed with various Polish agencies, including the Ministry of Privatization, where an undersecretary of state has been appointed to handle delicate reprivatization questions. In the absence of clear legislative guidance, however, the government has been reluctant to proceed. Because of Poland's history under Nazism and communism, the potential program is massive and the supporting documentation minuscule.

Complicated infrastructure, devastation of the property, abandonment, expropriation, and many substantial problems of a political, social, and economic nature all have contributed to the complexity of the issue. Any attempts to resolve this problem must weigh the interests of former owners with the rest of society. Most proposals of reprivatization strategies represent two competing solutions.

One proposal presented by the government stipulated that 5 percent of the stock issued by state-owned enterprises (SOEs) privatized within the mass privatization program would be set aside to create the so-called reprivatization reserve. From this reserve, people whose property was illegally expropriated would receive payment or stock. This payment would be commensurate with the value of the illegally nationalized property.

A competing proposal, termed the Consultative Council's Proposal, was formulated by the "political-right" faction of the Sejm. It insisted on returning real assets equivalent to the nationalized property to all people whose property was expropriated in the 1940s and 1950s. The proposal does not differentiate between individuals whose property was nationalized legally and those whose property was nationalized illegally. All would receive real assets.[42]

As Professor Slay reported, "Reprivatization generated almost as much controversy as the mass privatization program." All five of Poland's post-1989 governments avoided action on reprivatization and consistently resisted well-orchestrated pressures for the return to former owners of property confiscated by various government actions. Slay offered an explanation for reluctance on the part of the government to become involved in this complex economic, social, and political issue. Fiscal considerations played a large role, since restitution of properties that might otherwise be sold would reduce budgetary revenues that privatization was expected to produce, while compensation for former owners would clearly be a further budgetary strain. There was a fear that reprivatization would produce a "bureaucratic morass" that would forestall other forms of privatization. Policies pursued from 1990 to 1993 only sanctioned the return of properties if expropriation was clearly illegal at the time of seizure, and if restitution was not "clouded" by issues of physical alteration or modernization.

As of mid-1994, no reprivatization program had succeeded in gaining parliamentary approval,[43] and reprivatization has remained an issue before each succeeding government. It is only a matter of time before some compromise solution will come before the Parliament and eventually be enacted as a statement of public policy.

"SMALL" PRIVATIZATION

One of the earliest forms of privatization in most of the nations of Central and Eastern Europe was classified as "small" privatization. In their study of privatization, Earle, Frydman, Rapaczynski, and Turkewitz made this important distinction: small privatization refers to the process of ownership transformation in retail trade, catering, and service sectors, and not to the privatization of smaller enterprises, which, in the context of the region, may mean manufacturing firms with as many as 200 employees. What van Brabant termed "petty" privatization corresponds to this application of "small" privatization to retail trade, catering, and service sector enterprises. Earle, Frydman, Rapaczynski, and Turkewitz offer two important reasons for these cases of privatization.

First, the essential aspect of the privatization of most state stores in Eastern Europe is not the transfer of a business but rather the conveyance of ownership or use rights in the real estate on which the businesses are located. Second, this shift of emphasis blurs the distinction between "privatized" stores and new "start-up" businesses. These "start-ups" are often located on premises that had been previously owned or controlled by the state. The essence of the change in both cases is in the transfer of rights to commercial real estate.[44]

Earle, Frydman, Rapaczynski, and Turkewitz also stressed that the most important objective of small privatization is the rapid establishment of a large number of relatively small, owner-managed businesses that "can quickly adapt to changing circumstances, reallocate the existing stock of consumer goods, find new and better suppliers, as well as make room for numerous entrepreneurial individuals and create an important middle-class constituency for the new regime."[45]

Small privatization consists of setting up new private enterprises or purchasing small enterprises (or often parts of an enterprise) to form a new business. Even before 1989, Poland was noted for having the most developed private sector within the Soviet Bloc, consisting of private farmers and small shop owners. Seventy-five to 80 percent of Polish agriculture was in private hands; only 20 to 25 percent had been collectivized. Small shopkeepers also were able to participate significantly in small-scale privatization.

This distinction was based on the differences in the economic mobility of private farmers and small shopkeepers and their ability to participate in privatization processes. In Poland only the latter group managed to advance financially and therefore was able to participate significantly in what is called "small-scale privatization." Individually, these efforts are usually not significant; however, in total they have contributed very substantially to the change in the Polish economy.

While the privatization process for large firms came almost to a standstill in 1992, the privatization of small-scale firms (mainly retail outlets and other service establishments) proceeded rapidly. The three important legislative acts that facilitated the small-privatization process were not strictly privatization acts at all. Instead, small-scale privatization was carried out under the *1990 Amendment to the Housing Act of 1974* and the *Law on Local Self-government* (8 March 1990), together with the subsequent *Regulations Introducing the Law on Local Self-government* (10 May 1990). With these three legislative actions, local governments gained a significant distance and degree of autonomy from the central government and from government agencies.

COOPERATIVE AND *GMINA* PRIVATIZATION

Under the communist system, municipalities owned a significant portion of commercial property, especially in the cities. Municipal governments are known in Polish as *gmina*s. There are 2,400 *gmina*s in Poland. The process by which municipalities began disposing of a large number of retail, catering, and service outlets became known as "*gmina* privatization." But, the process was neither standardized nor uniform. It might be more accurate to say that there were 2,400 variations of *gmina* privatization.

The combination of actions authorized by the *Cooperative Restructuring Law of 1990* and the legislation relating to self-government facilitated small privatization to such an extent that no specific small privatization legislation was deemed necessary. Cooperative privatization and *gmina* privatization together served to transfer the majority of state-owned properties to the private sector.

COOPERATIVE PRIVATIZATION

There were some small specialized consumer cooperatives, but two retail giants, Spolem and Samopomoc Chlopska, controlled the majority of all retail shops and catering services in the socialized sector. However, they did not compete with each other. Spolem enjoyed a monopoly in cities and towns; Samopomoc Chlopska enjoyed a similar monopoly in the countryside and rural areas.

For example, Samopomoc Chlopska controlled over 11,000 purchasing points for cereals, potatoes, livestock, fruits, vegetables, and recycled materials. It operated 1,052 meat packing houses, 1,100 bakeries, 750 mineral water-processing plants, 225 feed-mixing mills, and 3,000 manure warehouses. The *Cooperative Restructuring Law of 1990* dissolved the central cooperative bodies and any related cooperative associations and mandated a transfer of cooperative assets to new owners. The law required local cooperatives to hold elections for governing board members by 31 March 1990.

The restructuring and subsequent privatization of the consumer cooperative movement involved four different processes. Earle, Frydman, Rapaczynski, and Turkewitz summarized the four processes:

1. The *Cooperative Restructuring Law of 1990* directly attacked the cooperative associations, privatized a significant portion of their property (which had a very significant impact on the wholesale and distribution systems), and released individual cooperatives from central control.
2. The 1990 *Housing Act* and restructuring of housing cooperatives caused a "hemorrhage of units from the consumer cooperative system."
3. Local cooperatives began selling or leasing stores and restaurants to private parties (most often their own members and employees) but sometimes to small outside entrepreneurs.
4. Local cooperatives themselves were privatized, in part through the stroke of a bureaucrat's pen, when they were simply reclassified as "private" and ceased to be socialized.[46]

The *Cooperative Restructuring Law of 1990* placed all associations into a form of receivership and initiated individual liquidation procedures for each. A liquidator was appointed by the Ministry of Finance or a local training representative. Liquidators were responsible for managing the assets during the transition period and for developing plans for the disposition of the assets of the cooperative. However, the liquidator first had to ascertain which plans and assets had been transferred without payment to the cooperative in the 1980 to 1990 period. Wherever possible these assets were to be returned to their rightful owners. Other assets of the cooperatives and any reserves or working capital were to be used to pay any association liabilities and to cover the cost of liquidation.

What were the patterns of cooperative privatization? Assets could be transferred to member cooperatives, with or without payment. "Preferred recipients" of the privatization of cooperatives were employees of the business associated with the assets to be transferred. If one-half the employees founded a new cooperative as a private enterprise, the assets might be transferred to them without payment. Assets not transferred to local member cooperatives or employees could be sold at public auction. Assets could be transferred to joint stock or limited liability companies established by former employees or cooperative members.

As in the case of spontaneous privatization, the distribution of assets was determined primarily by the liquidator, employees, and cooperative officials, and cases of illegal transfers appeared to be common, with the liquidators arranging for "unpublicized and often undocumented sales." In some cases, these same individuals became managers of the commercial partnerships that had been formed to purchase the assets of the previously dissolved associations.[47]

These same researchers discovered that upon the dissolution of the co-operative associations, local cooperatives experienced three categories of "serious difficulties." First, managers of local cooperatives lacked business experience. Confronted with a new business climate and a lack of directives from "central headquarters," and now facing competition for the first time, many managers were simply unable to manage, that is, to make decisions, especially in conditions of uncertainty and ambiguity. Second, the loss of subsidies from the central budget to the cooperatives resulted in a significant decline in revenues. Simultaneously, many valuable units were lost from some cooperatives to other municipal and housing cooperatives. Finally, the cooperatives now "inherited" many activities, projects, and programs (i.e., sports teams, guest houses, summer resorts) that were primarily social, and not economic, in nature. In the new environment, these allied activities could not be sustained.

How could these local cooperatives meet this challenge? First, they could decide the situation was so desperate as to preclude any possibility of survival, in which case they might choose to liquidate. Second, they could continue to operate, hoping to acquire additional capital and business acumen or managerial expertise as they continued operations. A third alternative would be to sell or lease assets to increase revenue.

What were the results? Cooperative privatization is, in essence, a category of small privatization. As such, it is a highly diversified and widely decentralized activity. Early data is limited and unreliable. Data from the Central Statistical Office (GUS) indicated that cooperatives were still operating some 43,000 stores at the end of 1992. The number of stores operated by consumer cooperatives had declined by approximately 51,000 units. Of these, between 27,000 and 29,000 (or 53 to 57%), were lost to communalization and housing cooperatives. A balance of 20,000 to 22,000 shops were left, repesenting a reasonable estimate of the number of units privatized by the consumer cooperatives themselves.[48]

Cooperatives tended to favor leases over sales, with first rental preferences given to employees. Often these leases had provisions that restricted the kind of future business that could be undertaken. Many contained a "noncompete" clause designed to protect units still being operated by the cooperative or by other lessees. The greatest effect of cooperative privatization was to expedite privatization in the small sector. The dissolution of cooperatives had a positive impact on small privatization. The process released extensive assets essential for the development of private wholesale and distributor outlets and simultaneously "decapitated" the state-dominated cooperative system. Local cooperatives were set adrift. The absence of any follow-up in the form of revised cooperative legislation in Poland left local cooperatives with persons in positions of authority who were imbued with the management mentality, policies, and practices of the communist system. Yet, the process effectively privatized assets of the local cooperatives by leasing and franchising them to private parties.

Cooperative privatization gave further credence to one of the major conclusions of the Central European University Privatization Project:[49] "[S]mall privatization is primarily a conveyance of interests in real estate on which small businesses are or may be located and ... the other commercial assets [are] controlled by state retail trade and service units and [are] of very limited value."[50]

GMINA PRIVATIZATION: LOCAL GOVERNMENTS JOIN THE PRIVATIZATION PROCESS

Gmina privatization had a similar effect upon economic transformation. Municipalities suddenly enjoyed real ownership of large parcels of commercial property, near total freedom from central control, and almost complete autonomy to determine the future purpose and use of these properties. This transfer process was called "communalization," and became the key element in the development of the private retail trade. As local governments began to claim ownership of these newly acquired properties, they immediately began to lease or sell them, thus creating their own small privatization process.

The Law on Local Self-government gave ownership and control over all divisible property in three categories:

1. Movable and immovable state properties that heretofore had been under central custody and control of territorial units of central administration;
2. Movable and immovable property of state enterprises and assets of other organizational units previously accountable to territorial units of central administration; and
3. State property that had been designated for public purposes and that previously was controlled by the voivodships or organizational units of the voivodships.

Voivodships are the largest territorial units of Polish government. There are 49 voivodships, each headed by a voivoda (prefect), or governor. As soon as the voivodships began to claim ownership, the small privatization process expanded exponentially. Even before the Law on the Privatization of State-owned Enterprises was enacted in July 1990, the program of gmina privatization was already "in full swing."[51]

Which groups were inclined to take advantage of the opportunities created by communalization of previously owned and controlled state properties, and what was their primary interest?

1. State enterprises and consumer cooperatives that had previously used these premises at administratively established low rentals;
2. Employees who quickly saw that communalization provided them with an opportunity to become proprietors—provided they could make "arrangements" with local authorities;
3. Local residents, especially local entrepreneurs with local ties and loyalties who did not want "outsiders" involved;
4. Unions defending the rights of insiders to continue operating their businesses;
5. *Gmina* officials themselves; and
6. "Outsiders" who were interested in acquiring newly communalized property.

Earle, Frydman, Rapaczynski, and Turkewitz have written extensively about the role of the *gmina* officials. They note that although new officials had been elected, the speed of the process of reform made it possible for large numbers of former *nomenklatura*, especially in the smaller *gminas*, to preserve their positions. Despite this, their tenure was unstable and their connections significantly influenced their behavior. The informality of the privatization process also offered officials opportunities for patronage and personal gain. The possibility of passing title of valuable properties to friends, family members, business associates, and colleagues was an important factor in the decisions affecting the disposition of *gmina* assets. In addition, local officials had a limited understanding of overall economic conditions and were not predisposed to change. Although they were quite willing to remove premises from state enterprises and consumer cooperatives, they were obviously more sympathetic to the claims of insiders employed in local units.[52]

The record shows that the decisions made with reference to communalized property and the speed at which *gmina* privatization occurred tended to favor insider-dominated arrangements.

HOUSING COOPERATIVES AND PRIVATIZATION

The Central European University Privatization Study revealed that small privatization in Poland was not especially influenced by any formal programs through which ownership or title to businesses previously run by the state and by cooperatives became private. Rather, the process was driven by changes in the real estate market. Changes in the real estate market involved a process in which businesses lost their prime asset—the premises leased to them at highly preferential rates, usually at a fee wholly unrelated to the potential value of the property on the open market. Before 1989 housing cooperatives were the next major real estate owners after the *gminas*. Housing cooperatives, like consumer cooperatives and municipalities, were destined to play a major role in the transfer of the use of commercial real estate into private hands. This transfer process constituted the essence of small privatization in Poland.

Yet, this small privatization movement came about in an indirect manner. The revision of the *Housing Act of 1974* gave real estate owners real rights to dispose of commercial property. Earle and his associates pointed out that this revision of the *Housing Act,* which was not explicitly concerned with privatization, was of greater importance in this connection than were many other aspects of the privatization program. The few simple paragraphs of the revision created a set of positive incentives for owners of real estate and released a truly spontaneous initiative toward better use of existing commercial space.[53]

The *Housing Act of 1974* controlled the use and disposition of the real properties of both state and private persons. The act gave the state a preemptive right to use any commercial property if it was judged that a state or cooperative enterprise needed the location to conduct business, or if the property was included in a "master plan" for the allocation of retail and/or service outlets in a given area. Rental agreements with socialized enterprises were subject to administrative review. This type of property could be further leased or sold only at prices established by the Council of Ministers. The system, in practice, became known as the "special renting mode." This system permitted a committee of local planning officials to decide on the "best" use of each available unit, regardless of private or state ownership. Then the local planning committee would choose an appropriate state company or consumer cooperative to run the particular business. The original *Housing Act of 1974* did not apply to housing cooperatives; but the 1982 *Law on Cooperatives* restricted their operations by obliging housing cooperatives to follow the "social economic plan" determined by the local planning committee.

In August of 1989, the situation was radically altered with the entry of the Mazowiecki government and the enactment of new laws and amendments. On first reading, the *1990 Amendment to the Housing Act of 1974* did not seem unusual. The amendment provided that henceforth commercial premises previously rented on the basis of administrative decisions were now to be governed by the appropriate provisions of the Civil Code. Innocuous as that amendment seemed, the subsequent interpretation of the amendment was to provide a whole new channel for rapid privatization. The Civil Code gave the owner of the property almost unlimited freedom to terminate any lease of indefinite duration. The 1990 Amendment released municipalities and cooperatives from existing administrative controls and gave them the right to freely dispose of what suddenly was a very valuable asset. Tenants were given three months to renegotiate their rental agreements or be evicted. Under the previous system there was no indication that housing cooperatives would ever be able to act independently of the Party or of the state, so it was rare to have negotiated a term lease. Suddenly, almost all tenants were vulnerable, and most premises were soon to be leased or sold competitively, creating a new and competitive real estate market almost overnight.

What were the consequences of the *1990 Amendment to the Housing Act of 1974*? First, the importance of the 1990 amendment on small privatization cannot be overestimated; and second, "in a relatively short period of time, a great majority of commercial premises in Poland were allocated to new users. The real estate market changed beyond recognition."[54] Despite controversy about the precise nature of the data, the small privatization process was essentially complete by the end of 1992.

The question of reprivatization, the effect of spontaneous privatization, the authorization of small privatization and the anticipation of privatization by liquidation, the various mass privatization plans, and the sectoral approach each contributed to establishing new initiatives and new patterns of private sector development.

FACTORS INFLUENCING PRIVATIZATION

Even before the Privatization Law of 1990 was adopted there were extensive debates that centered around questions of "closed" or "open" privatization and about systems for the distribution of shares of privatized companies. Under closed privatization, shares of the firm were to be available to employees of the firm and not available on the open market. Open privatization permitted shares to be sold on the open market, both foreign and domestic. One distribution scheme called for an essentially "free distribution" of shares, since most Polish citizens were simply too poor to buy shares. Another scheme proposed a variation of an Employee Stock Ownership Plan (ESOP) for employees; and a third favored a "fully commercial" privatization with shares selling on the open market.

In 1989, the Mazowiecki government attempted to promote a privatization program whereby SOEs would become joint stock companies, with the state as the sole owner. Workers' groups (most noticeably, Solidarity) forced the government to withdraw the plan because they feared the loss of power of the Workers' Councils and the eventual loss of employment.

Among the political factors influencing the privatization process had been the ill-defined ownership structures in Poland. Another consideration involved the spontaneous privatization of SOEs (discussed earlier), whereby members of the *nomenklatura* made "sweetheart" deals domestically or with a foreign partner. Once abuses were made known, citizen support for the privatization process began to erode and social consensus for the more generalized economic reforms weakened.

In his 1993 Lionel Robbins Lecture at the London School of Economics, Professor Sachs commented on this situation: "This process of spontaneous privatization accelerated the revolution in Eastern Europe because there was nothing more grating on the public than the notion that the Communists who had ruined the economy over the past forty years were about to steal it and become the Capitalist owners for the next forty years. In Poland, in 1989, just before the fall of the old regime, public angst over this kind of behavior was intense."[55]

The institutional framework within which structural reform and privatization were to be achieved has been outlined by Professor Lavigne, who observed that the governments of countries in economic transition are often reluctant to become too deeply involved with the privatization process. The institutional framework in such countries tended to be modest and dispersed over a number of agencies. Dispersion of the responsibility of ministers adds to the risk of administration delays, interagency rivalries, confused or contradictory communications, and the general limitations of the bureaucratic process.

Whatever the specific national situation, four institutional characteristics are common to the privatization process:

1. The existing government, no matter how it is constituted, is required to supervise or shepherd the process. University of Warsaw professor Jacek Kochanowicz pointed out that the state cannot simply wait for the transition to occur but must become the active agent of change.[56]

2. The question of ownership of state enterprises proved to be a major difficulty. For example, under the principle of socialist ownership of the means of production, the state was the owner of these enterprises and the only proper economic actor in the system. Was "the state" truly the individual owner of each enterprise? In retrospect, this question was superfluous. Whatever the technical or philosophical answer, it was the Communist party and its partners in the *nomenklatura* who exercised control and provided administrative direction to enterprises through the system of central planning. Individual ownership rights were never the issue. In 1994, Prime Minister Pawlak reorganized the Agency of Government Ownership, and eventually the Ministry of Privatization was transformed into a Treasury Ministry.[57]

3. Prior to the privatization process, state-owned enterprises were transformed into joint stock companies or limited liability companies. The terminology for this process varied. In Poland commercialization was the term most commonly used to describe this process. The term dates back to

1988–1989. Until the privatization process is complete, the treasury remains the sole owner of all the SOEs. Depending on the plan, different agencies (often with competing agendas) were involved in various oversight functions.

4. Professor Lavigne argued that in a centralized process of privatization, the process should not be initiated without several far-reaching economic and financial measures. Corporate assets must be carefully evaluated according to "generally accepted accounting standards." A determination should be made about the economic viability of the firm and whether it should be liquidated, restructured, and/or recapitalized. Firms proposed for the privatization process were generally required to develop an appropriate organizational restructuring and to produce a market feasibility or business plan. Restructuring often involves a process of separating, dividing, or divesting parts of firms and creating new firms.[58]

In Poland the privatization process was characterized by a tension between the proposals put forward by the various postcommunist governments that were "centralist" in their outlook and the pressure exercised by insiders in the firms who were seeking to retain control over ownership questions at the enterprise level. Solidarity, both as a trade union and as a "workers' movement," represented the second view. The leadership of Solidarity was influenced by a traditional liberal point of view. Many in this group believed that the main goal of the reforms was to establish a capitalist system that would put an end to the spontaneous, often illegal, appropriations of state property by the local *nomenklatura* and limit the powers of Workers' Councils at the enterprise level.[59] However, it would become apparent that even supporters of privatization within Solidarity fundamentally misunderstood the privatization process itself.

After the passage of the initial legislation of 1990, it was expected that privatization would be achieved quickly by using the process of commercialization. This process would confer a new legal legitimacy to the state enterprise sector. The process would then proceed to privatization. Circumstances soon revealed the fallacy of this early optimism. The privatization law proposed in July 1990 represented many compromises. The commercialization process began very slowly and moved ahead even less speedily. The range of privatization techniques finally adopted represented an effort to give the government both time and options in developing a general privatization plan. Major resistance arose from provisions in the legislation that gave insiders a large degree of choice about whether or not their enterprise would be included in the privatization program. Mirroring the unstable political climate, parliamentary divisions, and continuous tensions between and among the government, the Parliament, and the president increasingly delayed and politicized the privatization process.

Van Brabant reiterated that the main motivation for privatization has been negative—undercutting the power of the bureaucracy and, in a certain sense, "getting even" for almost 50 years of state socialism. Related motives may be to enhance personal and societal freedom and encourage the democratic process.[60]

Professor van Brabant divided the privatization process into stages. He contended that except in very extraordinary circumstances, state-owned enterprises can best be entrusted to one or more asset management agencies directly responsible to Parliament. He envisaged a four-step sequence. The first step is establishing reforms that alter the legal position of the SOE from being an agent of the state, subject to ad hoc bureaucratic interferences, into a joint stock or limited liability company.[61] Through *corporatization*, the firm acquires an independent legal status, with accompanying rights and obligations. However, the state retains ownership. In step two, the firm is either determined to be profitable and is *commercialized* or is determined to be unsalvageable and is liquidated.

A third stage involves what he defined as *usufruct divestment*.[62] Selected public assets are contracted to private producers through leases, franchising, management contracts, or subcontracting, whereby management receives the gains (the *usus fructus*) of its assets by virtue of the contract, while the state still retains the ultimate right of disposal (*abusus*). Van Brabant differentiated usufruct divestment from commercialization on the basis that under usufruct divestment, management will retain considerable autonomy, including determining the nature and method of production and which organizational form best serves the needs of the organization.[63]

The fourth and last step is total *divestment*. At this point, the state completely transfers the total property rights of a firm owned by the state to some other agency.

These steps confront policy makers with a wide range of choices about which of the various privatization formats are best under the circumstances. Some alternatives are more appropriate than others. How was this dilemma to be resolved?

Van Brabant suggested that before selecting any particular format, policy makers should consider responses to a series of policy considerations that are designed to provide useful parameters in defining and eventually deciding the "best option" for privatization decisions. His eight points include:

1. The speed of privatization, the types of firms to be privatized, and the extent of restructuring to be undertaken prior to privatization;
2. Whether to proceed primarily with sales or free distribution, and which method should be preferred for each class of assets;

3. To whom privatization should in the first instance be addressed (including the respective roles of foreigners, former owners, or other property claimants), the desirability of spreading ownership, and the possibility of concentrating ownership by allowing those with financial resources to acquire real assets, regardless of the provenance of their resources;

4. Whether the implicit property rights of enterprise managers and the *nomenklatura*, and the accrued and vested property rights of managers and workers that had derived from prior self-management, enterprise initiative, or Workers' Councils, should be recognized fully or only in part;

5. The role of financial institutions (such as banks, insurance companies, pension funds, mutual and investment funds, as well as holding companies) while intermediating between corporations and households;

6. The degree to which it is desirable for government to reserve shares for later sale and how these shares should be administered;

7. The role, if any, that policy makers may wish to assign to a core of established investors, that is, banks, insurance companies, venture capitalists; and

8. The desirability of pursuing an eclectic approach to privatization rather than viewing it as an alternative to a course motivated largely by ideological or purely technical considerations.[64]

Even with detailed analysis and careful study, not every decision whether to sell outright, enter into a domestic joint venture or a global joint venture, or recommend the firm be included in one of the National Investment Fund (NIF) portfolios will be perfect. Van Brabant pointed out that two forces were underplayed at the inception of the transition process. One is the need for a degree of pragmatism because time is short and "ideal solutions are just that." There is also the need to embrace a variety of strategies in removing the party-state-*nomenklatura* triad from decision making about asset use and in forging ahead with divestment.[65]

There seems to have been an orderly progression through these four stages of development: SOEs restructured as joint stock companies; evaluation of their profitability; usufruct divestment; and total divestment. At the same time, other options were proposed to help discern which is the best model for privatization, based on the individual corporation's vision of the future for the enterprise. The Balcerowicz Plan envisioned a quick and radical transformation to the market economy. Privatization was the centerpiece of the plans for economic transformation. Yet, in the fall of 1989 and in the first half of 1990, nothing happened. The implementation of privatization appeared to come to standstill. What contributed to the slowdown of the privatization process?

PRIVATIZATION STALLS

Barbara Blaszczyk, vice-chair of the Council of Ownership Transformation, and Marek Dabrowski, chairman of the Council of Ownership Transformation, offered a unique perspective, based on their operational experience. They noted that the political debate was the most important factor that stalled the privatization process at its inception. This debate was to some extent a continuation of earlier academic discussions held before the Round Table, although it was more ideological and political in nature than before. They asserted that the pattern selected was characterized by the adoption of only one viewpoint, often in its most radical version, with little willingness to compromise.[66]

Blaszczyk and Dabrowski also pointed out that from the very beginning there were four competing options for privatization:

1. Commercial privatization through the capital market;
2. Privatization mainly through employee ownership;
3. Privatization through "citizen ownership"; and
4. Privatization by institutional investors.

The privatization debate at the end of 1989 and the first half of 1990 concentrated on the role of employee ownership. That debate reached no satisfactory solution. They commented that as of the mid-1990s, the idea of commercial privatization had given way to the concept of citizen ownership. This could be seen as a "historical paradox," because the change took place just after the adoption of the *Law on Privatization of State-owned Enterprises* in July 1990. Although this law accepted the multitrack approach to privatization, it gave priority to commercial privatization through a public offering.[67]

By 1990, the entire privatization process had taken on a political context. The implementation of privatization was also affected by the rotation of ministry officials responsible for implementation. The first plenipotentiary for Ownership Transformation in the Mazowiecki government was Krzysztof Lis, who strongly opposed employee ownership schemes. Lis was succeeded by Waldemar Kuczynski (mid-September 1990–January 1991), who became minister for Ownership Transformation. Kuczynski attempted to push privatization through the capital market by arranging for the sale of five SOEs. He initiated the so-called liquidation privatization under Article 37 of the Privatization Law. His term of office lasted only four months because the government changed. Next to assume office was

Janusz Lewandowski in the government of Prime Minister Krzysztof Bielecki. Because of Lewandowski's prominent role as far back as 1986 in advocating the free distribution of privatization vouchers, it was assumed that he would immediately implement a mass privatization program. He did not do so.

Lewandowski concentrated on implementing the privatization option most readily available—privatization by liquidation. Initially, privatization was conducted either as capital privatization or liquidation privatization. Capital privatization was based on Chapters 2 and 3 of the *Law of Privatization of State-owned Enterprises*. Capital privatization proceeded in two phases. Initially the SOE was transformed into a "one-person" company, that is, a joint stock or limited liability company under the State Treasury. Then, during a second phase, shares in the company were offered to private investors. A public offering was organized, and investors were then selected or invited to take part in the bidding process.

The second method was called "liquidation privatization," or "privatization by liquidation," a term that is enigmatic and very misleading. Sachs pointed out that the term is confusing, since the liquidation in this case is not an actual splitting up of the firm's assets, but rather a legal winding up of the operations conducted as a state enterprise, with a subsequent leasing of the assets to the existing work force. Liquidation is a legal process whereby the SOE is transformed into a commercial company in which 100 percent of the equity is held by the State Treasury, and the company begins to carry out its business based on the *Commercial Code of 1934*. The term "privatization by liquidation" has been applied to both financially viable firms and to bankrupt operations. Privatization by liquidation is accomplished without the necessity of the firm undergoing the prior process of conversion into a commercial company. About 1,000 enterprises were privatized via liquidation during the first two years of privatization.[68] "Privatization by liquidation became the most popular means of ownership transformation"[69] and the most successful privatization strategy outside the field of the privatization of small units, such as retail stores and small workshops.[70] Legislation in 1990 permitted up to 20 percent of the stock to be offered to employees and some other smaller groups of stakeholders, and the remaining shares of stock were to be sold to the public.

There are SOEs that are in a relatively good economic and financial situation. The liquidation of these viable enterprises may be accomplished under Article 37 of the *Law on Privatization of State-owned Enterprises.*In this process the firm is closed and deleted from the official register of state enterprises. The assets of the viable firm may be sold or transferred to a new enterprise or leased to another company.

Blaszczyk and Dabrowski explained that this type of privatization (apart from different procedures and decision-making bodies) differs essentially from capital privatization.[71] There is no transition period during which the enterprise has been transformed into a company operating under the *Commercial Code,* simultaneously remaining entirely under the ownership of the State Treasury.

The second type of privatization by liquidation corresponds more accurately to the traditional interpretation of the term. This process applies to firms that are not viable, or are judged to be in such adverse financial situation as to be unsalvageable, or firms that are, in fact, bankrupt. This liquidation process takes place under Article 19 of the *Law on State Enterprises of 1981.* In these cases, an official "liquidator" is appointed to oversee the liquidation of the firm. Whatever assets remain are sold to the highest bidder. The funds derived from the sale of assets are applied to pay off the outstanding obligations of the firm.

Privatization by liquidation was a popular form of privatization from the very first legislation in August 1990. By the end of 1992, the process of transformation had been initiated for 2,478 out of 8,454 state-owned enterprises. Nearly 30 percent (1939) of these transformations were in the nonagricultural sector. Of those involved, 480 enterprises were transformed into capital companies (commercialized) and the remaining 1,459 (or 75.2%) came under one or the other of the Articles of Liquidation privatization (662 on the basis of conversion under the privatization law and 797 truly liquidated on the basis of the *Law on State Enterprises*).[72]

Privatization by liquidation peaked in the second half of 1991, and slowed down thereafter. There were an increasing number of firms within the group that were designated for "real" liquidation due to substandard economic performance. They were simply not viable in a free market environment.

Blaszczyk and Dabrowski suggested that several different factors contributed to this slowdown. The worsening financial condition of enterprises being considered for privatization and political instability caused popular support for the process to decline. Lack of consistency and continuity in the privatization policy of successive governments, together with inadequate inventiveness and lack of determination in introducing and supporting unconventional methods of privatization, has also played an important role.[73]

Frydman, Rapaczynski, and Earle explained that the popularity of privatization through liquidation is due to the advantage this method offers to insiders of the privatized enterprises, who gain an ability to control and manipulate the process to their benefit. They further observed that while this type of privatization is much more controlled than the spontaneous privatization during the closing days of the pre-Solidarity regime, it is also an outlet for continuing pressure for further decentralized and "spontaneous" forms of ownership transformation.[74]

PRIVATIZATION BY LIQUIDATION: SOLVENT ENTERPRISES' PRIVATIZATION BY LEASING

Leasing, rather than selling, has proven to be the most common path of privatization through the liquidation process.[75] First, all privatizations by liquidation are initiated by a sponsoring agency (called the "founding organ"), which usually is an industry-related or sectoral ministry, a local authority, or the Workers' Council of the enterprise itself. The consent of the Ministry of Privatization is also required. In the case of leasing, the concurrence of the Workers' Council is mandatory. The lease is made to a joint stock or limited liability company. The majority of the employees of the state enterprise to be liquidated must be shareholders in the new enterprise.[76] Also, the new joint stock or limited liability company must be capitalized at the level of at least 20 percent of the value of the enterprise being liquidated at the time of the leasing arrangement.

Leases are usually written for five to 10 years. There are three types of lease contracts: (1) lease and sale; (2) tenancy with an option to purchase; and (3) tenancy without the option to purchase.

Leasing involves reaching a consensus among management, the Workers' Council, and the unions, all of which are "interested parties" to the lease negotiation. This interaction has led to considerable jockeying around the issue of the value of the assets, and opens the way for actions and decisions that, while technically legal, may not be quite so ethical.

Frydman, Rapaczynski, and Earle noted that an inherent moral hazard is that insiders, who have access to information and control over a company's operations, may be interested in arriving at a low valuation prior to executing the leasing contract. This arrangement creates an incentive for the insiders to reduce the enterprise's cash flow, since valuation is often based on the firm's discounted future cash flows.[77]

As a result of experiences similar to those described above, the government inaugurated procedures to modify and establish new procedures for asset valuations to reduce the extent of insider collusion.

Privatization by Lease and Sale

In the lease and sale arrangement, several steps are defined by law. When the lease contract is signed, the new company acquires only a leasehold on the assets of the firm being liquidated. Concurrently, the parties involved sign a contract obligating the founding organ of the former state enterprise to give title to the new company (lessee) at the end of the lease period, provided the new company has made all the agreed-upon payments and satisfied any other terms of the lease. It is in this second contract that the price of the assets being acquired is specified and the yearly terms of payment are indicated. The payments are calculated in such a way that the assets are fully paid for at the conclusion of the lease.[78] When the lease expires, and all payments and conditions have been satisfied, title to the enterprise passes from lessor to lessee by a special notarial act.

Tenancy with Option to Purchase

The second alternative, tenancy with the option to purchase, is quite similar to the lease and sale plan. The difference relates to the amount and manner of payments. Instead of the schedule of payments being equal to the value of the assets, payments are smaller with a possibility to purchase the assets at the end of the lease period by a "balloon payment." If the lessee chooses this option and at the end of the lease wishes to purchase the firm, the price is determined by the market value prevailing at that time. The amounts paid during tenancy are deducted from the purchase price.

Tenancy without Option to Purchase

The third alternative, tenancy without the option to purchase, involves an arrangement whereby the lessee pays only an amount equal to the interest payments on the lease and sale price. Then, at the conclusion of the lease, if the lessee decides to purchase the enterprise, the purchase price is established at full market value.

Although three options were possible, for all practical purposes, all leasing arrangements were in the lease and sale category. Purchasers are disinclined to risk an increase in the market price during the leasing period. Once the lease is signed, oversight by the founding organ or by the Ministry of Privatization usually has been limited to collecting payments. An exception could arise if the employees of the new company lodge almost any kind of complaint with the founding organ or the ministry. While such a possibility exists, this type of problem has not generally arisen.

PRIVATIZATION BY LIQUIDATION: INSOLVENT ENTERPRISES

The above three options apply to privatization by liquidation of solvent or viable enterprises. What about the privatization by liquidation of firms judged already insolvent, or potentially insolvent, or already bankrupt? The *Law on State Enterprises* provided that in such cases of "insolvency liquidations," the assets of the enterprise were to be sold to either natural or legal persons. Again, the initiative for sale belongs legally to the founding organ or the Ministry of Privatization. However, in practice, the ministry requires that the director of the enterprise and the Workers' Council be consulted. The *Law on State Enterprises* and the *Privatization Law* both give the director and the Workers' Council the right to question and sometimes to challenge this decision.

Liquidation sales are public. They must be advertised in the local and the national press. Prospective bidders may request and receive detailed information about the sale and may also visit the enterprise, inspect operations, and examine the books. In order to ensure a fair minimum price and guarantee more accurate valuation, the founding organ or the ministry may use outside experts and consultants in the process. Interestingly, the winning bid need not be the highest bid in monetary terms. A bid received from the employees of the company being sold under insolvency liquidation receives "special consideration." Likewise, the credibility of the buyer or the credit-worthiness of the bidder are also taken into consideration.

When these initial models of privatization were being introduced, a particularly pressing economic problem also existed. There was a distinct shortage of capital in the Polish domestic market. To overcome this paucity of capital and to make possible active bidding in the liquidation of state-owned assets, the Ministry of Privatization and the Ministry of Finance developed a support package to assist perspective buyers. The Ministry of Privatization, in cooperation with the Ministry of Finance, offered the following arrangements to assist potential buyers during the initial shortage of domestic capital:

1. The purchase price of an enterprise is payable partly in cash (no less than 40% of the total) with the rest payable in 16 equal installments, payable quarterly over four years, with the possibility of a one-year grace period;
2. The sums payable in cash are considered to have a value 1.25 times greater than the sums payable in installments;
3. The same interest terms as those made available in the case of leasing arrangements (see above) are provided.

PRIVATIZATION BY LIQUIDATION: "QUICK PRIVATIZATION"

Another aspect of the liquidation privatization effort is a Ministry of Privatization effort called "quick privatization" or simply "quick sale." The program was launched in July 1991 for the purpose of making a "quick sale" of small- or medium-size state enterprises. The founding organ takes the initiative. Potential investors are invited to enter into negotiations for purchase. Investors may be individuals, including employees, or corporate groups, but only Polish nationals may bid. Companies in the quick privatization program were put together in groups of six, and the sales were conducted simultaneously. Sales were subject to the approval of the Ministry of Privatization. Sales were made on a cash-and-credit basis, with a minimum of 40 percent in cash and the balance and interest payable in installments. This program made only a modest contribution to Polish privatization. Between July 1991 and March 1992, only 46 enterprises were privatized through this approach.

THE SECTORAL APPROACH

The sectoral approach to privatization is not, strictly speaking, privatization. Rather it is a process of deciding which privatization model and which restructuring tools are best for individual companies, determined through a "sector by sector" analysis of an industry. The sectoral approach involves the grouping together of a number of enterprises in a given branch of industry for the purpose of systematic analysis. The process involves not necessarily all, but between five and 30 industries. The purpose of the analysis is to determine their real potential for privatization.

Frydman, Rapaczynski, and Earle observed that

> in launching the sectoral privatization program, the ministry was attempting to achieve a number of objectives. To begin with, the failure of the capital privatization program and its very high cost made authorities look for a way of combining the analysis of a number of enterprises, in order to save costs and develop more pressure from both insiders and outsiders to privatize certain sensitive areas, such as the tobacco industry, and may have felt unsure how to handle a complex situation. Sectoral privatization allowed it to postpone immediate privatization in some cases, while at the same time preparing an "industrial policy" of sorts that would allow it to proceed with more confidence and expertise at a later date.[79]

By the fall of 1993, more than 350 enterprises, divided into 20 sectors, had been prepared for privatization using the sectoral approach. There are two steps in the process. First, a "lead advisor" is selected by competitive tender. The lead advisor must perform a domestic and international analysis of the sector and each company within the sector. The lead advisor may be drawn from an accounting firm, a consulting firm, or from the field of investment banking. Lead advisors may be domestic or foreign or a consortia of Polish and overseas firms. The lead advisor also contacts potential investors to inquire about their interest and solicits their ideas about the future development of the sector and how to make it profitable. The advisor then prepares a strategy for the sector and a plan of action leading either to the privatization or the restructuring of the companies.

In the second step the ministry representing the government receives, evaluates, and approves the recommendation of the lead advisor. The government then may take action, using several possible channels: public offering, tender sale, restructuring, or privatization.

As an example of the scope of these efforts, the Capital Privatization Department of the Ministry of Ownership Transformation (Ministry of Privatization) undertook 20 sector studies to analyze and evaluate companies within each sector for possible privatization. These 20 sectors are included: ball bearings (with 4 companies for sale), breweries (8), cable and wire (10), cement and lime (26), confectionery (16), construction (30), cosmetics and detergents, electronics and telecommunications (10), furniture manufacturing (2), glass (26), machine tools (34), meat (23), mechanical and electrical, automotive components (28), paints and lacquers (5), power engineering (2), pulp and paper (6), rubber and tire manufacturing (8), shoes (36), manufactured gases (8), and tobacco (7).

The sectoral approach was designed to be especially attractive to foreign investment. Professor Jacek Klich offered the opinion that "this new concept of sectoral privatization is more attractive not only because it covers sectors of special interest to American investors. The United States is on the top of the list of foreign investors in Poland."[80]

Frydman, Rapaczynski, and Earle concluded that sectoral privatization has not yet yielded the intended results. While the lead advisors have produced extensive papers diagnosing industry conditions, few actual privatizations have flowed from their reports. Given the high costs and low returns of the sectoral approach, the government is not especially interested in an immediate expansion of this program.[81]

CHALLENGES YET TO BE OVERCOME

The privatization process throughout Central and Eastern Europe continues to face certain common constraints and challenges. Professor Lavigne offered this classification of constraints:

1. *Economic constraints,* of which the lack of domestic capital is the most substantial, especially under deflationary macroeconomic policies that still affect investment more than consumption.
2. *Technical constraints,* among them the lack of proper accounting rules and experience. All the big accounting and consulting companies have opened offices in Eastern Europe, as well as a host of smaller companies, often set up as joint ventures. These institutions absorb a significant share of the revenues of privatization (up to 20% according to some statements), and also a large share of the technical assistance granted to the countries in transition.
3. *Institutional constraints,* related to central and local government

involvement in the process. The specific institutions that have been set up are constantly criticized for their action, overcommitted, and unable to meet the deadlines; often they are accused of conflict of interests and insider trading.[82]

Poland has experienced these economic, technical, and institutional constraints. Privatization tends to lead to polarization. Those SOEs most capable of adjusting to environmental changes either were already privatized or were about to be privatized. Many of the remaining SOEs would be increasingly difficult to privatize because, although large in scale, they did not represent sufficient value for prospective investors. The most common problems faced by SOEs in 1993 were bad locations; or they represented unprofitable industries (steel, mining, etc.); or they included firms that lacked export possibilities because of inferior quality, marketing inexperience, or continued governmental interventions that further damaged profitability. The giant SOEs (the WOGs) tended to be outdated, if not completely obsolete, highly politicized, and unionized. Resistance to privatization was intense on the part of both management and workers, primarily because they feared loss of their jobs as a result of privatization.

The SOEs that are not privatized or restructured are increasingly visible and create significant political tension. The commercialization of these SOEs and their eventual privatization or restructuring involves substantial costs and constitutes a significant drain on an already precarious state budget.

The initial optimism with which privatization was introduced has been eroded and diminished by delay. Delays were caused by frequent policy changes and changes in government leadership, quixotic attitudes of the Sejm, and the maneuverings of bureaucrats, which allowed time and eventually gave impetus for SOE managers and workers to develop strong resistance to privatization and restructuring.

In Polish publications, media, and newspapers, opinions began to be expressed that some SOEs should remain under the control of the state. Some argued that privatization should be promoted only in areas where competition was necessary or desirable. In other sectors, such as natural monopolies, utilities or military-related industries, domestic competition may not be essential to good performance. It was argued that firms operating in these areas need not and should not be privatized.[83]

A CHANGE IN PRIVATIZATION STRATEGY: TRANSITION TO THE MASS PRIVATIZATION PROGRAM (MPP)

The experiences of the period from 1989 to 1993 proved that privatization would indeed be a long-term process. It would involve depoliticizing economic decisions by separating enterprises from the state and creating an institutional structure of corporate governance.[84]

As Jeffrey Sachs has pointed out, Poland's economic transformation must be viewed from two perspectives: the timing and content of the reforms themselves and the timing and content of the actual restructuring. Sachs estimated a three-to-five-year time period for the introduction of the reforms. He also noted that restructuring will last for a much longer period, presumably for a decade or more.[85]

Frydman and Rapaczynski added that privatization is not merely a change of ownership. Rather, it is "a complex social and economic transformation, which is supposed to change the way every company is run and every business decision is made."[86]

It is not surprising, then, that certain issues have persisted in the privatization process:

1. The speed at which privatization should be introduced and the sequencing of the privatization process. How does a country in transition stabilize uncertainty?[87]
2. Restitution of property to legitimate owners. As mentioned earlier, Poland is one of the only Central and Eastern European countries that did not pass a reprivatization program. The Ministry of Privatization has an undersecretary responsible for reprivatization matters.
3. One of the several aims of privatization in transition economics is the concern for equity. In Poland equity considerations have been rather dominant. In so many instances of privatization of SOEs, workers have been given a preferential share of the assets of the company being privatized.

At the outset, the Mazowiecki government advocated a multitrack privatization program and the public responded positively. However, four major interest groups each had very different expectations about privatization and promoted essentially different solutions. These groups are:

1. Former owners of property nationalized legally and illegally (on the grounds of the existing laws);
2. Workers and management of SOEs;
3. Prospective investors, both domestic and foreign; and
4. Other social groupings (i.e., public sector employees paid from the state budget, teachers, doctors, public administrators, etc.) with expectations different from the interests of the three groups mentioned above.

Investors who were willing to participate in privatization wanted the situation to be as clear as possible. Therefore, they demanded that the "legal status of property" be clarified and stabilized. Investors who had already participated in the privatization program wanted their rights to privatized property guaranteed. Sometimes this position was at odds with the interest of former owners of nationalized property.

The government and other political structures in Poland, especially the Sejm, had to balance the interests of the above four groups. As a democratically elected body, especially after 1991, the Sejm was expected to act as an agent of the public interest in the privatization processes. Agency, in this case, is a very delicate and ambiguous notion. The acceleration or slowdown of privatization in Poland relates to the way each succeeding government has defined the concept of public interest in relation to privatization.

In chapter 7, we will consider the privatization process in the period from 1993 to 1995, with special emphasis on mass privatization programs.

▨ *Chapter Seven*

Polish Mass Privatization

Proposals, Plans, and Progress

"The Polish privatization experience is full of paradoxes."
Ben Slay

OVERVIEW

Chapter 7 will examine the road to the Polish Mass Privatization Program (MPP) from the initial discussions through 1995. This chapter will examine the variations and the annual (sometimes political) revisions that have created a cycle of delays, beginning with the initial proposal (1990), the legislative delays and amendments (1991 and 1992), the revised proposal (1992), the privatization law itself (1993), and the subsequent years of administrative delays (1994 to 1995).

Leszek Balcerowicz observed that "political resistance has interfered with the whole privatization process ... and especially the program ... mass privatization ... I consider the main reason for delays in the privatization process to be frequent changes in governments."[1]

Privatization is not a new idea in Poland. In the mid-1980s, economists initiated privatization discussions and by 1988, fully a year before the Round Table, public discussion focused on a program of vouchers, exchangeable for shares in enterprises. Two prominent economists who proposed such a program were Janusz Lewandowski and Jan Szomburg, both of the Gdansk Institute for Research into Market Economies.[2] Mass privatization was a campaign issue in the first presidential election in 1990. In that election Lech Walesa considered mass privatization to be a key issue.

Privatization has been further complicated by unresolved issues related to the question of reprivatization (discussed in chapter 6), presenting a formidable obstacle affecting every proposal for privatization. It represents the most poignant example of the inability of the political system to articulate interests and forge a consensus. "Everybody understands that delay in this area constitutes one of the most important barriers to privatization and to the entrance of foreign capital, [but] there is still . . . no legislation in this field."[3]

The pre-Solidarity *Law on State Enterprises* (25 September 1981) and the *Law on Economic Activity* (31 December 1988) provided directors of SOEs considerable latitude relating to the assets of these enterprises. This legislation gave directors the right to dispose of property to newly established commercial enterprises—even to companies in which they were partners or directors. Directors took full advantage of this legislation, and without considering issues of conflict of interest, took ample advantage of the opportunities given them. These pre-Solidarity laws were amended in 1990 and 1991 to eliminate examples of what is now derisively called "spontaneous privatization."

The post-Solidarity *Law on Privatization of State-owned Enterprises* (13 July 1990) allowed "privatization by liquidation," whereby the SOE will cease to exist and all of its assets and liabilities will be transferred to a newly established limited liability company. In this manner, the SOE is transformed into a 100 percent State Treasury–owned commercial company, which in turn is authorized to offer up to 20 percent of its shares to employees and other groups of stakeholders.

Another road to privatization is to declare the SOE bankrupt, liquidate its assets, and contribute them to a new commercial company. Early success was achieved by privatization through liquidation, the method considered most appropriate for small enterprises. In September 1990, the Ministry of Ownership Changes prepared and published its Privatization Program. The *Privatization Law* envisaged three main routes to privatization:

1. Commercialization or corporatization of state-owned enterprise, to be followed by a sale of shares to the public;
2. The liquidization route, involving the dissolution of the enterprise as a legal entity and privatization of its assets; and
3. Small-scale privatization, mainly in trade and services.[4]

Political controversy significantly delayed MPP enactment. In 1991 and 1992, the proposed privatization act languished in various parliamentary committees and was frequently amended. By June 1992, the ministry had proposed an MPP with 270 larger-than-average SOEs ready and willing to participate in the process. Previously, the minimum goal had been set at 600 SOEs. The MPP called for free distribution of certificates to all Polish adults age 18 and over, for a total distribution of over 27 million certificates. These certificates could be exchanged for shares in companies selected for the plan.

Under the original proposal, National Investment Funds (NIFs), comprising 25 to 30 enterprises each, were to be established as joint stock companies under the Polish *Commercial Code.* Twenty such NIFs were originally envisaged.

The proposed ownership structure of the companies privatized within MPP was envisioned as follows:

1. 60 percent of the share capital allocated to an NIF, of which one lead shareholder has a 33 percent stake, and the remaining 27 percent, a minority shareholding;
2. Up to 10 percent allocated to employees in a free distribution; and
3. 30 percent at the disposal of the ministry.

Enactment of MPP in 1992 proved to be unrealistic because the Sejm diverted its attention elsewhere. Yet, despite domestic distractions, the government recognized the need for some action on the MPP. Finally, in 1993, the Polish Privatization Program, with a voucher component, passed the Sejm (30 April) and the Senate (7 May) and was signed into law (18 May). Legislative enactment is one process; implementation is quite another case!

What were some of the problems delaying the law until 1993? Jan Bossak, currently the board chairman for NIF No. 2, cited six problem areas: (1) political controversy over privatization itself; (2) political compromise between two prime objectives—efficiency and social equity; (3) privatization revenues were disappointing; (4) Warsaw Stock Exchange listings fell below expectations; (5) criticism that the voucher system has become an autonomous component of the reform package; and (6) "the dramatic deterioration of the financial standing of many SOEs and privatized enterprises, a liquidity squeeze . . . large bad credit portfolios by Polish state banks extending easy loans to insolvent state enterprises and the real threat of a chain reaction of failures of SOEs and commercial banks if not supported by the government."[5]

There have been other obstacles to privatization, some anticipated, others unexpected. The lack of both experience and managerial skills was anticipated, but the lack of clear vision and rules, rising unemployment, declining living standards, and less job security all served to increase worker anxiety and resistance. Privatization entailed dismantling Workers' Councils and eliminating many management prerogatives. The fear of downsizing and massive layoffs fueled the anxiety of workers. Lack of capital and access to credit was of concern to private investors. The general recession and the poor performance of already privatized companies caused a negative attitude toward privatization in the mind of the public.

Rapacki and Linz observed that "the anticipated barrier of lack of experience and skills in conventional financing, accounting techniques and methods of valuation of assets due to the distorted financial environment, lack of an efficient capital market, unreliable accounting systems, deepening recession and growing social suspicion created an atmosphere of mistrust of the Ministry and consulting companies."[6]

THE MPP REVISION OF 1992

In June 1992, the Ministry of Ownership Changes introduced a revised MPP proposal. The purpose of the revision was to achieve an acceleration of the privatization process and to provide for greater public participation.

The MPP of 1992 called for privatization through commercialization. Commercialization, however, is an intermediary step before actual privatization. Commercialization is the transformation of a state-owned company into a joint stock or limited liability company, controlled solely by the State Treasury. This approach was intended to: (1) provide a clear decision-making and control structure; (2) adjust the legal status of the SOE to the market environment; (3) create pressure for market-oriented restructuring; and (4) prepare the enterprise for privatization. The concept of commercialization provoked further delays, especially in the wake of the 1993 parliamentary elections.

MASS PRIVATIZATION LAW: OWNERSHIP CHANGES AND POLITICAL UPHEAVAL

The *Mass Privatization Law* was passed 30 April 1993. The law provided for three activities: the commercialization of SOEs, the establishment of NIFs, and the payment of participation fees.

1. *Commercialization of SOEs.* Plans called for the privatization of about 600 state-owned large- and medium-sized companies, transforming them into joint stock companies. Some of these companies would include firms in better-than-average financial conditions.

Under the final provisions of the 1993 law, the structure of ownership for each company closely paralleled earlier proposals and was as follows: 60 percent of the stock will be allocated to the NIFs, with 33 percent of the stock given to the leading NIF, and 27 percent of the stock distributed among all other NIFs; 30 percent of the total stock will be held by the State Treasury; and 10 percent of the total stock will be given for free to the employees of the company involved in the program of mass privatization.

2. *Establishment of NIFs.* The MPP provided that each fund could enter into management contracts, including special remuneration provisions, with experienced and professional fund management firms. The major task of the management firms would be to increase the value of their portfolios by increasing the market value of the firms to be privatized. Other duties of the fund managers were to represent shareholders' interests, increase management effectiveness, restructure companies (where appropriate), and attract both foreign and domestic investment capital.

In the March 1992 proposal, each of the 20 NIFs was to hold stocks in all of the 600 SOEs proposed for commercialization. These 600 would be divided into 20 groups of 30 companies each. The number of firms was later reduced to 444.

Governmental delays, particularly those occasioned by the 1993 parliamentary elections, prevented the implementation of the NIFs in the summer of 1993, as had been originally proposed. The implementation of the NIFs was delayed further until the fall of 1994 and actually was not fully implemented until 1995.

3. *The Registration Fee.* The registration fee was set at 10 percent of an average monthly salary (slightly above 200 USD). Certificates were to be available after one year of NIF operation. Stocks of the funds, as well as certificates not converted into stocks, would be traded on the secondary market.

The legal provisions governing the establishment of the NIF and the distribution of certificates and trading share certificates are specified in the law. Ewa Freyberg, former undersecretary of privatization and now undersecretary of state at the Polish Treasury, explained the various procedures as follows:

1. *Establishment of National Investment Funds.* In March 1994, the Selection Commission was given the responsibility to chose firms and consortia that could best manage the property of the National Investment Funds. Contracts were to be signed with these firms by the Supervisory Boards of each fund. Originally, 72 management groups bid for the management of 20 NIFs. Eventually over one-half withdrew, leaving 33 international consortia as candidates to manage the proposed 20 funds. The number of funds was later reduced to 15. The Selection Commission was also charged with the responsibility to select candidates for the Supervisory Boards of each fund. The number of members on each board was established by executive order at twelve. This candidate selection process was originally scheduled to be concluded by June 1994. However, the Ministry of Ownership Changes received over 7,000 applications for membership on the Supervisory Boards. The first members of the Supervisory Boards and Boards of Directors of National Investment Funds were to be appoint-

ed by the ministry and were scheduled to be appointed in July 1994. The complexity of the process and the volume of applicants considerably delayed action by the ministry.

At the same time, the Council of Ministers was scheduled to assign specific companies to a particular fund. After the council had approved these allocations, Supervisory Boards were authorized to sign contracts with managing firms.

2. *Distribution of Share Certificates.* At the time the NIFs were established, preparations were begun in May and June 1994 to select firms to print and distribute the share certificates.

3. *Trading in Share Certificates, National Funds' Stocks, and Stocks of Partnerships Participating in the Program.* The Ministry of Privatization drafted legislation to prepare capital markets for the changes in securities trading required by the implementation of the entire privatization program. The most important bills involved the establishment of a fiscal agent, a Common Electronic Data Processing (EDP) Center for brokerage houses, and over-the-counter trading in share certificates. The Mass Privatization Program was mainly financed from assistance provided by the World Bank, PHARE, USAID, and the British Know How Fund. A contribution from the European Bank for Reconstruction and Development (EBRD) was also expected.[7]

After evaluating the situation, Freyberg concluded that "the unique character of [the voucher system] consists in its comprehensiveness, especially the close relation between the process of restructuring and privatization. The success of the program will hinge not only on the improvement of enterprise positions and thus an increase in the value of share certificates, but also on the mass access of further companies to the program."[8]

The ownership changes in the Polish economy in 1993 included an increase in the number of sales of Treasury-owned companies, a simultaneous slowdown in the process of transformation of state-owned enterprises into Treasuty-owned companies, commencement of the practical implementation of the NIF program, and advancement of the process of transfer of state farms to the Treasury Agricultural Property Agency. There was a reduction of over 42 percent in the number of enterprises granted permission to embark on the liquidation route and a 19 percent decrease in the number of enterprises that underwent liquidation because their economic condition proved to be nonviable.[9]

What are some of the facts related to ownership changes in 1993?

1. The privatization process encompassed 4,035 state-owned enterprises, 46 percent of the total reported as of 30 June 1990. Of these, 522 enterprises had been transformed into Treasury-owned companies, and in 202 cases the equity share capital had been paid into the National Investment Funds (NIFs). By December 1993, 165 additional enterprises had applied for inclusion in the NIF program, bringing the total to 367.

2. Four hundred and thirty state-owned enterprises went into liquidation. Of these 265 were closed, and 165 were transformed into new private entities.

3. The Ministry of Privatization decided that a vote must be taken at the enterprise level before any enterprise could begin the process of privatization. Not all enterprises voted to participate. The prime minister also had the right to veto enterprise participation in the process of privatization or to exclude certain enterprises on the basis of the "public interest." At year's end, Prime Minister Pawlak had exercised this prerogative and declared nine firms in "the public interest" and removed them from the privatization pool.

4. The government decided to encourage employee buyouts of state-owned enterprises. After May 1993, employee-owned companies acquired title to the corporate assets after paying one-half the installments. This situation made for a substantial improvement in their corporate credit rating because these enterprises could now offer lenders the security required for long-term credits. There were over 720 employee-controlled companies in Poland, employing almost 250,000 persons.

5. The number of companies quoted on the Warsaw Stock Exchange increased from 16 to 21.

6. Capital privatization involved the sale of 43 companies, which was almost double the number in 1992. In the second half of 1993, a distinct acceleration of selloffs occurred, accompanied by a slowdown in the conversion of state-owned enterprises into Treasury corporations, primarily because there was a backlog of 200 Treasury companies waiting for privatization. Some of these enterprises had been waiting for as long as two years.

Why had there been this delay in Treasury companies becoming privatized and in the implementation of the legislation?

The Suchocka government was plagued by labor unrest, union dissatisfaction, and even Solidarity-led strikes. The government attempted to appease worker dissatisfaction and to counter the resurgence of membership in official government unions and the pressure created by them. The *Pact on the State Enterprise in the Process of Transition* was signed on 22 February 1993 by representatives of the government, trade unions, and employees. The pact included an agreement to amend seven laws, all designed to guarantee greater rights to workers. Among the laws to be amended was the *Privatization Act of 1990*. However, actual and perceived government inaction and the slowness of reforms prompted Solidarity to accuse the government of failure to honor its commitments under the terms of the pact. This growing dissatisfaction contributed to an unexpected parliamentary crisis in June 1993. The Sejm was dissolved and the legislative process was interrupted. Privatization plans suffered from governmental paralysis.

The 1993 elections resulted in a newly elected Parliament and a new government under Prime Minister Waldemar Pawlak, as the Democratic Left Alliance (SLD), with direct ties to the former Communist party, and the former communist-dominated Polish Peasants party (PSL) gained sufficient seats to form a majority coalition in the Parliament.

During the campaign, other political parties had attacked the SLD and the PSL as the reincarnation of the previous communist-controlled and communist-dominated parties. Opposition parties were so preoccupied attacking the SLD and the PSL that they failed to put forth their own programs for social and economic reform. While claiming to be different from their predecessors, the SLD and PSL did not themselves advance any particularly concrete programs. The government began to negotiate with trade unions in an attempt to fulfill the original terms of the State Enterprise Pact, especially with respect to the *Privatization Law of 1990*. However, 1993 ended without the differences between the union demands and the amendments proposed by the government being resolved.

Jan Bossak observed that this stalemate had a negative impact on the attitude of the unions toward privatization. Demands of unions in large enterprises, which fought for an expansion of employee privileges, and in particular "free distribution" of 15 percent of an enterprise's equity share capital, led a large number of state-owned enterprises to delay the choice of a method of privatization. One result was a decline of interest in the NIF program and in transformation of state-owned enterprises through the capital route or through liquidation.[10]

An analysis of the election results suggested that the public appeared to have lost enthusiasm for economic transformation and indicated a decline in approval for the movement toward a free enterprise system. One current of public opinion began to project arguments that the privatization program was a misappropriation of public property. There was evidence in the election of a certain nostalgia for state intervention and for the security of the earlier system.

Waldemar Pawlak of the PSL was elected prime minister, although the SLD was clearly the senior partner in the coalition. The Pawlak government proved to be a disaster with reference to economic reform. Pawlak was especially negative toward mass privatization initiatives. Pawlak was hesitant, indecisive, and reticent under the guise of being prudent, consultative, and circumspect. At the outset, his administration portended to offer a period of stability. In retrospect, it proved to be a period of stagnation and procrastination.

Jerzy Baczynski, editor in chief of *Polityka,* wrote: "If we can discern any political reason for the Prime Minister's silence, it would be a general reluctance to change anything. His favorite words are 'stability, perfection and seeking better solutions' which in practice means maintaining the status quo."[11] The programs most impacted by inaction and indecision were the MPP, especially the voucher program.

1994: THE TORTOISE PACE OF PRIVATIZATION

The movement toward any form of privatization was so slow that President Walesa chided the government for "the tortoise pace" of MPP implementation. Nineteen ninety-four was truly a year of inaction. Andrzej Goldberg, editor in chief of *Tygodnik Solidarnosc,* wrote: "The most important economic issue dealt with by every post-1989 government with only meager results is privatization. Waldemar Pawlak has to take all the blame today, especially for the constantly postponed mass privatization. The Mass Privatization Program prepared by the previous government has been waiting for Pawlak's signature for the past twelve months."[12]

The priorities of the Pawlak administration were, not surprisingly, directed more toward agricultural policy than business policy. They were also heavily tilted toward developing an improved social safety net for citizens most severely impacted by the economic transition.

The Pawlak government took a rather populist stance and suggested that SOEs could be better managed by national rather than foreign managers; that foreign investors would profit at Poland's expense; and that the state had an obligation to maintain control over entire sectors of the economy. This was the position taken by Bogdan Pek, chairman of the Sejm Privatization Committee. Specifically, paying fees to foreign advisors for NIF services became a major issue for Pawlak that, in turn, contributed to the delay of mass privatization. These attitudes reflected Pawlak's acceptance of the mentality of state central planning as "conventional wisdom."

On 26 September 1994, the minister of privatization, Wieslaw Kaczmarek, protested publicly that the "delay in implementing the Mass Privatization Program is costing the country many billions of zlotys and is hurting Poland's reputation abroad."

Stung by this open disagreement within his cabinet and the consistent criticism of his failure to act, on 1 October 1994, Prime Minister Pawlak made a television response defending his inaction. He claimed that he had "good reasons for not making a quick decision despite pressures from various lobbies." Pawlak stressed that he had no intention of withdrawing his support from voucher privatization and that he, indeed, expected to implement this program "soon." Meanwhile, he asserted that mass privatization legislation should be further amended: "At stake is the fact that the National Investment Funds would be managed mainly by foreign companies, which would be paid handsomely but not held responsible for their work." In addition, Pawlak maintained that the lack of proper evaluation of the assets of state-owned enterprises was a problem. Likewise, "it is not true that enterprises participating in the [MPP] are all losing money." Pawlak denied press rumors that not implementing the voucher system by September jeopardized relations with the International Monetary Fund (IMF).[13] Finally, he declared that he "decided not to sign the program quickly because there was no consultation with provincial governors on this issue."[14]

Another maneuver of the Pawlak government, designed to circumvent privatization, involved the action of the Council of Ministers in October 1994 to approve the Stabilization-Restructuring Privatization Program. Struggling state-owned enterprises with good development prospects were to receive access to new credit lines and government loan guarantees. Restructuring, including significant management changes, was offered as an intermediate step toward later privatization.

The stabilization aspect of this program was designed to stop the deterioration of SOEs. Restructuring was offered as an alternative to privatization by politicians not favorably disposed to privatization in the first place. Restructuring sought to retain worker control through Workers' Councils and labor unions. The Stabilization-Restructuring Privatization Program was ambiguous, but entirely consistent with the prevailing political philosophy of the SLD/PSL coalition. These alternatives to privatization played on the rising sense of supernationalism, on the increasingly unfavorable perception of privatization, on a growing conviction that the state should retain control over some segments of the economy, on the emotion of disgruntled workers and union members, and on a feeling that Poles were being manipulated in the discussions on privatization.[15]

The question of how to administer the NIFs preoccupied the government for more than two years. Finally, in November 1993, the NIFs began with 202 enterprises chosen in two stages. Later, 165 more enterprises applied, bringing the total to 367 enterprises.

Another concern was how NIF managers were to be "controlled." How much freedom should they have? Pawlak wanted tight control. He also wanted "Polish" control through the appointment of a majority of Polish citizens to every Supervisory Board. The decision was ultimately made that at least two-thirds of the Supervisory Board, including the chairman, must be Polish citizens.

Throughout the process, however, it became evident that the Pawlak government preferred commercialization as the alternative to privatization. In the classical concept of privatization, commercialization is only one step. "The spirit and the letter of the law foresee commercialization as the beginning of a process that is to end in privatization, and not simply a change in the governance structure of state firms."[16] Now, commercialization was being offered as an end in itself. Commercialization preserves state control, strengthens the status quo, and demands a minimum change in the management or structure of commercialized companies.

A major concern about commercialization is that the process inevitably "breeds complacent managers." Professor Adam Lipowski, of the Institute of Economic Sciences of the Polish Academy of Sciences, noted that "current announcements about introducing commercialization have led to a decreased activity among founding authorities in implementing recovery and liquidation procedures (because of) expectations among company management boards regarding cheap loans, debt clearing, tax breaks and protective duties in connection with privatization."[17]

Leszek Balcerowicz, in an interview in *Wprost* (25 September 1994), observed:

> The dangers of mass commercialization, if it is not connected with a concurrent increase in the speed of privatization, are increased further when accompanied by the grouping of state enterprises and companies into various concerns and holding companies. The rationale for forming these is the catchy phrase of the state owner's increased control. The result is the creation of entities which may hamper privatization, regardless of the real intentions of those who set them up.[18]

In early 1995, the public began to ask whether the Pawlak government would continue to slow down privatization or even try to stop the privatization process at the commercialization stage? As it turned out, the proper question should have been whether the government itself, based on the unnatural coalition of the SLD and the PSL, would survive.

Interparty rivalry, differences in agenda and leadership styles, slow progress toward economic reform, and eventually, pressure from the president and Parliament brought about the collapse of the Pawlak government. On 6 February 1995, President Walesa gave the Parliament an ultimatum to change the government or face dissolution. The next day Waldemar Pawlak was history! He was replaced by Jozef Oleksy, speaker of the Sejm, and a former high-ranking Communist party official.

As a result of the change in government, Poland joined Hungary, Bulgaria, Slovakia, and Lithuania as former East Bloc countries where reconstructed communists have regained control of their governments. In each instance, the change reflected a backlash against the negative impact of market reforms, especially the process of privatization.

PRIVATIZATION: SOME OBSERVATIONS

After two years of starting and stopping, the zigzag policies related to privatization provide ample data to compare expectations with reality. As early as 1993, Jan Bossak offered certain preliminary conclusions:

1. The privatization program should be an element of overall economic strategy.
2. Privatization and private sector development should be better harmonized with financial and structural policies.

3. The Polish lesson clearly indicates that delay in reform of the financial and tax system and lack of a structural policy lead to new distortions and higher costs that prolong the adjustment process.
4. The higher costs and slower pace of reform and privatization are undermining social and political support for the reform, including the privatization program.
5. It is important to pay more attention to the privatization program, not only as a legal and management issue, but also a complex economic, social, and political problem.
6. Social and political support is of crucial importance. Thus, it is very important to reduce apprehension and attract employees to participate in the program.
7. A recessionary environment slows down the privatization process and discourages foreign investment.
8. The positive lesson of the Polish privatization is confirmation of the usefulness of different methods.[19]

Many issues surrounding commercialization, NIF operations, and implementation needed to be negotiated. In retrospect, delay and changes in the implementation of the MPP, as viewed in the light of Professor Bossak's critique, not only doomed Pawlak to failure, but also created risks that the Oleksy government had to face. These risks included:

1. *Risks of Diminishing Interest.* The government privatization proposals had generated only limited interest. Recession was a factor. Another was the public perception of the reduced opportunity for quick personal gain. Fear also existed among workers that privatization meant a loss of jobs, a lower standard of living, and less job security. Social consensus appeared to be weakening. Society, indeed, was hovering at the "brink of social endurance."

2. *Risk of Worsening Financial Conditions of SOEs.* Yves Fortin, representative of the European Bank for Reconstruction and Development (EBRD) in Warsaw, commented in *Zycie Gospodarcze* that "due to delay in program planning and approval, the financial situation of many enterprises deteriorated, changing the conditions of their access to capital."[20]

3. *Risk of Diminishing Interest of Foreign Investors.* Wieslaw Rozlucki, chairman of the board of the Warsaw Stock Exchange, commented on 28 November 1994 in *Gazeta Wyborcza* that "foreign investors don't like the fact that the Mass Privatization Program hasn't gotten off the ground. At some point, this became the symbol of Polish impotence. They are also worried about political disputes and the plan to introduce a tax on the sale of stocks."[21] Moreover, these same investors may now have other options in Central and Eastern Europe and Russia.

4. *Risk of Straining Relations with World Bank/IMF.* In October 1994, the World Bank issued a report on the Polish economy. The report

was "largely positive on the overall situation," but indicated "that the existing opportunities must be taken advantage of fully, in order to maintain the momentum for change." The report also noted "several dangers," including "the slow-down in the pace of privatization."

Paul Knotter, World Bank representative in Poland, cited major areas of concern in the World Bank Report, stressing that "privatization is one of the main policies to achieve the goal (greater productivity). It is therefore of critical importance that privatization be accelerated rather than slowed down." The report itself noted that among the problems that must be addressed was that privatization had progressed more slowly than desired. "It needs a decisive push forward to prevent stalling."[22]

THE MPP

The Mass Privatization Program (MPP) had been designed to privatize the large SOEs of Polish industry, known as the WOGs. MPP had been languishing for nearly six years. The voucher plan was an early intention of the reformers, and voucher privatization theory even pre-dated Solidarity. Privatization, including the novel system of awarding ownership certificates to every citizen, was on the agenda of the Round Table discussions (5 February–5 April 1989) and a centerpiece in Lech Walesa's 1990 presidential campaign. The creation of the Ministry of Privatization (then called the Ministry of Ownership Transformation) was one of the first acts of Tadeusz Mazowiecki when he became prime minister on 1 August 1990. The Ministry of Ownership Transformation began to function on 1 January 1991. Its first minister was Janusz Lewandowski, considered to be the father of MPP through the *certificate and voucher* method.

MPP was incorporated in the September 1990 package of privatization proposals of the ministry to the Sejm. In the legislative process the proposed *Privatization Law* underwent 18 drafts before it finally passed the Sejm (30 April 1993) and the Senate (7 May 1993)—and then only by a slim margin. The *Law on Privatization of SOEs* was signed into law 18 May 1993 by President Walesa.

Between 1993 and 1996, MPP fell victim to politics and to changing, often contradictory, attitudes about privatization on the part of successive governments. Finally, on 30 November 1994, procedures and mechanisms essential to the implementation of the legislation were authorized. Thus, 30 November 1994 is the date the Ministry of Privatization considers to be the official beginning of the MPP Program. Even then, the introduction of many key policies, procedures, and processes for implementing the MPP were delayed into late 1995 and early 1996.

At last, what is termed "the nonconventional" voucher privatization program became operative. Then, MPP received a new name. The former

MPP is now officially called the National Investment Fund (NIF) Program.

In order to deal with the NIF Program, the government itself was reorganized by President Kwasniewski in October 1996. The Privatization Agency was assigned to the Ministry of Treasury, with yet another new minister to be appointed. By this time, all of the preliminary and organizational aspects of the NIF Program had been accomplished. Kwasniewski promised to make the NIF Program work. The infrastructure was in place and prospects were generally encouraging.

The mass privatization process has been described as complex by Strong, Reiner, and Szyrmer, "involving a number of laws; state legislative, administrative and judiciary authorities; local governments, political parties; social organizations (labor unions and organizations of employers); managers and workers of enterprises; domestic and foreign buyers, and restitution claimants."[23] The interplay of these factors and players contributed to the almost six-year delay in the implementation of this particular phase of privatization.

Leszek Balcerowicz had devised a transition plan for economic reform that came in time to be called the Balcerowicz Plan. It included a form of mass privatization that would be required to transform the SOEs. He called this program *transformational privatization.* He concluded that "in the inherent conditions of the European post-socialist economies a rapid rate of transformational privatization can only be achieved if the techniques of mass privatization are used."[24] The techniques of mass privatization to which Balcerowicz referred are the *nonconventional techniques of privatization certificates and vouchers,* which allowed citizens to obtain shares in state companies at a nominal or symbolic price. Early in the process, Poland adopted in voucher-type MPP theory, but it was the last of the former Eastern Bloc countries to implement it.[25]

As Frydman and Rapaczynski pointed out: "The presupposition of all the mass programs is that effective privatization must be based on a free or nearly free distribution of privatized assets, since only in this way can the scarcity of capital and valuation problems be overcome. . . . All mass privatization programs foresee the creation of some intermediary institutions that could concentrate the dispersed citizen holdings and [which] exercise monitoring and supervisory powers on behalf of the small stakeholders."[26]

Lavigne suggested that the free transfer of shares to the public involves two main variants: (1) distribution of vouchers, or coupons, to be converted into shares in operating companies; and (2) distribution of shares in investment funds or holding companies that in turn have shares in companies.[27] Poland chose the second variant as the basis for its mass privatization program. However, technical constraints and political obstacles gravely impeded developments in Poland from the initial 1990 Mass Privatization Program (MPP) to the newly named and currently operative

1996 National Investment Fund (NIF) Program. As it was finally constituted, the NIF Program involved 512 state-owned companies, representing most industrial sectors, out of the 3,000 companies that the state continued to own to 1996.

Van Brabant pointed out a phenomenon that was certainly operative in the case of Poland: Policy makers invariably understated the dimensions and nature of various "adjustment problems." Moreover, powerful forces of inertia and the resistance of the central-planning system thwarted the operation of a market economy.[28]

A chronology in the form of a life cycle analysis of the MPP/NIF from inception, conception, birth, infancy, early childhood, a period of benign neglect and near death, resuscitation, revival, and adulthood appears at the end of this chapter.

THE NIFS

Under the NIF Program 15 funds have been established as joint stock companies. Firms qualifying for the NIF Program are first transformed into joint stock companies with both a Supervisory Board and a Management Board. The largest stockholder is the Treasury. The Treasury transfers the majority of its shares to the NIF pool according to the previously established formula.

The NIF Program is designed to transfer a significant part of the assets of the state sector to all adult citizens of Poland for a nominal fee. (The creation of the NIFs answers one question: how to create capitalism in a nation without capital or capitalists?) The NIF Program helps effect this transfer while at the same time it focuses on the *restructuring of SOEs*, enhancing their competitive capacities. "The National Investment Fund [Program] in Poland therefore differs from the mass privatization programs executed in some Central and Eastern European (countries) and Russia. Their voucher programs have achieved a quick transfer of companies to the private sector but without any specific mechanism for their restructuring."[29] Because of this restructuring provision, the NIF plays an important role in economic reform in Poland.

The reason for the nominal fee for certificates is explained by Professor Bossak: "A fee of zl. 20, much less than their attributable book value, partly compensates [for] the losses incurred by the population at the turn of the eighties and nineties due to inflation in the value of saving deposits and additionally [is] an element of social justice."[30] Zl. 20 was equivalent to an $8.00 purchase price.

The national budget set aside significant capital for each of the 15 funds. In addition, the NIFs have access to a loan facility with the Bank of Poland. That arrangement permitted financing the first two years of the fund manager fees (up to $3.2 million per fund), using proceeds from a World Bank/European Bank for Reconstruction and Development (EBRD) Loan. Piotr Stefaniak, director, Ministry of Privatization, NIF and Mass Investment Programs Department, indicated: "The idea from the outset has been to rely on self financing, the basic cost is payments to the management companies, which come in two parts: a fixed portion, or 15 percent of profits 10 years after selling NIF shares, and a flexible portion, which depends on the profits the funds register."[31]

Jan Bossak, board chairman of NIF No. 2, reported that over 8 percent of Polish industry, construction, and commerce is represented in the NIF portfolios. He detailed the situation as follows: In terms of sales, the largest group of companies is represented by the food industry (8%); the largest group in number is from electro-engineering (16%); the largest portion of a branch of national production is represented by light industries (25%); and over 20 percent of mineral production is included in the NIF.[32]

Investors could participate in the MPP/NIF Program in three ways: (1) purchasing shares in the individual companies participating in MPP; (2) purchasing universal certificates for eventual conversion; and (3) purchasing shares in NIFs when they are listed on the stock exchange.

The MPP/NIF Program had only just begun to be implemented by the time the Oleksy government was organized. Addressing an *Economist*-sponsored Warsaw conference, Prime Minister Oleksy assured his audience that "reducing inflation and speeding up the pace of privatization are the two key problems his government now faces." He commented that when he took over as prime minister, "he found that Poland's privatization program had stalled . . . we must speed up the pace of privatization."[33]

What Oleksy did not detail were his specific ideas about privatization. However, the perspective of the SLD became clearer with the passage of new privatization legislation. Admittedly, the Act of 1990 needed updating and revising. An attempt had been made during the Suchocka government. The 1995 revision of the legislation, according to *Warsaw Business Journal* commentator Marek Matraszek, "goes a long way to undermining the achievements of the past four years. Hailed as a step forward in the privatization process, the draft legislation is in fact a highly repressive step that politicizes the process and disperses responsibility for its being carried through."[34]

The *1995 Act on Privatization and Commercialization of State-owned Enterprises* was introduced to supersede the *1990 Act on Privatization of State-owned Enterprises*. The most important and the most controversial provisions of the 1995 act related to (1) a new approval process for the commercialization and the privatization of nearly 4,000 SOEs; (2) changes more favorable to employees; (3) commercialization "for purposes other than privatization"; and (4) more explicit rules for direct and indirect privatization. Direct privatization referred to the sale or lease of SOE assets directly to a private sector firm. Indirect privatization referred to the sale of shares in a commercialized firm. The 1995 legislation included a number of new routes to privatization: (1) commercialization by debt conversion; (2) SOEs that have already been commercialized may be managed by third parties under contract; and (3) employee ownership with Treasury participation. The 1995 act provides for multiple incentives and preferential terms to encourage the involvement of domestic investors.

The 1995 legislation required that any privatization involving alcohol, airports, arms, banks, energy, insurance, or telecommunications must be approved by the Sejm. Any decision to begin commercialization requires approval of the Council of Ministers. Previously, commercialization was initiated by the minister of privatization under the rules of the *Commercial Code* (1934).

Those who favored the 1995 law argued that it furthered the stabilization and restructuring efforts begun in the Pawlak administration. In reality, this 1995 enactment reflected a legislative desire to *slow down* the privatization process. Employee rights were enhanced. Employees now gained a 15 percent share of commercial companies for free rather than a 20 percent share at half price. Moreover, they gained one employee-elected seat on the Management Board in all companies of over 500 employees. The 1995 act provided that employees had the right to two-fifths worker membership on the Supervisory Board. The right of Workers' Councils to veto the commercialization/privatization process, one of the complicating provisions of the 1990 act, was eliminated.

What then was the basis for the widespread criticism from Solidarity, the Freedom Union (UW), and the Business Center Club, Poland's largest entrepreneurial organization? What was the reason for President Walesa's veto of the act of 1995? The most highly disputed provision of the 1995 legislation centered on the issue of commercialization. Commercialized firms would now come under the jurisdiction of provincial governors, who had very little incentive to move commercialized firms into the private sector. Under the provisions of the 1995 act, governors acquired the right to nominate managing directors and employee board representatives for the commercialized firms. Governors gained the unique opportunity to reward political allies, former party members, and *nomenklatura* with choice appointments. The 1995 act widened the opportunity for political favoritism in the privatization process. The role of the national minister of privatization would be reduced to simply carrying out whatever privatization decisions were made at the *voivodship* level.

Matraszek stated it succinctly: "Firstly, it makes privatization much less certain. By failing to establish that commercialization of state enterprises is only the first step to privatization, it makes [it] more likely that a commercialized enterprise will stay that way. . . . Secondly, the law politicizes the privatization process by making it much more dependent on interministerial bargaining." He continued: "Most commentators agree that the law is a disaster, and that its success rests on the good intentions of the coalition parties. However, these good intentions . . . do not seem to exist."[35] Another concern was that the law would open the privatization process to special interests by requiring permissions from the full Council of Ministers and the Sejm. This process would give political groups, like the PSL, a significant opportunity to exercise a negative influence on the process.

The *1995 Act on Privatization and Commercialization of State-owned Enterprises* passed the Parliament on 21 June 1995. President Lech Walesa vetoed the legislation. The Sejm overrode his veto by three votes. That action required the president to either sign the legislation or refer it to the Constitutional Tribunal. President Walesa chose the latter option. Walesa contended that some of the provisions of the new law infringed upon the constitutional principle of separation of powers. In his letter of transmittal to the Tribunal, the president cited 11 provisions that he believed did not conform to the Constitution. While the appeal was before the Tribunal, the *1990 Privatization Law* remained in force.

The time required for Tribunal consideration made it impossible for it to respond immediately. The Tribunal eventually rendered its opinion but not until after the November 1995 presidential elections. The Tribunal agreed that three provisions of the legislation were violations of the separation of powers and were unconstitutional. They were: (1) conferring on the Sejm the authority to privatize select sectors of the economy and requiring specific industries to seek permission of the Sejm to privatize; (2) conferring on the Council of Ministers the right to sell shares in SOEs without specific regulations; and (3) permitting the Council of Ministers to lease SOEs to employees without specific regulations. New legislation, the *Act of 30 August 1996 on Commercialization and Privatization,* approved 20 December 1996, would resolve these constitutional issues by providing that each of these processes would still be controlled by the Sejm, but only indirectly and only after receiving proposals from the Treasury Privatization Section of the Ministry of Economy.

Meanwhile, during the fall of 1995, the impending presidential elections became the focus of public attention.

PRESIDENTIAL CANDIDATES SPEAK OUT
ON PRIVATIZATION

In the presidential election of 1990, a program of mass privatization had been a key element in the campaign of Lech Walesa. The privatization issue persisted throughout the 1990 to 1995 period. In the first round of 1995 presidential elections, scheduled for 5 November 1995, 17 persons declared as candidates, although two candidates withdrew before 30 October. All 15 candidates were questioned by *The Warsaw Voice* about their positions on various national issues, especially privatization.

Three candidates, each of whom ran as independents, had their own mass privatization plan—including President Lech Walesa, who continued to float his earlier proposal of an outright gift to every Pole of zl. 100 million (old).

Two other former prime ministers were among the candidates. Jan Olszewski, representing the Movement for the Polish Republic (ROP), favored "Solidarity's enlarged share-voucher proposal." Former prime minister Waldemar Pawlak of the Polish Peasants party (PSL) stressed that "fast privatization (is) harmful" in that it "fails to maximize property values." The remaining nine minority candidates held various views on privatization from "modest" support to outright opposition.[36] Finally, Aleksander Kwasniewski, representing the Democratic Left Alliance (SLD), supported the present privatization law, but expressed the belief that all popular share-holding schemes were "unrealistic."

The range of views of presidential aspirants reflected the variety of positions held by most average Poles. They suggested a certain ambivalence, hesitancy, and scepticism of the public at large about the whole privatization process.

Kwasniewski and Walesa gained the highest support in the first round of voting (5 November 1995) and thus were the finalists in the second round (19 November 1995). Kwasniewski was elected and was inaugurated as president on 23 December 1995.

Analysts believed that the time had come for Poland to update its privatization strategy and to develop a comprehensive time-bound plan that would embrace the many enterprises still remaining. President Kwasniewski committed his administration to renewed privatization efforts, especially implementing mass privatization. By now the multitrack approach had functioned long enough to have successes and failures that would be valuable benchmarks for developing refined strategies. As 1995 closed, the possibility existed that the momentum generated by the resolution of the long-awaited MPP and the excitement and the potential of the emerging NIF Program would be just that incentive. Polish transformation still needed increased foreign investment, a government commitment to more aggressive privatization, recharging of social consensus, increased public interest, and further citizen education about the long-term effects of the market economy.

The Polish MPP finally emerged renamed and revitalized. The expectation existed that the NIF Program, fully implemented and wisely administered, would be a key mechanism for further economic development as

Poland looked ahead to the year 2000 and increased citizen involvement in the emerging free market system.

Chronology of Life Cycle of MPP/NIF

Inception	Mid-1980s by Solidarity economists.
Conception	Round Table (7 February–6 April 1989).
Gestation	Semi-free Election Campaign (May–June 1989).
	Balcerowicz Program adopted (December 1989).
	Ministry of Ownership Transformation established (April 1990).
	Law on Privatization of SOEs introduced (July 1990).
	(Seven months of debate and 18 drafts amended to satisfy left-wing deputies.)
Birth	Ministry proposes first MPP legislation (September 1990).
Infancy	Presidential election. Walesa wins, favors rapid MPP (December 1990).
	Lewandowski, father of MPP, becomes minister of privatization (1 January 1991).
	PPP and MPP languish in Parliament committees (1991–1992).
	Jan Olszewski elected PM (23 December 1991). No action on MPP.
	Ministry unveils detailed MPP legislation (August 1992).
	Law defining establishment, operation, and privatization of NIFs adopted (30 April 1993).
Childhood	PPP (with MPP) passes the Parliament (Sejm) (30 April 1993).
	PPP (with MPP) passes the Senate (7 May 1993).
	PPP (with MPP) signed into law (18 May 1993).
Near Death	Bogdan Pek, Sejm privatization chair, calls for cancellation of MPP aspect of PPP (July 1993).
Benign Neglect	Waldemar Pawlak elected PM (September 1993).
	Pawlak and his Peasant party opposed to MPP/NIF plans.
	Pawlak delays all MPP/NIF until 30 November 1994.
Resuscitation	Pawlak signs MPP/NIF authorization/action on NIF Supervisory Councils (24 November 1994).
	Kaczmarek now permitted to sign NIF incorporation documents (30 November 1994).
Revival	30 November 1994 considered the real starting date for NIF.
	Candidates for NIF boards selected (December 1994).
	15 NIFs authorized by Notarial Act (19 December 1994).
	Choosing and signing agreements between Supervisory Council and management firms Arrangements concluded (12 July 1995).
	Allocation of the original 413 enterprises to 15 NIFs (July 1995).
Adulthood	NIF is implemented, universal certificates distributed (22 November 1995).
	Additional 99 firms approved, added to NIF (December 1995) as joint stock companies.

11 million certificates sold by March 1996.
Certificates traded on Warsaw Stock Exchange (15 July 1996).
26 million certificates sold by 22 November 1996.
NIF Program now in full operation.

Note: PPP—Polish Privatization Program; MPP—Mass (voucher) Privatization Program; NIF—National Investment Fund

Chapter Eight

Economics and Politics after Shock Therapy

"This is perhaps one more proof of the historical rule according to which revolutions tend to devour their children."

Ryszard Rapacki

OVERVIEW

The initial euphoria over political developments in Poland since August 1989 has in many ways turned to somber realism, as attention has been focused on the practicality of reforming society and restructuring the economy in the postcommunist era. Prominent Solidarity activist Zbigniew Bujak noted: "There is no fast, easy transition from totalitarianism to democracy."[1]

On the political side, Poles seem a bit wary of their fragile "experiment with democracy." Many have demonstrated an impatience with the pace and results of reforms. The Polish electorate has exhibited some of the same characteristics as their neighbors in Romania, Bulgaria, Albania, and Lithuania have. Continued political, ethnic, and religious strife in the former Soviet Union (Armenia, Chechnya, Azerbaijan) and the slow death of Yugoslavia and Albania as unified nation-states have not added to sustained optimism.

In 1992, James Wedel noted that trade and investment were critical factors for assuring success in the process of economic transformation. Short-term "quick fix" solutions or endless rounds of political squabbling would not suffice. Wedel added that the region was "in danger of becoming a playground for consultants and a dumping ground for surplus commodities of only marginal value."[2]

Nearly at the end of the twentieth century, Poland has certainly made considerable strides in the process of transformation into a Western, democratic, and capitalist nation. In this regard, Poland has been part of a more generalized process of renewal and reform that has gripped the entire region. In some nations, the process has been accomplished at a far lesser speed or embarked upon with a far lesser degree of democratic enthusiasm than in Poland. Yet, in varying degrees, all of the nations of Central and Eastern Europe shared fundamental objectives, which became part of the core process of Polish reform, begun in August 1989 with the selection of Tadeusz Mazowiecki as Poland's prime minister.

OBJECTIVES OF THE REFORM

1. *Attaining political stability and pluralism, through holding free and multiparty elections.* This goal was accomplished in Poland as early as 1991, and to a large degree in all nations of the region by 1992 to 1994. The process of democratization was critical in order to "create working, sustainable [political] institutions that can promote the process of reform."[3]

2. *Implementing a program of real economic reform with the evolution to a full market economy.* The process was well on its way in Poland by 1991 but is still ongoing in other nations of the region. It involves an emphasis on the development and nurturing of a substantial private sector and a parallel reduction of the state sector through a program of privatization in a multitrack process.

3. *Assuring the development of strong democratic institutions in a true "civil society."* This will nurture a genuine respect for internationally recognized human rights, the rule of law, and the protection of minorities.[4] The attainment of this objective is a special concern in the former Soviet Union, Bulgaria, Albania, and Yugoslavia.

4. *Creating and nurturing basic institutions of capitalism.* These include banking systems, credit institutions, customs and clearing houses, currency exchanges, a viable stock market, and investment funds and vehicles.

5. *Creating a political and diplomatic process, dedicated to encouraging friendly relations with the United States, Western Europe, Russia, and the former members of the Warsaw Pact.*

In attempting to join the family of Western European nations, a major foreign policy objective for Poland has involved its potential entry into NATO. The process, discussed seriously as early as 1991, was begun in earnest in December 1966. In this context, it is important to note that Aleksander Kwasniewski, who defeated President Lech Walesa for reelection, was quick to reaffirm that Poland's goal was to become one of the "central pillars" of the alliance, and not merely an outpost.[5]

In reviewing the nascent period of Polish economic reform and transformation, First Secretary Gorbachev provided an umbrella to the reform process by removing the specter of Soviet military intervention from the political equation. By the time of the Round Table in 1989, Gorbachev had renounced the Brezhnev Doctrine. Later, by advocating a radical reform, or *perestroika*, of the economic and political systems in the Soviet Union, Gorbachev removed the Soviet Union as a conservative ally of the opponents of reform.[6] Polish reformers were free to operate in an atmosphere of confidence that their efforts would not meet with Soviet military intervention. Speaking at a Czechoslovak-Soviet Friendship Rally in April 1987, Gorbachev outlined the basis for this important change. He stated: "No one has the right to lay claim to a special position in the socialist world."[7]

SHARED GOALS

While nations in the region stand at various stages of development, political pluralism, and economic progress, it is generally agreed that three goals were shared in common:

1. Stabilization of the economy to suppress hyperinflation;
2. Transformation of the socialist, monocentric economic system into a market economy, with fundamental changes in ownership and the demonopolization of the state sector of the economy; and
3. Privatization of the economy through creation of new shareholding companies, joint stock companies, joint ventures, the sale of state assets, the creation of national investment funds, and the creation of small business enterprises.[8]

In many ways, the Polish experiment in democracy and in creating a market economy stands as the bellwether for all of the nations of Central and Eastern Europe.[9] Shock therapy reforms instituted in the period 1990–1991 were a bold attempt to overcome the crises and upheavals that had gripped Poland for nearly all of its 45-year history under communism. The *Wall Street Journal* recognized this preeminent fact in a feature article in 1990, "In East Europe, only Poland makes hard decisions."[10]

Zbigniew Brzezinski also underscored the importance of Poland in the drama of Central and Eastern Europe: "The failure of its [Poland's] experiment would provide a disastrous lesson for others."[11] From a closer perspective still, Tadeusz Mazowiecki, the first democratically elected prime minister in the region, spoke eloquently of the Polish experiment: "For the past six years, we have been carrying out a program of transition to a market economy. We have paid the high and inevitable price of a drop in production and in our standard of living. However, let us keep in mind that this price is something temporary, while the positive results will be long lasting."[12]

IMPEDIMENTS FACING ECONOMIC AND POLITICAL REFORMERS

In evaluating the political and economic situation, several impediments to prospects for long-range success existed in varying degrees in all of the nations of the region. They must be addressed before sustained economic progress could be assured:

1. *The possible reemergence of hyperinflation.* This would threaten the societal consensus necessary to sustain reform efforts.

2. *The disequilibrium created by a rapid rise in unemployment and the existence of underemployment.* This is especially pronounced in the industrial-working class, as society continues to hover at or near the "barrier of social endurance."

3. *The lack of a mature capital market and savings, the problem of evaluation and assessment of assets being prepared for the mass privatization process (the Lenin Shipyard in Gdansk comes immediately to mind),*[13] *and the existence of severe "bottlenecks" in settling foreign accounts.*

4. *The pressure to increase nominal wages in the face of price increases.* Poland, as well as many of the nations in the region, still experienced "market-clearing Western prices and Eastern wages."[14]

5. *The existence of the nomenklatura,* a privileged class in an officially "classless society," in the governmental bureaucracy, and in a host of private enterprises, businesses, banks, and foreign trading corporations organized since the demise of the authoritarian communist system, is problematical.

6. *Continued political instability.* Twenty-nine political parties competed in Poland's first national election campaign in 1991. In the 1993 parliamentary elections, there were six national tickets.[15] For some, political instability was seen as a more serious problem than economic uncertainty.[16] This instability manifested itself into a literal revolving door of postcommunists (sometimes acting in coalition governments) taking the reigns of democratically elected governments throughout the region.

While no one predicts that any of the nations of the region will somehow "fall back into communism," many observers are concerned that the region might lapse into a protracted period of cynicism, deflated expectations, ethnic or religious violence, or hopelessness—a time reminiscent of the Poland of 1981 to 1989, before the Round Table bargain led to the demise of the closed communist system.

It is now apparent that the entire region was standing at another crossroads. On one hand, if the reforms failed, the region faced an endemic "Balkanization" of the type witnessed in Yugoslavia or Albania, or in several of the Russian republics. On the other hand, many saw the region on the verge of the "threshold of success," which was being made possible by the opening up of the system.

It is against this backdrop that an analysis of the state of the Polish economy and politics in the period 1990 to 1995 will be undertaken. In chapter 9, "Quo Vadis, Poland?" we will offer our views on the future of Poland as it advances toward the new millennium.

POST TRANSITION ECONOMICS

How did the Polish economy perform in light of these substantial impediments? By 1995, the World Economy Research Institute believed that the role of the private sector had been firmly secured. In 1995, it further increased as the private sector contributed nearly 58 percent of GDP, compared to 56 percent in 1994, 50 percent in 1993, and less than 30 percent in the period 1990 to 1992. The share of the private sector in employment stood at nearly 60 percent.[17] However, the road to generally positive economic news has not always been steady.

Gross Domestic Product (GDP) increased by 2.6 percent in 1992; 4.6 percent in 1993; and 5.2 percent in 1994. After a disastrous drop of 11.9 percent in 1991, industrial output increased by 2.8 percent in 1992; 6.4 percent in 1993; a hefty 12.1 percent in 1994; and a respectable 9.4 percent in 1995. Equally as important, productivity increased 5.5 percent in 1992; 5.6 percent in 1993; 4 percent in 1994; and 6.8 percent in 1995. The Central Statistical Office (GUS) reported that following the steep plunge from 1990 to 1993, there was an increase in total real income in both 1994 and 1995. This was true of both wages and salaries (an average 5.5% increase) and social security payments (5.1% increase). In the period 1990 to 1993, however, private farmers and industrial wage earners in state-owned enterprises were the two groups most severely hit by the deep recession. From 1990 to 1993, real incomes of farmers fell by half, while those of blue-collar wage earners tumbled by 35.7 percent below the 1989 levels.

In absolute and relative terms, the deterioration in the position of wage earners and private farmers from 1990 to 1993 may best explain the steady erosion of broad public support for changes in society. Rapacki noted somewhat wryly that it is indeed a paradox that blue-collar workers and farmers, the dual core of the Solidarity movement, were the "main losers at the beginning of the road from central planning to the market." While it is certainly true that the situation of farmers has marginally improved (output improved by 16% in 1995), but it was still 12.6% below the 1989 level. Rapacki continued, "This is perhaps one more proof of the historical rule according to which revolutions tend to devour their children."[18] The privatization program saw a decrease in worker authority over enterprises, the dismantling of Workers' Councils, and the loss of co-management perquisites guaranteed to workers by the *1981 Law on Workers' Self-management* and the *1990 Privatization Law.*

Pensioners grumbled the loudest about social and economic change, complaining that they were the "forgotten class" in Poland's march to the market. Yet, until 1995 pensioners marginally benefited from the unusually high and rising proportion of pensions to wages: 45 percent in 1989; 55 percent in 1990; 58.6 percent in 1991; 59.2 percent in 1992; and 74 percent in 1993 and 1994. In 1995, the percentage slipped to 70.4 percent of the average monthly employment compensation.[19]

POLAND'S ECONOMY IN 1995—A DETAILED LOOK

In their report on the Polish economy in 1995, the World Economy Research Institute commented:

1. "1995 was another successful year for the Polish economy. This is undoubtedly a result of the systemic reforms and stabilization program launched six years [ago] and the economic policies pursued by successive governments.
2. Another year of dynamic economic growth [a 7% rate of growth of real GDP] has brought an easing of one of the gravest social problems: high unemployment.
3. The year was also characterized by good results in Poland's international economic relations."[20]

Several observations may be made that highlight the cumulative effect of the transformation process:

1. Nineteen ninety-five exhibited the *fastest rate of growth in the Polish economy since 1992*.[21] Poland's GDP grew by just under 7 percent. Industrial production increased by 10.2 percent, and investment increased by an impressive 19 percent. GDP totaled some 115 billion USD, or $2,988 per capita.

2. *Inflation* continued to be problematic, although there was a "relatively small drop" in the inflation index from 1994 (29.5% to 27.8%).

3. *Unemployment* fell by 225,000 individuals—from 16.5 percent to

15.2 percent; however, the problem of discouraged workers and underemployed workers continued to persist.

At the end of 1995, total employment stood at nearly 15 million individuals in the official labor market. However, one of the main characteristics of the labor market has been the high percentage of unregistered employment in the gray, or second, economy. Interestingly, even the Central Statistical Office (GUS) has begun to study this phenomenon and published its findings in 1995.[22] According to GUS, more than two million individuals were employed in the gray market in 1995, with major sectors including agriculture, construction, repairs, retailers, and neighborhood services (child care, small-scale repairs, small shops).

During 1995, the government made an effort to change laws affecting the labor market. Legislation will shift the priorities from traditional "passive measures" (such as providing unemployment benefits and early retirement incentives) to more "active" measures (such as job training, vocational education, and increasing the minimum wage). The government hopes that widening the difference between the size of benefits (zl. 260) and a larger minimum wage will make work more attractive.[23]

4. The main sources of Polish *household income* included wages and other forms of employment compensation and social security payments (old age and disability pensions and unemployment benefits). Capital gains (interest and dividend payments made to individuals) have had little effect on income growth, although the Pioneer First Trust Fund, Poland's first mutual fund company, maintained more than 250,000 active individual accounts.

After a steep drop in the period from 1990 to 1993, *incomes increased by 5.3 percent in 1995*. Both wages and salaries (5.5%) and social security payments (5.1%) increased.[24] At the end of 1995, gross monthly income increased by 32.8 percent in absolute terms, reaching zl. 726.97 or $302.90. For the first time since 1989, all sectors of the economy saw an increase in compensation in real terms. Overall, wages and salaries increased by 3.4 percent in the corporate sector and 3.7 percent in the government sector, taking into account the inflation index.

In 1995, nearly 9.1 million Poles collected old age and disability pensions. The average gross monthly pension was zl. 511.69 ($213.20), 70.4 percent of the average monthly compensation. The average monthly pension for farmers was the lowest at zl. 298.89 ($124.54). In real terms, 1995 saw an increase of 3.3 percent in gross old age and disability pensions, brought about in substantial terms by two inflation-indexed adjustments in March and December. Social security benefits and welfare payments increased by 9.9 percent to zl. 5.5 billion (nearly $2.3 billion). Reflecting the change in government policy toward a more activist bent of education and training, there was a 42.8 percent increase in aggregate unemployment benefits, which totaled zl. 3.6 billion ($1.5 billion). GUS also determined that there was a 0.5 percent increase in real per capita income in 1995. The largest increases were registered among farmers (6.4%) and the self-employed (3.6%).

5. In terms of *consumption expenses,* households spent an incredibly high 40.4 percent of their incomes on food in 1995. Housing expenses, including heating and energy, also continued to *take up a disproportionate share of household budgets.* Statistics indicate one ominous trend. Incomes and consumption of the richest 20 percent of Polish households[25] are five times as high as the incomes and consumption of the poorest 20 percent. These households are comprised mainly of families with more than two children and the unemployed.

When considering the performance of the economy during 1995, several conclusions can be drawn. First, there is no doubt that the short-term macroeconomic performance of the economy has improved, despite somewhat of an "underperformance in the inflation area." Yet, alarmingly, public perception was changing and confidence was on the wane.[26]

Second, it may be argued that economic policy displayed more continuity and congruity under postcommunists from 1993 to 1995 than it did in the period 1990 to 1993 during a variety of Solidarity or Solidarity-protected governments.[27]

Third, 1995 witnessed a failure on the part of the government to sustain "radical, systemic, and structural reforms." There were still 3,610 state-owned enterprises. Three hundred eighty-six Treasury companies were being prepared for privatization.[28] Many of the larger retail organizations (including Cefarmy, Domy Towarowe Centrum, PHS, Ruch, Pewex, Baltona) were likewise being readied for privatization, as were LOT Airlines and the Cegielski railway engineering works in Poznan (the site of the 1956 worker riots). As part of continuing efforts to reform the financial sector, 19 banks and other financial institutions were "in line for privatization." Because of the scope of the efforts that remained, it was critical for the government to act boldly and decisively. The government was also called upon to pursue vigorously the privatization process begun in the chemical, brewing, cement and lime, and electro-engineering industries.

Yet, in 1995, the government undertook several actions that were incompatible with market mechanisms. These actions had the potential to "unleash strong disincentives for economic agents to behave according to the logic of a competitive environment."[29] Chief among these actions was the increase of "direct government intervention[s]" into the private market. One observer stated: "I would be more optimistic if the state would take its hands off business."[30] The government expanded the number of public agencies being financed from revenues of the central budget and attempted to renationalize some key sectors of the economy, such as banking, "[with] clear trends to set up and strengthen state-owned or state-controlled holdings and cartels in industry" (including the Polish State Railways and the coal mining industry).

There was once again a distinct possibility that schizophrenic governmental actions might lead to another period of the "lost opportunities" or "misused chances" that characterized both the Gomulka (1956–1970) and Gierek (1970–1980) regimes.

Marek Lubinski of the WERI offered some insight into the nature of the dilemma that faced Poland: "One of the crippling legacies of the past is the structures of the economy with its prevalence of heavy industry [the WOGs]. Restructuring is always a long and costly process and in Poland it is additionally handicapped by strong political pressures."[31] Support for reform was declining in the midst of a "depressed economic mood," whether or not justified by the facts. Many were skeptical that the government of Wlodzimierz Cimoszewicz would have the political will to continue to press for difficult economic goals[32] that may not meet with widespread societal approval. In essence, would Poland continue to "make the hard choices"?

POLITICS SINCE SHOCK THERAPY

Ryszard Rapacki provided a context to a discussion of the politics since shock therapy. Rapacki concluded that during the initial period of the transformation process, "the number of social groups who may be deemed losers far exceeded the number of gainers."[33] Forty-three percent of wage earners slid below the poverty line in the first half of 1992.[34] In 1993, GUS reported that a third of the population lived under the poverty line. Is there any wonder that a skillful combination of reconstructed communists, joined by their newfound Peasant party partners, and aided by their allies in the *nomenklatura,* could appeal to the fears of those who had been left behind in the process of transformation?

As early as 1990, Zbigniew Brzezinski noted that "the failure of its [Poland's] experiment would provide a disastrous lesson for others."[35] We now see that despite initial optimistic predictions, the process of transformation has proved much more costly, wrenching, and socially disorganizing than originally envisioned. It has had a profound effect on Polish politics.

Skepticism is rampant. Many believe that the government (no matter whether it is led by Mazowiecki, Bielecki, Olszewski, Suchocka, Pawlak, Oleksy, or Cimoszewicz) and the presidency (whether filled by Walesa, Kwasniewski, or perhaps even the enigmatic Tyminski) somehow represent "phantom interests." Many Poles also believe that politicians were acting on behalf of "future generations" rather than meeting the needs of existing social groups in society.[36] The situation has produced an endemic political instability (seven governments in less than seven years), political posturing, and demagogy. It has given successive governments very little room to maneuver with critics on both the right and the left. In retrospect, the 1991 candidacy for president of the Canadian emigre Stanislaw Tyminski and his "Party X," which dealt a staggering defeat to the presidential hopes of Tadeusz Mazowiecki and the charges of spying leveled against both Prime Minister Jozef Oleksy and former President Lech Walesa stand as marquee examples of the ingrained political turmoil and chaos that have gripped Poland.

Mazowiecki, Bielecki, Olszewski, Suchocka, Pawlak, Oleksy

Jan Olszewski had come into office in December 1991 as the leader of a five-party coalition government. President Walesa had strongly resisted pressure to name Olszewski as prime minister, but finally relented when it became apparent that none of his choices were likely to win parliamentary approval. Olszewski was a founding member of the Christian National Union (ZCh-N), a party with a reputation for extremism and sometimes fanaticism. It was a strongly nationalistic party, allied closely to the Roman Catholic Church. The ZCh-N stressed the critical importance of family and moral values. During its brief tenure, it introduced legislation to criminalize abortion and to introduce religious instruction into Polish public schools.

Olszewski was determined to make a "clean break with Poland's communist past" and to end the "forgive and forget" policy of Tadeusz Mazowiecki and Jan Krzysztof Bielecki. Olszewski believed that Mazowiecki and Bielecki had cheated Poles of the "fruits of their victory over communism" by failing to decommunize. Soon, Olszewski became embroiled in a bitter personal struggle with President Walesa, asserting that Walesa himself had "succumbed to communist influence."[37]

On the economic side, the Olszewski government offered a somewhat critical appraisal of the Balcerowicz Program. It attacked the Balcerowicz Program as being too liberal, and for not taking into account the negative impact of the resulting recession. It offered a program of greater state intervention, promising to implement what it termed would be a "breakthrough" or a "radically different strategy." However, Olszewski recognized that economic reality left very little room for maneuvering, and the government began to "concentrate its efforts primarily on the domestic political sphere."

Olszewski's tenure in office was marked by constant turmoil. Olszewski's minister of defense, Jan Parys, was forced to resign when he claimed that President Walesa had been preparing a military coup with disgruntled officers. The confrontation between Olszewski and President Walesa over the issue of decommunization came to a head. In June 1992, the Olszewski government literally collapsed after a clumsy attempt on the part of one of its ministers, Antoni Macierewicz, an ex-member of ROP-CiO, to disclose the names and identities of certain communist secret agents and "close collaborators" in state institutions. After the nomination of Peasant party leader Waldemar Pawlak failed to win approval in the Sejm, a new government led by Hanna Suchocka of the Democratic Union was formed.

Suchocka was a devout Catholic who had been a professor of state law at Poznan University. Suchocka had previously served in the Sejm (1980–1985) as a member of the Democratic party (one of the two official minority parties during the communist period); however she strongly supported Solidarity during this period. She was an experienced politician who had been elected to the Sejm as a member of the Solidarity Civic Committee (1989) and later the Democratic Union (1991). As prime minister, she was a realist about the fragmented political equation. Her government was a coalition of two pro-reform parties, a fundamentalist Catholic party and two small peasant parties. She attempted to practice what has been called "normal politics," supporting moderate political and economic reforms. Balcerowicz noted that the Suchocka government continued the program started three years earlier. It tried to strengthen macroeconomic stabilization, to maintain the essential liberal character of the economic system, and to speed up the privatization process.[38] Her government was confronted by a series of industrial strikes, demonstrations organized by farmers, and spirited opposition by some in Solidarity to her privatization program.

Suchocka was forced to make concessions to farmers concerning the introduction of a degree of agricultural protectionism and was also politically coerced into granting farmers subsidies for fuel. Reacting to labor unrest, the Suchocka government entered into a social pact with trade unions that modified wage controls and increased workers' rights in the privatization process. Rapacki commented about the dilemma confronting the Suchocka regime: "It [could] either meet the demands thus making the same economic problems reappear later in a more acute form, or stick to its declared policy line and risk being overthrown by a populist-oriented party/coalition."[39] The Suchocka government surprisingly lost a "no confidence" vote in the Sejm by a single vote in May of 1993 and was forced to submit its resignation. Suchocka agreed to continue in office until the 19 September parliamentary elections. Hanna Suchocka is still generally thought of as a "personable and highly regarded professional woman" whose personal reputation for competency and integrity was not damaged during her tenure as prime minister.

THE TURNING POINT: PARLIAMENTARY ELECTIONS OF 1993

By the time of the 1993 elections to the Sejm, the political situation in Poland had crystallized. In March 1992, more than 129 political parties had been officially registered in democratic Poland,[40] giving weight to the oft-repeated political joke: "Wherever there are two Poles, there surely are at least three political parties." In the 1993 elections there were, by contrast, only six national tickets.

One of the national tickets was the Democratic Left Alliance or SLD. The SLD was itself a coalition of the Social Democracy of the Polish Republic (SdRP) and the Polish Socialist party (PPS), both with strong ties to the communist past. The SLD, however, supported market reforms and the privatization program, but demanded a greater consideration for the interests of labor and for continued "central intervention" into the economy in order to reduce the social costs of transformation.

A second non-Solidarity party was the Polish Peasant party (PSL), which as a traditional agrarian party represented the interests of farmers and courted the support of the Roman Catholic Church.[41] To the surprise of many observers, the electorate decidedly swung to the left and to non-Solidarity parties. Contrary to most pre-election polls, the overall turnout was 10 percent higher in 1993 than in 1991, with 52 percent of eligible voters participating.

Post-Solidarity parties polled an aggregate 48.1 percent of the vote, a 7 percent drop-off from 1991. However, because of Poland's unique electoral system, of the 460 seats in the Sejm, post-Solidarity parties captured only 131: Democratic Union (UD), 10.6 percent—74 seats; Union of Labor (UP), 7.3 percent—41 seats; and President Walesa's Non-Party Bloc to Support the Reforms (BBWR), 5.4 percent—16 seats. The SLD gathered 20.4 percent of the vote and held 171 seats in the Sejm. Its partner, the PSL compiled 15.4 percent of the vote and captured 132 seats. Leszek Moczulski's Confederation for an Independent Poland (KPN) polled 5.4 percent and elected 16 deputies. A German-minority party also elected four members.

The most dramatic defeat was suffered by parties that had formed the core of the four post-Solidarity governments from 1989 to 1993. Only the Democratic Union, which had supported the Suchocka government, maintained its representation in the Sejm. Janusz Golebiowski commented that the "net result [of the 1993 elections] was a vote for the continuation of democratic change and rule of law, but with a definite slowdown in the pace of market reforms and a greater degree of state intervention."[42]

As a result of the elections, a "left-coaltion" government was formed. It was led by Waldemar Pawlak, the leader of the PSL. Pawlak had led the PSL Program Alliance in the 1991 parliamentary elections, winning 48 seats in the Sejm and seven in the Senate. (A rival peasant group, Solidarity

Peasant Alliance, took 28 seats in the Sejm in the 1991 election. In the 1993 elections, both of these Peasant parties would join together in a united party group.) In 1992, Pawlak's nomination to succeed Jan Olszewski failed when he was unable to win majority support in the Sejm. In 1993, Pawlak assumed the position of prime minister in a partnership with the postcommunist SLD, the senior party in the ruling coalition. The SLD leader, Aleksander Kwasniewski, remained outside of the formal government structure.

As could be anticipated, Pawlak's government was a mass of contradictions. It was confronted by enormous pressures to reduce the social costs of transformation and satisfy pent-up social demands in such areas as pensions, unemployment insurance, and nominal wages. It was also pressured to meet more populist demands to protect the position of farmers, reduce foreign participation in the economy, and raise business taxes and customs duties in order to provide revenues for social spending and state subsidies. As discussed in chapter 6, Pawlak introduced measures that slowed down the privatization process. He was forced to bow to workers' demands to retain the powerful Workers' Councils and to provide shares to workers in privatized enterprises, measures viewed as disincentives to foreign investments.

However, in retrospect, the tenure of the Pawlak government was a period of relative social and economic stability, marked by a decided decrease in industrial unrest and labor militancy. The SLD-PSL coalition seemed more prepared than its Solidarity predecessors to cope with labor unrest, even with the major strikes that occurred in state-owned enterprises, in the transportation sector, and in public service areas such as education and health services. Golebiowski concluded that the reason for the decline was the change that had occurred in the structure of the economy. A majority of Polish workers now worked in the private sector where unions were much weaker and where workers exhibited a reluctance to strike. Golebiowski noted that even in public service areas, economic transformation had made workers keenly aware of the link "between their welfare, and above all job security, and the health of the firm."[43]

By the midpoint of 1994, the "radical-left" government had turned out to be neither very "left" nor "very radical." It billed itself instead as a "strong supporter of privatization." It announced that it would "push ahead with a mass privatization scheme in 1994." Perhaps, as the *Financial Times* reported, it was true that "senior SLD members' experience in running a bankrupt communist economy converted them to the virtues of private enterprise."[44]

In the end, however, Pawlak would become embroiled in endless personal and political conflicts with President Walesa and his SLD partners. In the summer of 1994, President Walesa embarked upon a course of conduct that would destabilize the political scene. Perhaps reacting to public opinion polls that indicated a sharp drop in his own popularity (down from 70% to about 27%), the president indicated that he no longer had confidence in the prime minister. The SLD likewise made it known that it felt a reconstruction of the government was necessary. Finally, in February 1995, President Walesa publicly announced that Pawlak was simply "not up to the job." After President Walesa vetoed a number of acts passed by the Sejm, including the crucial Budget Act, Pawlak was forced to resign. Pawlak's resignation led to the accession of Jozef Oleksy to the post of prime minister. No one could deny Oleksy's direct ties to Poland's communist past.

Oleksy had served as head of the Social Democracy of the Polish Republic (SdRP), the successor to the Polish United Workers' party. It counted among its leadership such individuals as Aleksander Kwasniewski, Leszek Miller, Slawomir Wiatr, and Wlodzimierz Cimoszewicz. Oleksy had been speaker of the Sejm and was known for his administrative abilities. Oleksy publicly favored a "go slow" policy on privatization and protectionist economic policies.[45] In fact, economic policies remained quite stable under the leadership of Finance Minister Grzegorz Kolodko, an economist with no direct political affiliations who had been appointed during the tenure of Prime Minister Pawlak. Poles looked forward to a period of relative political stability and continued economic growth.

Once again, however, events would overwhelm intentions. In December 1995, allegations surfaced that Prime Minister Oleksy had collaborated with Soviet and later Russian intelligence officers. This crisis led to the resignation of Oleksy and the elevation of Wlodzimierz Cimoszewicz of the SLD to the post of prime minister.

Political Configurations

An analysis of the political groupings prevalent from 1991 to 1995 may help to place the political situation in proper context as Poland prepared for the 1995 presidential election.

Political groupings in Poland might quite reasonably be described as either *post-Solidarity*, that is, parties "genetically descended from the Solidarity mass movement of the eighties," and *non-Solidarity*, that is, parties with "other than Solidarity ancestry."[46] In 1989, the Solidarity bloc had smothered all opposition and won 70 percent of the votes cast. More than 62 percent of voters turned out in this election. Just a year later, despite a "war at the top" between Prime Minister Mazowiecki and Solidarity leader Walesa, Solidarity candidates polled just over 60 percent on the first ballot in the presidential elections. The non-Solidarity candidate, Stanislaw Tyminski, captured 23.1 percent on the first ballot. Wlodzimierz Cimoszewicz polled 9.21 percent in the 1990 election as the candidate of the postcommunist left. In the 1991 elections for Parliament, post-Solidarity parties captured a solid 55 percent of the vote.

A Splintered Solidarity

Within the post-Solidarity camp,[47] it was possible to identify a left, a traditional "social democratic" grouping in the Union of Labor (UP); a center, composed of the Democratic Union (UD) and the Liberal Democratic Congress (KL-D); and a right, composed of the Polish Convention and the Christian National Union (ZCh-N).

The Democratic Union (UD) was perhaps the most influential and prominent post-Solidarity group. It had inherited the mantle of the Democratic Action Civic movement (ROAD), which was founded by Zbigniew Bujak and Wladyslaw Frasyniuk. ROAD had been established with the support of Bronislaw Geremek and Jacek Kuron. In 1990, ROAD had opposed the candidacy of Lech Walesa for president and supported the candidacy of Prime Minister Mazowiecki.

The UD was a broad coalition of the left (on such issues as shock therapy and maintaining a strong social safety net) and the right (rejecting nonmarket socialist solutions). In 1991, the UD emerged as the strongest party, capturing 62 seats in the Sejm and 21 in the Senate. However, the UD captured only 12.31 percent of the popular vote. The KL-D (also called the Smallholder party) won 37 seats in the Sejm and six in the Senate. It was headed by Jan Krzysztof Bielecki, elected to the Sejm in 1989 as a member of the Solidarity Civic Committee, and Janusz Lewandowski, minister of ownership transformation. Bielecki succeeded Mazowiecki as Poland's second democratically elected prime minister.

On the right, the main party was the ZCh-N, described as a "strongly authoritarian Catholic party marked by a fanatical intolerance"[48] It polled nearly 9 percent in the 1991 elections, capturing 49 seats in the Sejm and nine in the Senate. The ZCh-N provided Poland's third postcommunist government, that of Jan Olszewski. The ZCh-N strongly supported the reintroduction of religious instruction into public schools and the criminalization of both abortion and birth control.

This configuration was essentially maintained as post-Solidarity parties entered the 1993 elections. Late in the cycle, however, President Walesa formed the Non-Party Bloc to Support the Reforms (BBWR), positioned on the center-right of the spectrum.

Within the non-Solidarity grouping, the left was composed of the postcommunist Social Democracy party (SdRP), the successor to the Polish United Workers' party (PZPR), which had dissolved itself in January 1990. The party gained 60 seats in the Sejm and four in the Senate in the 1991 elections, garnering 11.98 percent of the vote and emerging as the second strongest party. The SdRP was joined by the Polish Socialist party (PPS), whose "radical wing," led by Jozef Cyrankiewicz, had collaborated with the Polish Workers' party to create the PZPR in 1948. The historian and Solidarity biographer Jan Jozef Lipski helped to refound the PPS in 1987. The SdRP allied with certain of the trade unions and a portion of the PPS to create a "bloc" called the Democratic Left Alliance (SLD). The SLD abandoned central planning and supported a wide range of market reforms and the fragile privatization program. However, it demanded a greater concern for the interests of Polish workers and more direct governmental intervention in the market to preserve the economic position of the unemployed and pensioners.

The non-Solidarity group also included the Polish Peasants party, a typical agrarian party, which had evolved from the peasant movement in Poland. During "People's Poland," the communists reorganized the Peasant party in 1947 as the United Peasant party or the ZSL. This party was represented in substantial numbers in the Sejm and enjoyed a false public persona as an independent political force. After 1989, the ZSL was led by Roman Jagielinski, who opposed a broad-based privatization program. Major rival parties within the peasant tradition (one with the name PSL) existed. One was led by Roman Bartoszcze, a rural Solidarity activist. Bartoszcze had been a candidate for president in the 1991 presidential elections, but managed to win only 7.15 percent of the popular vote. There was also a PSL-Solidarity group, led by Jozef Slisz and Henryk Bak, which ironically favored capitalist development in the countryside and Poland's entry into the European Community.

In the 1991 elections, the Peasant party was divided. The PSL Program Alliance, led by future Prime Minister Waldemar Pawlak, took 48 seats in the Sejm and seven in the Senate, with a total of 8.73 percent of the vote. The Solidarity Peasant Alliance captured 28 seats in the Sejm, winning 5.46 percent of the popular vote.

The "radical" populist and nationalist right in the non-Solidarity camp was composed of the Confederation for an Independent Poland (KPN), initially formed in 1979. The KPN had fiercely opposed the Round Table as a sellout of Polish interests. Led by Leszek Moczulski, a co-founder of ROPCiO in 1979, the party based its existence on nationalism (a frequently scrawled slogan seen on vacant walls was "Polska dla Polakow"), economic protectionism, preservation of the social safety net, and continued opposition to a rapprochement with the Soviet Union or its Russian successor state. Moczulski received a personally disappointing 2.5 percent of the vote in the 1990 presidential election. However, growing popular discontent with the Balcerowicz Program pushed the KPN vote to 8.7 percent in 1991, an election in which it captured 44 seats in the Sejm and four in the Senate.

There were also three other minor parties: the fiercely anticommunist Realpolitik Union (UPR) on the extreme anarchist right; Tyminski's "Party

X," which won four seats in the Sejm, and the Party of Self-Defence; and one other political grouping that merits brief attention—the Polish Party of the Friends of Beer (PPPP)—founded in 1990 by the actor and political satirist, Janusz Rewinski. The PPPP won 3.27 percent of the vote in the 1991 parliamentary elections and elected 16 of its members to the Sejm. It has engendered widespread popular interest in postcommunist Poland as a group that pokes political fun at the more traditional political parties and institutions. It counts members on both the left and right.

PRESIDENTIAL POLITICS

The resurgence of postcommunists in 1993 and the accession of Jozef Oleksy to the position of prime minister led to rampant public speculation (strongly encouraged by President Walesa himself) that somehow Poland might slip back into communism. This would become a flash point in the presidential election of 1995.

Lech Walesa had assumed the presidency in December 1990 after considerable pressure had forced General Jaruzelski to resign from the post. Walesa and his supporters were no longer content with the bargain struck at the Round Table that had been reduced to a simple slogan: "Your President, Our Prime Minister."[49]

The presidential election of 1990 resulted in the "War at the Top" in Solidarity ranks, approximating the worker-intelligentsia split of pre-1980. Walesa's accession to the post of president, a position that did not carry any major executive powers under General Jaruzelski, began a period of nearly five years of protracted struggles with the Sejm and succeeding governments.

President Walesa sought to change the political situation from a cabinet- to a presidential-type government. Under President Walesa's vision, the president would exercise broad powers over the executive and the legislative branches. The president would be able to issue decrees having the full force of law, would oversee both the judiciary and the office of public prosecutor, and would possess even wider powers to dissolve Parliament. President Walesa insisted on his interpretation of the Constitution that invested the president with "general authority in the field of external and internal security of the state." The president thus claimed the authority to appoint or at least veto appointments of the ministers of defense, interior, and foreign affairs. These ministries were commonly referred to as the "presidential ministries." Walesa vetoed bills on six occasions and exercised his lawmaking powers on 10 separate occasions. He asserted his "dominance over the National Broadcasting Council, and established within the security services (UOP) and armed forces informal powers of command and his own advisory apparatus."[50]

President Walesa forced the resignation of Defense Minister Piotr Kolodziejczyk and continued to press for the appointment of a minister of foreign affairs who was clearly unacceptable to the SLD-PSL ruling coalition.

Nineteen ninety-five was a presidential election year. Walesa understood that his position in Poland had seriously eroded since the early days of Solidarity. His presidential powers had been limited by the passing of the Little Constitution of 17 October 1992, stripping him of legal power to recommend the dismissal of the prime minister or members of the cabinet. The Little Constitution also limited presidential authority to dissolve Parliament, unless the legislature failed to pass the critical budget bill within three months of submission by the government, or unless the Parliament was unable to produce a majority government.

The 1995 Presidential Election

As the presidential election approached, Walesa was the frequent butt of political and personal jokes. Individuals commented about his inability to speak "proper Polish." In the summer of 1994, Walesa ranked 19 out of 20 in popularity among Polish politicians and his approval ratings hovered around 5 percent. John Pomfret of the *International Herald Tribune* noted that Walesa's precipitous "slide from grace reflects the profound ambivalence many Poles feel for the revolutionary fire sparked by their leader. While Mr. Walesa is still hailed abroad as a great revolutionary, in Poland he gets little credit for the benefits brought by his revolution."[51]

In February 1995, President Walesa publicly spoke out in favor of the resignation of Prime Minister Waldemar Pawlak, whom Walesa said "was not up to the job." Walesa embarked on a negative strategy of "trench warfare" with Parliament. He vetoed legislative acts, including the critical Budget Act, and referred them to the Constitutional Court. Walesa played both the SLD and the PSL against each other and precipitated a cabinet crisis in March 1995. A new prime minister, Jozef Oleksy, was selected. Oleksy promptly agreed to Walesa's candidates for the three presidential ministries and the immediate crisis receded. Throughout the period, however, while the political situation remained in turmoil, events did not significantly upset public policy. Economic policy remained under the firm control of Finance Minister Grzegorz Kolodko, who generally followed the path setdown by his predecessor, Leszek Balcerowicz.

At the outset of the presidential campaign, numerous candidates stood forward to replace Lech Walesa, chief among them Jacek Kuron, and SLD leader Aleksander Kwasniewski. Kwasniewski had been General Jaruzelski's chief negotiator at the 1989 Round Table. Kuron had undertaken an extensive fact-finding/fund-raising tour of the United States in 1994. Former Prime Minister Hanna Suchocka likewise tested the political waters through an American lecture tour. Most observers gave President Walesa practically no chance of reelection.

As the spring progressed, however, it became obvious that the real challenge for post-Solidarity parties would be to defeat Kwasniewski, who emerged as the candidate representing the "broad perspective of the left." Kwasniewski maintained roughly a 20 percent level of support in public opinion polls, as he announced formally for the presidency in mid-May. Walesa had bounded back to a 10 percent level.

By the fall of 1995, society was severely polarized between negative "anti-Walesa" and "anti-Kwasniewski" camps. The anti-Walesa group focused on the personality quirks of the president. Golebiowski described Walesa's style as "crude and aggressive," "divisive," "hectoring," and "unstatesmanlike." In comparison, Kwasniewski was characterized as "businesslike," "unruffled," "moderate," and "appealing."[52] Walesa was criticized for "overreaching and meddling" into parliamentary politics, and for antics of the coterie who surrounded the president (the "Belweder Group"), seen as both corrupt and venal. Anti-Kwasniewski sentiment focused on his relative youth, problems with his personal background (he had falsely stated that he had an advanced university degree), and most importantly, by fears that the election of Kwasniewski would "return Poland to communism."

Fifteen candidates originally declared for the presidency. Two candidates, Marek Markiewicz and Lech Kaczynski, withdrew as of 30 October. The first round of voting on 5 November 1995 proved to be inconclusive. Five of the major candidates polled as follows: Waldemar Pawlak (Peasant party/PSL)—4.31 percent; Jan Olszewski (Movement for the Reconstruction of Poland/ROP)—6.86 percent; Jacek Kuron (representing the Union of Labor/UP and the "leftist" wing of the Freedom Union/UW)—9.22 percent; Lech Walesa—33.11 per cent; and Aleksander Kwasniewski (Democratic Left Alliance/SLD)—35.11 percent.

Despite predictions by the Center for Social Opinion Research (CBOS) that Walesa would in fact win the runoff, Kwasniewski emerged victorious in the final round on 19 November 1995 by a count of 51.72 percent to 48.28 percent. Contrary to the prevailing view that the election would not engender much public interest, a million more people voted in the runoff than had voted in the first round.

The closeness of the election reflected the deep divisions that existed in society. Kwasniewski was most successful in appealing to those who had suffered the greatest from the economic transformation and who by 1995 had certainly reached or exceeded the "barrier of social endurance." These included residents of small towns and rural areas, and workers who experienced the highest rates of unemployment and falling incomes. Many of these same individuals were workers in state-owned firms, or workers in declining industries like mining, metallurgy, shipbuilding, and heavy industry in general (the WOGs). They had formed the backbone of the Solidarity movement in 1980–1981. Initially, they were very optimistic and enthusiastic about future democratic and capitalist prospects for Poland. Kwasniewski also successfully appealed to the youth vote. He had raised his own version of the character issue by questioning Walesa's failure to pay appropriate income taxes. Kwasniewski was vague on specifics of his economic program, but promised a "kinder, gentler" transformation process.

President Walesa proved to be an especially bitter loser. Supporters contested the election, claiming that Kwasniewski's misinformation about his background had violated election rules. They urged that the election be invalidated. The Constitutional Court received over 600,000 individual petitions. It, however, ruled (9–5) that while Kwasniewski had indeed violated election protocols, the violations were insufficient to invalidate the election. When Kwasniewski was inaugurated as president on 23 December 1995, Lech Walesa refused to attend.

The election of Kwasniewski to the presidency underscored that there was a basic confusion of "capitalism" and "democracy" by the citizenry at large. When the economic reality of shock therapy hit, an acute expectations gap arose in society. Support for the program of shock therapy steadily declined from 45 percent in favor in October 1989 to about 20 percent in 1991.[53] The electorate experienced a decided downturn in public enthusiasm, exasperated by an increasingly acrimonious public debate in society that involved the president, the Parliament, trade unions, and the reconstructed communists, now marching under the democratic-capitalist banner of the SLD.

In this atmosphere, Solidarity and its most visible embodiment, Lech Walesa, became the object of electoral frustration. The 1993 election was clearly meant to be a "warning shot" to Solidarity and President Walesa. The results of the presidential election indicated that the lesson had yet to be learned.

At the conclusion of 1995, Poles joined many of their Central and Eastern European neighbors in opting for what we have termed "policy and performance over politics." Voters demonstrated their desire for concrete results and for a new breed of politicians "who promised to listen to them and help them make sense of the new economic realities."[54] Poles could no longer be persuaded to cast their votes for or against candidates based on political stereotyping, harsh propaganda that condemned out-of-hand the entire period of "People's Poland,"[55] or veiled threats by the hierarchy of the Roman Catholic Church. The Church's overt involvement in politics was feared by many as a sign of unwelcome expansionism into purely civil matters.[56]

In the period 1989 to 1995, Poles were probably naive in believing that the collapse of the former communist regime would instantly bring about a democratic-capitalist regime that would protect the rights and economic position of those who had brought about the 1989 revolution. By the end of this period, however, there seemed to be a growing public consensus that Poland's future did not lie in the hands of ancient rivalries, reconstituted conflicts between civil and religious authorities, or ongoing political dramas.[57] A consensus was developing on the importance of constructing a new and vibrant middle class that is nonideological, and not particularly political. Such a society would be dedicated to *political democracy,* Poland's *return to Europe,* a *principled consumerism* (reflecting Poland's strong religious tradition), and *overcoming the devastations* of the *command-and-control economy* that had inhibited creativity, spontaneity, and real prospects for economic and political progress for more than four decades.

In the next chapter, we shall discuss the important question, "Quo Vadis, Poland?" in light of the development of this new consensus.

Chapter Nine

"Quo Vadis, Poland?": The Polish Economy and Solidarity in Perspective

Looking Forward to the Third Millennium in Poland and in Central and Eastern Europe

"The Polish people do not respond to autocratic commands, whether Communist or otherwise."
Raphael Shen, in *Economic Reform in Poland and Czechoslovakia*

A RETROSPECTIVE

As early as 1993, Ryszard Rapacki of the World Economy Research Institute underscored the importance of Poland "as a reference point for other post-communist countries in Eastern and Central Europe to arrive at more universal lessons and to make the learning curve in these countries steeper."[1] Among the various aspects of the learning curve has been the inherent "irrationality" of the command-and-control economy, which we have identified as the root cause of the collapse of the political and economic systems in the 1970s. Some of the negative characteristics of the monocentric system include:

1. Labor was viewed as a nondynamic entity that would mechanically respond to central commands and directives.

2. Inevitable shortages of goods, endless lines or queues, the absence of consumer choice, and perhaps most importantly, a lack of optimism about overcoming the crisis led to ingrained worker dissatisfaction and frustration. Low worker morale led to declines in productivity, the inefficient use of capital, and production substantially below expectations of planners.

3. Wages bore no reasonable relationship to productivity, quality, price, or consumer satisfaction. Workers consistently "maximized" their personal utility by "minimizing" their effort. The system of central planning accentuated other weaknesses in the working classes that have been described by Professor Richard Hiscocks. These included absenteeism, drunkenness, theft, embezzlement, and corruption, as well as the view that "the misappropriation of state property . . . was not such a serious offense as the theft of private property."[2] Sectorial wage increases were often tied to political rather than economic considerations; for example, the exorbitant wages paid to miners in Silesia, or the massive increases promised by Prime Minister Rakowski in the period leading to the elections of 1989. We have termed this process the "triumph of politics over policy."

4. Every aspect of the manufacturing process—production, distribution, pricing, and consumption—was tightly planned and orchestrated. This left little or no room for delays, breakdowns, shortfalls, or for innovation, quality control, worker input, or a host of other "human" factors. The process became inflexible, arbitrary, and totally irrational. In this atmosphere, overproduction became the overreaching "good." Compliance with the plan meant worker bonuses, perquisites, and other monetary and social indicia of success.

5. External "realities" (membership in COMECON and the Warsaw Pact, and intricate commercial treaty obligations entered into with "fraternal socialist" states, most especially the Soviet Union) dictated that domestic production would be geared toward exports. Consumers bore the brunt of inferior quality products and an almost nonexistent emphasis on what is termed today as "service marketing."

6. International competitiveness was retarded. The economy proved incapable of earning convertible currencies in sufficient quantities to alleviate the lack of products in the domestic market. In the 1970s, the economy was unable to produce revenues sufficient to pay the interest on the accumulation of foreign debt amassed by the wasteful Gierek regime. Central planning led to the dollarization of the economy and to the existence of a horde of special shops (Pewex, Baltona) for use by the elites, most especially the *nomenklatura*. Ordinary Poles were forced to convert zlotys to dollars at a fraction of their worth on the black or second market, which thrived throughout the region in one form or another, and in a fairly open fashion in Poland.

7. Management perspectives were discouraged and innovation was seen as an unnecessary disruption to the socialized plan. Normal entrepreneurial curiosity regarding cost savings, productivity-enhancing techniques, and technological advances was met with a lack of enthusiasm by those further up the planning ladder, whose only "job" was to secure submission, and not innovation. Hiscocks added: "The number of workers and staff employed was frequently higher than was necessary, and

there was great reluctance to carry out the necessary reductions."[3]

8. Risk taking was discouraged and a robotlike mentality was encouraged and rewarded.

9. Financial considerations were ignored or minimized. Cost accounting, unit pricing, credit considerations, input analysis, banking relationships, cost effectiveness, product value, opportunity costs, and other economic factors essential to the functioning of a free market were infrequently considered or rejected by decision makers charged with creating the "rationality" of the central plan.

10. The system created a class of bureaucrats who possessed excellent technical education and skills, especially in the fields of engineering, science, and mathematics. Many individuals in the state-planning bureaucracy were educated at the prestigious Main School of Planning and Statistics in Warsaw and received graduate training in Western universities. However, they lacked basic management skills and were never schooled in techniques of organizational leadership or in innovative concepts such as "total quality management."

In the context of changing the economic system from the monocentric model, the Polish experiment would be unique. If successful, it would overcome the crisis generated by the breakdown in the economic system, establish a free market economy, and create a political democracy.

On the negative side, changes resulted in deep contractions of output, growing and persistent unemployment, rapid rises in inflation, and declining real incomes and consumption. In short, society suffered sometimes dire political, social, and economic distortions and paradoxes, all occurring at approximately the same time. These contradictions have only in the period from 1995 to 1997 fundamentally subsided. The economy has begun to see sustained, positive results and growth. Society has begun to settle into normal patterns.

Looking at the effects of politics and economics on society, the transition from central planning to the market had no historical precedents in terms of the expected sequence of events[4] or intended timetables. The transition resulted in pervasive popular disenchantment and discontent.[5]

The change in public opinion, which galvanized most acutely in 1995, did not materialize overnight. In 1993 the Center for Public Opinion Research (OBOP) poll reported that "no one represents workers' interests in the workplace."[6]

The growing societal frustration resulted in a head-on clash between heightened expectations and a sometimes "sour economic reality" and in the creation of a severe expectations gap. It also resulted in a tragic splintering of Solidarity. The reluctance on the part of the Mazowiecki government to tackle the decommunization problem became a major point of contention in society, an issue that persists until today.[7]

It may only be now that we might attempt to understand the schizophrenic nature of Polish society—struggling for renewal and reform in a series of endemic crises (1956, 1968, 1970, 1976, 1980, 1989), and yet reacting negatively to the results of that very process. For, as the Polish economist Kazimierz Laski noted: "People believed that the removal of the odious communist dictatorship and the indolent command economy would soon bring about a viable democratic regime and a flourishing Western-type economy."[8]

LOSERS IN THE TRANSFORMATION PROCESS

In the transition period from the historic Round Table to 1993, the social costs were truly enormous. For Poles brought up after World War II, open unemployment was a virtual unreality. "The standard of living in real socialism was poor, but life was relatively secure, the rules governing everyday activity comprehensible."[9] Janusz Golebiowski of the WERI wrote that "Societies grew used to relatively egalitarian distribution, regular and secure, though poorly rewarded; employment and free education and health services."[10]

In December 1989, the number of registered unemployed amounted to a minuscule 0.03 percent of the labor force. One year later, the rate reached 6.5 percent. At the end of 1993, unemployment stood at a staggering 16.4 percent of the work force. Many feared that unemployment might rise to 17 percent by the end of 1994, although "officially" it never did. By the end of 1995, unemployment stood at 14.9 percent.[11] The upward trend had subsided but many Poles had been permanently scarred by the experience.

A wide cross section of Poles has been especially hard hit by the so-called big bang or shock therapy program, initiated under the scrutiny of the IMF and the World Bank. One such group has been Poland's youth, where the percentage of unemployed (under age 24)—34.3 percent in 1993—was the highest in Europe, except for Spain.[12]

From a review of the economic data and social statistics from 1989 to 1993, the period during which the attitudes of many Poles were formed regarding the economic transformation, it is possible to identify many broad social groups who were clearly the losers in Poland's march toward the market:

1. Employees of state-owned firms [the WOGs], heavily dependent on the Soviet or COMECON market;[13]
2. Regions with high structural employment (over 20%);
3. Predominantly young and unskilled blue-collar workers in state-owned enterprises, who were the "mainspring of Solidarity's victory" in 1980 and 1989;

4. Sectors and industries most strongly affected by the persistent recession (for example, the textile industry in Lodz or the mining industry in Silesia—nearly 30%);
5. Declining industries like mining, metallurgy, shipbuilding, and all heavy industry, in general;
6. Other unskilled and semiskilled workers; and
7. Rural and small town residents, whose economic prospects were severely limited by a combination of factors—geography, the lack of affordable housing, the inability to move freely in society, cultural and religious traditions, and the lack of educational opportunities.

In the period 1989 to 1993, Poles were confronted by the reality of severe price increases, a drop in the real incomes of most Polish citizens, and a drastic cut in state spending for social welfare programs. While most Poles came to despise the communist system, they nevertheless supported many of the major aspects of the social safety net. Economic dysfunctions put in jeopardy the futures of pensioners, the unemployed, and the beneficiaries of the education system. The lack of central budget support dashed hopes for an overhaul of the fragile health care system, or the cleanup of the environment, badly neglected through nearly five decades of unchecked planned, yet socially destructive, industrial development.

Why was the transformation process so difficult? Prior to the Round Table, the opposition movement was both divergent (linking blue- and white-collar workers, farmers, students, and the intelligentsia) and essentially negative (focused almost exclusively on overthrowing the existing regime). Unlike "Gorbachev communists" in the Soviet Union who believed that the system could be successfully reformed (or their Hungarian counterparts who conceived the notion of "goulash communism"), opposition leaders in Poland had given up any idea of reforming the system. This was especially true after the brutal murder of Father Jerzy Popieluszko in October 1984, an event which we recognize as a turning point in the struggle to rid Poland of communism.

However, Dariusz Rosati, foreign minister in the Kwasniewski government, noted that society ignored or was unaware that economic and political transformations would impose a substantial cost on all of the major groups who initially supported the process.[14] In 1990, Lidia Kolarska-Bobinska insightfully wrote that in pre-1989 Poland, only the "myth of the free market" was prevalent in contrast to the "existing misery" and as a symbol of the prosperity in the West, especially in the United States.[15] Janusz Golebiowski of the WERI added: "The market was symbolized by the abundance of goods in the West, not hard work and the possibility of unemployment, the necessity of retraining, individual initiative and responsibility for one's welfare or greater social differentiation."[16] The phrase "they pretend to pay us and we pretend to work" exemplified a system verging on total collapse.

It is now clear that neither the average Pole, who would be urged to stoically accept the most difficult aspects of the reform, nor the government, which often attempted to operate "above politics," understood an essential and basic reality: Poland was a nation where there was little capital or private property, where there existed a basic aversion to risk taking, decidedly antimeritocratic attitudes, and poor work habits ingrained over a period of nearly 45 years. "The necessary implications of the market in terms [of private] ownership, job insecurity and work attitudes were yet to be learned and internalized."[17]

When expectations were not met with speedy results (after all, democracy was created "overnight," why could the same not be true of capitalism?), "confusion, uncertainty, disillusionment and a withdrawal syndrome" set in.[18]

In October 1991, only 42 percent of the population would participate in the completely free parliamentary elections. Popular support for the shock therapy of the Balcerowicz Plan declined steadily from 45 percent in favor in October 1989 to about 20 percent in favor in 1991.[19]

The expectations gap was exaggerated by an increasingly public rivalry for power among five competing political forces: the president and the "Belweder" faction; successive Solidarity governments; the Parliament (Sejm), with 29 political parties represented, but with no one party commanding more than 12 percent support; the trade unions, which showed an increasing willingness to use their strike weapon; and the reconstructed communists, now marching under the banner of the Democratic Left Alliance.

The stunning success of the SLD/PSL coalition[20] in the parliamentary elections of 19 September 1993 was astonishing but not altogether unexpected, given the enormity of the rising expectations gap and a keen sense of disappointment that had arisen in society. In retrospect, the parliamentary elections of 1993 should have been seen as a clear "warning shot" to both Solidarity and President Walesa that society had indeed reached the precarious "barrier of social endurance."

It is clear that from 1990 to 1993, Poland was immersed in a transformation illusion. It faced a critical conflict between the necessity for strong and dynamic central leadership, which was required to sell the difficult process of reform to an exhausted and discouraged population, and a strong tradition in which central executive power (often foreign) was seen as a vehicle for coercion. A fundamental mistrust of government, born out of nearly 125 years of partition, the interwar authoritarian period under Pilsudski, the period of Nazi occupation and brutality (1939–1945), and the more recent communist period (1945–1989), existed. These experiences resulted in an almost complete collapse of the economy and the society under Edward Gierek. They also led to the literal disintegration of the demoralized and fragmented Polish Communist party in the period immediately preceding the Round Table in the spring of 1989. Ironically, the Communist party had been the one institution, in addition to the Roman Catholic church, that had been a constant during the preceding 50 years. Now it too had disappeared from the political stage. However, few mourned its passing!

WINNERS IN THE "NEW POLAND"

Not all segments of Polish society have seen their economic fortunes decline since the onset of economic and political reforms. Among those who have gained from the transformation process have been entrepreneurs in the nonagricultural private sector (+8.5 percent in wages) and beneficiaries of social security (pension) payments (+5.3 percent), amounting to 9.1 million Poles, nearly a quarter of the population.

A new capitalist class has emerged in the nonagricultural private sector, especially in joint venture companies,[21] and in subsidiaries and branches of foreign enterprises. Bogumila Brocka-Palacz of the WERI noted that total aggregate foreign direct investment at the end of 1991 amounted to 700 million USD.[22] In 1995, foreign direct investment amounted to $2.1 billion, and can be further compared to $4.3 billion in the whole 1988 to 1994 period. The number of joint ventures rose from 4,796 at the end of 1991 to 10,131 at the end of 1992.[23] In 1994, there were more than 1.8 million private, nonagricultural firms in Poland, employing fully 30 percent of Poland's work force. By 1995, this figure had jumped to 2,061,291 firms, with 49,419 public sector firms remaining.[24] The contribution of the private sector has been steadily growing since the process of privatization began in 1990. In 1989, the private sector contributed 31.4 percent of GDP; in 1990—45.3 percent; in 1991—47 percent; in 1992—53.5 percent, in 1993—53.5 percent; in 1994—57.8 percent; and in 1995—60 percent.

In this regard, however, the largest barriers to sustained progress may be the unstable political situation, the abuse of political democracy, and the uncertainty of systemic arrangements in such areas as legal, tariff, banking, tax, and exchange rates.[25] Only in 1996 had the political situation somewhat stabilized as two major political forces (the Democratic Left Alliance, SLD, and the Solidarity Election Action, AWS) became major combatants in the political arena.

In the current business environment, the winners in the transformation process can be identified as follows:

1. The newly emerging business class, ranging from small, individual entrepreneurs, distributors, franchisees, and traders (more than

two million) to a small number of successful "billionaire business people." These individuals often base their operations on a networking culture, "exploiting the inconsistencies of the new regulatory framework."[26] In short, many of the winners include the *nomenklatura* elite who have reappeared sporting Western business suits and Western business attitudes;

2. A growing middle class (reported to number more than six million) immersed in the "culture of business";

3. Semiskilled and skilled personnel in high-tech industries (electronics, data processing, management information systems, computers);

4. The financial services sector, including banking and all of the other facets of the growing capital market; and

5. Accounting, legal, real estate, and other business-consulting services.

SOLIDARITY REVISITED

On 10 November 1980, the Solidarity trade union (NSZZ Solidarnosc) was officially registered in Warsaw.[27] Official communist unions, which were organized in the Central Council of Trade Unions (CRZZ), were abandoned by their formerly docile and pliant membership. By the spring of 1981, as many as 10 million workers (over 80 percent of the work force) had joined Solidarity. Solidarity was organized on a regional basis, a configuration intentionally established to be separate and distinct from the 49 provinces of the communist state. Its most important regional headquarters were in Mazowsze (Warsaw), Lower Silesia (Dabrowa-Silesia), "Little Poland" (Krakow), "Greater Poland" (Poznan), and Gdansk.

Solidarity was a divergent grouping of traditional trade unions. It was a distinct social movement clamoring for the reemergence of a civil society. It was also a loosely organized political organization that only later became dedicated to taking political power in the Polish state.

During its initial period (1980–1981), Solidarity was frequently embroiled in acerbic internal disputes and in a series of bitter battles with communist authorities fearful of losing their power and authority. One of the most notable of these battles concerned the initial conflict over registration (Would Solidarity recognize the "leading role" of the Communist party?), the dispute over "free Saturdays," and the "Bydgoszcz affair," where radical Solidarity activist, Jan Rulewski, was severely beaten by state security police.

Solidarity was banned under martial law, but it was not legally abolished until October 1982. Many of its organizers were rounded up, interned, or actually imprisoned. Martial law authorities were headed by the

Military Council on National Salvation (WRON), composed of 22 members. They used the ZOMO (armed police) and the army to break up strikes and other "illegal" activities. Solidarity was forced underground. It only later emerged as an effective resistance-opposition force under such leaders as Zbigniew Bujak, Wladyslaw Frasyniuk, Bogdan Lis, and Bogdan Borusewicz. Walesa and most other internees were released by the end of 1982. Martial law was officially ended on 31 December 1982; however, other emergency regulations continued in force for the next two years, during which time many Solidarity activists were again imprisoned. A complete amnesty was finally announced for early 1986. Poland was effectively ostracized by the West, most especially the United States.

How had Solidarity changed? The "first Solidarity" (1980–1981) was essentially a "bottom up" mass social movement. The "second Solidarity," however, was organized on a "top down" basis, under the auspices of a National Executive Committee chosen in October 1987 and chaired by Lech Walesa. The Executive Committee ceded most of its authority to the Civic Committee (KO), established in December 1988. The Civic Committee represented the "Solidarity viewpoint" in the Round Table and presented a Solidarity slate of candidates in the June 1989 semifree parliamentary elections. (Each candidate's name was displayed proudly on a poster featuring a smiling and confident Lech Walesa.) The Civic Committee played a critical role in the Mazowiecki government. A leading Solidarity activist, Henryk Wujec, was the secretary of the Civic Committee until June 1990.

Solidarity became more mainstream in the period after Mazowiecki assumed the position of prime minister. It established a weekly newspaper, *Tygodnik Solidarnosc,* and a daily, *Gazeta Wyborcza* [Electoral News], which is under the current editorship of Jacek Kuron. However, Solidarity quickly became divided on ideological lines. Leftist radicals like Stefan Jurczyk's "Solidarity 1980" criticized Solidarity's "corrupt deal" with the communists as a sellout. Kornel Morawiecki's "Fighting Solidarity" wing later galvanized itself into the Freedom party (PW).

The Solidarity trade union reelected Walesa as its chair in 1990, with over 77 percent of the vote. It generally supported Walesa in the presidential race of 1990 (most especially in the second and decisive round). However, Walesa's own position began to seriously erode. This erosion was seen most acutely in the defeat of Walesa's choice, Lech Kaczynski, to succeed him as chair and the election of Marian Krzaklewski to the post. (Kaczynski, along with his twin brother, Jaroslaw, would later become bitter personal critics of Walesa.) Krzaklewski announced that henceforth Solidarity would reject "politics," feel free to oppose governmental "financial, social, and economic restructuring measures," and instead embark upon a more traditional trade union course of action.

"Solidarity," as a distinct political party, won only 5 percent of the vote in the 1991 parliamentary elections, capturing 21 seats in the Sejm and five in the Senate. Despite announcing its intention to return to the principles that had guided the period of the "first Solidarity," Solidarity strongly supported the Suchocka government in its early period. Solidarity later turned away from this support and opposed the government's privatization program, which Krzaklewski maintained "threatened the position of workers."

Quo Vadis, Solidarity?

What is the proper role of the first popularly based political institution outside the control of the Communist party in the whole of Eastern Europe? Can Solidarity effectively defend workers' rights in the new entrepreneurship system? Can Solidarity once again gain the support of the electorate in the fall 1997 elections? Some, like Juliusz Urbanowicz of *The Warsaw Voice*, as early as 1993 wondered aloud if "Solidarity [was] a spent force."[28]

In the increasingly procapitalist environment of the early 1990s, Solidarity faced a deep dilemma: What could the trade union movement do as it saw rising unemployment, the real value of its members' wages plummet, and the poorest members of society undergo increasing economic strain and hardship? Raphael Shen wrote: "During Poland's first two and a half years of economic reform, industrial production plummeted, tax revenues fell below projections, unemployment rose, bankruptcies multiplied, and social discontent mounted, all contributing to the destabilization of Poland's young democracy."[29]

During the period 1989 to 1993, Solidarity was faced by a precipitous drop in its membership, a surprising resurgence in membership in the official government unions, and the realization that workers were increasingly reluctant to take part in Solidarity-led strikes. Members were convinced that union leaders had abandoned traditional goals of fighting for improvements in working conditions in favor of playing "political games" or in seeking personal advancement. In practical terms, Solidarity was viewed by many as an obstacle to reform.[30] It was able to topple governments (Bielecki, Olszewski, Suchocka), but it was unable to find a place for itself in the growing private sector, especially in small private businesses that did not rely upon a large pool of unskilled or semiskilled workers. Sadly, like the dinosaurs of *Jurassic Park*, the movement was more at home in the WOGs that flourished in the system of state subsidies and overemployment.

Shortly after Marian Krzaklewski assumed the leadership of Solidarity in 1991, he announced that the protective umbrella that the union held over Solidarity-bred governments would be removed in favor of a vigorous defense of workers rights, aimed at the "completion of the Solidarity revolution in Poland." However, no one, especially in Solidarity, knew what this would mean in practical terms, or could foresee that it might shortly lead to the reemergence of the communists as the dominant force in both parliamentary and presidential politics.

It is only now recognized that Solidarity had no clear-cut program of economic transformation in the immediate period after June 1989. The situation that existed in 1989 was strikingly reminiscent of the earlier period after the Gdansk Accords in August 1980 when Solidarity maintained its members were "workers" and not "economists." Solidarity seemed more intent on reforming the closed political system than the failed economic policies as it literally came to power in 1989.

Yet, economic transformation became the province of Leszek Balcerowicz and his team of economists who had perspectives very different from those of many rank-and-file Solidarity members. This group would later be scorned as "that group from Warsaw," whose attitude indicated to many that "the Polish people are simply instructed to sink or swim."[31] To many, this was a stark reminder of the days of the worker-intelligentsia split prior to the "Polish August" of 1980. The fact remained that while "the movement and its leaders remain[ed] immersed in both the political and economic spheres," society, as a whole, began to gravely doubt the course chosen for economic transformation and reform.[32] One prominent Solidarity leader, Jan Rulewski, likened Solidarity to a "political Frankenstein monster." Quo vadis, Solidarity?

The Future of Solidarity

Electoral support for Solidarity dropped from a high of more than 70 percent in 1989 to just over 52 percent in 1991 and less than 5 percent in 1993. The sharp decline may help to explain the difficult road faced by Solidarity in contemporary Polish society.

"Where Solidarity had proved over seven years of Martial Law that it could not be broken by the police truncheon,"[33] wrote Lawrence Goodwyn in 1991, it has yet to prove that it can be translated into a *democratic governing force*. A key to resolving the dilemma lies in looking at the many facets of Solidarity itself. In reality, there was no one Solidarity even in its incipient stages, and there is no one Solidarity today. Janusz Golebiowski has provided valuable insights into the nature of Solidarity and society in the postcommunist period.

There is a "liberal" Solidarity, favoring a radical transformation of the economy on the order of the reforms implemented by Leszek Balcerowicz in 1990–1991. There is an "interventionist" Solidarity, supporting the "third way," the Hungarian or Czech "dual economy" model. This interventionist model was recently suggested by Chancellor Helmut Kohl as a method for overcoming the deep crisis in the former East Germany. The interventionist model anticipates a large, gradually decreasing public sector alongside a *gradually growing private sector.* Such an approach is characterized by a "considerable degree of government intervention, powerful mechanisms preventing excessive income differentiation, and preservation of the welfare system" in such areas as housing, pensions, education, and health care, on the order of proposals put forth by Waldemar Pawlak, or more recently, by Wlodzimierz Cimoszewicz.[34]

There is a Solidarity dedicated to parliamentary democracy, and to maintaining its place in the political process. This facet of Solidarity maintains a belief in the rule of law, separation of church and state, respect for human rights, political pluralism, and a continued movement toward Western European values and markets, as Poland enters the greater European community. Bronislaw Geremek is a representative of this group.

There is a Christian Democratic Solidarity, led by former Prime Minister Tadeusz Mazowiecki. A significant part of this vision is the Christian National Union, led by former Prime Minister Jan Olszewski. This Solidarity seeks to uphold the position of traditional Catholic values within civil society.

There is a faction of Solidarity that wants itself totally divorced from the political process. It believes that Solidarity should remain always and preeminently a "labor union." It is apolitical and militant in pressing for a traditional union agenda.

Ominously, there is also an authoritarian Solidarity that believes that the process of economic transformation must be shielded and "guided" in a period of limited authoritarian rule, not unlike the historical experience of Pilsudski's interwar period after the coup of May 1926—or the more modern versions found in Chile, Taiwan, and South Korea.

A VIEW TO THE FUTURE

The success of the former communists and their allies in September 1993 and November 1995 is an indication that society had indeed reached a breaking point, that allusive "barrier of social endurance." It is also true that Poland has made great strides in the past seven years. Poland today enjoys a currency that is practically convertible. It has seen the virtual elimination of hyperinflation, and of the permanent shortages seen in the monocentric economy. Poles' purchasing power "far outstrips anything one would estimate from income statistics."[35]

In terms of international/external relations, agreements reached with the London and Paris Clubs allowed Poland to return to international capital markets.[36] Substantial progress has been reached concerning entry into the European Union—perhaps by the year 2000—and the OECD.[37] Discussions regarding NATO membership are moving to a rapid conclusion.

Proponents of Polish membership, among whom can be counted President Kwasniewski, see full NATO membership as another strong signpost of Poland's emergence as a full member-nation of the greater European community, the "common European home" envisioned by Russian president Mikhail Gorbachev.[38]

On the economic front, macroeconomic indicators pointed in a positive and sustainable direction. Nineteen ninety-five saw the fastest rate of growth since the economic recovery began in 1991. Gross domestic product increased by just under 7 percent in 1995; inflation stood at 21.6 percent (fully 10% lower than in 1994). Nominal corporate earnings rose by 32.1 percent. Janusz Golebiowski reported optimistically: "That the economy is performing well is not disputed by anyone in Poland."[39]

Approaching yet another election cycle in 1997, opposition forces argue that the present SLD coalition is reaping the hard-won benefits of programs enacted and implemented by their predecessors. Opponents of the postcommunist coalition (most notably, former Finance Minister Leszek Balcerowicz) assert that current economic policies may in fact be "sapping" these successes and worsening the outlook for sustained future growth and development.

Society likewise has settled into more normal patterns, unlike the cataclysmic and cyclical events of previous decades. Labor strikes were a less frequent occurrence in 1995. A middle class of more than six million is developing with a greater interest in acquiring the trappings and lifestyles of Western contemporaries than in engaging in endless debates over politics. Nineteen ninety-five also saw an increase in consumption by 4.5 percent and a rise in the real value of pensions and average wages (outside the still lagging agricultural sector), which recorded increases for the first time since 1991. After six years of increases, unemployment fell to 14.9 percent, from a high of 16.4 percent in 1993.

In reviewing the period of slightly more than 50 years, it is possible to look at the successes and failures of the process of reform through the "eyes" and actions of many of its major players. We have attempted to tell the story of contemporary Poland through the lives and characters of individuals whom we have identified as critical to their age and era. Some like Lech Walesa and Fr. Jerzy Popieluszko have become our personal heroes. Some like Leszek Balcerowicz and Tadeusz Mazowiecki, as well as many individuals we have come to know personally as friends and colleagues such as Edward Cyrson, Jacek Klich, and Jan Bossak are viewed as true visionaries. Some, like Wladyslaw Gomulka and Edward Gierek are tragic figures in a drama that in both cases began with hope and ended in dashed spirits and in calamity for Poland. Others, like Jacek Kuron, Adam Michnik, Anna Walentynowicz, and Jan Rulewski stand out as men and women of courage and insight in the face of hardship, persecution, and prison.

General Jaruzelski stands as a "shadow figure" whose role is yet to be fully delineated. Only recently has the role of John Paul II been explored for its historical importance.

All of the events discussed must likewise be seen in light of the deficiencies that existed in the economic system that have made the transitional process so difficult, often contradictory, and at times, irrational.

GENERALIZED CONCLUSIONS AND OBSERVATIONS

What general conclusions can be drawn from the past half century? What sense can be made of this period, which began in victory over the Nazis and which ended, somewhat ironically, at the Warsaw campaign headquarters of President Walesa, whose supporters sat in stunned silence in unexpected defeat, asking a simple yet profound question: What went wrong?

First, it is critical that reformers minimize negative consequences of reform efforts (especially severe unemployment) as much as possible. Well-intentioned reformers, even of the superior personal and intellectual caliber of Leszek Balcerowicz and his economic team, underestimated the extent of immediate harm that the transformation process would have on the economy and especially upon the workers who were the backbone of Solidarity in its formative period. In the words of Raphael Shen, "Polish people [were] simply instructed to sink or swim by designers of the shock therapy."[40] Over time, shock was transformed into frustration, despair, anger, cynicism, and denial—what we have termed the "expectations gap." Citizens turned away from support of reform efforts toward individuals or groups who offered "glib" solutions to ponderous economic and social dysfunctions.

Second, reformers essentially made the same mistake as did their central-planning predecessors. They *assumed* a degree of automatic responsiveness on the part of economic actors. Shock therapy was implemented in a spirit of "democratic euphoria," long before any "war at the top," or the emergence of more than a hundred political parties and groupings, all fighting for the attention of society. What was forgotten was that Polish workers were not automatons or robots.

The experiences of the past half century indicate that Poles do not respond well to automatic commands, whether bellowed by communist authorities, all-knowing bureaucrats of the *nomenklatura,* or members of a capitalist "transformation team." Economic revolutionaries in the intelligentsia or from a university setting never cultivated sufficient grass-roots support for reform efforts. Reformers clearly understood where they wanted the economy to go, but only in the broadest and most general sense.

Reformers ignored the fact that nearly 50 years of communism had literally traumatized and exhausted the population. In many cases, reformers in the Ministry of Finance separated their efforts from Poland's history, culture, and religious and political traditions. All too often, they forgot that reform of the economy was designed to better the material lives of the Polish working class. Goodwyn wrote most insightfully and perhaps tragically: "On the night of December 13 [the day of the imposition of Martial Law], many in the Warsaw intelligentsia discovered that in all the months of freedom that dated back to the Polish August, they had not set foot in the house of a worker."[41] In ignoring the social costs of the transformation, and in assuming docile compliance by an energized and awakened working class, the leaders of the transformation process dramatically misread their own people.

Third, economic performance is irretrievably connected to the culture, religion, politics, history, values, beliefs, and sense of "nationhood" of the people. Economic transformation cannot be separated from any of these intercepts. At its core, Solidarity stood for democracy, freedom, and equality. Solidarity also stood for an indomitable human spirit and for the innate, uncompromising dignity of the individual. Solidarity was more than a labor union, more than just "one" of the economic actors—it was a true revolutionary "movement" of principles, ideas, and ideals. In creating Solidarity, Polish workers, aided by their academic advisors, priests, engineers, and lawyers, brought Poland from the darkness of repression into the light of a civil society.

Fourth, the process of transformation will be difficult, socially wrenching, confusing, and oftentimes misunderstood. Essentially, however, the process will work. The success of the economic transformation and of the process of privatization has truly been amazing. Price liberalization, successful anti-inflation measures, a radical opening of the economy to foreign trade and investment, and thus away from autarchy, the establishment of the institutions of capitalism (banks, clearing and settlement houses, the stock exchange), the creation of a convertible currency, demonopolization of the state sector, efforts at the privatization of a great number of state-owned enterprises, and the successful launching of the National Investment Fund (NIF) Program are powerful testaments to the success of the reform efforts. The 7 percent growth in the GDP is impressive by any standard. This growth has been coupled with investment expansion, modernization of existing plants, purchases of machinery and equipment, and an increase in the growth of exports and foreign exchange reserves. These actions are designed to assure growth, future expansion of employment, and a rise in the standard of living for Poles.

Fifth, the political landscape still remains a veritable minefield. Politics is fraught with dissension, disunity, shifting alliances, new configurations, old grudges being replayed, and so forth. However, this is the quintessential Poland! As the electorate braces for another parliamentary election in 1997, it appears that voters may be confronted by relative stability. As early as 1995, two major viewpoints began to come forward to court the attention and allegiance of voters.

The Solidarity Election Action (AWS) and the Democratic Left Alliance (SLD) seem poised to confront each other directly over a wide range of important issues. This clash will help to resolve questions concerning the future course of economics and politics, economic transformation, privatization, restructuring, and maintaining the social safety net for those who were only marginally served by the "egalitarian" tendencies of the former system.

What economic and social challenges confront society as Poland enters its third millennium? What are the "great issues" that Poland will face in attempting to continue on its march to the market?

IMPERATIVES FOR THE FUTURE

1. Attention must be refocused on the *development of human capital* by improving declining educational and health care systems, by encouraging basic scientific research, and by increasing the emphasis on management and entrepreneurial training. Institutions must be developed to improve the long-neglected natural environment and to encourage responsible consumerism, cultural traditions, societal tolerance, and diversity.

2. *The pension and social insurance system must undergo substantial reform* in order to assure its viability in a capitalist framework that often exhibits an institutional hostility towards those who are unable to provide for themselves in an increasingly "go it alone" environment.

3. The government must insist upon continued *demonopolization* of society and its institutions, most especially the insurance sector, railways, transportation, and banking, to assure the deepening role of the market in Polish society.

4. Policies must be put in place to *restructure and reform the banking and financial sector* and the emerging financial service market. Regulators must insist on the creation of a suitable accounting, regulatory, legal, and supervisory framework. The banking sector must be fully privatized, with allowances for State Treasury involvement at some levels to assure socially conscious practices, creditworthiness, and an ability to compete successfully with more experienced and more highly capitalized foreign banks.

In the centrally planned economy, banking was completely centralized. What was considered to be a commercial bank was no more than a branch of the Central Bank. Balcerowicz has described this as a monobank system. The Central Bank in the Polish system was a key instrument of state planning and control. Through its local branches, the Central Bank was expected "to assure that the enterprises maintained such balance between investment, wages, and working capital as the state considered desirable."[42]

Mondschean and Opiela described the situation as follows:

> Under Communist control from the end of World War II to the end of the 1980's, Poland's banking system primarily served as a conduit for transferring funds between the central government and the various state enterprises that controlled the country's economic life. The National Bank of Poland (NBP) served as both central bank and supplier of credit to key industries. [It made] decisions on monetary policy, the allocation of credit to borrowers and the scope of NBP's operations that were made by the central government.[43]

Mondschean and Opiela concluded that "the main problem facing Polish banks today is not that they are too small but [that] they do not have enough capital." The absence of a domestic capital market presents a persistent challenge. "Thus, using foreign sources of funds seems to be a necessary ingredient in achieving the goal of an efficient and sound banking system."[44]

5. Emphasis must be placed on *assuring Poland's reentry into Europe* through institutional arrangements with the OECD, the EU, and NATO. In addition, Poland must continue its efforts to strengthen economic, political, and cultural ties with the Baltic Sea Region[45] (Lithuania, Estonia, Latvia, Denmark, Finland, Germany, and Sweden), as well as continuing the excellent relations forged with the Visegrad Group (Poland, Hungary, the Czech Republic, Slovakia, and Slovenia). At the same time, Poland must continue to make it clear that its interest in NATO membership is not at the expense of friendly relations with Russia or Ukraine or Belarus.

6. The government must insist on improvements in the *efficiency of industry and a restructuring of certain key sectors* of the economy, such as mining, the chemical industry, oil processing, metallurgy, and shipbuilding. It is important for both psychological as well as political reasons that the disaster that befell the Lenin Shipyard and its workers in the fall of 1996 is not repeated in other basic industries.

7. Policies must be encouraged that will *bring unemployment down* to at least half its current level (projections still foresee unemployment in the range of 13–14%), and that will meet the expected increase in the supply of labor in the next century. Planners must insist on the implementation of programs encouraging job growth, increasing the availability of jobs through demonopolization of public employment, encouraging the development of small businesses that exhibit a high degree of labor intensiveness (most likely, a further expansion of franchise and entrepreneurial opportunities). Programs must be developed that provide workers with on-the-job training, extensive training courses, and an expansion of vocational education.[46]

8. The basic strategy at the macrolevel must remain centered around *reducing inflation* (in the range of 15–17% or lower). The strategy must aim at increasing corporate profits, constraining the budget deficit, promoting sustainable growth in the range of 5–6 percent, and increasing individual consumption in the range of 2–3 percent. It should also center on increasing exports in the range of 6–7 percent; and increasing industrial output in the range of 8–9 percent, 6 percent in construction, and 4 percent in agriculture (still the largely forgotten sector). Any strategy must also assure that "real" incomes of Polish citizens will be increased.

9. *Foreign Direct Investment (FDI) should be encouraged.* Leszek Balcerowicz believed that a liberal foreign trade regime was a vital complement to the privatization process and an important precondition to increasing the overall efficiency of the economy. Administrative bottlenecks and legal restraints should be eliminated. Strategic alliances with domestic partners and joint venture activities should be encouraged through liberalization of access to the market and through a revision of laws relating to the ownership of land by foreign nationals and companies. Tariff levels should be reduced or completely eliminated (of course, on a reciprocal basis). Tax and foreign exchange regulations should likewise be liberalized to conform to EU, EFTA, CEFTA, and WTO guidelines and directives, with a minimum of "exceptions."[47]

10. The *privatization program must be maintained, revitalized, and re-energized.* Programs for the disposal or sale of state-owned assets, admission of NIF participation certificates to full trading on the stock exchanges, and the enactment of legislation related to "commercialization and privatization of state-owned enterprises, investment funds, and companies with a foreign capital stake"[48] should be completed.

Social acceptance of the privatization process is essential to its success. Yet, an ambivalent attitude toward privatization was apparent almost from the outset of the process. People expected that privatization would bring about significant improvements in society. What many Poles did not understand was how gradual, how long, and at what price the process might be accomplished. The experts may have understood the time required to convert from one economic system to another, but the complexity of economic reasoning and "systems redesign" were neither known nor understood by the public at large.

Other limitations exist in the privatization process and it will take time for changes to be introduced, to develop, and to mature. These limitations include:

1. A developed market infrastructure is absent.[49] Market research and market analysis, as well as the availability of advisory and consulting services, are preconditions for an effective system of marketing.

2. Recognized procedures for property evaluation are absent.[50]

3. Traditional indices, like return on investment or investment time

lag, which are ordinarily used to measure the performance of a firm and its profitability, are either unavailable or are unreliable. Only now are benchmarks for valuation beginning to emerge.

4. The financial infrastructure is severely limited or in some cases is entirely missing. The capacity to raise domestic capital is problematic. Since reliable data on the profitability of newly privatized firms are still limited, the experience of Polish citizens in investing is very new. Public offerings have not been as great a source of new capital as had been anticipated.[51]

5. The stock market is in its infancy. It has yet to demonstrate that it has the capacity to be a major vehicle for privatization. A strong capital market depends on a mature and developed stock market. The success of the NIFs is tied to the future success of the Warsaw Stock Exchange and the WIG.

6. The quality of the civil service is problematic. Under the former system, civil servants were often "appointed on the basis of their political reliability and lack of personal independence. The new [Eastern European] governments have started to exchange the old personnel, but the process is slow and the new people are often without much experience."[52]

7. There exists a serious shortage of experienced and skilled managers. It was simply an illusion that incumbent managers, steeped in the traditions and practices of the command-and-control system, could be retrained or could be replaced by a cadre of "real" managers. There never was an army of managers trained in the free market simply waiting in the wings; nor can the skills of effective management be instantly acquired. Van Brabant commented that the assumption that new managers will allocate their services properly and will automatically begin to maximize the net worth of their assets is "a vastly unrealistic assumption as few individuals in PETs [Political Economies in Transition] have had proper managerial experience. . . . Managerial skills and experience cannot be acquired quickly in an MBA program, certainly not in an accelerated, compressed version that is at times proposed to PETs."[53]

Looking back at this half century, we believe that the imperatives of transformation and reform indicate a clear course of action for Poland. Poland must adopt a policy for balanced and sustainable growth that embodies a strategy built around five pillars: (1) an economic policy that supports private sector development; (2) increased investment in human development and technology in order to increase productivity; (3) an improved social safety net, assuring an equitable distribution of the gains reaped since the opening of the system in 1989; (4) more effective management of public finances; and (5) an improvement in the governance of the Polish state by reducing endemic political instability.

Realistically, of course, only time will tell the final story of the struggle, begun inauspiciously by the defiant "leap of faith" of an activist, acutely religious electrician at the Lenin Shipyard in Gdansk. Nearly at the end of the twentieth century, it remains to be seen whether the irrepressible spirit of Poland, as part of the larger community of nations of Central and Eastern Europe, may yet prove worthy of the challenge of the postcommunist era.

Chapter Ten

Epilogue

"Poland is coming home."
    President Bill Clinton speaking in Warsaw, July 1997

Since the defeat of President Walesa and the collapse of the Oleksy government in late 1995, several important issues have been resolved and progress has been made on several fronts.

ECONOMIC FOUNDATIONS

Grzegorz Kolodko was the deputy prime minister and minister of finance in the governments of Prime Minister Waldemar Pawlak and Wlodzimierz Cimoszewicz (1994–1997). Kolodko authored the economic program termed "Package 2000." The program linked systemic changes with long-term policies for economic development. Kolodko's policies introduced reforms in the financial sector and demanded fiscal discipline in the state sector. This strategy involved a continuation of Balcerowicz's "hard budget" regime, ending subsidies to state-owned enterprises, requiring that bank credits only be offered on the basis of financial data, and creating real rates of interest for commercial loans. Package 2000 continued the privatization program (albeit at a slower pace), with an emphasis on improvements in the governance of public sector enterprises. The program fostered institutional support for developing entrepreneurship, based upon a sound industrial policy, restructuring of industries, job retraining, and a reduction of unemployment and underemployment.

Kolodko provided an important insight to the period after the defeat of President Walesa in the fall of 1995. Kolodko wrote that "Poland is the only post-socialist economy that has recovered its pre-transition level of output."[1] He offered the following evidence, upon which we will amplify with a review of economic data from 1996 through the midpoint of 1997.[2]

1. Poland's GDP stands 12 percent higher than in 1989, due to an average growth of 6 percent a year from 1994 to 1997. After an increase of 7.0 percent in 1995, GDP growth was recorded at 5.5 percent in 1996. At the start of the year, the Ministry of Finance predicted a 5.5 percent growth in 1997. However, at the midpoint of 1997, Poland's GDP was growing at a 7.3 percent rate, clearly outpacing other nations in the region.[3] Poland is frequently referred to as the "tiger of Eastern Europe."

2. About 80 percent of Poland's foreign trade is now with members of the OECD. Poland was admitted to the OECD on 11 July 1996, an action that validated the transformation process and was a "major psychological boost for its increasingly healthy economy."[4] OECD experts asserted that Poland scored the greatest success of any nation in the region in fundamental restructuring of its economy. However, the growing trade deficit ($12.7 billion in 1996, narrowing to $9.8 billion at the midpoint of 1997) continues to be a major concern. While exports increased by a respectable 7 percent in 1996, imports increased by an alarming 28 percent! Poland must work hard to avoid a new indebtedness trap.

Poland's main export trading partners in 1996 were Germany ($8.41 billion—34.3 percent); Russia ($1.65 billion—6.8 percent); and Italy ($1.30 billion—5.3 percent). On the import side, Germany ranked first ($9.16 billion—24.7 percent); Italy ($3.68 billion—9.9 percent); and Russia ($2.52 billion—6.8 percent). The United States was not ranked in the export category but placed sixth with imports of $1.63 billion—4.4 percent. The increase in the trade deficit can be partially explained by the rise in the value of the zloty, the drop in inflation, the continued lack of real export possibilities, and the decreasing value and demand for commodities such as copper, coal, and coke. In addition, Poland experienced a consumption boom as optimism for the future of the economy rose[5] and long-awaited real pay raises in the public sector materialized for the first time in nearly six years.

3. Poland continues in its march to full membership in the EU. Poland must continue its path of reform, reduce its growing foreign trade deficit, speed up privatization, and continue to "rein in the bureaucracy."[6] Poland's advantages include its large market and its already high rate of compliance with EU requirements.[7] For the fifth consecutive year, the budget deficit will be below the Maastricht target of 3 percent of GDP. The Eu-

ropean Bank for Reconstruction and Development (EBRD) estimates that the budget deficit will reach 2.8 percent in 1997.

4. The Maastricht Criteria require that public debt not exceed 60 percent of GDP. Public debt has been reduced from 86 percent of GDP in late 1993 to less than 50 percent, and 48.7 percent is expected in 1997.

5. The annual inflation rate has experienced a steady decline from 37.6 percent in 1993 to 29.5 percent in 1994; 21.6 percent in 1995; and 18.5 percent in 1996. The EBRD predicted an inflation rate of 18.1 percent in 1997. Kolodko, however, predicted that inflation would be 13.0 percent. At the end of May 1997, inflation stood at 14.6 percent, computed on an annual basis.

6. At the start of 1994, unemployment stood at 16 percent. It was reduced to 14.8 percent in 1995; 13.4 percent in 1996; and was projected by the Ministry of Finance to decline to 12.9 percent in 1997. The EBRD projection was 13.5 percent. Kolodko suggests it will be "slightly less." At mid-year 1997, the unemployment rate stood at 12.2 percent. A change in the social insurance system for unemployment, which significantly tightens the rules for insurance beneficiaries, is expected to reduce the unemployment rate even further.

7. Foreign direct investment is continuing to flow into Poland. In fact, "foreign direct investment has fueled Poland's economic growth so far, and is key to its future success." Nineteen ninety-six saw the greatest influx of foreign direct investment since the onset of the economic transformation. In 1996, foreign direct investment totaled $5.2 billion, compared with $10.1 billion invested in the entire period between 1989 and 1996. According to Waldemar Dabrowski, president of PAIZ, the National Agency for Foreign Investment, "Investing in Poland is no longer a business risk for the world's leading entrepreneurs. Instead, it is sound business sense."[8]

There are several reasons to invest in Poland. According to a PAIZ survey of 864 foreign investors, four factors have been paramount in spurring foreign investors to make firm commitments: first, Poland has significantly lower labor costs in comparison to most Western European nations; second, the size of Poland's potential domestic market (a population of more than 39 million); third, the prospects for continued economic growth; and fourth, the availability of a highly skilled and educated work force. In addition, Poland is considered to be a very stable base from which nations may enter former Soviet markets that have proved quite difficult to penetrate. (For once in its history, Poland's proximity to Russia may turn out to be a distinct advantage!)

The Warsaw Voice Business and Economy Yearbook reported that "foreign investors have seen a boom in sales revenues in recent years. . . . Poles appear to feel that there are areas for which foreign investment is particularly important, including construction, agriculture, telecommunications, recycling and health care."[9]

On the negative side, investors surveyed by PAIZ listed the following areas as problematic: the enigmatic legal, regulatory, and tax environment; the uneven operation of the banking and insurance systems; and inadequacies in the telecommunications and transportation infrastructure.

What is apparent is that Poland has matured as it prepares to further integrate with the European Community and the OECD. Poland's progress on the economic front indicates that it is now inextricably tied to Europe, as its economic, political, and legal institutions have been "systematically harmonized" with those of the West. Yet, several important questions remained unanswered, especially concerning what Professor Clothier has termed as "various hardships" in the privatization of the remaining SOEs. These hardships are manifested in characteristics of the already privatized SOEs, many of which are seen as unrestructured, grossly overmanned in both administration and direct labor, oversized and overcomplicated, saddled with inefficient and inappropriate buildings and out-of-date equipment, and supported by totally inadequate finance.[10]

POLITICAL MACHINATIONS

Maciej Letowski of *Tygodnik Solidarnosc* wrote of the paradox that faced Polish society as it approached the 1997 parliamentary elections: "Before 1993, Solidarity and the center-right had everything: the Sejm, the Senate, the government and the presidency. After 1993 and 1995, nothing remains: Everything is held by postcommunists."[11]

The political situation has remained fractured and contradictory. The scandal that surfaced in late 1995 concerning Prime Minister Jozef Oleksy continued to cast its shadow into 1996. In December 1995, Oleksy was accused of cooperating with Soviet and then Russian intelligence services. The charge was brought by Andrzej Milczanowski, Oleksy's minister of internal affairs who had been appointed by President Walesa. Oleksy and his entire cabinet was forced to resign in January. Wlodzimierz Cimoszewicz, who had been a candidate for president in the 1990 presidential elections representing the ex-communist left, became the new prime minister.[12] His cabinet "represented something for everyone." The PSL gained greater control over economic matters, but lost in their bid to replace Wieslaw Kaczmarek as minister of privatization.

Nineteen ninety-six was also a year of constant turmoil within the governing coalition. The crisis seemed to come to a head when Cimoszewicz (with the urging of President Kwasniewski) fired PSL member, Jacek Buchacz, as minister of foreign economic affairs without the slightest consultation with his PSL partners. The prime minister claimed that Buchacz had passed state funds to private companies connected to the PSL.[13] Another crisis loomed when the Sejm approved a four-bracket tax scale, disregarding the government's three-bracket proposal. The PSL abandoned its partners and unexpectedly voted for the four-bracket proposal. Both the deputy finance minister and Finance Minister Grzegorz Kolodko, as well as the head of the Council of Minister's Office, Leszek Miller, threatened the PSL with dissolution of the Sejm if this action was not reversed. PSL deputies, unwilling to risk early elections (and their seats), capitulated to SLD demands and adopted the three-bracket proposal.

Toward the Parliamentary Elections

During the first half of 1997, seven political configurations and/or parties were prominent. Six were traditional players on the political scene: the Democratic Left Alliance (SLD), led by Cimoszewicz and Oleksy; the Solidarity Election Action (AWS), led by Marian Krzaklewski; the Freedom Union (UW), led by Leszek Balcerowicz, and supported by former Prime Ministers Mazowiecki, Bielecki, and Suchocka; the Polish Peasants' party (PSL), led by Waldemar Pawlak; the Movement for the Reconstruction of Poland (ROP), led by former Prime Minister Jan Olszewski; and the Union of Labor (UP), a traditional "social democratic" party, with leaders such as Zbigniew Bujak and Tomasz Nalecz. A seventh party has recently surfaced and could mean serious problems for both the Left and Right. The National Party of Old-Age and Disability Pensioners (KPEiR) was founded in 1994 to play "the role of a trade union for pensioners." It has attracted interest among many of those who have been clear "losers" in Poland's economic transformation. At the midpoint of 1997, the KPEiR, colloquially known as the "Polish Gray Panthers," was collecting the support of approximately 7 percent of the Polish electorate.[14]

In the summer of 1997, Poland approached the fall parliamentary elections. Two major political configurations, the SLD and the AWS, were poised to confront each other for the support of the Polish electorate. Stunned by their defeat in 1993 by an odd coalition of postcommunists in partnership with the Peasant party, many in Solidarity felt that the fruits of their revolution had been stolen from them. Balcerowicz argued that the postcommunist coalition was reaping the hard won benefits of shock therapy.

There is, of course, some truth to Balcerowicz's complaint. There are also reasons why society turned against the reformers. A combination of interminable internecine warfare and a literal revolving door of post-Solidarity governments resulted in confusion about issues such as privatization, decommunization, and the role of foreigners in the development of the economy. In addition, the perception that as "president," Solidarity "hero" Lech Walesa was both meddling and ineffective led many to turn away from the course begun so optimistically after the Round Table and the equally stunning Solidarity victory in the contract Parliament elections of June 1989.

Society had in fact reached the "barrier of social endurance," presaged by Mieczyslaw Nasilowski, who envisaged that too many changes might literally overwhelm Polish society. Intentionally misled by the postcommunists, insightfully described as "merchants of nostalgia,"[15] society grew impatient with both the pace and results of reform. Many Poles saw their incomes erode and jobs disappear. They saw the bulk of capitalist firms (most especially banks and newly privatized companies) firmly in the hands of prominent members of the *nomenklatura,* who now had a "collective amnesia" about their questionable behavior in "People's Poland." Many Poles saw the government impose harsh measures on its own population and then blithely adopt a "sink or swim" attitude.

Throughout the entire transformation process, society was engaged in a transformation illusion that confused democracy with capitalism, success with struggle, and perhaps most unfortunately, values with material possessions. After nearly 50 years of conflict with the psychological, social, and economic effects of communism, society became exhausted when the revolution did not bring immediate results.

CHALLENGES OVERCOME CHALLENGES REMAINING

We have chosen to consider four topics as we close our study of the past 50 years of Polish economics and politics: church-state relations; the adoption of the new Constitution; the NIFs; and, Poland's acceptance into NATO.

Church-State Relations

Several issues have clouded relations between the Roman Catholic Church and the SLD-PSL coalition. One of the major points of contention was the liberal abortion law passed by the Sejm in October 1996; another has been the long-awaited *Concordat* between the government and the Vatican.

Poland in 1997 is much different from the days of its communist past when religiosity was equated with patriotism and opposition to atheistic communism. Pope John Paul II noted that under communism, the Catholic Church had offered "a space where individual and nation could defend their rights."[16] Despite growing materialism and disillusion with a Church that frequently interferes in purely secular political matters, 35 percent of Poles still attend mass weekly. According to a recent poll, nearly 90 percent of all Poles said that the pope was an authority for them in "religious, national, moral and intellectual matters." Fully two-third of all Poles also saw the pope as an authority in "social and political issues."[17]

The abortion law was especially prominent in the minds of many as the pope began his seventh visit to his native land (31 May–10 June 1997). On 28 May 1997, Poland's Constitutional Tribunal, its highest court, declared that the abortion law passed on 24 October 1996 violated Poland's constitution because it did not protect the "right to life." The court noted that "the highest value in a democracy is human life, which must be protected from its beginning to the end." The Sejm will now have a period of six months to either change the law or attempt to override the decision by a two-thirds majority.[18]

During his 11-day visit to Poland, the pope may have disappointed politicians who had hoped to use his visit to galvanize opposition to the ruling coalition. Instead, the pontiff was praised by both the Left and the Right for avoiding any direct involvement in politics, instead stressing values that would unite all Poles. However, John Paul spoke out forcefully against the evils of abortion. He repeated the words he had spoken after the Sejm had enacted an abortion law that permitted abortion for "social reasons": "A nation that kills its children becomes a nation of the past. It isn't easy for me to say that about Poland because I want it to have a great future." The pope's words guarantee that the abortion question will remain in the forefront of political discussions for the immediate future.

The Holy Father also spoke forcefully about issues of social and economic justice, arguing against an economic system that would exploit workers and deprive them of the "right to rest and take care of his family's spiritual life." The pontiff called attention to the growing problem of homelessness and challenged the government to pass laws "and guide the national economy in such a way that these painful phenomena of social life find a proper solution."[19]

The second issue in contention was the *Concordat*, originally signed on 28 July 1993 in the waning days of the Suchocka government. The *Concordat* is controversial. Deputies from both the SLD and the Union of Labor have voiced opposition to its ratification. Their opposition centers around three unusual issues: burials of nonbelievers, the civil validity of church weddings, and religious education in public schools.[20] A final resolution has been delayed (perhaps until after the results of the fall elections are known), as SLD members asked the Constitutional Court to determine the legality of the *Concordat* in light of Poland's new Constitution.

The Constitution

Although the Roman Catholic Church, elements of Solidarity, and their allies urged a negative vote (or a boycott) on the question of ratification of Poland new Constitution, 52.71 percent of Poles voted in favor of ratification on 25 May 1997. (The turnout was approximately 40%.) The original draft had been rejected by Catholic bishops in May 1996.[21] The bishops objected to the document's "moral relativism," which they said would result in the creation of a "secular, atheistic state." In December of 1996, the Sejm accepted a second draft of a compromise preamble, written by former Prime Minister Tadeusz Mazowiecki. Mazowiecki argued that most Church demands had, in fact, been accepted by SLD deputies—including a pledge that church-state relations would be guided by "respect for autonomy, independence and cooperation for the common good." In addition, the Constitution would contain no specific language providing for the right to an abortion. The final version was overwhelmingly approved by the Sejm on 2 April 1997 by a decisive vote of 451 in favor and 40 against.

The new Constitution contains the following provisions:

1. Parliament will consist of a 460-member Sejm and a 100-member Senate;
2. Parliamentary elections will be "universal, equal, direct and proportional";
3. The president will be chosen in a general election and will serve a five-year term;
4. The president will first designate a prime minister (who will select a cabinet). The Sejm will elect the prime minister. If the vote to confirm the President's choice fails, the Parliament itself will choose the prime minister and cabinet. Upon a failure of the Parliament, the initiative will return to the president;
5. The president can dissolve Parliament after three such unsuccessful attempts or if the Sejm fails to approve an on-time budget;
6. The president has 21 days to sign a law, refer it to the Constitutional Tribunal, or veto it. A three-fifths majority of the Sejm is sufficient to overturn a presidential veto;
7. Deputies in the Sejm may adopt a vote of "no confidence" in the government, but then must designate a new prime minister;
8. The "Presidential Ministries" have been abolished;
9. Only the government may announce a draft budget;
10. No individual can be compelled to reveal his or her religious beliefs;
11. Private ownership and private business is guaranteed;
12. The central bank has been strengthened as it will have the "exclusive right to issue money and set and carry out monetary policy";
13. All citizens have the right of equal access to health care, and free education in public schools.[22]

The new Constitution, signed on 16 July 1997, will take effect in mid-October.

The National Investment Funds

The NIF program was described in detail in chapter 7. The NIF Program involved 512 individual companies within the Mass Privatization Program (MPP). By July 1995, certificates were being freely traded in the unregulated securities market and were quoted for the first time on 15 July 1996 on the Warsaw Stock Exchange (WSE) at a value of zl. 104. Before the listing, certificates traded as high as zl. 115 in early March 1996, and as low as zl. 70 in June 1996. Even after listing on the WSE, certificate prices have vacillated considerably. By October 1996, the high for certificates was zl. 167 ($59.65) with heavy trading. In mid-November the secondary market certificate price held between zl. 140 and zl. 150. "Experts believe Polish banks have already soaked up more than 40% of new certificates," which prompted, among other factors, the opinion that "the Polish Mass Privatization project—despite its opponents past and present—is slowly beginning to gain a reputation as the best program of this type in a post communist country."[23]

On 16 April 1997, certificates were quoted as zl. 150.5. In April 1997, the Securities Commission approved the public trading of 15 NIF stocks on the Warsaw Stock Exchange. On 12 May, conversion began of the MPP "universal share certificates" into NIF shares. Citizens who are holders of the approximately 27.4 million certificates (purchased for zl. 20) will receive one share of each of the fifteen NIF stocks for each certificate held.

By June 1997, NIF stocks were listed on the WSE. This action concluded an important phase of the MPP. The entry onto the WSE of the 15 funds with assets approaching zl. 5.9 billion (nearly $2.4 billion) will increase its capitalization on and will attract a greater number of foreign investors. Moving the remaining SOEs to private ownership or into a similar voucher type system will be the next major challenge facing the government.

NATO

On 8 July 1997, NATO foreign ministers extended an invitation to three former Soviet Bloc nations (Poland, the Czech Republic, and Hungary) to join the alliance in time for NATO's 50th anniversary in 1999. On 10 July 1997, President Bill Clinton spoke to a jubilant crowd in Warsaw's Castle Square and announced that "Poland is coming home." Clinton was flanked by Polish president Aleksander Kwasniewski, who had made a personal point of supporting Poland's entry into NATO, even when this position was strenuously opposed by Russia. President Clinton played a decisive role in gaining the support of NATO members for Polish membership, and in rejecting calls for further expansion to include both Romania and Slovenia at this time.

Through speeches in both Madrid and Warsaw, President Clinton put the NATO debate into its proper historical and political context. President Clinton addressed the question of Poland's isolation behind the Iron Curtain, accomplished as a result of the divisions after World War II.[24] The president noted that "never again will your fate be decided by others. Never again will the birthright of freedom be denied you."[25] In the audience was former President Lech Walesa and former Prime Minister Tadeusz Mazowiecki, sitting in places of honor to recognize their roles in the transformation of Polish society. This was a day when both enemies and friends could exult in the joy of this historic celebration.

The admission of Poland into NATO, however, contains meaning far beyond its military and security implications. It represents Poland's symbolic return to the West and to Western democratic values. It recognizes that Poland has chosen the path of democracy and market reform. In short, Poland's acceptance into NATO is a tangible sign of the rebirth of the civil society that had inspired Polish revolutionaries—workers and intellectuals alike—since the first brave Poles of Poznan took to the streets in 1956, clamoring for dignity and freedom.

PERSISTENT QUESTIONS

Since the opening up of the economic and political systems, three important questions have persisted. One is economic, one is political, and one is sociological.

First, how would it be possible to build a capitalist system in a nation where there was neither capital nor capitalists? Activities undertaken by successive governments were designed to restore private property and to create capitalism in Poland. Included in these activities has been the creation of a strong private banking system to replace the monobank, the genesis of a vibrant stock market, and the founding of other institutions of capitalism. In building and sustaining capitalism, successive governments from Tadeusz Mazowiecki through Wlodzimierz Cimoszewicz have attempted to break the monopoly of state power and to empower individual Polish citizens, although some with less enthusiasm than others. Would the process continue after the 1997 elections?

Actions have included the introduction of a detailed and complex (often contradictory) process of privatization, especially of the large and inefficient state-owned enterprises (SOEs), creation of the NIFs, and expansion of employee ownership through ESOP options—actions carefully scripted to transform the monocentric, command-and-control system into a participative and economically democratic one. The process has seen the creation of a new entrepreneurial class as owners of more than two million small- and medium-sized businesses. It is the emergence of this new class that has fueled the real "economic revolution" in Poland.

Second, what is the proper role in society for post-, now reconstruct-ed-communists and for former members of the *nomenklatura*? The osten-tatious positioning of former *nomenklatura* in the government and in a host of private businesses ensures that this controversy would remain a public concern and would be bitterly contested in the fall 1997 parliamen-tary elections.

From the current rhetoric emanating from the ruling SLD coalition and its chief rival, the AWS, it is obvious that society has never fully come to grips with the issues of decommunization and the role of the *nomen-klatura* in postcommunist Poland. Society remains deeply divided. Many Poles still appear perplexed with the policy of "let bygones be bygones," which permitted the *nomenklatura* to resume a public role in both business and politics. Others fundamentally hold that a democratic government cannot appropriately exclude a class of persons from democratic participa-tion solely on the basis of their associations in the former system. It may be difficult, however, to convince the average Pole that individuals who in their minds "ruined Poland" should now be reaping the benefits of Poland's revolution in such an open and personal way.

Third, what should society do about the position of workers and oth-ers who have seen incomes plummet, industries closed, and the social safe-ty net rapidly disintegrate? Under the former system, society came to ac-cept many of the benefits of socialism. Yet, Polish workers began to feel increasingly alienated from their work in a system that treated labor simply as another impersonal cog in the economic wheel. How ironic that in "People's Poland," the totalitarian state diminished the dignity of its most important actors. In his June 1997 visit to Poland, Pope John Paul II spoke eloquently to this paradox: "Human labor must not be regarded merely as a force necessary for production. Man must not be seen as an instrument of production. Man creates and initiates work. We must do everything to ensure that work does not lose its proper dignity. We must not forget that it is work that serves man, and not man who serves work."[26]

Polish workers (sometimes with and sometimes without the support of the intelligentsia or students) rose up and literally fought their "communist masters" in a series of battles in 1956, 1968, 1970, and again in 1980. The events of 1980, however, were very different. In 1980 society was uniquely united, as workers, farmers, intellectuals, and students joined in solidarity to create a revolution. Even martial law, internments, provocations, prison, the murder of Fr. Popieluszko, and police brutality could not crush Solidar-ity or its ideals of democracy and freedom. In 1989–1990, society was supremely hopeful and confident that things would change dramatically for the better.

When the transformation of the political and economic systems did not result in immediate benefits to Polish workers who had "made the rev-olution," acute frustration and bitterness set in. Bogdan Borusewicz, one of the co-founders of the Solidarity Trade Union, insightfully noted that even Solidarity itself was not above a pointed criticism concerning this societal frustration. Borusewicz stated that beginning in 1989 Solidarity had created its own "elite" that became quite literally immersed in politics. This elite also strongly backed the economic reforms proposed by the intellectuals in the Ministry of Finance. The shock therapy program failed to keep unemployment within the targets of 300,000 to 400,000 people. Nearly 3.2 million Poles left the public sector between 1990 and 1993, but the private sector was able to absorb only 600,000 of these displaced workers. Unemployment continued to rise, and by the end of 1994, more than 2.5 million people were counted in the ranks of the unemployed.

At the same time, actions undertaken by Solidarity in 1993 in calling strikes, especially in the large public sector, spawned calls for limitations on the rights of trade unions and opposition to the State Enterprise Pact. The pact had originally energized Polish workers in the belief that they too would fairly share in the fruits of the capitalist revolution.[27] However, it never lived up to its optimistic potential.

Some like Kazimierz Ujazdowski (a member of the Conservative party) argued that Solidarity's dabbling in politics was the major "threat to Polish democracy." As early as July of 1993, Ujazdowski predicted that Solidarity "could have major problems crossing the five percent [threshold] for votes to enter the Sejm."[28] In retrospect, how prophetic! Both Ujazdowski and Borusewicz underscored the warning of Professor Mieczyslaw Nasilowski who warned that a true "economic or political shock" might drive Polish workers to the "barrier of social endurance." Reaching that barrier would certainly push voters to abandon Solidarity politicians in favor of parties or candidates with clear ties to "People's Poland." Many of these individuals would claim a certain myopic amnesia about the role they had played during the former period.

Society had certainly reached this barrier by the time of the parliamentary elections of 1993, and even more acutely by the time of the presidential election of 1995, when President Walesa went down to a stunning defeat at the hands of Aleksander Kwasniewski. Kwasniewski no longer needed to shelter or explain his communist associations or past.

POSTSCRIPT ON THE 1997 PARLIAMENTARY ELECTIONS

On 21 September 1997, the Solidarity Election Action (AWS), an amalgam of three dozen parties around Solidarity, defied pre-election polls and won first place with 33.8 percent of the vote, capturing 201 seats in the Sejm. Solidarity's victory was engineered by Marian Krzaklewski, a computer scientist with strong ties to the Roman Catholic church, who has strongly supported Poland's entry into both NATO and the European Union.

The AWS entered into a coalition with the market-oriented Freedom Union (UW), led by Leszek Balcerowicz, which captured 13.4 percent of the vote and 60 seats. The SLD suffered a surprising defeat, taking 26.8 percent of the votes and 164 seats.

On 15 October, the coalition nominated Jerzy Buzek to become prime minister. Buzek is a chemistry professor from Silesia who helped organize Solidarity's underground movement after martial law was imposed in 1981. Included in the new center-right Polish government were Bronislaw Geremek as foreign minister, Hanna Suchocka as Minister of Justice, Janusz Onyszkiewicz as defense minister, and Emil Wasacz, who as treasury minister, will be an charge of the privatization effort. Wasacz had been a Solidarity member, a manager of a steel mill, and a manager of an NIF. Also entering the cabinet will be Leszek Balcerowicz, who will be a deputy prime minister and finance minister.

As a result of their electoral defeats, the PSL dismissed Waldemar Pawlak as its chair. The PSL polled only 6.9 percent of the vote, losing 80 percent of its seats. The PSL also ousted Jozef Zych, the speaker of the Sejm. The Movement for the Reconstruction of Poland (ROP) suspended its entire executive board, including former Prime Minister Jan Olszewski. The Union of Labor (UP) likewise temporarily suspended the entire leadership of the party, including its leader, Ryszard Bugaj.

Marian Krzaklewski preferred to remain outside of the government, but made no secret of his plans to challenge President Kwasniewski for re-election in the year 2000.

◈ Endnotes

CHAPTER 1

1. The Catholic church was not officially represented at the Round Table, in keeping with the "strategic position" announced by Cardinal Glemp. For a discussion of the role of the Catholic church during the Round Table period, see Krzysztof Kosela, "The Polish Catholic Church and the Elections of 1989," *Religion in Communist Lands*, Vol. 18 (1990), pp. 124–137.

2. John Tagliabue, "Warsaw Opens Parley with Solidarity," in Bernard Gwertzman and Michael T. Kaufman (eds.), *The Collapse of Communism* (New York: Times Books, 1990), p. 18.

3. John Tagliabue, "Poland Sets Free Vote in June, First Since '45; Solidarity Reinstated," in Gwertzman and Kaufman (eds.), *Collapse of Communism*, pp. 33–36.

4. For a variety of materials on KOR [Komitet Obrony Robotnikow], see Robert Zuzowski, *Political Dissent and Opposition in Poland: The Workers' Defense Committee "KOR"* (Westport, Conn.: Praeger, 1994); Roman Laba, *The Roots of Solidarity: A Political Sociology of Poland's Working-Class Democratization* (Princeton, N.J.: Princeton University Press, 1991), emphasizing the role of workers as opposed to intellectuals; David Ost, *Solidarity and the Politics of Anti-Politics: Opposition and Reform in Poland since 1968* (Philadelphia: Temple University Press, 1990); and Michael M. Bernhard, *The Origins of Democratization in Poland: Workers, Intellectuals, and Oppositional Politics, 1976–1980* (New York: Columbia University Press, 1993). Both Ost and Bernhard emphasize the role of intellectuals in KOR. Perhaps of most interest is the view offered by an insider, Jan Jozef Lipski, *KOR: A History of the Workers' Defense Committee in Poland, 1976–1981*, trans. Olga Amsterdamska and Gene M. Moore (Berkeley: University of California Press, 1985). Of special note is Lawrence Goodwyn, *Breaking the Barrier: The Rise of Solidarity in Poland* (New York: Oxford University Press,

1991). This book was reviewed by Richard J. Hunter, *The Mid-Atlantic Journal of Business*, Vol. 28, No. 3 (December 1992), pp. 283–284. For a review of the Zuzowski book, see Jan Kubik, *The Polish Review*, Vol. 40, No. 3 (1995), pp. 357–361.

5. One of the most notable losers was Jerzy Urban, the former ubiquitous government spokesman, who has recently resurfaced as editor of the controversial review magazine *Nie* [No].

6. Zbigniew K. Brzezinski, "Beyond Chaos: A Policy for the West," *The National Interest*, No. 19 (Spring 1990), p. 9.

7. Leszek Balcerowicz, "Lessons from Economic Transition in Central and Eastern Europe," in Jan W. Bossak (ed.), *Poland: International Economic Report 1993/94* (Warsaw: World Economy Research Institute, Warsaw School of Economics, 1994), pp. 193–200, summarizing a lecture given on 1 December 1993. See also Leszek Balcerowicz, *Socialism, Capitalism, Transformation* (New York: Central European University Press, 1995), Chapter 9, pp. 145–151.

8. Bill Keller, "Gorbachev's Hope for Future: A Common European Home," in Gwertzman and Kaufman (eds.), *Collapse of Communism*, pp. 270–276.

9. Eugeniusz Smilowski, "Pentor Poll. Pessimism Takes the Lead," *The Warsaw Voice*, 10 November 1996, p. 6. A positive change in voter perception is discussed in chapter 10, *infra*.

10. For a discussion of the "Yalta system," see William L. Neumann, *After Victory: Churchill, Roosevelt, Stalin and the Making of the Peace* (New York: Harper & Row, 1967). See also William Larsh, "Yalta and the American Approach to Free Elections in Poland," *The Polish Review*, Vol. 40, No. 3 (1995), pp. 267–280, concluding that Yalta guaranteed the fate of Poland for the next half-century; Anna M. Cienciala, "Great Britain and Poland before and after Yalta (1943–1945): A Reassessment," *The Polish Review*, Vol. 40, No. 3 (1995), pp. 281–313. Lloyd Gardner adopts the view that "the partition of Europe had been largely accomplished before the cold war began." Lloyd C. Gardner, *Spheres of Influence: The Great Powers Partition Europe, from Munich to Yalta* (Chicago: Ivan R. Dee, 1993). This view is shared by Daniel S. Buczek, "The Coordinating Committee: A Neglected Chapter of World War II," *Polish American Studies*, Vol. 53, No. 2 (1996 Autumn), pp. 5–56. Buczek cites the 22 February 1944 speech of Prime Minister Churchill, noting that Soviet frontier demands on Polish territories were both "reasonable and just" (p. 23). For a view from the American perspective, see Arthur Bliss Lane, *I Saw Poland Betrayed* (Indianapolis, Ind.: Bobbs-Merrill, 1948). Lane was the American ambassador to Poland.

11. Prime Minister Mazowiecki set the tone for his policy of "let bygones be bygones" in a 5 July 1990 speech before the Sejm. Mazowiecki referred to "the full observance of individual rights, including the rights of those who sinned against the law for many decades. We want to accomplish this within the framework of the law." "A Plea for Self Control," *Gazeta International*, 19 July 1990, pp. 1–2.

12. See Balcerowicz, "Lessons," in Bossak (ed.) (1994), p. 194.

13. See Christine Spolar, "Romanians Go with Flow of the East's Reform Wave," *International Herald Tribune*, 5 November 1996, pp. 1, 8.

14. John Pomfret, "Poles Cooling towards Walesa in Policy Drift," *International Herald Tribune*, 6 July 1994, pp. 1, 4.

15. Janusz Golebiowski, "Political Changes in Poland and the Region," in

Bossak (ed.) (1994), p. 16. For a view of the left-center coalition in its early period, see "The Fading of Red," *The Economist*, 15 January 1994, p. 56.

16. Not all agree with the U.S. decision to "expand" NATO eastward. See, e.g., Thomas Friedman, "Not Yet," *New York Times*, 24 March 1997, p. A11. For a discussion of Poland membership in the EC, see Anne Wagner-Findeisen, "From Association to Accession—An Evaluation of Poland's Aspirations to Full Membership in the European Community, 1989–1992," in M. B. Biskupski and James S. Pula (eds.), *Poland and Europe: Historical Dimensions*, Vol. I (New York: Columbia University Press, 1993), pp. 243–281.

17. Reported in Jan W. Bossak, "Economic Performance of Central and Eastern Europe," in Bossak (ed.) (1994), p. 37, citing *Selected Economic Indicators* (Warsaw: IMF, January 1993).

18. See Balcerowicz, "Lessons," in Bossak (ed.) (1994), p. 197.

19. Adapted from ibid. See also Robert E. Norton, "The Americans Out to Save Poland," *Fortune*, 29 January 1990, pp. 129–134.

20. "Poland Invited to Join OECD," in *Economic and Legal Information from Poland*, Vol. VI, No. 3, p. 1 (New York: Embassy of the Republic of Poland, Commercial Counsellor's Office, June–August 1996).

21. "Polish Enterprises Looking for Partners," in ibid., p. 15, detailing joint venture opportunities.

22. See Imre Vajda, *The Second Five Year Year Plan in Hungary* (Budapest: Government Press, 1963), p. 28. See also Frederick Bernard Singleton, *Background to Eastern Europe* (London: Pergamon Press, 1965).

23. The yard was closed on 6 March 1997, causing the loss of the remaining 3,600 jobs. Solidarity stated that the closure was "politically motivated" and responded with a protest attended by more than 1,000 workers. The shipyard was reportedly more than $150 million in debt.

24. For a discussion of "losing and winning groups" in Poland's march to the market, see Richard J. Hunter, Leo V. Ryan, and Andrew Hrechak, "Out of Communism to What?: The Polish Economy and Solidarity in Perspective," *The Polish Review*, Vol. 39, No. 3 (1994), pp. 328–329, 333–335. This discussion is amplified in chapter 9, *infra*.

25. See, e.g., Richard J. Hunter and John Northrop, "Management, Legal and Accounting Perspectives: Privatization in Poland," *The Polish Review*, Vol. 38, No. 4 (1993), pp. 407–420.

26. Constantinos G. Grigoriadis, "The Future Is Here," in Rupert Wright (ed.), *The Central European Handbook: 1996/1997* (London: Euromoney Publications, 1996), pp. 62–74. See chapter 7, *infra*, for a full discussion on the NIFs. See also "Central and Eastern European Equities: Poland," *Euromoney*, February 1997, pp. 7–9. For a discussion of the mass privatization program, see Piotr Stefaniak, "Mass Privatization Programme," in *Encyclopaedia of Polish Industry* (London: Sterling Publications, 1997), pp. 22–24.

27. The term "WOG" is a Polish acronym for Wielkie Organizacje Gospodarcze. It refers to the large state-owned enterprises. See Paul Lewis, "Political Consequences of Changes in Party-State Structures under Gierek," in Jean Woodall (ed.), *Policy and Politics in Contemporary Poland* (London: Frances Pinter, 1982).

28. For a controversial biography of John Paul II, see Carl Bernstein and Marco Politi, *His Holiness, John Paul II and the Hidden History of Our Time*

(New York: Doubleday, 1996). See also Tad Szulc, *Pope John Paul II: The Biography* (New York: Charles Scribner's Sons, 1996).

29. Quoted in Bill Keller, "Gorbachev in Finland, Disavows Any Right of Regional Intervention," in Gwertzman and Kaufman (eds.), *Collapse of Communism*, pp. 163–166.

30. The quote is attributed to Gorbachev but it was actually spoken by Foreign Minister Gennadi Gerasimov in a conversation with the president of Finland, 25 October 1989.

31. Gwertzman writes insightfully: "At every turn, he [Gorbachev] did nothing or actually appeared to support those in Eastern Europe seeking more freedom and an end to Communist domination and seemed to lend his personal prestige to the ouster of such veteran Eastern European leaders as Erich Honecker in East Germany, Milos Jakes in Czechoslovakia, Todor Zhivkov in Bulgaria, and Nicolae Ceausescu in Romania. He tolerated, if not encouraged, the opening of the Berlin Wall, Solidarity's taking over the government in Poland, and the Hungarian Communists' setting elections which may lead to their own political suicide." Bernard Gwertzman, "Introduction," in Gwertzman and Kaufman (eds.), *Collapse of Communism*, p. vii.

32. Trevor Hall and Kathryn Spink, *Pope John Paul II: A Man and His People* (New York: Exeter Books, 1985), pp. 149, 324.

33. See George Sanford and Adriana Gozdecka-Sanford, *Historical Dictionary of Poland* (Metuchen, N.J.: Scarecrow Press, 1994). Professor M. B. Biskupski reviewed this book in *The Polish Review*, Vol. 40, No. 3 (1995), pp. 361–363.

CHAPTER 2

1. See "Hand to Mouth," *The Economist* (London), 28 March 1981. See also *Maly Rocznik Statystyczny* [Short Version Statistical Yearbook] (Warsaw: GUS, 1981–1983).

2. George Blazyca, "The Degeneration of Central Planning in Poland," in Jean Woodall (ed.), *Policy and Politics*, p. 124. See also *Trybuna Ludu*, 4 June 1981.

3. Adam Gwiazda, "Poland's Trade with the West: Past Trends and Future Prospects," *Coexistence*, Vol. 22 (1985), pp. 79–90.

4. Abecor Country Report, *Poland* (London: April 1984), p. 1. See also *Rocznik Statystyczny* [Statistical Yearbook] (Warsaw: GUS, 1984), No. 7, pp. 2, 4, 36.

5. Pawel Bozyk, *Dreams and Reality or an Anatomy of the Polish Crisis* (Warsaw: PIW, 1983). Bozyk was the chief economic advisor to Edward Gierek.

6. See Czeslaw Bobrowski, "Stopien swobody wyboru: Uwagi na marginesie wytycznych rozwoju gospodarczego na lata 1961–1965" [The Scope of the Freedom of Choice: Remarks on the Peripheral Guidelines for Economic Development for 1961–1965], *Gospodarka Planowa* [Planned Economy], Nos. 1–2 (1986), pp. 6–7.

7. Quoted in Lawrence Weschler, *Solidarity: Poland in the Season of Its Passion* (New York: Simon and Schuster, 1982), p. 68 (italics added).

8. For a most prescient discussion of the postcommunist system, see Zbig-

niew K. Brzezinski, *The Grand Failure: The Birth and Death of Communism in the Twentieth Century* (New York: Charles Scribner's Sons, 1989).

9.   Wladyslaw Gomulka, 1945–1948; Boleslaw Bierut, 1948–March 1956; Edward Ochab, March 1956–October 1956; Gomulka, 1956–1970; Edward Gierek, 1970–1980.

10.   See, e.g., Mid-European Research and Planning Center, *The Sovietization of Culture in Poland* (Paris: MERPC, 1953). See also Krzysztof Krygier (ed.), *System zaopatrzenia w gospodarce planowej* [The Procurement System in the Planned Economy] (Warsaw: PWG, 1955).

11.   John M. Montias, *Central Planning in Poland* (New Haven: Yale University Press, 1962). This work is still the classic analysis of the stages of central planning in Poland.

12.   *Zycie Gospodarcze* [Economic Life], No. 1 (1946). See also Oskar Halecki, *A History of Poland* (New York: Roy Publishers, 1956, 1966), p. 330. The original Halecki work was updated by Thaddeus V. Gromada (ed.) (1992) (New York: Dorset). See also *Dziennik Ustaw Rzeczpospolita* [Journal of the Laws of the Republic], No. 3, Item 17 (1946).

13.   Nicolas Spulber, *The Economies of Communist Eastern Europe* (Westport, Conn.: Greenwood Press, 1976), p. 57.

14.   Ernest Skalski, "Powojenna odbudowa" [Postwar Reconstruction], *Tygodnik Powszechny*, No. 21 (1985). The three-year Plan of Reconstruction surpassed the immediate prewar levels by 110 percent. See also Ivan T. Berend and Gyorgy Ranki, *Economic Development in East Central Europe in the 19th and 20th Centuries* (New York: Columbia University Press, 1974), who noted that direct state intervention was "greatly facilitated" because a considerable part of the Polish economy was owned by the state.

15.   See Z. Charlap and E. Szturm, "Statystyka Karteli w Polsce" [Statistics of Cartels in Poland], *Statystyka Polski* [Statistics of Poland], Series c, No. 28 (1935), p. 37; Ferdynand Zweig, *Poland between Two Wars: A Critical Study of Social and Economic Changes* (London: Secker and Warburg, 1944). See generally, e.g., Halecki, *A History*.

16.   Zbigniew K. Brzezinski, *The Soviet Bloc: Unity and Conflict* (Cambridge, Mass.: Harvard University Press, 1971), p. 14.

17.   For the most authoritative overview of the history of the Polish Communist party, see Marian K. (M. K.) Dziewanowski, *The Communist Party of Poland: An Outline of History* (Cambridge, Mass.: Harvard University Press, 1959, 1976).

18.   Halecki, *A History* (1966), p. 336; see also generally, Dziewanowski, *Communist Party of Poland*; Richard Hiscocks, *Poland: Bridge for the Abyss?* (London: Oxford University Press, 1963), Chapter 4, "Polish Communism up to 1944," pp. 65–89.

19.   See Goodwyn, *Breaking the Barrier*, p. 47, discussing the early "nonsuccess" of communists in the immediate postwar period. See also Jean Malara and Lucienne Rey, *La Pologne: D'une occupation a l'autre 1944–1952* [Poland: One Occupation to the other 1944–1952] (Paris: Editions du Fuseau, 1952), pp. 131–134.

20.   See Montias, *Central Planning*, pp. 190-219.

21.   Goodwyn, *Breaking the Barrier*, p. 187.

22. See Irwin T. Sanders (ed.), *The Collectivization of Agriculture in Eastern Europe* (Lexington: University of Kentucky Press, 1958).

23. See "Abrakadabra cen" [The Abracadabra of Prices], *Zycie Gospodarcze*, No. 19 (1956), p. 12. See also Franciszek Kowalski, "System cen fabrycznych w przemysle srodkow spozycia" [The System of Factory Prices in the Consumer Goods Industry], *Gospodarka Planowa*, No. 6 (1954), p. 37; Zbigniew Augustowski, "Ceny srodkow produkcji" [Prices of Means of Production], *Gospodarka Planowa*, No. 1 (1953), pp. 42–47.

24. See Bozyk, *Dreams and Reality*, p. 10.

25. Bronislaw Minc, "W sprawie metod planowania" [On Planning Methods], *Trybuna Ludu*, 20 March 1956.

26. Montias, *Central Planning*, pp. 37–38. See also S. Kuzinski, *Glowne proporcje rozwoju gospodarczego Polski Ludowej* [Chief Proportions in the Economic Development of People's Poland] (Warsaw: KiW, 1960), p. 42.

27. *Trybuna Ludu*, 8 June 1956.

28. Oskar Lange, *Funkcjonowanie gospodarki socjalistycznej* [The Functioning of the Socialist Economy] (Warsaw: PWE, 1960). For a spirited criticism of Lange, see Montias, *Central Planning*, p. 267.

29. See Edward Lipinski, *Rewizje* [Revisions] (Warsaw: PiW, 1956).

30. Wladyslaw Balicki, "The Theory of Disequilibrium in Centrally Planned Economies," Instytut Gospodarki Swiatowej [World Economy Institute], Working Paper (August 1981), p. 11. For a more complete discussion of Balicki's theories, see Wladyslaw Balicki, *The Theory of Disequilibrium of Demand* (Warsaw: The Institute of Planning, 1979).

31. Quoted in Singleton, Chapter 2, *Background*, p. 156.

32. *Trybuna Ludu*, 20 July 1956.

33. Polish United Workers' Party, Seventh Plenary Session, July 1956.

34. Reported in Goodwyn, *Breaking the Barrier*, p. 74.

35. Norman Davies, *God's Playground: A History of Poland*, Vol. II, *1795 to the Present* (New York: Columbia University Press, 1982), p. 547.

36. Ibid., p. 548.

37. Ibid., p. 563. The agreement was reached in Berlin between Polish and British representatives of the Combined Repatriation Executive. See Beate Ruhm von Oppen, *Documents on Germany under Occupation, 1945–54* (London: Royal Institute of International Affairs, 1955), pp. 107–110.

38. Goodwyn, *Breaking the Barrier*, p. 47.

39. Davies, *God's Playground*, p. 570, citing Aleksander Bregman (ed.), *Faked Elections in Poland as Reported by Foreign Observers* (London: Polish Freedom Movement, 1947).

40. Goodwyn, *Breaking the Barrier*, p. 50.

41. Davies, *God's Playground*, p. 573.

42. Reported in Goodwyn, *Breaking the Barrier*, p. 75. See Andrzej Micewski, *Cardinal Wyszynski: A Biography* (San Diego: Harcourt Brace Jovanovich, 1984). Cardinal Wyszynski offers a most personal note in Stefan Wyszynski, *A Freedom Within: The Prison Notes of Stefan, Cardinal Wyszynski* (London: Hodder & Stoughton, 1985), chronicling the earlier period of conflict with the Polish state. See also Hiscocks, *Poland: Bridge*, pp. 130–133.

43. For a discussion of the Gomulka era, see Nicholas Bethell, *Gomulka: His Poland, His Communism* (New York: Holt, Rinehart and Winston, 1969).

44. See generally, George Blazyca, "Economic Reform in Polish Industry: The Experience of the 1970's," Dissertation, University of Sussex (UK) (1978). See also M. Kalecki, "Podstawowe zagadnienia planu piecioletniego na lata 1961–1965" [Fundamental Problems of the Five-Year Plan for the Years 1961–1965], *Gospodarka Planowa*, Nos. 1–2 (1959), pp. 1–4.

45. See, e.g., Balcerowicz, *Socialism*, pp. 52–55.

46. Davies, *God's Playground*, p. 588.

47. Ibid., p. 589. For a discussion of the *Dziady* episode of 30 January 1968 in the larger context of communist ideology, see Andrzej Flis, "Crisis and Political Ritual in Postwar Poland," *Problems of Communism*, Vol. 37, Nos. 3–4 (May-August 1988), pp. 43–54. For a view of the topic of "real socialism," see Andrzej Flis, "From Marx to Real Socialism: The History of Utopia," *Poznan Studies in the Philosophy of the Sciences and the Humanities*, Vol. 36 (1994), pp. 19–30.

48. Goodwyn, *Breaking the Barrier*, p. 112.

49. Davies, *God's Playground*, p. 591.

50. *Rocznik Statystyczny 1975*, p. 80.

51. Quoted in Blazyca, "Economic Reform," p. 103.

52. George Sanford, "The Response of the Polish Communist Leadership to the Continuing Crisis: Personnel and Policy Change," in Woodall (ed.), *Policy and Politics*, p. 35. For a defense of the Gierek era, see Janusz Rolicki, *Edward Gierek: Przerwana dekada* [Edward Gierek: The Interrupted Decade] (Warsaw: Wydawnictwo FAKT, 1990).

53. Wieslaw Rydygier, "Zludzenia i rzeczywistosc" [Illusion and Reality], *Zycie Gospodarcze*, No. 41 (1980). See also Gwiazda, "Poland's Trade," p. 79.

54. Gwiazda, "Poland's Trade," p. 85.

55. Jan Drewnowski, "The Anatomy of Economic Failure in Soviet Type Systems," in Jan Drewnowski (ed.), *Crisis in the East European Economy: The Spread of the Polish Disease* (London: Croom-Helm, 1982), p. 72.

56. Blazyca, "Economic Reform," pp. 64–65.

57. Goodwyn, *Breaking the Barrier*, p. 125.

58. J. B. de Weydenthal, "The End of the Gierek Era," in William Robinson (ed.), *August 1980: The Strikes in Poland* (Munich: Radio Free Europe Research, 1980), p. 191.

59. Radio Warsaw, 6 September 1980, reported by J. B. de Weydenthal, "New Party Leader Appeals for Trust," in Robinson (ed.), *August 1980*, p. 198.

60. Andrzej Walicki, "Totalitarianism and Detotalitarization in Poland," *The Review of Politics*, Vol. 58, No. 3 (Summer 1996), p. 519.

61. Woodall (ed.), *Policy and Politics*, p. xiii.

62. Richard J. Hunter, "The Management Perspective on Poland's Economic Crisis and Recent Attempts at Reform," *The Polish Review*, Vol. 31, No. 4 (1986), pp. 299–313.

63. See Paul Lewis, "Political Consequences," in Woodall (ed.), *Policy and Politics*, p. 84. See also Andrzej Matysiak, "Funkcja przedsiebiorstwa w systemie WOG" [The Function of the Businessman in the WOG System], *in Mechanizm tworzenia akumulacji w gospodarce socjalistycznej* [Mechanism of Creating

Accumulations in the Socialist Economy] (Poznan: Akademia Ekonomiczna [Academy of Economics], 1984), Ch. 3.8.

64. Tadeusz Wrzaszczyk, Chairman of the Planning Commission 1975–1980, in discussions at the Sixth Plenum of the Party in September 1980, reported in *Nowe Drogi* [New Paths], Nos. 10–11 (1980), p. 97.

CHAPTER 3

1. Goodwyn, *Breaking the Barrier*, p. 150. For an insightful view of the early Solidarity period, see Timothy Garton Ash, *The Polish Revolution: Solidarity* (London: Jonathan Cape, 1983).

2. Quoted in John Darnton, "60 Days That Shook Poland," in William P. Lineberry (ed.), *Poland* (New York: H. W. Wilson, 1984), p. 37.

3. Balcerowicz, *Socialism*, p. 52.

4. For a discussion of the *nomenklatura* in the "changed" business environment, see Richard J. Hunter and Leo V. Ryan, "Uwaga! (Watch Out!) Opportunities and Pitfalls for an American Doing Business in Poland: The Political and Economic Scene," *The Polish Review*, Vol. 36, No. 3 (1991), p. 359.

5. Balcerowicz, *Socialism*, p. 52.

6. Walicki, "Totalitarianism," p. 519.

7. Weschler, *Solidarity*, p. 46.

8. See Richard J. Hunter, Artur Nowak and Leo V. Ryan, "Legal Aspects of the Transformation Process in Poland: Business Association Forms," *The Polish Review*, Vol. 40, No. 4 (1995), pp. 387–401. Many of the legal terms used in chapters 5 to 7, *infra*, are defined and explained in this article.

9. See Janos Kornai, "The Soft Budget Constraint," *Kyklos*, No. 1 (1986), pp. 3–30.

10. See generally J. Beksiak and U. Libura, *Rownowaga Gospodarcza w Socjalizmie* [Balanced Economy in Socialism] (Warsaw: PWN, 1974).

11. Balcerowicz, *Socialism*, p. 54, note 3.

12. This issue was explored at length in Richard J. Hunter, "Options and Perspectives for Today's Poland," Paper, 45th annual meeting of the Polish Institute of Arts and Sciences of America (PIASA), Hunter College, New York, 30 May 1987.

13. Quoted in Darnton, "60 Days," in Lineberry (ed.), *Poland*, p. 35.

14. Goodwyn, *Breaking the Barrier*, p. xxiv.

15. See Radio Free Europe (RFE) Research, "Polish Situation Report/28," 2 December 1977, Item 3a, reported by Roman Stefanowski, "The Free Labor Union Movement in Poland: A Short Background," in Robinson (ed.), *August 1980*, p. 60.

16. RFE, "Polish Situation Report/6," 3 March 1978, Item 4.

17. RFE, "Polish Situation Report/12," 30 May 1978, Item 3c.

18. Lech Walesa (with Marek Zaleski), *A Way of Hope: An Autobiography* (New York: Henry Holt and Co., 1987), p. 96.

19. Goodwyn, *Breaking the Barrier*, p. 141.

20. Roman Stefanowski, "The Free Labor Union Movement," in Robinson (ed.), *August 1980*, p. 60.

21. RFE, "Polish Situation Report/23," 30 October 1979, Item 2 (italics added).

22. Walicki, "Totalitarianism," p. 520 (italics added). See also generally Lipski, *KOR: A History*; Ost, *Solidarity and Politics*.

23. Goodwyn, *Breaking the Barrier*, p. 193; see also Lipski, *KOR: A History*, pp. 73, 77, 161–165, 346.

24. The Confederation for an Independent Poland (KPN) reminds listeners that Leszek Moczulski, the organization's founder, published a book in 1979, *Revolution without Revolution*, urging citizens to create institutions "independent" of the party.

25. Goodwyn, *Breaking the Barrier*, p. 194.

26. Ibid., p. 198.

27. Walesa, *Autobiography*, p. 149.

28. Leszek Kolakowski, "Tezy o nadziei i beznadziejnosci" [Theses about Hope and Hopelessness], *Kultura*, No. 6 (1971). For a personal view of the "new left," see Leszek Kolakowski, "The Concept of the Left," in Carl Oglesby (ed.), *The New Left Reader* (New York: Grove Press, 1969), pp. 144–158.

29. William Robinson, "Adam Michnik," in Robinson (ed.), *August 1980*, p. 334.

30. Walicki, "Totalitarianism," p. 521.

31. Walesa, *Autobiography*, p. 522.

32. Quoted by Goodwyn, *Breaking the Barrier*, p. 322.

33. Ibid., quoting Adam Michnik.

34. See generally ibid., pp. 322, 323.

35. The RFE dispatches were often summaries of other news services' reports. RFE was largely responsible for generating the *August 1980* volume, edited by William Robinson.

36. Ewa Celt, "Strikes Taking on a Political Dimension," in Robinson (ed.), *August 1980*, p. 49, noting that many in KOR "privately" believed that the government "had no intention whatsoever of using police or military forces to quell the unrest."

37. Concerning the demand for free and independent trade unions, Kuron reportedly said: "I thought it was impossible, it was impossible, and I still think it was impossible." Kuron certainly opposed the first demand "when he heard about it, opposed it upon reflection, and still opposed it while under police detention." Goodwyn, *Breaking the Barrier*, pp. 216–217.

38. Walesa, *Autobiography*, p. 99.

39. Stan Persky, *At the Lenin Shipyard: Poland and the Rise of the Solidarity Trade Union* (Vancouver, B.C.: New Star Books, 1981), p. 62.

40. J. B. de Weydenthal, "Worker-Management Bargaining in Poland," in Robinson (ed.), *August 1980*, pp. 38–41; RFE Series, Radio Broadcast/181, 21 July 1980.

41. Anna Kowalska, *The Sun* (Baltimore, Md.), 10 August 1980, cited by Ewa Celt, "Polish Labor Unrest: A Progress Report," in Robinson (ed.), *August 1990*, pp. 42–44.

42. Quoted in the *New York Times*, 18 August 1980.

43. Roman Laba, "The Roots of Solidarity," Unpublished Dissertation, University of Wisconsin (1989). Laba noted that "with dozens of tanks, armored trans-

ports and automatic weapons trained at the shipyard gates, this was a powerful incentive indeed to have an occupation strike." Quoted in Goodwyn, *Breaking the Barrier*, p. 114, note 17.

44. Ewa Celt, "Strikes Taking on a Political Dimension," in Robinson (ed.), *August 1980*, p. 49.

45. Anna Sabbat, "Strike Situation: Continuing Uncertainty," in Robinson (ed.), *August 1980*, p. 53.

46. *Biuletyn Informacyjny KSS "KOR"* [KOR Information Bulletin], January 1979; *Robotnik Wybrzeza* [The Coastal Worker], January 1979.

47. Reported in the *New York Times*, 20 August 1980.

48. UPI, 20 August 1980; also reported in *Le Figaro*, 21 August 1980.

49. William Robinson, "Lech Walesa," in Robinson (ed.), *August 1980*, p. 340, quoting a broadcast by ARD (the West German TV channel), 2 September 1980.

50. Goodwyn, *Breaking the Barrier*, p. 228, citing various "Gdansk Transcripts."

51. See Lipski, *KOR: A History*, pp. 421–422.

52. See Goodwyn, *Breaking the Barrier*, p. 40. See also Jadwiga Staniszkis, *Poland's Self-Limiting Revolution* (Princeton, N.J.: Princeton University Press, 1984); Jadwiga Staniszkis, "On Some Contradictions of Socialist Society: The Case of Poland," *Soviet Studies*, Vol. 31, No. 2 (April 1979), pp. 167–187.

53. "The Renewal of the Trade Union Movement" (editorial), *Trybuna Ludu*, 28 August 1980.

54. Anna Sabbat and Roman Stefanowski, "Chronology," in Robinson (ed.), *August 1980*, p. 21.

55. J. B. de Weydenthal, "Workers and the Government Reach Tentative Agreement," in Robinson (ed.), *August 1980*, p. 77, citing the Associated Press (AP), 30 August 1980.

56. Anna Sabbat and Roman Stefanowski, "Chronology," in Robinson (ed.), *August 1980*, pp. 22–23.

57. See *Solidarnosc*, No. 11, 30 August 1980. This was the "official" Solidarity publication during the Polish August. *The Gdansk Agreement* (The Protocol) of August is reprinted in full with commentary in Abraham Brumberg (ed.), *Poland: Genesis of a Revolution* (New York: Vintage Books, 1983).

58. Darnton, "60 Days," in Lineberry (ed.), *Poland*, p. 31.

59. An unidentified staff member at the Warsaw Solidarity office, quoted in Weschler, *Solidarity*, p. 64. See also David S. Mason, *Public Opinion and Political Change in Poland 1980–1982* (Cambridge: Cambridge University Press, 1985), pp. 199–299, for a discussion of "three myths held by Solidarity."

60. Quoted in Weschler, *Solidarity*, p. 64.

61. Ibid.

62. Darnton, "60 Days," in Lineberry (ed.), *Poland*, p. 40.

63. Seweryn Bialer, "Poland and the Soviet Imperium," *Foreign Affairs*, Vol. 59 (April 1981), p. 526. See also Adam Bromke, "Policy and Politics in Gierek's Poland," in Maurice D. Simon and Roger E. Kanet (eds.), *Background to Crisis: Policy and Politics in Gierek's Poland* (Boulder, Colo.: Westview Press, 1981), pp. 15–21.

64. Goodwyn, *Breaking the Barrier*, p. 135.

65. Said the filmmaker Andrzej Chodakowski: "It can't get any worse than what we've got. Anything would be an improvement over *nomenklatura*," quoted in Weschler, *Solidarity*, p. 106. See also George Kolankiewicz, "Employee Self-Management and Socialist Trade Unionism," in Woodall (ed.), *Policy and Politics*, p. 139. Kolankiewicz notes that the fight with the system had the support of even rank-and-file party members who had "often seen their own reputations marred by totally unacceptable appointments."

66. Goodwyn, *Breaking the Barrier*, p. 283.

67. Kolankiewicz, "Employee Self-Management," in Woodall (ed.) *Policy and Politics,* p. 143.

68. See *Glos Pracy*, 30 June 1981, and 1 and 2 July 1981.

69. Karol Modzelewski, the Polish historian, became national press spokesman for Solidarity in 1980. He eventually broke with Walesa in April 1981 over a disagreement concerning Walesa's "autocratic and incompetent leadership style." Modzelewski noted the tremendous "danger and tension" that strikes brought to pre-martial law Poland. See Weschler, *Solidarity*, p. 106.

70. Ibid., p. 101. See, e.g., George Kolankiewicz, "The Working Class," in David S. Lane and George Kolankiewicz (eds.), *Social Groups in Polish Society* (New York: Columbia University Press, 1973), pp. 88–151. See also Stanislaw Lipinski, "Losy" [Chances], *Zycie Gospodarcze*, No. 21 (1980); *Zycie Gospodarcze*, No. 30 (1980).

71. Robert Ball, "Poland's Economic Disaster," *Fortune*, Vol. 104, 7 September 1981, p. 47. See also Oskar Lange, "Polskie gospodarstwo narodowe w drugim roku planu 6-letniego" [The Polish National Economy in the Second Year of the Six-Year Plan], *Ekonomista* [The Economist], Second Quarter (1951), pp. 39–62, describing the early results of state planning; *Pisma ekonomiczne i spoleczne 1930–1960* [Economic and Social Writings] (Warsaw: PWN, 1961); *Funkcjonowanie gospodarki*, providing a theoretical basis for Lange's critique.

72. Quoted in Weschler, *Solidarity*, p. 126. As a summary before his martial law address, Jaruzelski said: "Our country is on the edge of an abyss. Achievements of many generations, raised from the ashes, are collapsing into ruin," p. 126.

73. See "Worldgram," *U.S. News & World Report*, 29 March 1982, pp. 33–34. For a persuasive rebuttal of the factual basis for the imposition of martial law, see Darnton, "Poland: Still Defiant," in Lineberry (ed.), *Poland*, p. 153. ("But they [the authorities] have difficulty mustering evidence to support these claims.") This period has been explored by Carl Bernstein and Marco Politi, *His Holiness, John Paul II and the Hidden History of Our Time* (New York: Doubleday, 1996), arguing that Jaruzelski's actions avoided a more serious Soviet intervention and were caused by his honest view that Solidarity was guilty of attempting to destroy the Polish State.

CHAPTER 4

1. Herbert Reed, "Poland's Stormy August," in Robinson (ed.), *August 1980*, p. 184.

2. Walicki, "Totalitarianism," p. 507.

3. Ibid., p. 514.

4. These terms were coined by Jaff Schatz, *The Generation: The Rise and Fall of the Jewish Communists of Poland* (Berkeley: University cf California Press, 1991), p. 322.

5. Walicki, "Totalitarianism," p. 514.

6. See Hanna Swida-Ziemba, "Stalinism i polskie spoleczenstwo" [Stalinism and Polish Society], in Jacek Kurczewski (ed.), *Stalinism* (Warsaw: OUP, 1989), pp. 86–87.

7. Walicki, "Totalitarianism," p. 515.

8. Ibid., p. 519.

9. Ibid., p. 520.

10. Reed, "Poland's Stormy August," in Robinson (ed.), *August 1980*, p. 186.

11. John Darnton, *New York Times*, 31 August 1980, citing a "former high official" in the Gierek government.

12. See Ryszard Kuklinski, "Wojna z narodem widziana od srodka" [War with the Nation Seen from Within], *Kultura* (April 1987), pp. 3–57.

13. Ibid., pp. 34–35.

14. Goodwyn, *Breaking the Barrier*, p. 284. See also Henry Norr, "Solidarity and Self-Management," *Poland Watch*, No. 7 (May–June 1985), pp. 102–104.

15. Norr, "Solidarity and Self-Management," pp. 112–113.

16. Quoted in Goodwyn, *Breaking the Barrier*, p. 308.

17. Ibid., p. 310.

18. See Hunter, "Management Perspective," p. 307.

19. Balcerowicz, *Socialism*, p. 273, quoting *Kierunki Reformy Gospodarczej* [Directions of Economic Reform] (Warsaw: GUS, 1981).

20. Ibid., p. 273, citing *Kierunki Reformy Gospodarczej*, p. 23.

21. COMECON (also known as the CMEA) was the "Eastern version" of the EU. It largely "depended on the decision of one country, the former Soviet Union." Balcerowicz, *Socialism*, p. 172. This situation had not radically changed in more than four decades. Isaac Deutscher, *Stalin: A Political Biography* (New York: Oxford University Press, 1967), p. 587, commenting on the early stages of establishing control in Eastern Europe, in his monumental biography of Stalin. For a chronology of COMECON, see Wytold Zygulski, "Farewell to COMECON. Timely Death," *The Warsaw Voice*, 7 July 1991, p. 4.

22. Marian Guzek, "Economic Reform in Poland and Prospects for Cooperation with the West," Lecture, Adam Mickiewicz University, Poznan, Poland, 26 July 1985, reported in Hunter, "Management Perspetive," p. 312.

23. Noted by Bialer, "Poland and the Soviet Imperium," p. 531. See also Bela A. Balassa, *The Hungarian Experience in Economic Planning: A Theoretical and Empirical Study* (New Haven: Yale University Press, 1959), Chapter 5; Joseph S. Berliner, *Factory and Manager in the U.S.S.R.* (Cambridge, Mass.: Harvard University Press [Russian Research Center], 1957).

24. See Ball, "Poland's Economic Disaster," p. 42.

25. See *Maly Rocznik Statystyczny* (1981–1986). See also "Selected Data on Polish Foreign Trade" (Warsaw: Foreign Trade Research Institute, 1990); Wharton Econometric Forecasting Associates, *Centrally Planned Economies Outlook*, Vol. 8, No. 1 (April 1987), pp. 73–76. Wharton, among others, casts doubts on some of the "reported data," and notes that "totals do not match because of discrepancies in official Polish figures."

26. *Rocznik Statystyczny* (1986), p. 118. See also *Maly Rocznik Statystyczny* (1989).

27. See Jerzy Babiak, "Agricultural Policy in Contemporary Poland," Unpublished paper, Poznan, 1984, reported in Hunter, "Management Perspective," p. 309. See also *Maly Rocznik Statystyczny* (1986), pp. xxxiv–xxxv.

28. See *Maly Rocznik Statystyczny* (1986–1989).

29. Gwiazda, "Poland's Trade," p. 80 (italics added). See also *Polish Foreign Trade in 1984: Annual Report* (Warsaw: Foreign Trade Research Institute, 1985), p. 9.

30. Przemyslaw Gajdeczka, "Polish Economic Results in 1986 and Early 1987: Dilemmas of Economic Reform," in Wharton Econometric Forecasting Associates, "Polish Economic Performance in 1996 and early 1989; Dilemmas of Economic Reform," Vol. 6, No. 14 (12 May 1987), p. 7.

31. Christopher Bobinski, "Poles Protest over Prices," *The Financial Times*, 20 March 1987, p. 2.

32. U.S. Helsinki Watch Committee, *Violations of the Helsinki Accords: Poland* (New York: The Helsinki Watch Committee, 1986), p. 45.

33. Goodwyn, *Breaking the Barrier*, p. 313. See also Roger Boyes and John Moody, *The Priest Who Had to Die: The Tragedy of Father Jerzy Popieluszko* (London: Victor Gollancz, 1986); Paul Lewis, "Turbulent Priest: The Political Implications of the Popieluszko Affair," *Politics*, Vol. 5, No. 2 (1985), pp. 33–39.

34. Cited in Goodwyn, *Breaking the Barrier*, p. 434, note 4.

35. Walesa, *Autobiography*, p. 306.

36. Quoted in Weschler, *Solidarity*, p. 221. Lipinski, the 93-year-old economist and founding member of KOR, expressed these words before the Solidarity Congress, in KOR's "last will and testament."

37. Kazimierz Poznanski, "Economic Adjustment and Political Forces: Poland since 1970," *International Organization*, Vol. 40, No. 2 (Spring 1986), p. 488.

38. For a discussion of the role of the "left" in Polish politics, see Leszek Kolakowski, "The Concept of the Left," in Oglesby (ed.), *New Left Reader*, pp. 144–158.

39. Maria Hirszowicz, *Coercion and Control in Communist Society: The Visible Hand in a Command Economy* (New York: St. Martin's Press, 1986). See also *Raport: Polska piec lat po sierpniu* [Report: Poland Five Years after August] (London: ANEKS Publishers, 1986).

40. Congressional Research Service, John P. Hardt and Jean F. Boone, *Poland's Renewal and U.S. Options, a Policy Reconnaissance* (Update) (Washington, D.C.: Library of Congress, 5 June 1987), p. 24.

41. Ibid., p. 29. For a discussion of the relationship between the Soviet Union and Poland concerning proposed reforms, see "Gorbachev's Policy and Soviet Programs," pp. 29–34. General Secretary Gorbachev stated in Prague in April 1987: "No one has the right to lay claim to a special position in the socialist world. Each party's independence, its responsibility before its people, and its right to independently decide questions of the country's development . . . ." Speech at the Czechoslovak-Soviet "Friendship Rally," 10 April 1987, translated in *FBIS Daily Report: USSR*, 14 April 1987, pp. F10–11. Contrast this view to that represented in a *Pravda* editorial of 22 August 1978, "Defense of Socialism Is the Highest Inter-

national Duty." The editorial continued: "History has evolved in such a way that the Soviet Union bears enormous responsibility for the security of the socialist camp."

42. "Solidarnosc Looks to Lead Again," *Polish American Journal*, June 1988, pp. 1, 3. The United States Department of State reaffirmed its "longer range process of reengagement" in three stages. Congressional Research Service, "Advancing the Step-by-Step Approach: Options for U.S. Policy," *Poland's Renewal*, p. 35.

43. *Trybuna Ludu*, 5 May 1987 (concerning the second phase of the reform).

44. *Political Report* delivered by Wojciech Jaruzelski to the 10th PZPR Congress, Warsaw, 29 June 1986, translated in *FBIS Daily Report: Eastern Europe*, 1 July 1986, p. 18. For a full discussion of the reforms proposed by General Jaruzelski, see Wharton Econometric Forecasting Associates, Centrally Planned Economies Service, "Summary of the Theses for the Second Stage of Economic Reform in Poland Presented by the Commission for Economic Reform," Vol. 6, No. 14 (12 May 1987), pp. 17–20.

45. *Zycie Gospodarcze*, p. 44, quoted in Richard J. Hunter, "An Analysis of the Second Stage of Economic Reform," Paper, 46th annual meeting of PIASA, Georgetown University, May 1988, pp. 1–2.

46. *Polish Perspectives*, quoted in Hunter, "Management Perspective," p. 1.

47. The *Law on Social Consultation and Referenda* required a majority of eligible voters for the results to be binding. Since the vote in favor of the first question was 44.29 percent of the total electorate and on the second question was 46.29 percent, the results on either question were not binding.

48. See generally, Balcerowicz, *Socialism*, pp. 286–287.

49. The *1982 Law on Prices* distinguished *administrative*, *regulated*, and *contracted* prices. Administrative prices were set by an administrative bureau or agency; regulated prices were set by the sellers themselves who were required to comply with a price formula determined by the government; contracted prices would be fixed by "negotiations" between the parties. In the early period of reform, contrary to expectations, administrative prices increased. See Balcerowicz, *Socialism*, p. 280.

50. See "Czapka na miare" [The Hat that Fits], *Zycie Warszawy*, No. 3 (1988), p. 3.

51. Goodwyn, *Breaking the Barrier*, pp. 332–333.

52. See, e.g., A. Parkola and R. Rapacki, "II etap reformy w handlu zagranicznym" [The Second Stage of the Reform of Foreign Commerce] (Warsaw: Instytut Gospodarki Swiatowej [World Economy Institute], Working Paper Serials, 1987).

53. Balcerowicz, *Socialism*, p. 287.

54. Goodwyn, *Breaking the Barrier*, p. 341.

55. Ibid., p. 344.

56. John S. Earle, Roman Frydman, Andrzej Rapaczynski, and Joel Turkewitz, *Small Privatization* (New York: Central European University Press, 1994), p. 200.

57. By the end of 1989, 30 percent of the volume of all sales of consumer goods were made at totally free-market prices.

58. P. Tamowicz, T. Aziewicz, and M. Stompor, *Small Privatization: Polish*

Experiences (Gdansk: The Gdansk Institute for Market Economies, June 1992), p. 32.

59. See Goodwyn, *Breaking the Barrier*, p. 342.

60. Ibid., p. 333.

61. The *New York Times* reported in "On the Recent Strife in Poland," *Polish American Journal*, June 1988, p. 2, quoted in Hunter, "Management Perspective," pp. 11–12.

CHAPTER 5

1. Kazimierz Poznanski (ed.), *Stabilization and Privatization in Poland: An Economic Evaluation of the Shock Therapy Program* (Boston: Kluwer Academic Publishers, 1993), p. 2. For a detailed analysis and supporting statistics about the "near collapse" of the Polish economy, see Elzbieta M. Jagiello, "The Economic Situation in 1989," in Marian Paszynski, Josef Soldaczuk, and Stanislaw Falkowski (eds.), *The International and the Polish Economy in 1989 and 1990* (Warsaw: Foreign Trade Research Institute, 1990), pp. 67–80; Branko Milanovic, "The Decomposition of the System, October 1988–September 1989," in Poznanski (ed.), *Stabilization*, pp. 50–55. Milanovic concludes that "the legacy of the Rakowski government is ambiguous," p. 50.

2. Branko Milanovic, "Poland's Quest for Economic Stabilization, 1988–1991: Interaction of Political Economy and Economics," in Poznanski (ed.), *Stabilization*, p. 59.

3. Ibid., p. 56.

4. Jeffrey Sachs, *Poland's Jump to the Market Economy* (Cambridge, Mass.: MIT Press, 1993), p. 33.

5. Jan Mujzel, "Privatization in Poland—Its Achievements, Weaknesses and Dilemmas," in Yilmas Akyuz, Detlef J. Kotte, Andras Koves, and Laszlo Szamuely (eds.), *Privatization in the Transition Process: Recent Experiences in Eastern Europe* [United Nations Conference on Trade and Development (UNCTAD) and Foundation for Economic Research, Budapest (KOPINT-DATORG)] (Geneva: United Nations, 1993), p. 119.

6. Jan W. Bossak (ed.), *Poland: International Economic Report 1989/90* (Warsaw: World Economy Research Institute, Main School of Economics, 1990b), p. 15.

7. Ibid., p. 17.

8. Professor Janos Kornai has written the classic, standard, and most comprehensive analysis of the structure of socialist economies. See Janos Kornai, *The Socialist System: The Political Economy of Communism* (Princeton, N.J.: Princeton University Press, 1992).

9. Sachs, *Poland's Jump*, p. 44.

10. Adapted and quoted from ibid., pp. 12–13.

11. Aleksander M. Vacic, "Comments on Papers on Polish Privatization," in Akyuz et al. (eds.), *Privatization in Transition*, p. 176.

12. Ibid.

13. Sachs, *Poland's Jump*, p. 43.

14. Balcerowicz, *Socialism*, p. 342. This section is based on his "Conclusions:

Personal Reflections on Poland," Chapter 17, pp. 340–343. Also cf. Leszek Balcerowicz, *800 dni* [800 Days] (Warsaw: Polska Oficyna Wydawnicza "BGW," 1992); Mario I. Blejer and Fabrizio Coricelli (eds.), *The Making of Economic Reform in Eastern Europe: Conversations with Leading Reformers in Poland, Hungary and the Czech Republic* [Studies of Communism in Transition] (Brookfield, Vt.: Edward Elgar, 1995).

15. The "Balcerowicz Team" consisted of Marek Dabrowski, deputy in the Ministry of Finance until the summer of 1990; Stefan Kawalec, first chief advisor and then deputy in the same ministry, responsible for financial institutions; Janusz Sawicki, deputy at the Ministry of Finance, responsible for foreign debt negotiation; Andrzej Podsiadlo, who oversaw the state enterprises in the ministry; Grzegorz Wojtowicz, first deputy chairman of the Polish National Bank and its chairman in 1991, all graduated the same year in the Faculty of Foreign Trade of the Central School of Planning and Statistics. Wojciech Misiag and Ryszard Pazura, deputies in the Ministry of Finance, also graduated from the Central School of Planning and Statistics. Later, this same group would be referred to as "that gang from Warsaw" by those who had become disenchanted with reforms.

16. This group included both foreign advisors—Jeffrey Sachs, David Lipton, Wladyslaw Brzeski, Stanislaw Gomulka, Jacek Rostowski, and Stanislaw Welisz—and Polish ones—Karol Lutkowski, Andrzej Stanislaw Bratkowski, Antoni Kantecki, Adam Lipowski, Andrzej Parkola, and Andrzej Ochocki. Most of the foreign advisors were of Polish origin, so-called Polonia academics.

17. Sachs, *Poland's Jump*, p. 9.

18. Ben Slay, "The Polish Economic Transition," in John P. Hardt and Richard F. Kaufman (eds.), *East-Central European Economies in Transition* [Joint Economic Committee, Congress of the United States] (Armonk, N.Y.: M. E. Sharpe, 1995), p. 465.

19. Balcerowicz, *Socialism*, p. 307.

20. Cf. Sachs, *Poland's Jump*, pp. 45–46.

21. Balcerowicz, *Socialism*, p. 311.

22. Ibid., p. 351. Balcerowicz presents an interesting analysis of his own administrative style and how he chose his "team" and established "the rules of the game" in his autobiographical essay, which appears as chapter 17 of *Socialism*, esp. pp. 348–353.

23. Slay, "Economic Transition," in Hardt and Kaufman (eds.), *Economies in Transition*, p. 466.

24. Balcerowicz, *Socialism*, p. 352.

25. Ibid.

26. Ibid., p. 359.

27. Ibid., p. 310.

28. Richard D. Bartel, "Charting Poland's Economic Rebirth: Interview with Jeffrey D. Sachs," *Challenge*, January–February 1990, p. 27.

29. Ibid., p. 22 (italics in the original).

30. See Balcerowicz, *Socialism*, p. 353.

31. Marian Paszynski, "Prospects for the Current Year," in Paszynski, Soldaczuk, and Falkowski (eds.), *The International and the Polish Economy*, p. 80.

32. Sachs, *Poland's Jump*, pp. 45–46.

33. Adapted from Leszek Balcerowicz, Barbara Blaszczyk, and Marek

Dabrowski, "The Polish Way to the Market Economy," in Wing Thye Woo, Stephen Parker, and Jeffrey D. Sachs, *Economies in Transition: Comparing Asia and Eastern Europe* (Cambridge, Mass.: MIT Press, 1997), p. 138.

34. For an extensive discussion of "Poland: Land and Housing in Transition," see Ann Louise Strong, Thomas A. Reiner, and Janusz Szyrmer, *Transitions in Land and Housing: Bulgaria, the Czech Republic, and Poland* (New York: St. Martin's Press, 1996), pp. 135–235.

35. Jan W. Bossak, "The Program for Stabilization and System Reforms," in Bossak (ed.) (1990b), pp. 56–57.

36. Sachs, *Poland's Jump*, pp. 46–47.

37. For a further elaboration of these programs and more specifics related to phases I, II and III, see Bossak, "The Program," in Bossak (ed.) (1990b), pp. 57–59.

38. Cf. Leo V. Ryan, "The Tempestuous Warsaw Stock Exchange: 1991–1996," in Khosrow Fatemi (ed.), *International Business in the New Millennium: International Capital Markets and Economic Integration*, Vol. III (Laredo, Tex.: Texas A&M International University, 1997), pp. 687–706.

39. Cf. Janusz Fiszer, "Polish Parliament Approves New Foreign Investment Law of 1991," *Tax Notes International*, July 1991, pp. 721–725.

40. Olivier Blanchard, Rudiger Dornbusch, Paul Krugman, Richard Layard, and Lawrence Summers, *Reforms in Eastern Europe* (Cambridge, Mass.: MIT Press, 1992), p. 17.

41. Ibid., p. 20.

42. Ibid., p. 21.

43. Ibid., p. 29.

44. Marian Paszynski "Prospects for the Current Year," in Paszynski et al. (eds.), *The International and the Polish Economy*, pp. 82–84.

45. Stefan Kurowski, quoted by Dariusz Filar, "Poland on the Free Market Road," *Wall Street Journal* (Europe), 13 March 1989.

46. Paszynski, "Prospects," in Paszynski et al. (eds.), *The International and the Polish Economy*, p. 84.

47. Jacek Kochanowicz, "Transition to Market in a Comparative Perspective," in Poznanski (ed.), *Stabilization*, p. 243.

48. See generally, Filar, "Poland on the Free Market Road."

49. Jeffrey Sachs, "The Economic Transformation of Eastern Europe: The Case of Poland," in Poznanski (ed.), *Stabilization*, pp. 210–211.

50. Sachs notes that "the term hyperinflation is sometimes casually tossed about Poland's hyperinflation in 1989 was just the fourteenth occurrence in world history." Sachs, *Poland's Jump*, p. 40.

51. Wieslaw Otta, Lecture, Adam Mickiewicz University, Poznan, 25 July 1990.

52. Sachs, "Economic Transformation," in Poznanski (ed.), *Stabilization*, p. 211.

53. The subsequent governments and their tenure include Bielecki, January–December 1991; Olszewski, December 1991–May 1992; Suchocka, July 1992–October 1993; Pawlak, September 1993–February 1995; Oleksy, March 1995–January 1996; Cimoszewicz, January 1996–September 1997 elections; Buzek, 1997 to present.

54. Poznanski (ed.), *Stabilization*, p. 1.

55. Sachs, "Economic Transformation," in Poznanski (ed.), *Stabilization*, p. 210.

56. Kochanowicz, "Transition," in ibid., p. 242.

57. Tsuneaki Sato, "Comment," in Akyuz et al. (eds.), *Privatization in Transition*, p. 167.

58. Mujzel, "Privatization Achievements," in ibid., p. 121.

59. John P. Hardt and Philip J. Kaiser, "Country Studies: Overview," in Hardt and Kaufman (eds.), *Economies in Transition*, p. 459.

60. Sato, "Comment," in Akyuz et al. (eds.), *Privatization in Transition*, p. 168.

61. Hardt and Kaiser, "Country Studies," in Hardt and Kaufman (eds.), *Economies in Transition*, p. 459.

62. Slay, "Economic Transition," in ibid., p. 476.

63. Ibid., p. 477.

64. Ibid., p. 472.

65. Keith Crane, "Taking Stock of the 'Big Bang'," in Poznanski (ed.), *Stabilization*, p. 81.

66. Ibid.

67. Ibid., p. 82.

68. Poznanski, in Poznanski (ed.), *Stabilization*, p. 36.

69. Crane, "Taking Stock," in Poznanski (ed.), *Stabilization*, p. 82.

70. Slay, "Economic Transition," in Hardt and Kaufman (eds.), *Economies in Transition*, p. 479.

71. Balcerowicz, *Socialism*, p. 368.

72. Ibid., p. 307.

73. Ibid., pp. 307–308.

74. Ibid., p. 337.

75. Adapted and quoted from ibid., pp. 336–337.

76. Barbara Blaszczyk and Marek Dabrowski, "The Privatization Process in Poland," in Akyuz et al. (eds.), *Privatization in Transition*, p. 113.

77. The impact of conversion of municipal and housing cooperatives was equally important in the development of small businesses and private property.

78. Jozef van Brabant, "The Hobbled Transition: Mined Privatization Paths in the East," in Akyuz et al. (eds.), *Privatization in Transition*, p. 79, pp. 78–79 (italics in the original).

79. Jozef van Brabant, "The New East and Old Trade and Payment Problems," in Poznanski (ed.), *Stabilization*, p. 80.

80. Van Brabant, "The Hobbled Transition," in Akyuz et al., *Privatization in Transition*, p. 80. For a further analysis of "Open Invitation to Chicanery," see Leo V. Ryan, "The New Poland: Major Problems for Ethical Business," *Business Ethics: A European Review*, Vol. 1, No. 1 (January 1992), pp. 9–15, reprinted in Max L. Stackhouse, Dennis McCann, Shirley J. Roels, and Preston N. Williams (eds.), *On Moral Business: Classical and Contemporary Resources for Ethics in Economic Life* (Grand Rapids, Mich.: William B. Eerdmans Publishing Company, 1995), pp. 765–770.

81. Slay, "Economic Transition," in Hardt and Kaufman (eds.), *Economies in Transition*, p. 473.

82. Charles S. Maier, "Democracy and Its Discontents," *Foreign Affairs*, Vol. 73, No. 4 (July/August 1994), p. 55.

83. Poznanski (ed.), *Stabilization*, p. 9.

84. Slay, "Economic Transition," in Akyuz et al. (eds.), *Privatization in Transition*, p. 479.

85. Balcerowicz, *Socialism*, p. 358.

86. Ibid., p. 331. The Ten Systemic Outcomes represent our abbreviated summary of the discussion. See "Systemic Outcomes," in ibid., pp. 328–331.

87. Ibid., p. 331.

88. Poznanski (ed.), *Stabilization*, p. 10.

89. Vacic, "Comments," in Akyuz et al. (eds.), *Privatization in Transition*, pp. 181–182.

90. Ibid., p. 181. The results of the 1993 parliamentary election proved Vacic to be quite prophetic.

CHAPTER 6

1.   Blanchard et al., *Reforms in Eastern Europe*, p. 59.

2.   Sachs, "Economic Transformation," in Poznanski (ed.), *Stabilization*, p. 198.

3.   Jan Mujzel, "Some Practical Problems of Privatization—Through Polish Eyes," in Walter D. Connor and Piotr Ploszajski (eds.), *Escape from Socialism: The Polish Route* (Warsaw: IFIS Publishers, 1992), p. 29.

4.   Wladyslaw Jermakowicz, *Privatization in Poland: Aims and Methods* (Warsaw: Centrum Prywatyzacji [Privatization Center], 1992), p. 7.

5.   Marie Lavigne, *The Economics of Transition: From Socialist Economy to Market Economy* (New York: St. Martin's Press, 1995), p. 155.

6.   Sato, "Comment," in Akyuz et al. (eds.), *Privatization in Transition*, p. 169.

7.   Van Brabant, "The Hobbled Transition," in ibid., p. 62.

8.   Ibid., p. 64. *Usufruct* derives from the Latin *usus fructus*, referring to the right to use the returns from legally recognized assets (i.e., property).

9.   PETs include Bulgaria, Czechoslovakia, the former German Democratic Republic (GDR), Hungary, Poland, Romania, and the Soviet Union. The term PETs was coined by van Brabant, who defined the term as follows: "These economies aim at radically transforming themselves and doing away with virtually the entire wherewithal of traditional central planning, including its macro- and microeconomic approaches and the institutions and instruments associated with them." Jozef M. van Brabant, *Remaking Eastern Europe: On the Political Economy of Transition* (Boston: Kluwer Academic Publishers, 1990), p. 11.

10. Blanchard et al., *Reforms in Eastern Europe*, p. 57.

11. Sachs, *Poland's Jump*, pp. 56–57.

12. Balcerowicz, *Socialism*, p. 181.

13. Sachs, *Poland's Jump*, p. 80.

14. Ibid., p. 82.

15. Ibid., p. 83.

16. Wojciech W. Charenza, "East European Transformation: The Supply Side," in Poznanski (ed.), *Stabilization*, p. 167.

17. Van Brabant, *Remaking Eastern Europe*, p. 125.

18. Tadeusz Kowalik, "Privatization in Poland—Social Progress or Another Shock," in Akyuz et al. (eds.), *Privatization in Transition*, p. 150.

19. Louisa Vinton, "Domestic Politics and Foreign Policy, 1989–1993," in Ilya Prizel and Andrew A. Michta (eds.), *Polish Foreign Policy Reconsidered: Challenges of Independence* (New York: St. Martin's Press, 1995), p. 35.

20. Roman Frydman, Andrzej Rapaczynski, John S. Earle et al., *The Privatization Process in Central Europe* (New York: Central European University Press, 1993), p. 176.

21. Vacic, "Comment," in Akyuz et al. (eds.), *Privatization in Transition*, p. 178.

22. Ibid., p. 174.

23. Poznanski (ed.), *Stabilization*, p. 1.

24. Slay, "Economic Transition," in Hardt and Kaufman (eds.), *Economies in Transition*, p. 463.

25. Sachs, *Poland's Jump*, p. 84. Sachs writes: "In the British privatizations, leading merchant banks prepared careful valuations of each enterprise, in order to set an appropriate price for the sale of the state's shares. Then, typically, a long public relations campaign was undertaken to explain the specific privatization to the public, and to attract potential investors. In some cases the enterprise itself was restructured in preparation for the privatization. Then, after restructuring, valuation, and a public campaign, the firm was sold, typically through a public offering of shares. Within Eastern Europe, this approach has come to be called the British model."

26. Ibid., p. 85.

27. Jacek Klich, "The Concept of Mass Privatization in Poland: Theoretical and Practical Considerations," Working Paper (Krakow: Academy of Economics, June 1993), pp. 2–3.

28. Roman Frydman and Andrzej Rapaczynski, *Privatization in Eastern Europe: Is the State Withering Away?* (New York: Central European University Press, 1994), pp. 14–15.

29. Ministry of Privatization, *Program Powszechnej Prywatyzacji* [Program of Mass Privatization] (Warsaw: Ministry of Privatization, 1990), quoted in Janusz Golebiowski (ed.), *Transforming the Polish Economy* (Warsaw: World Economy Research Institute, 1993), p. 179.

30. Van Brabant, "The Hobbled Transition," in Akyuz et al. (eds.), *Privatization in Transition*, p. 69.

31. Frydman, Rapaczynski, Earle et al., *Privatization in Central Europe*, p. 181.

32. Blanchard et al., *Reforms*, p. 33.

33. Ibid.

34. Transfer pricing refers to the pricing of property or products transferred among divisions of a firm. "A 'transfer price' is the price attached by a business enterprise to transactions between different divisions in affiliates under its ownership." See "transfer pricing," in Peter Newman, Murray Milgate, and John Eatwell

(eds.), *The New Palgrave Dictionary of Money & Finance*, Vol. 2 (New York: Stockton Press, 1992), p. 690. Many managers of SOEs established highly favorable transfer prices for units of their enterprises, and then exercising their newly acquired authority under the *Law on Economic Activity*, sold the more profitable units of the SOEs to newly established private enterprises, in which these same managers quite often had a proprietary interest. Economists Mark Hirschey and James L. Pappas admit that "a vexing difficulty encountered is the problem of setting an appropriate price for the transfer of goods and services among divisions." Mark Hirschey and James L. Pappas, *Managerial Economics*, Eighth Edition (New York: The Dryden Press, 1996), p. 661. In the Polish transition-economy, which lacked recognized systems of cost accounting, managers were able to take additional advantage of these lacunae when establishing the prices at which they sold various profitable enterprise units. This approach proved to be the route by which many *nomenklatura* left their state-appointed managerial positions and became "instant capitalists" and managers in the new and emerging free market system.

35. Frydman and Rapaczynski, *Privatization in Eastern Europe*, p. 62.

36. L.V. Ryan and A. Nowak, "Patterns of Polish Private Sector Development," in Mordechai E. Kreinin (ed.), *Contemporary Issues in Commercial Policy* (Tarrytown, N.Y.: Pergamon, 1995), p. 110, Note 1. Cf. The *Law of State-owned Enterprises of 25 September 1981*, as amended in 1990–1991, especially Arts. 42, 46a, and 46b. Also cf. Richard J. Hunter, Artur Nowak, and Leo V. Ryan, "Private Ownership in Poland: Former Laws, Present Legislation," in Khosrow Fatemi (ed.), *The Globalization of Business in the 1990's: Implications for Trade and Development*, Vol. I, Part IV, National Studies (Laredo, Texas: Texas A&M International University, 1992), pp. 207–229; Richard J. Hunter, Artur Nowak, and Leo V. Ryan, "Legal Aspects of the Transformation Process in Poland: Business Association Forms," *The Polish Review*, Vol. 40, No. 4 (1995), pp. 387–401.

37. Lavigne, *Economics of Transition*, p. 169.

38. Sachs, *Poland's Jump*, p. 32.

39. Lavigne, *Economics of Transition*, p. 169.

40. Ibid.

41. Ibid., p. 170.

42. M. Rajska, "Raj Utracony" [Paradise Lost], *Gazeta Bankowa*, 17 September 1994, No. 38, p. 8.

43. Slay, "Economic Transition," in Hardt and Kaufman (eds.), *Economies in Transition*, p. 472. See also Jacek Klich, "Reprivatization in Poland: 1991–1994," *Przeglad Organizacji*, Special Issue (1995), pp. 26–27, discussing the legal status, scope, structure, and forms of reprivatization.

44. Earle, Frydman, Rapaczynski, and Turkewitz, *Small Privatization*, pp. xvi, xviii–xix. The Privatization Study cited here refers to a survey conducted by the authors to provide empirical evidence concerning the performance of privatized trade and service establishments in the Czech Republic, Hungary, and Poland and to identify the main driving forces of successful privatization in those three countries. An explanation of the survey and an analysis of the results appears as "Part IV: The Survey," pp. 239–301.

45. Ibid., p. xvii.

46. Ibid., p. 230.

47. Ibid., pp. 232–233.

48. Central Statistical Office [GUS] data, reported in ibid., pp. 235–236.

49. The Central European University is a private, independent, and nonpartisan educational institution located in Prague. The Central European University Privatization Project conducts research and analysis to provide policy makers and analysts, primarily in Eastern Europe but also elsewhere, with current, comprehensive, and reliable information and interpretation concerning the state of privatization in the region (including the former Soviet Republics).

50. Earle, Frydman, Rapaczynski, and Turkewitz, *Small Privatization*, p. xxvii (italics in the original).

51. Ibid., p. 205.

52. Ibid., p. 209.

53. Ibid., pp. 201–202.

54. Ibid., pp. 203, 205.

55. Sachs, *Poland's Jump*, p. 33.

56. Kochanowicz, "Transition," in Poznanski (ed.), *Stabilization*, p. 243.

57. In 1996 the Cimoszewicz government further reorganized ministries. It dissolved the Privatization Ministry itself and transferred privatization activities to an "agency portfolio" under the new State Treasury, and further relegated control of privatization to the Treasury. Steven Anderson and Tomasz Stepien, "Shuffling the Deck," *Warsaw Business Journal*, 7–13 October 1996, pp. 1, 12. Also see Steven Anderson and Tomasz Stepien, "The Grand Ministry Plan," *Warsaw Business Journal*, 7–13 October 1996, p. 12.

58. Quoted and adapted from Lavigne, *Economics of Transition*, pp. 160–162.

59. Frydman, Rapaczynski, Earle et al., *Privatization in Central Europe*, p. 176.

60. Van Brabant, *Remaking Eastern Europe*, p. 127.

61. Van Brabant, "The Hobbled Transition," in Akyuz et al. (eds.), *Privatization in Transition*, p. 64.

62. Keith Cowling points out that the term "privatization" is "neither comprehensive nor precise enough" since privatization, while concerned with the transfer of assets, often "says nothing about the transfer of property rights." He explains these property rights as "the right of utilization of such assets *(usus);* the right of return from such assets *(usus fructus);* and the right of disposal of such assets *(abusus)*—and privatization is incomplete without the transfer of rights." Keith Cowling, "Reflections on the Privatization Issue," in Ha-Joon Chang and Peter Nolan (eds.), *The Transformation of the Communist Economies: Against the Mainstream* (New York: St. Martin's Press, 1995), p. 164.

63. Van Brabant, "The Hobbled Transition," in Akyuz et al. (eds.), *Pivatization in Transition*, p. 64.

64. Ibid., pp. 70–71.

65. Ibid., p. 71.

66. Blaszczyk and Dabrowski, "Privatization Process," in Akyuz et al. (eds.), *Privatization in Transition*, p. 86.

67. Ibid., p. 87.

68. Sachs, *Poland's Jump*, p. 86.

69. Irena Grosfeld, "Comments on Papers on Polish Privatization" in Akyuz et al. (eds.), *Privatization in Transition*, p. 166. The term "LLC" is now widely used in the United States.

70. Frydman, Rapaczynski, Earle et al., *Privatization in Central Europe*, p. 187.

71. Blaszczyk and Dabrowski, "Privatization Process," in Akyuz et al., *Privatization in Transition*, p. 98.

72. See ibid., pp. 99–105, for details and analysis on the number of firms in each category.

73. Ibid., p. 103.

74. Frydman, Rapaczynski, Earle et al., *Privatization in Central Europe*, pp. 187–188.

75. Ibid., p. 188.

76. There is also a provision that if the employees do not exercise their right to purchase shares in the new joint stock or limited liability company within two months after the Workers' Council decision, the lease can proceed without the majority vote of the employees.

77. Ibid., p. 189.

78. The yearly payments on the lease are governed by a special regulation of the minister of finance of 10 November 1990 (No. 43, item 334.)

79. Frydman, Rapaczynski, Earle et al., *Privatization in Central Europe*, p. 198.

80. Jacek Klich, "Privatization and Financial Investment in Poland," in Arian Kaandorp and Jacek Klich (eds.), *Privatization and Restructurisation in East-Central Europe* (Krakow: Jagiellonian University [Tempest Programme], 1993), p. 97.

81. Frydman, Rapaczynski, Earle et al., *Privatization in Central Europe*, p. 199.

82. Lavigne, *Economics of Transition*, p. 170.

83. Janusz J. Tomidajewicz, "Przedsiebiorstwa panstwowe w procesie budowania gospodarki rynkowej" [State-owned Businesses in the Process of Building a Market Economy], *Ruch Prawniczy, Ekonomiczny i Socjologiczny*, Kwartal IV (Poznan: Wydawnictwo Naukowe UAM, 1991), pp. 136–141. This idea was an extension of the policy first enunciated as early as the second stage of economic reform under General Jaruzelski. Early reforms contemplated a lasting state presence in key industries or key industrial sectors.

84. Sachs, "Economic Transformation," in Poznanski (ed.), *Stabilization*, p. 198.

85. Ibid.

86. Frydman and Rapaczynski, *Privatization in Eastern Europe*, p. 40.

87. Ibid.

CHAPTER 7

1. Leszek Balcerowicz, *Rzeczpospolita*, 22 June 1992, reported in Golebiowski (ed.), *Transforming the Polish Economy* (1993), pp. 193–194.

2. Martin R. Myant, *Transforming Socialist Economies: The Case of Poland and Czechoslovakia* (Brookfield, Vt.: Edward Elgar, 1993).

3. Jan Szomburg, "The Decision Making Structure of Polish Privatization," in John S. Earle, Roman Frydman, and Andrzej Rapaczynski (eds.), *Privatization in the Transition to a Market Economy: Studies of Preconditions and Policies in Eastern Europe* (London: Pinter; New York: St. Martin's Press, 1993), pp. 73–85.

4. Ministry of Privatization, *Program Powszechnej Prywatyzacji* (Warsaw: Ministry of Privatization, 1990), encompassing the full range of privatization efforts.

5. Jan Bossak, "Privatization," in Golebiowski (ed.), *Transforming the Polish Economy*, p. 185.

6. R. Rapacki and S. J. Linz, "Privatization in Transition Economies: Case Study of Poland," Working Paper (East Lansing, Mich.: Mich. State University, Department of Economics, 1992), quoted in ibid., p. 186.

7. Ewa Freyberg, "Mass Privatization Program," in Bossak (ed.) (1994), pp. 212–215.

8. Ibid., p. 215.

9. Jan Bossak, "Private Sector Development and Privatization," in ibid., pp. 125–135.

10. Ibid., p. 135.

11. Jerzy Baczynski, "Year of Stability Was Really Stagnation," *Polityka*, quoted in *The Warsaw Voice*, 16 October 1994, p. 6.

12. Andrzej Goldberg, "Privatization Blockage Could Backfire on Pawlak," *Tygodnik Solidarnosc*, quoted in *The Warsaw Voice*, 16 October 1994, p. 6.

13. In an agreement signed with the IMF in August 1994, Poland declared the Mass Privatization Program would be implemented by September and that the first NIF would be registered by the end of 1994. Neither target date was met.

14. *The Warsaw Voice*, 9 October 1994, p. B1.

15. A. Kowalik, "Prywatyzacja–Niezbedna Pozyteczna czy Szkodliwa" [Privatization—Indispensable Advantage or Harm], *Rzeczpospolita*, No. 282, 1994, p. 1.

16. Szomburg, "Decision Making," in Earle, Frydman, and Rapaczynski (eds.), *Privatization in Transition*, p. 81.

17. Adam Lipowski, "Commercialization Makes Managers Complacent," *Nowa Europa*, 26–27 November 1994, quoted in *The Warsaw Voice*, 11 December 1994, p. B2.

18. Balcerowicz, quoted in *The Warsaw Voice*, 9 October 1994, p. B2.

19. Bossak, "Private Sector Development," in Golebiowski (ed.), *Transforming the Polish Economy*, pp. 188–189.

20. Yves Fortin, "Financing Badly Needed for Mass Privatization," *Zycie Gospodarcze*, quoted in *The Warsaw Voice*, 11 December 1994, p. B2.

21. Wieslaw Rozlucki, "Foreign Investors Waiting Clear Mass Privatization Signals," *Gazeta Wyborcza*, 28 November 1994, quoted in *The Warsaw Voice*, 11 December 1994, p. B2.

22. Paul Knotter, quoted in *Nowa Europa*, 14 October 1994, p. 1.

23. Strong, Reiner, and Szyrmer, *Transitions in Land and Housing*, p. 193.

24. Balcerowicz, *Socialism*, p. 200.

25. Cf. Myant, *Transforming Socialist Economies*. Czechoslovakia was the

first country to launch a "voucher type" or "coupon" system in the privatization process.

26. Frydman and Rapaczynski, *Privatization in Eastern Europe*, p. 160.

27. Lavigne, *The Economics of Transition*, p. 166. See also D. Mario Nuti, *Mass Privatization: Costs and Benefits of Instant Capitalism* (London: London Business School, May 1994).

28. Van Brabant, *Remaking Eastern Europe*, p. 25.

29. Jan W. Bossak, "National Investment Fund's Program," in Marek Lubinski (ed.), *Poland: International Economic Report 1995/1996* (Warsaw: The World Economy Research Institute, 1996) p. 237.

30. Ibid.

31. "Privatization: National Investment Funds," *The Warsaw Voice 1996 Business and Economy Yearbook* (Warsaw: The Warsaw Voice, 1996), pp. 68–69.

32. Bossak, "NIF Program," in Lubinski (ed.) (1996), p. 239.

33. David Osterhout, *Central European Business Weekly*, 23–29 June 1995.

34. Marek Matraszek, *Warsaw Business Journal*, 7–13 July 1995, p. 9.

35. Ibid.

36. *The Warsaw Voice*, "Election Day Arrives: An Excess of Choice," 5 November 1995, pp. 16–17.

CHAPTER 8

1. Krzysztof Leski, "The Heat Is On!" *Gazeta International*, 9 August 1990, p. 1. For an article on the creation of Democratic Action, see Steve Crawshaw, "The Action Man of Solidarity," *The Independent*, 26 July 1990, p. 3.

2. James Wedel, "Getting U.S. Aid Right: Learning a Lesson from Poland," *Polish American Journal*, June 1992, p. 2.

3. Ibid., p. 2, quoting Jacek Poznanski, USAID coordinator of aid to Poland.

4. United States Department of State, *U.S. Assistance to Central and Eastern Europe: An Overview* (Washington, D.C.: United States Department of State, 1991). A concise statement of the conditions required for Poland's entry into the EU is found in Euromoney, *The 1997 Guide to Preparing for EMU* (London: Euromoney Publications, 1997), p. 4. The *Maastricht Criteria* are spelled out in Euromoney, *1997 Guide*, p. 5.

5. See generally Keller, "Gorbachev's Hope," in Gwertzman and Kaufman (eds.), *Collapse of Communism*, pp. 270–276. See also Steven Lee Myers, "NATO Takes Steps to Expand Ranks Into Eastern Europe," *New York Times*, 11 December 1996, pp. 1, A9.

6. See generally Congressional Research Service, *Poland's Renewal*, p. 29.

7. Translated in *FBIS Daily Report: USSR*, 14 April 1987, pp. F10–11.

8. Ministry of Privatization, *Information Guide to the Ministry of Privatization* (Warsaw: Studio G&Z, 1991). For a discussion of NIF Certificates, see Lidia Sosnowska-Smogorzewska, "Massively Popular Privatization," *The Warsaw Voice*, 1 December 1996, p. 9; "Emerging Securities Markets: Poland," *Central European*, December 1996/January 1997, p. 35.

9. Richard J. Hunter and Leo V. Ryan, "The Polish Experiment in Democra-

cy and a Free Market: Its Importance for Eastern and Central Europe," *Mid-Atlantic Journal of Business*, Vol. 28, No. 3 (December 1992), pp. 231–234.

10. *Wall Street Journal*, 5 June 1990, p. 13. For a view of these "hard decisions," see Jeffrey Sachs and David Lipton, "Poland's Economic Reform," *Foreign Affairs*, Vol. 69, No. 3 (Summer 1990), pp. 47–66.

11. Brzezinski, "Beyond Chaos," p. 9.

12. *Gazeta International*, 19 July 1990, p. 1.

13. See, e.g., Richard J. Hunter and John Northrop "Management, Legal and Accounting Perspectives: Privatization in Poland," *The Polish Review*, Vol. 38, No. 4, pp. 407–420. For a discussion of tax issues related to the privatization process, see generally Richard J. Hunter and Mark S. Blodgett, "Tax Aspects of Doing Business in Central and Eastern Europe: New England Implications," *International Tax Journal*, Vol. 23, No. 1 (Winter 1997), pp. 62–70; "The Polish Tax System," *Encyclopaedia of Poland Industry*, pp. 12–13, discussing current tax issues; Jerzy Wandecki, "The VAT Landscape. The Uncertain Tax," *The Warsaw Voice* (Business), 18 July 1993, p. B1; Deloitte Touche Tohmatsu International, *Meeting Tax Obligations in Central and Eastern Europe* (Amsterdam: International Bureau of Fiscal Documentation, 1994).

14. See "Economic Indicators," *Central European*, September 1996, pp. 50–51, citing data from PlanEcon, Washington, D.C.

15. Janusz Golebiowski, "Political Changes in Poland and the Region," in Bossak (ed.) (1994), p. 15.

16. See, e.g., Robert Strybel, "Crisis Is Deepening," *Polish American Journal*, June 1992, p. 10.

17. For a discussion of key labor issues, see Mieczyslaw Kabaj, "Industrial Relations, Labor Market and Unemployment," in Lubinski (ed.) (1996), pp. 65–70.

18. Ryszard Rapacki, "Political Economy of Transformation," in Golebiowski (ed.) (1993), p. 13.

19. See, e.g., *Rzeczpospolita*, 14 December 1992, reporting on the economic data from 1992; *The Economist*, 30 April 1994; Marzenna Weresa, "Incomes, Social Services and Consumption," in Lubinski (ed.) (1996), pp. 71–76.

20. Marek Lubinski, "Preface," in Lubinski (ed.) (1996), p. 7. See William A. Stoever, "Revamping Business Education in a Post-Communist Country: The Warsaw School of Economics," *The Polish Review*, Vol. 41, No. 2 (1996), pp. 173–194, discussing the Warsaw School of Economics.

21. A statement of the economic data for GDP, inflation, unemployment, and personal incomes for the 1989–1997 period is included in the Appendix.

22. See *Monitoring rynku pracy, praca nierejestrowana W Polsce w 1995* [Monitoring the Labor Market, Unregistered Employment in Poland in 1995] (Warsaw: GUS, 1995); M. Kalaska and J. Witkowski, *Unregistered Employment in Poland* (Warsaw: CSO, 1996), p. 47.

23. The *Employment and Unemployment Act* was passed on 22 December 1995.

24. *Raport o sytuacji spoleczno-gospodarczej kraju. Rok 1995* [Report about the Social-economic Situation of the Nation. 1995] (Warsaw: GUS, 30 January 1996), p. 43. See also Louisa Vinton, "Poland's Social Safety Net: An Overview," *RFE/RL (Radio Free Europe/Radio Liberty) Research Report*, Vol. 2, No. 17 (April 1993), pp. 3–11.

25. The issue of "winners" and "losers" was discussed at length in Richard J. Hunter, Leo V. Ryan, and Andrew Hrechak, "Out of Communism to What?: The Polish Economy and Solidarity in Perspective," *The Polish Review,* Vol 39, No. 3 (1994), pp. 334–335, pp. 328–329.

26. Smilowski, "Pentor Poll," p. 6.

27. See George Blazyca and Ryszard Rapacki, "Continuity and Change in Polish Economic Policy: The Impact of the 1993 Election," *Europe-Asia Studies,* Vol. 48, No. 1 (1996), pp. 85–100.

28. For a discussion of business association forms, see Hunter, Nowak, and Ryan, "Legal Aspects," pp. 387–401. See also Charles Blishen, "Only the Best Need Apply," *Central European,* September 1996, pp. 10–14, discussing the issue of Polish conglomerates as "targets" for leveraged buyout attempts.

29. Ryszard Rapacki, "Development Trends and Economic Policy," in Lubinski (ed.) (1996), p. 46.

30. Jane Perlez, "A Bourgeoisie Blooms and Goes Shopping. Poland's Market Reforms Take Hold," *New York Times,* 14 May 1996, pp. D1, D6.

31. Marek Lubinski, "Economic Outlook and Policy in 1996," in Lubinski (ed.) (1996), p. 152.

32. The Pentor Poll was reported in Smilowski, p. 6.

33. Ryszard Rapacki, "Political Economy of Transformation," in Golebiowski (ed.), *Transforming the Polish Economy,* p. 15.

34. *Zycie Gospodarcze,* No. 49 (1992).

35. Brzezinski, "Beyond Chaos," p. 9.

36. Dariusz Rosati, "The Politics of Economic Reform in Central and Eastern Europe," Mimeograph (Minneapolis: University of Minnesota, November 1991), cited in Hunter, Ryan, and Hrechak, "Out of Communism," p. 335.

37. For a discussion of the turmoil that surrounded the frequent changes in government, see Anna Sabbat-Swidlicka, "Poland: A Year of Three Governments," *RFE/RL (Radio Free Europe/Radio Liberty) Research Report,* Vol. 2, No. 1 (January 1993), pp. 102–107. Adam Michnik has taken the brunt of many of these criticisms of the "nonretaliation process." See Alain Besancon, "Adamowi Michnikowi w odpowiedzi" [In Response to Adam Michnik], *Kultura,* No. 6 (1990), pp. 126–128. Vladimir Bukowsky saw the entire process as a "victory for the communists." Vladimir Bukowsky, "Totalitarianism in Crisis: Is There Any Smooth Transition to Democracy," in E. F. Paul (ed.), *Totalitarianism at the Crossroads* (New Brunswick, N.J.: Crossroads Books, 1990), p. 13–14.

38. Balcerowicz, *Socialism,* p. 300. For a discussion of the policies of the Suchocka regime, see Louisa Vinton, "Polish Government Faces New Strike Challenge," *RFE/RL (Radio Free Europe/Radio Liberty) Research Report,* Vol. 2, No. 21 (21 May 1993), pp. 25–30.

39. Rapacki, "Political Developments," in Golebiowski (ed.) (1993), p. 17.

40. Raphael Shen, *Economic Reform in Poland and Czechoslovakia* (Westport, Conn.: Praeger, 1993), p. 8. For an informative article on political configurations locked in a "struggle against the communists," see Romuald Szeremietiew, "Independent Movements in Poland," *Perspectives,* Vol. 19, No. 2 (March/April 1989), pp. 3–5. Fr. Shen's book is especially insightful and comprehensive.

41. Janusz Golebiowski, "Political Changes in Poland and the Region," in Bossak (ed.) (1994), pp. 9–18.

42. For a discussion of political developments in 1993 and 1994, see ibid., p. 15.

43. Janusz Golebiowski, "Political Changes in Poland," in Jan Bossak (ed.), *Poland: International Economic Report 1994/1995* (Warsaw: World Economy Research Institute, Warsaw School of Economics, 1995), p. 11.

44. *Financial Times*, 18 March 1994, p. iv.

45. Janusz Golebiowski, "Political Developments in Poland and in the Region," in Lubinski (ed.) (1996), p. 11.

46. Golebiowski, "Political Changes," in Bossak (ed.) (1994), p. 12.

47. See generally, George Sanford and Adriana Gozdecka-Sanford, *Historical Dictionary of Poland* (Metuchen, N.J.: Scarecrow Press, 1994).

48. Ibid., p. 49.

49. See "A Storm Around the President," *Gazeta International*, 9 August 1990, p. 1. Speaking at a meeting of the Warsaw Civic Committee, Lech Walesa said: "A president of the past, a 35 percent prime minister–is this democracy?" noted in Leski, "The Heat Is On," p. 1.

50. Golebiowski, "Political Changes," in Bossak (ed.) (1995), p. 12.

51. John Pomfret, "Poles Cooling," pp. 1, 4. This article appeared fully seventeen months *before* the presidential elections of 1995. See generally, Donald E. Pienkos, "The 1995 Polish Presidential Election: A Step Toward Normalcy," *The Polish Review*, Vol. 42, No. 4 (1997), pp. 395–430.

52. Golebiowski, "Political Developments," in Lubinski (ed.) (1996), p. 13.

53. CBOS, November 1991, cited in Hunter, Ryan, and Hrechak, "Out of Communism," p. 330.

54. Spolar, "Romanians Go with Flow," pp. 1, 8.

55. See Walicki, "Totalitarianism," p. 526. In reaction to the view that *People's Poland* was no more than an "occupied country," Walicki writes: "Many people felt themselves offended, wounded in their patriotic pride, and decided to defend the meaning of their lives." Walicki takes the position that a wholesale delegitimization of the period of communist rule "would not have been supported in a free, popular referendum." Cf. Andrzej Walicki, "From Stalinism to Post-Communist Pluralism: The Case of Poland," *New Left Review* (January/February 1991), p. 121.

56. Cardinal Glemp, argues that the real import of communism was not anti-capitalism, but rather secularism—"striving to expel the church from the public sphere." Walicki, "Totalitarianism," p. 527, citing "Czy PRL trwa?" [Is the PRL Continuing?], *Gazeta Wyborcza*, 16 March 1995, p. 3.

57. The Walesa-Oleksy "soap opera" would continue well into 1996. See Konrad Niklewicz, "The Presidential Paper Chase," *The Warsaw Voice*, 10 November 1996, p. 6; Kuba Spiewak, "Marked Man," *The Warsaw Voice*, 24 November 1996, p. 7.

CHAPTER 9

1. Rapacki, "Political Economy of Transformation," in Golebiowski (ed.), *Transforming the Polish Economy*, p. 2.

2. Hiscocks, *Poland: Bridge*, p. 287.

3. Ibid., p. 287.

4. See especially, Leszek Balcerowicz, "Lessons from Economic Transition in Central and Eastern Europe," in Bossak (ed.) (1994), pp. 193–200.

5. Cf. *Polityka*, No. 51–52, 21–28 December 1991; Rapacki, "Political Economy of Transformation," in Golebiowski (ed.), *Transforming the Polish Economy* (1993), p. 1.

6. Juliusz Urbanowicz, "At the Crossroads. Solidarity in Today's Poland," *The Warsaw Voice*, 27 June 1993, p. 6.

7. Sabbat-Swidlicka, "Three Governments," pp. 102–107.

8. Kazimierz Laski, "Transition from Command to Market Economies in Central and Eastern Europe: First Experience and Questions," Mimeograph (Vienna: The Vienna Institute for Comparative Economic Studies, 1991), p. 2.

9. J. Kochanowicz, "Polish Fears," *Gazeta Wyborcza*, No. 47, 25 February 1992.

10. Janusz Golebiowski, "Democratic Poland: Dilemmas of Stabilization," in Golebiowski (ed.), *Transforming the Polish Economy*, p. 25.

11. "Survey Poland," *The Economist*, 16 April 1994, pp. 3–22. Additional economic data is based on information from the Central Statistical Office (GUS) for the cited year, *Economic and Legal Information from Poland*, and *The Sarmatian Review*, a publication of the Houston circle of PIASA.

12. See, e.g., Krzysztof Kaczynski, "Labor Market and Employment," in Bossak (ed.) (1993), pp. 111–115.

13. COMECON was founded in 1949 as the Soviet "version of the Marshall Plan," and later served as an economic and political counterbalance to the European Economic Community. Its headquarters was located in Moscow. COMECON was formally disbanded in Budapest on 28 June 1991, although it had ceased many of its "coordinating" duties as early as 1989.

14. See Rosati, "The Politics of Economic Reform."

15. Lidia Kolarska-Bobinska, "The Myth of the Market and the Reality of Reform," in Stanislaw Gomulka and Anthony Polonsky (eds.), *Polish Paradoxes* (London, New York: Routledge, 1990). For a discussion of the early period of economic reform, see Lucia Swiatkowski Cannon, "The Economic Shock Strategy in Poland, 1990–1992," in M. B. Biskupski and James S. Pula (eds.), *Poland and Europe: Historical Dimensions*, Vol. 1 (New York: Columbia University Press, 1993), pp. 231–241.

16. Golebiowski, "Social Perceptions of Market Reform," in Golebiowski (ed.), *Transforming the Polish Economy*, p. 48.

17. Stanislaw Gomulka, "Economic, Social and Political Problems of Economic Transformation: The Case of Poland, 1989–1992," Mimeograph (Warsaw, March 1992), quoted by Rapacki, in Golebiowski (ed.), *Transforming the Polish Economy*, p. 4.

18. Laski, "Transition," quoted in Hunter, Ryan, and Hrechak, "Out of Communism," p. 330. Cf. Rapacki, "Political Economy," p. 4.

19. November 1991, cited in Hunter, Ryan, and Hrechak, "Out of Communism," p. 330, as evidence of "declining public support," even in the early period.

20. For a discussion of Polish Peasants' party (PSL) politics in 1996, see Kuba Spiewak, "PSL Party Congress. Peasants' Revolt Fails," *The Warsaw Voice*, 1 December 1996, p. 5.

21. For a discussion of the importance of joint ventures to the Polish econo-my, see Dariusz Filar, "From Autarcky to Joint Ventures: Toward the Post-Commu-nist Opening of the Polish Economy," *Mid-Atlantic Journal of Business*, Vol. 27, No. 2 (June 1991), pp. 181–191.

22. Bogumila Brocka-Palacz, "Domestic and Foreign Investment," in Golebiowski (ed.), *Transforming the Polish Economy*, pp. 209–220.

23. See generally, Monika Sowa, "Foreign Trade and Foreign Direct Invest-ment," in Bossak (ed.) (1993b), p. 122.

24. See Adam Noga, "Private Sector Development and Privatization," in Lu-binski (ed.) (1996), p. 111.

25. Elzbieta Kawecka-Wyrzykowski, "Tariffs and Quotas in Polish Foreign Trade," in Golebiowski (ed.), *Transforming the Polish Economy*, pp. 231–238. See also IMF, Piero Ugolini, "National Bank of Poland. The Road to Indirect Instru-ments," Occasional Paper No. 144 (Washington, D.C.: International Monetary Fund, October 1996), presenting the experience of the National Bank of Poland (NBP) in transition from a "monobank" to a "market-based institution."

26. Rapacki, "Political Economy," in Golebiowski (ed.), *Transforming the Polish Economy*, p. 72.

27. This commentary is not meant to be a "history" of Solidarity. It is offered to provide a context to the discussion of the current political scene. For an impor-tant listing of bibliographic sources on Solidarity, see Edward J. O'Boyle, "Poland's Solidarity Movement: Some Likely Sources of Information," Paper (Baton Rouge, La.: Louisiana Tech University, September 1989).

28. Juliusz Urbanowicz, "At the Crossroads. Solidarity in Today's Poland," *The Warsaw Voice*, 27 June 1993, p. 6.

29. Shen, *Economic Reform*, p. 216.

30. See Przemyslaw Falczynski, "Operation Jobless," *The Warsaw Voice*, 11 July 1993, p. 11.

31. Shen, *Economic Reform*, p. 231.

32. Golebiowski, "Social Perception," in Golebiowski (ed.), *Transformation of the Polish Economy*, pp. 44–48.

33. Goodwyn, *Breaking the Barrier*, p. 339. For an insightful article about the "many faces of Solidarity," written in mid-1990, see Stanislaw Gebethner, "The Many Solidarities," *The Warsaw Voice*, 8 July 1990, p. 3.

34. For a comprehensive view of the issue of popular attitudes, see Golebiowski, "Social Perceptions," in Golebiowski (ed.), *Transforming the Polish Economy*, pp. 44–48, especially p. 44. On the topic of the "dual economy" (a phrase coined by Kornai), see Janos Kornai, *The Road to a Free Economy* (New York: Norton, 1990). Chancellor Kohl's proposals for state intervention were re-ported by the UPI wire, 1 January 1997.

35. "Partitioned Again," *The Economist*, 16 April 1994, p. 5.

36. Detailed information on the London and Paris Clubs agreements may be found in the Appendix.

37. The process moved very swiftly. Representatives of the Polish government and the OECD signed "official documents" on 11 July 1996 that assured Poland's invitation to become the 28th OECD member nation.

38. *The Warsaw Voice* published a special edition, "Polish Days in NATO," 28 April 1996, pp. 14–16. An important article was written by Dariusz Rosati,

then foreign minister, "NATO Expansion Is Russia Friendly," *The Warsaw Voice*, 28 April 1996, pp. 14–16.The U.S. Senate approved NATO expansion in May 1998 by a vote of 80–19.

39. Golebiowski, "Political Developments," in Lubinski (ed.) (1996), p. 9.

40. Shen, *Economic Reform*, p. 231.

41. Goodwyn, *Breaking the Barrier*, pp. 320–321.

42. Frydman and Rapaczynski, *Privatization in Eastern Europe*, p. 84.

43. Thomas S. Mondschean and Timothy P. Opiela, "Banking Reform in a Transition Economy: The Case of Poland," *Economic Perspectives* (The Federal Reserve Board of Chicago), Vol. XXI, Issue 2 (March/April 1997), p. 16.

44. Ibid., p. 28. Cf. Marie Lavigne, *Economics of Transition*, pp. 179–183.

45. See, e.g., Jacek Szlachta, "Poland and Baltic Regional Cooperation," in Lubinski (ed.) (1996), pp. 202–207. See also EuroFutures, *Perspectives for the Economic Development of the Baltic Sea Region* (Stockholm: Eurofund AB, 1994).

46. The main features of the employment program are discussed in Mieczyslaw Kabaj, "Labor Market Policies and Programmes for Counteracting Unemployment in Poland," in Michael Sinai (ed.), *Global Unemployment*, Vol. II (London: Zed Books [United Nations University, World Institute for Economic Development Research], 1995), pp. 216–234.

47. For a discussion of current tax issues in Poland, see Richard J. Hunter and William Jones, "An Update on the Polish Tax System," Paper, 55th annual meeting of PIASA, Fordham University, New York, June 1997.

48. Marek Lubinski, "Economic Outlook and Policy in 1996," in Lubinski (ed.) (1996), p. 156. See also Hunter, Nowak, and Ryan, "Legal Aspects," pp. 387–401.

49. Frydman and Rapaczynski, *Privatization in Eastern Europe*, p. 16.

50. Ibid., Appendix I, "Valuation of State Enterprises in the Polish Economy," pp. 41–43, offering a model and case study of the valuation process of a state-owned enterprise.

51. For a discussion of the need for capital markets as a precondition for privatization, see Lavigne, *Economics of Transition*, pp. 182–183.

52. Frydman and Rapaczynski, *Privatization in Eastern Europe*, p. 85.

53. Van Brabant, *Remaking*, p. 132.

CHAPTER 10

1. Letter of Grzegorz Kolodko, *The Economist*, 21 June 1997, p. 10.

2. General economic statistics for this period have been taken from the European Bank for Reconstruction and Development (EBRD) and the Main Statistical Office (GUS), cited in *The Warsaw Voice 1997 Business and Economy Yearbook* (Warsaw: The Warsaw Voice, 1997).

3. *The Economist*, 28 June 1997, p. 107; *The Economist*, 12 July 1997, p. 94. *The Economist* cites data from "national statistics offices, central banks and stock exchanges."

4. Jane Perlez, "Poland Joining O.E.C.D., A Step Further into Europe," *New York Times*, 11 July 1996, p. C3; Magda Sowinska, "Poland in the OECD," *The Warsaw Voice*, 21 July 1996, p. 9. See also Stanley J. Paliwoda, "Capitalizing on

the Emergent Markets of Central and Eastern Europe," *European Business Journal* 1997, Vol. 9, Issue 1, pp. 27–36.

5. Eugeniusz Smilowski, "The Pentor Poll. A Sunny Spring," *The Warsaw Voice*, 4 May 1997, p. 7.

6. Peter S. Green, "Rules on Reform Won't Be Bent, EU Tells Poland," *International Herald Tribune*, 19–20 October 1996, p. 2.

7. For a discussion of Poland's accession to the European Union, see Dariusz Styczek, "How Far, How Fast," *The Warsaw Voice*, 22 June 1997, pp. 16–17. The European Commission agreed on 10 July 1997 to recommend that the EU open membership talks with Poland, the Czech Republic, Hungary, Slovenia, Estonia, and Cyprus. This decision is termed the "Five plus One" agreement. Reuters, 10 July 1997.

8. "Foreign Investment: 'An Open Secret,'" *The Warsaw Voice 1997 Business and Economy Yearbook*, p. 16.

9. Ibid., p. 23.

10. See Anthony Clothier, "Central and Eastern European Privatizations are Different," *European Business Journal*, Vol. 9, Issue 1 (1997) pp. 37–42. For a discussion of the question of Russian privatization, see Marshall Goldman, "The Pitfalls of Russian Privatization," *Challenge*, Vol. 40, No. 3 (May–June 1997), pp. 35–49, noting that "[In Russia], little has been accomplished, and in Poland, privatization was under way for approximately five years before anything substantial was accomplished," pp. 35–36. A full discussion of Russian privatization issues may be found in Joseph R. Blasi, Maya Kroumova, and Douglas Kruse, *Kremlin Capitalism: The Privatization of the Russian Economy* (Ithaca, N.Y.: ILR, 1997).

11. Letter of Maciej Letowski, "A Chance for Order," *The Warsaw Voice*, 28 July 1996, p. 20. Letowski is editor of *Tygodnik Solidarnosc*. He believes that the current political turmoil is the "price for the incomplete revolution of 1989."

12. For a biography of Cimoszewicz, see Sanford and Gozdecka-Sanford, *Historical Dictionary*, pp. 49–50. For a discussion of the Cimoszewicz cabinet, see Kuba Spiewak, "Something for Everyone?" *The Warsaw Voice*, 18 February 1996, p. 5.

13. For an "insider" discussion of the "Buchacz Firing," see Kuba Spiewak and Lidia Sosnowska-Smogorzewska, "The PM's Quick Draw," *The Warsaw Voice*, 15 September 1996, p. 5. A practical perspective may be found in the letter of Stanislaw Cwik of *Trybuna*, the former Communist Party publication, in *The Warsaw Voice*, 15 September 1996, p. 20, urging a "common sense" approach that would guarantee the success and continuation of the SLD-PSL coalition. The strategy failed.

14. Kuba Spiewak, "Pensioner's Party. The Polish Gray Panthers?" *The Warsaw Voice*, 15 June 1997, p. 6.

15. "Poland. An AWSome Future?" *The Economist*, 31 May 1997, pp. 49, 52.

16. Jonathan Luxmoore and Jolanta Babiuch, "The Pope's Balancing Act," *The Tablet*, 28 June 1997, pp. 826–827.

17. "The Church in the World," *The Tablet*, 14 June 1977, pp. 781–782.

18. For a discussion of the passage of the abortion bill in the Sejm, see Magdalena Kulig, "Poland's Lawmakers Vote to Liberalize Restrictive Abortion Law," *The Star-Ledger* (Newark, N.J.), 25 October 1996, p. 6.

19. Anita Szarlik, "A Pope for All Poles," *The Warsaw Voice*, 15 June 1997, p. 15.

20. Kuba Spiewak and Piotr Lewandowski, "Concordat. Movement at Last," *The Warsaw Voice*, 27 April 1997, p. 5. The *Concordat* was again blocked on 27 June 1997 when UW and PSL deputies walked out of the Sejm in order to stop civil legislation on the status of religious education in schools. *The Warsaw Voice*, 6 July 1997, p. 6.

21. Jonathan Luxmoore, "Act VII: Enter Pope John Paul," *The Tablet*, 31 May 1997, pp. 296, 298–299.

22. See Kuba Spiewak, "C Is for Compromise," *The Warsaw Voice*, 26 January 1996, p. 5. For a discussion of key constitutional provisions, see Kuba Spiewak, "Now It's Up to 'We, the People,'" *The Warsaw Voice*, 30 March 1997, p. 7. For a comprehensive study on the issue of constitutionalism in Poland, see Mark Brzezinski, *The Struggle for Constitutionalism in Poland* (Oxford, St. Antony, 1998).

23. Lidia Sosnowska-Smogorzewska, "Last Chance to Cash In," *The Warsaw Voice*, 17 November 1996, p. 10.

24. A *Warsaw Voice* editorial noted that "after World War II, bound by the Soviet sphere of influence against our will, we found ourselves in the camp opposing our natural allies." *The Warsaw Voice*, 6 July 1997, p. 2.

25. Alison Mitchell, "Clinton Cheers Exultant Poles, and Vice Versa,"*New York Times*, 11 July 1997, pp. 1, A6.

26. Szarlik, "A Pope for All Poles," p. 15.

27. For a discussion of the State Enterprise Pact, see Krzysztof Markowski, "The State Enterprise Pact," in Jan W. Bossak (ed.), *Poland: International Economic Report 1992/1993* (Warsaw: The World Economy Research Institute, Warsaw School of Economics, 1993a), pp. 171–177.

28. For two very different views of the "future" of the trade union movement, see the interviews with Kazimierz Ujazdowski and Bogdan Borusewicz in *The Warsaw Voice*, 11 July 1993, p. 9.

Chronology of Significant Economic and Political Dates and Events

WORLD WAR II TO 1995

1939–45	*World War II*
1939	(23 August)—Nazi-Soviet Pact
1939	(1 September)—Hitler invades Poland
1939	(17 September)—USSR invades and partitions Poland on the basis of the Nazi-Soviet Pact
1941	(June)—Hitler invades Russia; Poles accept the Soviet Union reluctantly as the "ally of our allies"
1941	(5 December)—*Declaration of Friendship and Mutual Assistance* signed by Stalin and General Sikorski
1941/42	(end of December/beginning of January)—Polish Workers' party (PPR) established, Marceli Nowotko, general-secretary
1942	(November)—Nowotko shot, succeeded by Pawel Finder
1943	(16 January)—Soviets declare all people who lived in Soviet territory will be considered Soviet citizens
1943	(March)—Union of Polish Patriots in the USSR (ZPP) formed, with writer Wanda Wasilewska as chairman; ZPP calls for a program of reform, acknowledges the territorial claims of the Soviet Union, and demands "new territories" in compensation from Germany
1943	(March)—the PPR publishes its *manifesto* called "What We Are Fighting For," composed by Gomulka and Pawel Finder
1943	(app. March)—"Berling Army" created in the Soviet Union, the "Kosciuszko Division"
1943	(12 April)—Announcement of the discovery of the mass grave in the woods of Katyn (near Smolensk) of 4,321 Polish officers (in all, more than 8,000 were murdered)
1943	(26 April)—Stalin breaks off diplomatic relations with the London

government over the Katyn Affair after it requested the International Red Cross investigate the matter

1943   (4 July)—The death of General Sikorski at Gibraltar results in Stanislaw Mikolajczyk as head of the government-in-exile

1943   (28 November–1 December)—Teheran Conference adopts the Curzon Line as Poland's eastern frontier; no Polish representative is present

1943   (23 November)—Gomulka elected secretary of the PPR

1944   (1 January)—National Homeland Council (the KRN) provisionally established (Bierut as chairman of the presidium), aiming to establish a pro-Soviet "representative body" in Poland

1944   (4 January)—Soviet army crosses the pre-war Polish-Soviet frontier

1944   (22 February)—Churchill's speech to the House of Commons declares that Soviet territorial demands were both "reasonable and just"

1944   (June)—Gomulka officially forms the National Homeland Council (KRN) without Moscow's prior approval

1944   (mid-June)—Mikolajczyk visits Moscow; confronted by three conditions: recognition of the Curzon Line; withdrawal of "anti-Soviet accusations" regarding Katyn; resignation of anti-Soviet members of the London government, including Sosnkowski, Kukiel, and Kot

1944   (18 July)—Red Army crosses the Curzon Line at the Bug River

1944   (21 July)—Red Army captures Chelm, near Lublin

1944   (22 July)—The Polish Committee of National Liberation (PKWN) formed under Soviet auspices in Lublin; known as the *Lublin Committee*; composed of Osobka-Morawski (Chairman), Radkiewicz (security), Rola-Zymierski (defense), and Andrzej Witos (vice-chair and agriculture)

1944   (23 July)—Lublin named the temporary capital of Poland by the PKWN

1944   (1 August–2 October)—*Warsaw Uprising* takes 150,000 to 200,000 lives; Russian army remains at the outskirts of Warsaw

1944   (6 September)—*An Act on Land Reform* adopted by the PKWN; nationalization of all farms over 100 hectares in western Poland, and farms over 50 hectares in eastern Poland

1944   (2 October)—Home Army leader, Tadeusz Bor-Komorowski, surrenders to the Germans; the next day, the survivors capitulate, the remaining inhabitants are expelled from Warsaw, and the systematic destruction of the city begins

1944   (15 December)—Churchill's speech to Parliament indicates a "hardening stance" against Soviet territorial and political demands

1944   (31 December)—PKWN proclaims itself the Provisional Government of Poland

1945   (1 January to June)—Provisional Government of the Republic of Poland (RTRP) formed

1945   (4 January)—Provisional Government "recognized" by Stalin

1945   (4–11 February)—*Yalta Conference*; Allied leaders call for the "reorganization" of the Provisional Government, with "inclusion of democratic leaders from Poland itself and from Poles abroad"; elections to be held "as soon as possible"; implementation left to Vyacheslav Molotov, Sir Archibald Clark-Kerr, and W. Averell Harriman

1945   (March-April)—Prominent noncommunists arrested and sent to Moscow for detention

1945   (12 April)—President Roosevelt dies; succeeded by Harry S. Truman

1945   (21 April)—*Polish-Soviet Non-Aggression Pact* signed

1945   (28 June)—Provisional Government of National Unity (TRJN) formed as a result of the Yalta Conference; Osobka-Morawski continues as premier; Mikolajczyk, first deputy premier and minister of agriculture; Wincenty Witos, vice-president; and Gomulka, second deputy premier and minister for the recovered territories; Boleslaw Bierut becomes president. The "opposition" receives only five out of 20 cabinet posts. This government lasts until February 1947

1945   (29 June, 5 July)—Governments of France, the United States, and the United Kingdom recognize this "new" government

1945   (17 July–2 August)—*Potsdam Conference* fixes Polish-German frontier on the Oder and Western Neisse rivers

1945   (July)—*Potsdam Conference* recognizes the "political interests" of the Soviet Union in Central Europe; accepts *de facto* the Soviet-sponsored PKWN as the government of Poland

1945   (September)—a new Polish Peasant party (PSL) founded with Wincenty Witos as its chair; Witos dies in October, succeeded by Stanislaw Mikolajczyk

1945   (16 October)—Poland becomes the 51st nation to sign the United Nations Charter

1945   (6 December)—First Congress of the Polish Workers' Party

1946   (3 January)—*An Act on the Nationalization of Industry* and *An Act on Taking Over the Main Branches of the National Economy* effect the nationalization of all factories with 50 or more workers and the complete takeover of "basic industries"; provide the basis for socialized property in "People's Poland"

1946   (14 February)—Agreement reached between Polish and British representatives of the Combined Repatriation Executive, effecting the "transfer" of 5,057,000 Germans from east Pomerania, east Brandenburg, Silesia, Danzig, East Prussia, and central Poland

1946   (5 March)—Churchill's *Iron Curtain* speech at Westminster College in Fulton, Missouri: "From Stettin in the Baltic to Trieste in the Adriatic an iron curtain has descended across the continent." (A lesser-known aspect of this speech was his rejection of the Polish western frontier, and of "Slav penetration deep into German territory.")

1946   (30 June)—Referendum held; Mikolajczyk urges a "no vote" on question one, concerning abolishing the Senate; the government claims a 68 percent vote in its favor

1947   (January)—*Nowe Drogi* [New Roads], the theoretical organ of the

PPR's Central Committee, appears; the first article is "Strong in Unity," written by Gomulka

1947   (19 January)—Parliamentary elections held; communist-led Democratic Bloc captures 80 percent of the vote in a blatantly rigged election; British and American governments launch protests, but to no avail.

1947   (5 February)—Bierut elected president of the Republic

1947   (6 February)—Jozef Cyrankiewicz elected as premier, serves until 1972 (last nominal noncommunist to hold the post)

1947   (19 February)—The "Little Constitution" comes into force

1947   (October)—Mikolajczyk denounced as a "foreign spy" and "collaborator"; in November he escapes to London and eventually to the United States, where he dies in 1966

1948   (28 January)—*Polish-Soviet Trade Treaty* (Poland rejects Marshall Plan Aid)

1948   (3 September)—After a series of vicious attacks (led by Hilary Minc) at the Plenum of the Party's Central Committee, Gomulka replaced as first secretary by Boleslaw Bierut

1948   (4 September)—Minc announces the introduction of collectivization into Polish agriculture

1948   (15 December)—The Polish United Workers' party (PZPR) created

1949   Constantine Rokossowski appointed minister of defense and commander-in-chief of the Polish Army

1949   COMECON created

1951   (31 July)—Gomulka arrested in Krynica; spends three years under virtual "house arrest"

1952   (22 July)—Constitution proclaims the *Polish People's Republic* (PRL)

1953   (5 March)—Stalin dies

1953   (26 September)—Cardinal Wyszynski placed under arrest at a monastery in Komancza in the Bieszczady Mountains; later moved to Lidzbark, in northeast Poland

1955   (14 May)—Warsaw Pact is formed as a counterbalance to NATO

1956   (25 February)—Khrushchev's *Secret Speech* to the Twentieth Party Congress denounces Stalin's "crimes against the Party and the people," and Stalin's "cult of personality"

1956   (12 March)—President Bierut dies suddenly in Moscow, replaced by Edward Ochab on 21 March (date of death is in dispute)

1956   (June)—Workers at the (ZISPO) Cigielski Locomotive Factory in Poznan riot; demonstrators seize the District Offices of the government and Party; 74 are killed, 300 injured; workers clamor for "bread" and "freedom," amid cries of "Russians Go Home!"

1956   (9 October)—Minc resigns; Gomulka, opposed by the "Natolin Group," reappears in the Central Committee

1956   (17 October)—Imre Nagy readmitted to the Hungarian Communist party

1956   (19 October)—The Politburo of the Soviet Communist party (Khrushchev, Molotov, Mikoyan, Kaganovich, Koniev) arrive at

	Okecie Airport to "monitor" the situation
1956	(21 October)—Gomulka elected first secretary; Rokossowski ousted from the Politburo; the pro-Soviet "Natolin Group" (Rokossowski, Radkiewicz, Nowak) discredited
1956	(23–24 October)—Hungarian Revolution in full swing
1956	(October)—Government sets up the Conference of Workers' Self-Management in larger enterprises
1956	(28 October)—Cardinal Wyszynski returns to Warsaw and "blesses" the new regime
1956	(5 November)—Imre Nagy overthrown and arrested
1956–57	Leszek Kolakowski leads a group in creating the journal *Po prostu* in the climate of de-Stalinization
1957	(May)—A committee of the Economic Advisory Council, under the chairmanship of Oskar Lange, issues a "thesis" for a new economic model
1957	(June)—The Economic Committee of the Council of Ministers established to "coordinate" economic policy at the highest levels
1957	(2 October)—Adam Rapacki (foreign minister) proposes creating a nuclear-free zone in Poland, Czechoslovakia, and the two German Republics (the Rapacki Plan)
1957	(5 November)—The All-Polish Club of Progressive Catholic Intelligentsia established; the revived *Tygodnik Powszechny* appears in print on Christmas Day
1958	(September)—Government forbids members of religious orders from giving instruction in schools, unless "fully qualified" as teachers; orders removal of religious symbols from public classrooms
1960	(April)—Authorities announce that the Nowa Huta site for building a large church will be used for a school instead
1961	(Summer)—Religious instruction excluded from all public schools
1964	(15 October)—Khrushchev resigns as First Secretary
1964	Modzelewski, along with Kuron, write their *Open Letter to the Party*
1965	(18 November)—"Letter of Polish Bishops" to their German counterparts seeking an end to hostilities and a plea to Germans to "forgive and forget"
1966	(Spring)—Philosopher Leszek Kolakowski is expelled from the Communist party and is forced to leave Poland in 1968
1968	(March)—The closing of Adam Mickiewicz's *Dziady* [Forefathers' Eve] brings about a clash with students; workers rally to the side of the government and attack students; serious "antisemitic" overtones develop
1968	(Spring-Summer)—Events in Czechoslovakia conclude with a Warsaw Pact invasion, including Polish troops
1970	(7 December)—Treaty between the Federal Republic of Germany and Poland recognizes Poland's western frontier
1970	(12 December)—Crisis caused by decision of the government to increase food prices by as much as 20 percent; workers stage strikes

	in Szczecin, Gdynia, Elblag, and Gdansk; cries of "Gomulka Out" and "Hang Gomulka" are heard
1970	(20 December)—Central Committee accepts the "resignation" of Gomulka; Edward Gierek becomes first secretary
1976	(June)—Gierek announces a price hike for food by an average of 60 percent; workers at the Ursus tractor plant tear up a railway line; in Radom, the Party House is burned. Workers met by police brutality
1976	(September)—Committee for the Defense of Workers (KOR) formed, originally by 14 and later 30 members, led by Jacek Kuron
1976	(December)—Workers killed at Gate No. 2 of the Lenin Shipyard; demands call for trade unions "to be made up of non-Party members"
1977	(Spring)—Committee for the Defense of Human and Civil Rights (ROPCiO) founded
1977	(7 November)—KOR's journal, *Robotnik,* begins publication; a free "union cell" set up in Radom, by Leopold Gierek, editor of *Robotnik*
1977	(November-alternatively January 1978)—The creation of the "Society for Scientific Courses," the "Flying University" (under the "inspiration" of Andrzej Celinski)
1977	(December)—Gierek visits the Vatican and holds a private meeting with Pope Paul VI
1978	(29 April)—The Committee of Free Trade Unions for the Baltic Coast, centered in Gdansk, founded by Andrzej Gwiazda, Antoni Sokolowski, and Krzysztof Wyszkowski; a similar "free trade union" had been previously established in Katowice (23 February) in an appeal signed by Kazimierz Switon, Wladyslaw Sulecki, Tadeusz Kicki, and Roman Ksciuczek
1978	(16 October)—Cardinal Karol Wojtyla of Krakow elected as Pope John Paul II
1979	Creation of the Young Poland movement (RMP) (under the leadership of Aleksander Hall)
1979	Creation of the underground newspaper, the *Coastal Worker*
1979	(June)—First pilgrimage of Pope John Paul II to Poland
1979	Founding of the Confederation for an Independent Poland (under the leadership of Leszek Moczulski)
1979	(11 October)—Eight worker-activists from Szczecin set up an unofficial free labor committee for western Pomerania region
1979	(December)—KOR draws up the *Charter of Workers' Rights*
1980	(15 January)—Walesa and 14 other workers dismissed from their jobs at Elektromontaz
1980	(3 May)—Arrests of several members of the Young Poland movement and the Committee for the Defense of Human and Civil Rights
1980	*The "July Events"* (1 July)—Government announces price increases for meat (2 July)—First statement by KOR that it will act as a "strike

information agency"; first strike reported in Mielec, in an aircraft factory

(2–11 July)—Strikes spread to Ursus tractor plant near Warsaw, and to Tczew, Huta Warszawa, and Lodz; then to Wloclawek, Iwiczna, Mielec auto plant, Swidnik aircraft factory, Zeran auto factory, tram drivers in Warsaw

(11–19 July)—Strikes spread to Lublin, Poznan, Warsaw, Chelm, Krasnik, Stalowa Wola, Wroclaw; by 26 July, strikes affect 100 enterprises

(27)—July) Gierek departs for three-week vacation in the Crimea

(31 July)—Gierek meets with Brezhnev at the Crimea

1980   *Events of the "Polish August"*

(2 August)—Strikes spread to Gdansk (Lenin) Shipyard

(4 August)—First mention of "work stoppages" in *Trybuna Ludu;* 1,000 Warsaw garbage collectors strike

(5 August)—Three members of opposition arrested (Jan Litynski, editor of *Robotnik,* Piotr Kecik, and Stefan Kozlowski); helicopter factory workers in Swidnik strike

(7 August)—Anna Walentynowicz fired for "activism"

(8 August)—KOR offers strikers financial support; will henceforth serve as a "contact center" for the various strike committees

(12 August)—Warsaw bus drivers' strike spreads

(14 August)—Strikes take on a definite "political character"; workers at Lenin Shipyard stage all-out "occupation" strike; future strike leader Lech Walesa "climbs over shipyard wall" to be with striking workers, engaged in an occupation strike

(15 August)—Communications blackout in Gdansk, as the government seeks to "isolate" workers and strike leaders; Cardinal Wyszynski delivers important sermon at Jasna Gora; Wyszynski prays for the "spirit of freedom" and the "right of self-decision"

(16 August)—Interfactory Strike Committee (MKS) established in Gdansk, composed of two representatives from the Lenin Shipyard and the other 20 striking units (Walesa sets the date as 16–17 August)

(17 August)—Open-air mass celebrated at shipyard gate by Bishop Kaczmarek, attended by 3,000 strikers

(17 August)—Deputy PM Tadeusz Pyka appointed head of a government commission to examine the Gdansk situation

(17 August)—MKS (now representing more than 200,000 workers) draws up its list of 16 demands

(18 August)—Politburo meets; Jablonski and Kania go to Gdansk; strikes spread to Szczecin; the Party announces it would agree to "negotiate" with the MKS if Walesa, Walentynowicz, and Gwiazda ("hard ones") were eliminated

(19 August)—Strikes spread to entire Baltic coast, and to Nowa Huta in Krakow; Walesa emerges as the head of the MKS Presidium;

Deputy PM Barcikowski is sent to Szczecin as head of a Party-government commission

(20 August)—14 members of KOR rounded up and detained, including Adam Michnik and Jacek Kuron

(21 August)—*Appeal of 64* Polish intellectuals (drafted by the Mazowiecki-Geremek group); Moczulski detained; the number of activists under arrest reaches 24

(21 August)—Pyka replaced by Politburo member Jagielski as chief government negotiator

(22 August)—MKS represents 400 work facilities; pope offers mass for Poland; *Twenty-One Demands* strike bulletin posted

(23 August)—First round of talks ends without progress; number of workplaces involved in the strikes grows to 370

(24 August)—IV Plenum of PZPR meets in Warsaw; Gierek forced to accept the removal of many of his closest associates; major governmental and Party changes announced, including the prime minister, foreign minister, minister of finance, Planning Commission and Price Commission chairmen, Radio and TV Committee chair, and director of GUS

(25 August)—Seven "advisors" arrive in Gdansk to assist strikers in negotiations, including Geremek, Mazowiecki, Kowalik, Kubicki, Kuczynski, Wielowieyski, and Staniszkis; MKS now represents more than 400 factories

(26, 27 August)—Second and third rounds of Jagielski-MKS talks in Gdansk prove inconclusive; MKS founded at Nowa Huta

(28 August)—Walesa appeals for a temporary halt to spreading strikes to allow negotiators to work out a compromise; *Charter 77* movement (Czechoslovakia) releases statement in support of Gdansk strikers

(29 August)—*Appeal of 64* intellectuals now has 239 signatories

(30 August)—Walesa announces agreement on Point No. 1—the "right to free and independent trade unions"; Deputy PM Jagielski announces that he "accepts the formula for a new trade union"

(30 August)—Szczecin strike

(30 August)—Szczecin strike declared over; agreement signed by Barcikowski and Szczecin MKS chair, Marian Jurczyk

30 August)—10 Soviet human rights activists express sympathy for strikers in Poland, led by Andrei Sakharov

1980   (1 September)—Remaining dissidents released; Kuron reiterates his support for the "socialist system" and recognizes the Party's "leading role"

1980   (3 September)—Pope John Paul speaks on Poland's "moral right to independence, sovereignty, and self-determination"; strike of Silesian miners settled

1980   (5 September)—Gierek, "seriously ill," ousted as first secretary; replaced by Stanislaw Kania

1980   (6 September)—Kania appeals for "public trust" in radio address to the nation

1980   (14 September)—Poland's Council of State issues a decree on legal

	procedures for registration of new labor unions outside the jurisdiction of the official unions
1980	(November)—Registration of NSZZ Solidarnosc as the first legal independent trade union in a Soviet-controlled country
1981	(February)—Jaruzelski replaces Pinkowski as premier; retains the defense portfolio
1981	(16–19 March)—"Bydgoszcz Affair" begins with a sit-in by peasant activists at a Party headquarters; ends in beating of 27 Solidarity activists, including Jan Rulewski, regional chairman
1981	(March)—"National warning strike" takes place
1981	(March)—Creation of the "Network" (Siec) to assure worker control of enterprises
1981	(September)—First Congress of NSZZ Solidarnosc; Walesa elected president, defeating Andrzej Gwiazda (Gdansk), Marian Jurczyk (Szczecin), and Jan Rulewski (Bydgoszcz)
1981	(25 September)—Sejm passes a *Law on State-owned Enterprises,* providing for "independence, self-governance, self-financing, full legal personality" of enterprises.
1981	(September)—Sejm passes the *Law on Self-management of State-owned Enterprises,* guaranteeing worker participation in the management of state enterprises
1981	(28 October)—Solidarity calls for a one-hour general strike
1981	(13 December)—Imposition of martial law
1981	(18 December)—Pope John Paul sends a letter to Walesa: "I am heart and soul with you"
1982	(January)—Fr. Jerzy Popieluszko conducts "Mass for the Motherland" at St. Stanislaw Kostka Church in Warsaw
1982	(Spring)—Provisional Coordinating Committee of Underground Solidarity formed (TKK)
1982	(6 July)—*The Law on Principles of Conducting Economic Activity in Small Industry by Foreign Corporate Bodies and Private Persons* passes; it is part of the "economic reform" package
1982	(October)—Jaruzelski announces a series of "economic reforms" during the height of martial law
1982	(October)—NSZZ Solidarnosc delegalized and property confiscated
1982	(8 November)—Walesa writes to General Jaruzelski proposing a "reopening of a national dialogue," signed by a "Corporal Walesa"
1982	(11 November)—Walesa released from internment
1982	(November-December)—Regulations issued by minister of justice, minister of finance, chairman of the Council of Ministers, and minister of domestic trade on various aspects of the proposed economic reform
1983	(16–23 June)—Pope John Paul's second visit to Poland; the pope meets with Lech Walesa
1983	(5 October)—Announcement that Lech Walesa has been awarded the Nobel Peace Prize
1983	(July)—Martial law "officially" ends, although many restrictions remain (government sets the date as 31 December 1982)

1983	(July)—Jaruzelski creates the Ministry of Economic Reform
1983	(10 December)—Nobel Prize awarded to Lech Walesa; Walesa refuses to attend the ceremony because of fear he will not be permitted to return to Poland
1984	(19 October)—Fr. Popieluszko murdered while returning from a special workers' mass in Bydgoszcz; funeral attended by more than 350,000 people; Walesa says: "Solidarity lives on, because you have given your life for us"
1985	(November)—33 University presidents dismissed
1986	(January)—Limited amnesty declared by the government (Michnik, Lis, Frasyniuk, and Bujak released)
1986	(November)—Meeting between U.S. Assistant Secretary of State Ridgway and Polish Foreign Ministry official Jan Kinast in Vienna, discussing reopening ties
1987	(February)—U.S. Deputy Secretary of State Whitehead visits Poland and meets with Jaruzelski
1987	(March)—U.S. sanctions lifted; delegation from the Sejm visits Washington
1987	(October)—"Second Stage of Economic Reform" announced
1987	Third pilgrimage of Pope John Paul II; John Paul recognizes Solidarity's "eternal significance"
1987	(29 November)—Popular referendum results in "rebuff" to government
1988	(August)—General Kiszczak and Walesa meet in formal negotiations with no immediate results evident
1988	(November)—Walesa "humiliates" Alfred Miodowicz, head of the official trade unions, in a nationally televised debate
1988	(18 December)—Solidarity "Citizens Committee" gathers in Warsaw, with a final membership of 232 persons
1988	(23 December)—Sejm passes the *Law on Business Activity with the Participation of Foreign Parties* (Polish Foreign Investment Law)
1988	(23 December)—Sejm passes the *Law on Business (Economic) Activity,* providing for "equal rights" for all economic sectors
1989	(3 February)—Historian Roy Medvedev indicates that as many as 20 million died as victims of Stalin
1989	(6 February)—Round Table talks begin; actual talks take place 4 March–5 April
1989	(15 February)—Last Soviet troops leave Afghanistan
1989	(26 March)—Soviet voters participate in the "freest" elections since 1917; Yeltsin elected leader in Moscow
1989	(5 April)—*Round Table* agreement concluded with "power-sharing arrangement" in the "contract Parliament"
1989	(17 April)—Solidarity relegalized
1989	(5 June)—Semi-free elections to the contract Parliament result in rout of Communist party candidates
1989	(5 June)—General Jaruzelski invites Solidarity to join in a coalition government; Solidarity refuses

1989	(16 June)—Nagy given a solemn "hero's burial" in Budapest, 31 years after he was hanged and buried in a common grave
1989	(30 June)—Major changes in Polish banking system proposed as part of an economic program recommended by the World Bank and IMF
1989	(19 July)—General Jaruzelski elected president of Poland
1989	(19 August)—Tadeusz Mazowiecki nominated as prime minister, as the Kiszczak candidacy collapses
1989	(12 September)—Mazowiecki assumes position of prime minister of the coalition government; three main portfolios still controlled by communists
1989	(6 October)—Government announces plans for a "market economy"
1989	(25 October)—Gorbachev disavows the "Brezhnev Doctrine," renouncing any right of regional intervention
1989	(26 December)—Nicolae Ceausescu and wife Elena executed in Bucharest, Romania
1989	(27 December)—The Sejm passes the *Balcerowicz Program*
1989	(28 December)—More than 25 laws ("the big bang") for radical economic reforms passed by the Sejm
1989	(29 December)—The "leading role" of the Communist party in Polish Constitution abolished
1989	(29 December)—Vaclav Havel, Czech dissident and writer, elected president of Czechoslovakia by the Parliament
1990	(1 January)—Stabilization program begins
1990	(27 January)—Polish Communist party dissolved
1990	(16 February)—Agreement with Paris Club obtains debt relief until February 1990, $9.4 out of Poland's $39 billion debt
1990	(21 March)—*U.S.-Poland Treaty Concerning Business and Economic Relations* signed
1990	(5 July)—Prominent communist cabinet ministers dismissed, including Janicki (agriculture), Kiszczak (interior), Siwicki (Defense)
1990	(13 July)—*Law on Privatization of State-owned Enterprises* passed by the Sejm, involving 7,600 enterprises; creation of the Ministry of Ownership Transformation
1990	(14 November)—German and Polish foreign ministers sign a treaty permanently ratifying borders
1990	(26 November)—First round of presidential election eliminates Prime Minister Mazowiecki; Walesa and Tyminski face a runoff
1990	(December)—Lech Walesa (with 74%) elected president, defeating Stanislaw Tyminski
1991	(4 January)—Bielecki confirmed as the new prime minister
1991	(15 February)—Meeting of the Visegrad Group
1991	(20 April)—Negotiations with *Paris Club* result in reduction of 50 percent of Polish debt
1991	(14 May)—Central School of Planning and Statistics assumes its original name, Warsaw School of Economics
1991	(22 May)—10,000 Solidarity members march in Warsaw protesting the reforms and urging rapid decommunization

1991	(28 June)—COMECON formally disbanded in Budapest
1991	(1 July)—The Warsaw Pact is formally disbanded in Prague
1991	(July)—Warsaw Stock Exchange opened
1991	(14 July)—*Law on Companies with Foreign Participation* passed by the Sejm (new foreign investment law)
1991	(26 July)—Law on taxation of personal income passed
1991	(October)—Fully free democratic elections held
1991	(23 December)—Jan Olszewski becomes prime minister (government lasts only five months); Balcerowicz "ends his public service" after meeting with Prime Minister Olszewski
1992	(24 April)—Solidarity stages a "mass protest" in Warsaw; 70,000 workers take to the streets in protest over the economy
1992	(4 June)—Poland's third postcommunist government falls
1992	(5 June)—Waldemar Pawlak of the Polish Peasant's party nominated as prime minister
1992	(2 July)—Pawlak unable to form a government; government of Hanna Suchocka assumes power
1992	(August)—Ministry of Privatization unveils the "mass privatization" program
1992	(Fall)—First state-owned bank is privatized (Bank for Export Development)
1992	(December)—A wave of strikes (mainly in the coal mines) hits Poland
1992	(21 December)—Meeting of the CEFTA in Krakow
1993	(March)—Sejm passes the *Acts on Financial Restructuring of Enterprises and Banks*
1993	(March)—Agreement made with *London Club* (private debt management involving 500 Western banks) concluded
1993	(30 April)—Law sets forth the establishment, operation, and privatization of the NIFs
1993	(May)—Suchocka government loses "no confidence" vote in Sejm and is forced to resign
1993	(18 May)—*Polish Privatization Law* (PPP), with mass privatization aspect, signed into law
1993	(May)—*Law on National Investment Funds and their Privatization* passed by the Sejm
1993	(19 September)—Elections to the Sejm result in defeat for Solidarity-backed parties; Waldemar Pawlak of the PSL becomes prime minister
1994	(4 February)—Parliament passes a comprehensive copyright law
1994	(11 March)—Second agreement reached with *London Club* to restructure Poland's foreign debt
1994	(July)—President Clinton visits Poland
1994	(October)—World Bank gives Poland's economy a "largely positive" report
1994	(December)—Candidates for the NIF Boards selected
1995	(6 February)—Walesa gives the Sejm an "ultimatum" to either change the Pawlak government or face dissolution
1995	(7 February)—Pawlak government collapses

1995	(4 March)—Jozef Oleksy becomes Poland's prime minister
1995	(19 November)—Walesa defeated for reelection by Aleksander Kwasniewski, a leading member of the SLD
1995	(22 November)—NIF plan implemented; Universal Share Certificates distributed
1995	(21 December)—Oleksy accused of collaboration with Russian/Soviet intelligence
1995	(23 December)—Aleksander Kwasniewski inaugurated as president; Lech Walesa refuses to attend the ceremony
1995	(end)—GDP increases by approximately 7 percent
1995	(31 December)—2,110,710 economic entities registered in Poland (2,061,291 in the private sector; 49,419 in the public sector)

◈ Selected Economic Statistics

		1989	1990	1991	1992	1993	1994	1995	1996	1997 (Mid-Yr)
Inflation	(a)	251.1	585.8	70.3	43.0	35.3	32.2	27.8		
	(b)				37.6	29.5	21.6	18.5	14.6	
Real GDP	(c)	2	−11.6	−7.6	1.5	3.8	5.3	7.0		
Growth	(b)								5.5	7.3
Budget Surplus	(a)	−7.4	2.8	−2.0	−4.9	−2.3	−2.2	−1.8	−2.4 (d)	−2.8
Unemploy- ment	(a)	6.1	11.5	11.8	13.6	15.7	16.0	14.9		
	(b)							14.8	13.4	12.2
Debt	(a)	49.0	48.0	47.6	48.4	47.3	42.2	43.9	42.9 (d)	42.8

(a) National Bank of Poland figures, reported in Mondschean and Opiela, "Banking Reform in a Transition Economy: The Case of Poland," p. 20.
(b) Ministry of Finance, reported in The Warsaw Voice 1997 Business and Economy Yearbook, p. 15.
(c) GUS, reported in Mondschean and Opiela, p. 20.
(d) Expected, European Bank for Reconstruction and Development (EBRD), reported in The Warsaw Voice 1997 Business and Economy Yearbook, p. 10. The statistics cited also report as sources JP Morgan, Nomura Securities, and Investmentbank Austria Research. See also Euromoney, The 1997 Guide to Preparing for the EMU, p. 6. The Maastricht Criteria are found on p. 5.

Selected Economic Statistics

⊗ The Paris and London Clubs

1. Poland's largest Paris Club creditors (in USD billion):

Germany	5.94
France	3.63
Austria	3.60
United States	3.46
Brazil	3.00
Canada	2.64
U.K.	1.65
Italy	1.32
Japan	0.66

Poland's debt was reduced by at least 50 percent; France and the United States agreed to reduce their debt by 70 percent.

See "Reforms, Debt Relief, and Development Prospects," in Golebiowski (ed.) (1991), pp. 134–142.

2. Poland's London Club or private commercial debt of 13.2 USD billion was reduced by 45.2 percent, including a 37 percent reduction of interest and a 52 percent reduction in principal. The following nations housed institutions holding private debt:

Germany	24%
United States	18%
U.K.	10%
Japan	9%
France	8%
Austria	6%

Italy	4%
Switzerland	4%
Others	17%

Poland's largest creditors in the London Club are: Salomon Brothers Inc., BFG Bank, Commerz Bank, Swiss Bank Corp., Lloyd's Bank, BNP, Standard Chartered PLC, Westdeutsche Landesbank, Societe Generale, Bank of America, and Dresdner Bank.

See Jan W. Bossak and Krzysztof Kalicki, "Poland's Agreement with the London Club," in Bossak (ed.) (1994), pp. 201–207. The authors note: "Poland's agreement with the London Club is the crowning achievement of not only long and sophisticated negotiations, but also the effect of consistent implementation of economic reforms in Poland and their high evaluation by the G-7, the Paris Club, the IMF, and the World Bank," p. 203.

◈ Selected Bibliography*

BOOKS

Ash, Timothy Garton. *The Polish Revolution: Solidarity*. London: Jonathan Cape. 1983.

Balassa, Bela A. *The Hungarian Experience in Economic Planning: A Theoretical and Empirical Study*. New Haven: Yale University Press. 1959.

Balcerowicz, Leszek. *800 dni*. Warsaw: Polska Oficyna Wydawnicza "BGW." 1992.

———. *Socialism, Capitalism, Transformation*. New York: Central European University Press. 1995.

Balicki, Wladyslaw. *The Theory of Disequilibrium of Demand*. Warsaw: The Institute of Planning. 1979.

Beksiak, J., & U. Libura. *Rownowaga Gospodarcza w Socjalizmie*. Warsaw: Panstwowe Wydawnictwo Naukowe. 1974.

Berend, Ivan, & Gyorgy Ranki. *Economic Development in East Central Europe in the 19th and 20th Centuries*. New York: Columbia University Press. 1974.

Berliner, Joseph S. *Factory and Manager in the U.S.S.R.* Cambridge, Mass.: Harvard University Press. 1957.

Bernhard, Michael M. *The Origins of Democratization in Poland: Workers, Intellectuals, and Oppositional Politics, 1976–1980*. New York: Columbia University Press. 1993.

Bernstein, Carl, & Marco Politi. *His Holiness, John Paul II and the Hidden History of Our Time*. New York: Doubleday. 1996.

Bethell, Nicholas. *Gomulka: His Poland, His Communism*. New York: Holt, Rinehart and Winston. 1969.

Blanchard, Olivier, Rudiger Dornbusch, Paul Krugman, Richard Layard, &

*Translations can be found in the chapter endnotes.

Lawrence Summers. *Reforms in Eastern Europe*. Cambridge, Mass.: MIT Press. 1992.

Blasi, Joseph R., Maya Kroumova, & Douglas Kruse. *Kremlin Capitalism: The Privatization of the Russian Economy*. Ithaca, N.Y.: ILR. 1997.

Boyes, Roger, & John Moody. *The Priest Who Had to Die: The Tragedy of Father Jerzy Popieluszko*. London: Victor Gollancz. 1986.

Bozyk, Pawel. *Dreams and Reality or an Anatomy of the Polish Crisis*. Warsaw: Panstwowy Instytut Wydawniczy. 1983.

Brzezinski, Mark. *The Struggle for Constitutionalism in Poland*. Oxford: St. Antony. 1998.

Brzezinski, Zbigniew K. *The Grand Failure: The Birth and Death of Communism in the Twentieth Century*. New York: Charles Scribner's Sons. 1989.

———. *The Soviet Bloc: Unity and Conflict*. Cambridge, Mass.: Harvard University Press. 1977.

Davies, Norman. *God's Playground: A History of Poland*. Vol. II, *1795 to the Present*. New York: Columbia University Press. 1982.

Deutscher, Isaac. *Stalin: A Political Biography*. New York: Oxford University Press. 1967.

Dziewanowski, Marian K. (M. K.). *The Communist Party of Poland: An Outline of History*. Cambridge, Mass.: Harvard University Press. 1959, 1976.

Earle, John S., Roman Frydman, Andrzej Rapaczynski, & Joel Turkewitz. *Small Privatization*. New York: Central European University Press. 1994.

Frydman, Roman, & Andrzej Rapaczynski. *Privatization in Eastern Europe: Is the State Withering Away?* New York: Central European University Press. 1994.

Frydman, Roman, Andrzej Rapaczynski, John S. Earle, et al. *The Privatization Process in Central Europe*. New York: Central European University Press. 1993.

———. *The Privatization Process in Russia, Ukraine and the Baltic States*. New York: Central European University Press. 1993.

Gardner, Lloyd C. *Spheres of Influence: The Great Powers Partition Europe, from Munich to Yalta*. Chicago: Ivan R. Dee. 1993.

Goodwyn, Lawrence. *Breaking the Barrier: The Rise of Solidarity in Poland*. New York: Oxford University Press. 1991.

Halecki, Oskar. *A History of Poland*. New York: Roy Publishers. 1956, 1966. Thaddeus V. Gromada (ed.). New York: Dorset. 1992.

Hall, Trevor, & Kathryn Spink. *Pope John Paul II: A Man and His People*. New York: Exeter Books. 1985.

Hirschey, Mark, & James L. Pappas. *Managerial Economics*. Eighth Edition. New York: The Dryden Press. 1996.

Hirszowicz, Maria. *Coercion and Control in Communist Society: The Visible Hand in a Command Economy*. New York: St. Martin's Press. 1986.

Hiscocks, Richard. *Poland: Bridge for the Abyss?* London: Oxford University Press. 1963.

Jermakowicz, Wladyslaw. *Privatization in Poland: Aims and Methods*. Warsaw: Centrum Prywatyzacji. 1992.

Kalaska, M., & J. Witkowski. *Unregistered Employment in Poland*. Warsaw: Central Statistical Office. 1996.

Kornai, Janos. *Glowne proporcje rozwoju gospodarczego Polski Ludowej*. Warsaw: Ksiazka i Wiedza. 1960.

———.*The Road to a Free Economy*. New York: Norton. 1990.

———. *The Socialist System: The Political Economy of Communism*. Princeton, N.J.: Princeton University Press. 1992.

Laba, Roman. *The Roots of Solidarity: A Political Sociology of Poland's Working-Class Democratization*. Princeton, N.J.: Princeton University Press. 1991.

Lane, Arthur Bliss. *I Saw Poland Betrayed*. Indianapolis, Ind.: Bobbs-Merrill. 1948.

Lange, Oskar. *Funkcjonowanie gospodarki socjalistycznej*. Warsaw: Panstwowe Wydadnictwo Ekonomiczne. 1960.

———. *Pisma ekonomiczne i spoleczne 1930–1960*. Warsaw: Panstwowe Wydawnictwo Naukowe. 1961.

Lavigne, Marie. *The Economics of Transition: From Socialist Economy to Market Economy*. New York: St. Martin's Press. 1995.

Lipinski, Edward. *Rewizje*. Warsaw: Panstwowy Instytut Wydawniczy. 1956.

Lipski, Jan Jozef. *KOR: A History of the Workers' Defense Committee in Poland, 1976–1981*. Trans. Olga Amsterdamska & Gene M. Moore. Berkeley: University of California Press. 1985.

Malara, Jean, & Lucienne Rey. *La Pologne: D'une occupation a l'autre 1944–1952*. Paris: Editions du Fuseau. 1952.

Mason, David S. *Public Opinion and Political Change in Poland 1980–1982*. Cambridge: Cambridge University Press. 1985.

Matysiak, Andrzej. *Mechanizm tworzenia akumulacji w gospodarce socjalistycznej*. Poznan: Akademia Ekonomiczna. 1984.

Micewski, Andrzej. *Cardinal Wyszynski: A Biography*. San Diego: Harcourt Brace Jovanovich. 1984.

Montias, John M. *Central Planning in Poland*. New Haven, Conn.: Yale University Press. 1962.

Myant, Martin R. *Transforming Socialist Economies: The Case of Poland and Czechoslovakia*. Brookfield, Vt.: Edward Elgar. 1993.

Neumann, William L. *After Victory: Churchill, Roosevelt, Stalin and the Making of the Peace*. New York: Harper & Row. 1967.

Nuti, D. Mario. *Mass Privatization: Costs and Benefits of Instant Capitalism*. London: London Business School. May 1994.

Ost, David. *Solidarity and the Politics of Anti-Politics: Opposition and Reform in Poland since 1968*. Philadelphia, Pa.: Temple University Press. 1990.

Persky, Stan. *At the Lenin Shipyard: Poland and the Rise of the Solidarity Trade Union*. Vancouver, B.C.: New Star Books. 1981.

Rolicki, Janusz. *Edward Gierek: Przerwana dekada*. Warsaw: Wydawnictwo FAKT. 1990.

Sachs, Jeffrey. *Poland's Jump to the Market Economy*. Cambridge, Mass.: MIT Press. 1993.

Sanford, George, & Adriana Gozdecka-Sanford. *Historical Dictionary of Poland*. Metuchen, N.J.: Scarecrow Press. 1994.

Schatz, Jaff. *The Generation: The Rise and Fall of the Jewish Communists of Poland*. Berkeley: University of California Press. 1991.

Shen, Raphael. *Economic Reform in Poland and Czechoslovakia*. Westport, Conn.: Praeger. 1993.

Singleton, Frederick Bernard. *Background to Eastern Europe.* London: Pergamon Press. 1965.

Spulber, Nicolas. *The Economies of Communist Eastern Europe.* Westport, Conn.: Greenwood Press. 1976.

Staniszkis, Jadwiga. *Poland's Self-Limiting Revolution.* Princeton, N.J.: Princeton University Press. 1984.

Szulc, Tad. *Pope John Paul II: The Biography.* New York: Charles Scribner's Sons. 1995.

Tamowicz, P., T. Aziewicz, & M. Stompor. *Small Privatization: Polish Experiences.* Gdansk: The Gdansk Institute for Market Economies. June 1992.

Vajda, Imre. *The Second Five Year Plan in Hungary.* Budapest, Government Press. 1963.

van Brabant, Jozef M. *Remaking Eastern Europe: On the Political Economy of Transition.* Boston: Kluwer Academic Publishers. 1990.

von Oppen, Beate Ruhm. *Documents on Germany under Occupation, 1945–1954.* London: Royal Institute of International Affairs. 1955.

Walesa, Lech (with Marek Zaleski). *A Way of Hope: An Autobiography.* New York: Henry Holt and Co. 1987.

Weschler, Lawrence. *Solidarity: Poland in the Season of Its Passion.* New York: Simon and Schuster. 1982.

Woo, Wing Thye, Stephen Parker, & Jeffrey D. Sachs. *Economies in Transition: Comparing Asia and Eastern Europe.* Cambridge, Mass.: MIT Press. 1997.

Wyszynski, Stefan. *A Freedom Within: The Prison Notes of Stefan, Cardinal Wyszynski.* London: Hodder & Stoughton. 1985.

Zuzowski, Robert. *Political Dissent and Opposition in Poland: The Workers' Defense Committee "KOR."* Westport, Conn.: Praeger. 1994.

Zweig, Ferdynand. *Poland between Two Wars: A Critical Study of Social and Economic Changes.* London: Secker & Warburg. 1944.

JOURNAL AND OTHER ACADEMIC ARTICLES

Augustowski, Zbigniew. "Ceny srodkow produkcji," *Gospodarka Planowa*, No. 1, pp. 42–47. 1953.

Balicki, Wladyslaw. "The Theory of Disequilibrium in Centrally Planned Economies," *Instytut Gospodarki Swiatowej*, Working Paper, pp. 9–39. August 1981.

Bartel, Richard D. "Charting Poland's Economic Rebirth: Interview with Jeffrey D. Sachs," *Challenge*, pp. 22–30. January–February 1990.

Besancon, Alain. "Adamowi Michnikowi w opowiedzi," *Kultura*, No. 6, pp. 126–128. 1990.

Bialer, Seweryn. "Poland and the Soviet Imperium," *Foreign Affairs*, Vol. 59, pp. 522–539. April 1981.

Blazyca, George, & Ryszard Rapacki. "Continuity and Change in Polish Economic Policy: The Impact of the 1993 Election," *Europe-Asia Studies*, Vol. 48, No. 1, pp. 85–100. 1996.

Bobrowski, Czeslaw. "Stopien swobody wyboru: Uwagi na marginesie wytycznych rozwoju gospodarczego na lata 1961–1965," *Gospodarka Planowa*, Nos. 1–2, pp. 6–7. 1986.

Brzezinski, Zbigniew. "Beyond Chaos: A Policy for the West," *The National Interest*, No. 19, pp. 3–12. Spring 1990.

Buczek, Daniel S. "The Coordinating Committee: A Neglected Chapter of World War II," *Polish American Studies*, Vol. 53, No. 2, pp. 5–56. Autumn 1996.

Cienciala, Anna M. "Great Britain and Poland before and after Yalta (1943–1945): A Reassessment," *The Polish Review*, Vol. 40, No. 3, pp. 281–313. 1995.

Clothier, Anthony. "Central and Eastern European Privatizations Are Different," *European Business Journal*, Vol. 9, Issue 1, pp. 37–42. 1997.

Filar, Dariusz. "From Autarcky to Joint Ventures: Toward the Post-Communist Opening of the Polish Economy," *Mid-Atlantic Journal of Business*, Vol. 27, No. 2, pp. 181–191. June 1991.

Fiszer, Janusz. "Polish Parliament Approves New Foreign Investment Law of 1991," *Tax Notes International*, pp. 721–725. July 1991.

Flis, Andrzej. "Crisis and Political Ritual in Postwar Poland," *Problems of Communism*, Vol. 37, Nos. 3–4, pp. 43–54. May–August 1988.

———. "From Marx to Real Socialism: The History of Utopia," *Poznan Studies in the Philosophy of the Sciences and the Humanities*, Vol. 36, pp. 19–30. 1994.

Goldman, Marshall. "The Pitfalls of Russian Privatization," *Challenge*, Vol. 40, No. 3, pp. 35–49. May–June 1997.

Gwiazda, Adam. "Poland's Trade with the West: Past Trends and Future Prospects," *Coexistence*, Vol. 22, pp. 79–90. 1985.

Hunter, Richard J. "The Management Perspective on Poland's Economic Crisis and Recent Attempts at Reform," *The Polish Review*, Vol. 31, No. 4, pp. 299–313. 1986.

Hunter, Richard J., & Mark S. Blodgett. "Tax Aspects of Doing Business in Central and Eastern Europe: New England Implications," *International Tax Journal*, Vol. 23, No. 1, pp. 62–70. Winter 1997.

Hunter, Richard J., & John Northrop. "Management, Legal and Accounting Perspectives: Privatization in Poland," *The Polish Review*, Vol. 38, No. 4, pp. 407–420. 1993.

Hunter, Richard J., Artur Nowak, & Leo V. Ryan. "Legal Aspects of the Transformation Process in Poland: Business Association Forms," *The Polish Review*, Vol. 40, No. 4, pp. 387–401. 1995.

Hunter, Richard J., & Leo V. Ryan. "The Polish Experiment in Democracy and a Free Market: Its Importance for Eastern and Central Europe," *Mid-Atlantic Journal of Business*, Vol. 28, No. 3, pp. 231–234. Dec. 1992.

———. "Uwaga! (Watch Out!) Opportunities and Pitfalls for an American Doing Business in Poland: The Political and Economic Scene," *The Polish Review*, Vol. 36, No. 3, pp. 345–361, 1991.

Hunter, Richard J., Leo V. Ryan, & Andrew Hrechak. "Out of Communism to What?: The Polish Economy and Solidarity in Perspective," *The Polish Review*, Vol. 39, No. 3, pp. 327–344. 1994.

Kalecki, M. "Podstawowe zagadnienia planu piecioletniego na lata 1961–1965," *Gospodarka Planowa*, Nos. 1–2, pp. 1–4. 1959.

Karczmar, M. "Problemy reformy systemu kredytowego," *Finanse*, No. 3, pp. 12–25. 1957.

Klich, Jacek. "Reprivatization in Poland," *Przeglad Organizacji*, pp. 26–27. 1995.

Kolakowski, Leszek. "Tezy o nadziei i beznadziejnosci," *Kultura*, No. 6, pp. 3–21. 1971.

Kornai, Janos. "The Soft Budget Constraint," *Kyklos*, No. 1, pp. 3–30. 1986.

Kosela, Krzysztof. "The Polish Catholic Church and the Elections of 1989," *Religion in Communist Lands*, Vol. 18, pp. 124–137. 1990.

Kowalski, Franciszek. "System cen fabrycznych w przemysle srodkow spozycia," *Gospodarka Planowa*, No. 6, p. 37. 1954.

Kuklinski, Ryszard. "Wojna z narodem widziana od srodka," *Kultura*, pp. 3–57. April 1987.

Lange, Oskar. "Polskie gospodarstwo narodowe w drugim roku planu 6-letniego," *Ekonomista*, pp. 39–62. 1951.

Larsh, William. "Yalta and the American Approach to Free Elections in Poland," *The Polish Review*, Vol. 40, No. 3, pp. 267–280. 1995.

Lewis, Paul. "Turbulent Priest: The Political Implications of the Popieluszko Affair," *Politics*, Vol. 5, No. 2, pp. 33–39. 1985.

Maier, Charles S. "Democracy and Its Discontents," *Foreign Affairs*, Vol. 73, No. 4, pp. 48–64. July/August 1994.

Mondschean, Thomas S., & Timothy P. Opiela. "Banking Reform in a Transition Economy: The Case of Poland," *Economic Perspectives* (The Federal Reserve Board of Chicago), Vol. XXI, Issue 2, pp. 16–31. March/April 1997.

Norr, Henry. "Solidarity and Self-Management," *Poland Watch*, No. 7, pp. 102–113. May–June 1985.

Paliwoda, Stanley J. "Capitalising on the Emergent Markets of Central and Eastern Europe," *European Business Journal*, Vol. 9, Issue 1, pp. 27–36. 1997.

Parkola, A., & R. Rapacki. "II etap reformy w handlu zagranicznym," Warsaw: Instytut Gospodarki Swiatowej, Working Paper Series. 1987.

Pienkos, Donald. "The 1995 Presidential Election: A Step Toward Normalcy," *The Polish Review*, Vol. 42, No. 4, pp. 395–430. 1997.

Poznanski, Kazimierz. "Economic Adjustment and Political Forces: Poland since 1970," *International Organization*, Vol. 40, No. 2, pp. 455–488. Spring 1986.

Ryan, Leo V. "The New Poland: Major Problems for Ethical Business," *Business Ethics: A European Review*, Vol. 1, No. 1, pp. 9–15. January 1992.

Sabbat-Swidlicka, Anna. "Poland: A Year of Three Governments," *RFE/RL (Radio Free Europe/Radio Liberty) Report*, Vol. 2, No. 1, pp. 102–107. January 1993.

Sachs, Jeffrey, & David Lipton. "Poland's Economic Reform," *Foreign Affairs*, Vol. 69, No. 3, pp. 47–66. Summer 1990.

Staniszkis, Jadwiga. "On Some Contradictions of Socialist Society: The Case of Poland," *Soviet Studies*, Vol. 31, No. 2, pp. 167–187. April 1979.

Stoever, William A. "Revamping Business Education in a Post-Communist Country: The Warsaw School of Economics," *The Polish Review*, Vol. 41, No. 2, pp. 173–194. 1996.

Szeremietiew, Romuald. "Independent Movements in Poland," *Perspectives*, Vol. 19, No. 2, pp. 3–5. March/April 1989.

Tomidajewicz, Janusz J. "Przedsiebiorstwa panstwowe w procesie budowania gospodarki rynkowej," *Ruch Prawniczy, Ekonomiczny i Socjologiczny*, Kwartal IV. Poznan: Wydawnictwo Naukowe UAM, pp. 136–141. 1991.

Vinton, Louisa. "Poland's Social Safety Net: An Overview," *RFE/RL (Radio Free Europe/Radio Liberty) Research Report*, Vol. 2, No. 17, pp. 3–11. April 1993.

———. "Polish Government Faces New Strike Challenge," *RFE/RL (Radio Free Europe/Radio Liberty) Research Report*, Vol. 2, No. 21, pp. 25–30. May 1993.

Walicki, Andrzej. "From Stalinism to Post-Communist Pluralism: The Case of Poland," *New Left Review*, pp. 93–121. January/February 1991.

———. "Totalitarianism and Detotalitarization: The Case of Poland," *The Review of Politics*, Vol. 58, No. 3, pp. 505–529. Summer 1996.

GENERAL EDITED COLLECTIONS

Akyuz, Yilmas, Detlef J. Kotte, Andras Koves, & Laszlo Szamuely (eds.). *Privatization in the Transition Process: Recent Experiences in Eastern Europe*. Geneva: United Nations Conference on Trade and Development. 1993.

Biskupski, M. B., & James S. Pula (eds.). *Poland and Europe: Historical Dimensions*. Vol. I. New York: Columbia University Press. 1993.

Blejer, Mario I., & Fabrizio Coricelli (eds.). *The Making of Economic Reform in Eastern Europe: Conversations with Leading Reformers in Poland, Hungary, and the Czech Republic*. Studies of Communism in Transition. Brookfield, Vt.: Edward Elgar. 1995.

Bregman, Aleksander (ed.). *Faked Elections in Poland as Reported by Foreign Observers*. London: Polish Freedom Movement. 1947.

Brumberg, Abraham (ed.). *Poland: Genesis of a Revolution*. New York: Vintage Books. 1983.

Chang, Ha-Joon, & Peter Nolan (eds.). *The Transformation of the Communist Economies: Against the Mainstream*. New York: St. Martin's Press. 1995.

Connor, Walter D., & Piotr Ploszajski (eds.). *Escape from Socialism: The Polish Route*. Warsaw: IFIS Publishers. 1992.

Drewnowski, Jan (ed.). *Crisis in the East European Economy: The Spread of the Polish Disease*. London: Croom-Helm. 1982.

Earle, John S., Roman Frydman, & Andrzej Rapaczynski (eds.). *Privatization in the Transition to a Market Economy: Studies of Preconditions and Policies in Eastern Europe*. London: Pinter; and New York: St. Martin's Press. 1993.

Fatemi, Khosrow (ed.). *The Globalization of Business in the 1990's: Implications for Trade and Development*. Vol. I, Part IV. National Studies. Laredo, Tex.: Texas A&M International University. 1992.

———. *International Business in the New Millennium: International Capital Markets and Economic Integration*. Vol. III. Laredo, Tex.: Texas A&M International University. 1997.

Gomulka, Stanislaw, & Anthony Polonsky (eds.). *Polish Paradoxes*. London, New York: Routledge. 1990.

Gwertzman, Bernard, & Michael T. Kaufman (eds.). *The Collapse of Communism*. New York: Times Books. 1990.

Hardt, John P., & Richard F. Kaufman (eds.). *East-Central European Economies in*

Transition. Joint Economic Committee, Congress of the United States. Armonk, N.Y.: M. E. Sharpe. 1995.

Kaandorp, Arian, & Jacek Klich (eds). *Privatization and Restructurisation in East-Central Europe.* Krakow: Jagiellonian University. 1993.

Kreinin, Mordechai E. (ed.). *Contemporary Issues in Commercial Policy.* Tarrytown, N.Y.: Pergamon. 1995.

Krygier, Krzysztof (ed.). *System zaopatrzenia w gospodarce planowej.* Warsaw: Panstwowe Wydawnictwo Gospodarcze. 1955.

Kurczewski, Jacek (ed.). *Stalinism.* Warsaw: Open University Press. 1989.

Lane, David S., & George Kolankiewicz (eds.). *Social Groups in Polish Society.* New York: Columbia University Press. 1973.

Lineberry, William P. (ed.). *Poland.* New York: H. W. Wilson. 1984.

Newman, Peter, Murray Milgate, & John Eatwell (eds.). *The New Palgrave Dictionary of Money & Finance.* Vol. 2. New York: Stockton Press. 1992.

Oglesby, Carl (ed.). *The New Left Reader.* New York: Grove Press. 1969.

Paszynski, Marian, Jozef Soldaczuk, & Stanislaw Falkowski (eds.). *The International and the Polish Economy in 1989 and 1990.* Warsaw: Foreign Trade Research Institute. 1990.

Paul, E. F. (ed.). *Totalitarianism at the Crossroads.* New Brunswick, N.J.: Crossroads Books. 1990.

Poznanski, Kazimierz (ed.). *Stabilization and Privatization in Poland: An Economic Evaluation of the Shock Therapy Program.* Boston: Kluwer Academic Publishers. 1993.

Prizel, Ilya, & Andrew A. Michta (eds.). *Polish Foreign Policy Reconsidered: Challenges of Independence.* New York: St. Martin's Press. 1995.

Robinson, William F. (ed.). *August 1980: The Strikes in Poland.* Munich: Radio Free Europe Research. 1980.

Sanders, I. T. (ed.). *The Collectivization of Agriculture in Eastern Europe.* Lexington: University of Kentucky Press. 1958.

Simon, Maurice D., & Roger E. Kanet (eds.). *Background to Crisis: Policy and Politics in Gierek's Poland.* Boulder, Colo.: Westview Press. 1981.

Sinai, Michael (ed.). *Global Unemployment.* Vol. II. London: Zed Books (United Nation University, World Institute for Economic Development Research). 1995.

Stackhouse, Max L., Dennis McCann, Shirley J. Roels, & Preston N. Williams (eds.). *On Moral Business: Classical and Contemporary Resources for Ethics in Economic Life.* Grand Rapids, Mich.: William B. Eerdmans Publishing Company. 1995.

Strong, Ann Louise, Thomas A. Reiner, & Janusz Szyrmer. (eds.), *Transitions in Land and Housing: Bulgaria, the Czech Republic, and Poland.* New York: St. Martin's Press. 1996.

Woodall, Jean (ed.). *Policy and Politics in Contemporary Poland.* London: Frances Pinter. 1982.

Wright, Rupert (ed.). *The Central European Handbook: 1996/1997.* London: Euromoney Publications. 1996.

PUBLICATIONS BY THE WORLD ECONOMY RESEARCH INSTITUTE

Warsaw: The World Economy Research Institute
The Warsaw School of Economics
(Formerly the Main School of Economics)

Bossak, Jan W. (ed.). *Gospodarka Swiatowa i Gospodarka Polska w 1989 Roku*. 1990a.
――――. *Poland: International Economic Report 1989/1990*. 1990b.
――――. *Poland: International Economic Report 1992/1993*. 1993a.
――――. *Transforming the Polish Economy*. 1993b.
――――. *Poland: International Economic Report 1993/1994*. 1994.
――――. *Poland: International Economic Report 1994/1995*. 1995.
Bossak, Jan W., & Krzysztof Stupnicki (eds.). *Poland: International Economic Report 1987/1988*. 1988.
Ciamaga, Lucjan (ed.). *Europa '92–Polska*. 1990.
Golebiowski, Janusz (ed.). *Poland: International Economic Report 1990/1991*. 1991.
――――. *Poland: International Economic Report 1991/1992*. 1992.
――――. *Transforming the Polish Economy*. 1993.
Lubinski, Marek (ed.). *Poland: International Economic Report 1995/1996*. 1996.
――――. *Poland: International Economic Report 1996/1997*. 1997.

SERVICES, REPORTS, AND YEARBOOKS

Abecor Country Report. Poland. London: Abecor. April 1984.
Charlap, Z., & E. Szturm. "Statystyka Karteli w Polsce," *Statystyka Polski*. Series c, No. 28. 1935.
Congressional Research Service. John P. Hardt, & Jean F. Boone. *Poland's Renewal and U.S. Options, a Policy Reconnaissance* (Update). Washington, D.C.: Library of Congress. 5 June 1987.
Deloitte Touche Tohmatsu International. *Meeting Tax Obligations in Central and Eastern Europe*. Amsterdam: International Bureau of Fiscal Documentation. 1994.
Dziennik Ustaw Rzeczpospolita. 1946, 1947, 1989, 1991.
Economic and Legal Information from Poland. New York: Embassy of the Republic of Poland, Commercial Counsellor's Office. 1993–1997.
Encyclopaedia of Polish Industry. London: Stirling Publications. 1997.
EuroFutures. *Perspectives for Economic Development of the Baltic Sea Region*. Stockholm: Eurofund AB. 1994.
Euromoney. *The 1997 Guide to Preparing for the EMU*. London: Euromoney Publications. 1977.
Foreign Trade Research Institute. *Polish Foreign Trade in 1984: Annual Report*. Warsaw: Foreign Trade Research Institute. 1985.
――――. "Selected Data on Polish Foreign Trade." Warsaw: Foreign Trade Research Institute. 1990.

International Monetary Fund. *Selected Economic Indicators*. Washington, D.C.: International Monetary Fund. 1993.

International Monetary Fund. Piero Ugolini. "National Bank of Poland. The Road to Indirect Instruments." Occasional Paper No. 144. Washington, D.C.: International Monetary Fund. October 1996.

Kierunki Reformy Gospodarczej. Warsaw: GUS. 1981.

Mid-European Research and Planning Center. *The Sovietization of Culture in Poland*. Paris: MERPC. 1953.

Ministry of Privatization. *Information Guide to the Ministry of Privatization*. Warsaw: Studio G&Z. 1991.

————. *Program Powszechnej Prywatyzacji*. Warsaw: Ministry of Privatization. 1990.

O'Boyle, Edward J. "Poland's Solidarity Movement: Some Likely Sources of Information." Paper. Baton Rouge, La.: Louisiana Tech University. September 1989.

Radio Free Europe Research. "Polish Situation Reports." Munich: Radio Free Europe. 1978–1980.

Raport: Polska piec lat po sierpniu. London: ANEKS Publisher. 1986.

The Sarmatian Review. Houston, Tex.: Polish Institute of Arts and Sciences. January 1997.

United States Department of State. *U.S. Assistance to Central and Eastern Europe: An Overview*. Washington, D.C.: United States Department of State. 1991.

U.S. Helsinki Watch Committee. *Violations of the Helsinki Accords: Poland*. New York: The Helsinki Watch Committee. 1986.

The Warsaw Voice Business and Economy Yearbook. Warsaw: The Warsaw Voice. 1996, 1997.

Wharton Econometric Forecasting Associates. *Centrally Planned Economies Outlook*. Vol. 8., No. 1. April 1987.

————. "Polish Economic Performance in 1986 and Early 1987: Dilemmas of Economic Reform," Vol. 6, No. 14. 12 May 1987.

PUBLICATIONS BY GUS [CENTRAL STATISTICAL OFFICE]

Warsaw: GUS

Biuletyn Statystyczny. 1977–1996.
Maly Rocznik Statystyczny. 1977–1996.
Rocznik Statystyczny. 1977–1996.

Articles

"Monitoring the Labor Market, Unregistered Employment in Poland in 1995." 1995.

"Raport o sytuacji spoleczno-gospodarcego kraju. Rok 1995." 30 January 1996.

"Wstepna informacja o gospodarce 1995." 19 January 1996.

NEWSPAPER/MAGAZINE/PERIODICAL PUBLICATIONS*

The Associated Press
The Baltimore Sun
Biuletyn Informacyjny KSS/"KOR"
Central European
Central European Business Weekly
Challenge
The Economist
Ekonomista
Euromoney
FIBIS Daily Report: USSR
Le Figaro
The Financial Times
Fortune
Gazeta Bankowa
Gazeta International
Gazeta Wyborcza (Official Solidarity publication)
Glos Pracy (Official organ of the Central Council of Trade Unions)
The Independent
International Herald Tribune
New York Times
New York Times Magazine
Nowa Europa
Nowe Drogi (Theoretical and political organ of the Central Committee of the
    PZPR)
Nowy Swiat
Polish American Journal
Polish Business Times
Polityka (A weekly, originally very close to Wladyslaw Gomulka)
Pravda
Reuters
Robotnik Wybrzeza
Rzeczpospolita
Solidarnosc
The Star-Ledger (Newark, New Jersey)
The Tablet
Trybuna Ludu (Official Communist party newspaper; today, *Trybuna*)
Tygodnik Powszechny (Catholic publication of the "Znak" group in Krakow)
United Press International
U.S. News & World Report
Wall Street Journal
Wall Street Journal (Europe)
Warsaw Business Journal
The Warsaw Voice

*Individual citations found in chapter notes.

Zycie Gospodarcze (Semi-official publication dealing with economic questions)
Zycie Warszawy

BOOK REVIEWS

Biskupski, M. B. Review of the book *Historical Dictionary of Poland*. *The Polish Review*, Vol. 40, No. 3, pp. 361–363. 1995.

Hunter, Richard J. Review of the book *Breaking the Barrier*. *Mid-Atlantic Journal of Business*, Vol. 28, No. 3, pp. 283–284. 1992.

Kubik, Jan. Review of the book *Political Dissent and Opposition in Poland. The Workers' Defense Committee "KOR."* *The Polish Review*, Vol. 40, No. 3, pp. 357–361. 1995.

OTHER CONTRIBUTIONS

Babiak, Jerzy. "Agricultural Policy in Contemporary Poland." Unpublished paper. Poznan: Adam Mickiewicz University. 1986.

Blazyca, George. "Economic Reform in Polish Industry: The Experience of the 1970's." Dissertation. Sussex, U.K.: University of Sussex. 1978.

Gomulka, Stanislaw. "Economic, Social and Political Problems of Economic Transformation: The Case of Poland 1989–1992." Mimeograph. Warsaw. March 1992.

Guzek, Marian. "Economic Reform in Poland and Prospects for Cooperation with the West." Lecture. Poznan: Adam Mickiewicz University. 25 July 1985.

Hunter, Richard J. "An Analysis of the Second Stage of Economic Reform." Paper. 46th Annual Meeting of PIASA, Georgetown University, Washington, D.C. May 1988.

———. "Options and Perspectives for Today's Poland." Paper. 45th Annual Meeting of PIASA, Hunter College, New York. 30 May 1987.

Hunter, Richard J., & William Jones. "An Update on the Polish Tax System." Paper. 55th Annual Meeting of PIASA, Fordham University, New York. June 1997.

Klich, Jacek. "The Concept of Mass Privatization in Poland: Theoretical and Practical Considerations." Working paper. Krakow: Academy of Economics. June 1993.

Laba, Roman. "The Roots of Solidarity." Dissertation. Madison: University of Wisconsin. 1989.

Laski, Kazimierz. "Transition from Command to Market Economies in Central and Eastern Europe: First Experience and Questions." Mimeograph. Vienna: The Vienna Institute for Cooperative Economic Studies. 1991.

Otta, Wieslaw. Lecture. Poznan: Adam Mickiewicz University. 25 July 1990.

Rosati, Dariusz K. "The Politics of Economic Reform in Central and Eastern Europe." Mimeograph. Minneapolis: University of Minnesota. November 1991.

⬦ Index

About the Authors

RICHARD J. HUNTER, Jr., is Professor of Legal Studies at Seton Hall University. He has written extensively on Eastern and Central European business, politics, law, and economics and has served on the Board of Directors of the Polish Institute of Arts and Sciences of America.

LEO V. RYAN, C.S.V. is Professor of Management in the Kellstadt Graduate School of Business at DePaul University. He has also taught at the Poznan Academy of Economics and at the Polish-American Management Center, University of Lodz. His most recent books include *Human Action in Business* (1996) and *Etyka Biznesu* (1997).

ISBN 0-275-96219-9

90000>

EAN

9 780275 962197

HARDCOVER BAR CODE